Corruption in Business

Corruption in Business

Edited by Lester A. Sobel

Contributing editors: Mary Elizabeth Clifford,
Joseph Fickes, Christopher Hunt, Hal
Kosut, Stephen Orlofsky, Gerry Satter-
white

Indexer: Grace M. Ferrara

FACTS ON FILE, INC.   NEW YORK, N.Y.

Corruption in Business

Library of Congress Catalog Card Number: 76-41986
ISBN 0-87196-292-6

9 8 7 6 5 4 3 2 1
PRINTED IN
THE UNITED STATES OF AMERICA

Contents

Introduction

CORRUPTION IN BUSINESS IS FREQUENT, widespread and familiar. Corporation executives, bankers, secretaries and clerks are convicted disturbingly often of such acts as looting their own companies, cheating customers, bribing public officials and even plotting with out-and-out gangsters. Government employes, political leaders and labor union officers have accepted—or demanded—bribes, election campaign contributions and other favors from businessmen in return for legal or illegal considerations.

It is not always easy to determine who has done the corrupting or who has been corrupted; sometimes both sides appear to have started with an equal deficiency of ethics. American businessmen doing business abroad often assert that bribery is a ''way of life'' in many countries and that no wheels can turn in such lands until enough ''grease'' has been applied at the proper points. But foreign observers frequently claim that it is the American who is the instigator and master of corrupt business arrangements.

Americans are periodically confronted with developments that make them distressingly aware of the always present problem of corruption in business, in politics and in other areas of public life. In the mid-1970s, Watergate and the disclosure of questionable foreign payments by American corporations have again made the subject one of immediate concern.

Secretary of the Treasury W. Michael Blumenthal, while still president of the Bendix Corp., had discussed the situation in the May 25, 1975 issue of *The New York Times*. ''The public opinion polls continue to show that the proportion of the public that takes a critical or hostile view of business is growing,'' he noted.

1

". . . The news media have turned the spotlight on many questionable activities: political campaign contribution bribes to officials of
foreign countries, tax dodges, mishandling of pension funds, shod-
diness of product quality, improper financial practices, discrimination in employment and lack of concern for worker health and
safety—all of which tend to raise questions about the ethical standards of business and to lower public confidence.'' Blumenthal continued:

"Faced with reports of this kind, the instinct of most businessmen
is to rally to the defense of the business community. It is not true,
they protest, that this conduct is par for the course. Indeed, if the
misbehavior of a large corporation makes news, that is because the
majority of large corporations do not misbehave . . . All this is true
enough, but it misses the point. To leap to the defense of business
in general whenever some specific abuse is uncovered only tends, in
the public mind, to associate the one with the other. If businessmen
are ethically strong and morally clean, why should they not be the
first to denounce the abuses and malpractice that—far more than our
critics in the media—threaten the survival of the free-enterprise system?

"The business community needs a more intimate and meaningful
dialogue with its critics. . . . What we have today hardly deserves the
name of dialogue. On one hand, we have the scandals, the charges,
the countercharges and the suspicions so characteristic of the post-
Watergate atmosphere. On the other, we find business spokesmen
defending business as if it were a monolith, all of a piece, as if
every suggestion of corporate wrongdoing, every proposal for
change, were an attack on the free-enterprise system as a whole. . . .

"An entirely new approach is needed—a frankly moral approach
that would begin with business taking a long, hard look at itself.
This is not the sort of assignment that the public will entrust . . . to
any of the groups traditionally associated with the defense of business, however earnest, honest and competent they may be. We
would all benefit . . . if the members of the business community,
together with representatives of other segments of our society,
would organize an institute or association to promote the idea of responsibility and ethics in business practices in the broadest sense.
Business executives are professional people, but there is nothing in
business life that corresponds to the bar associations, the American
Medical Association, or the American Society of Architects. Why,
then, should business people not set up an association dedicated to
defining and maintaining the standards of their profession?

"Such a group would deal with concrete questions of business ethics—not as an advocate defending business right or wrong; not from the view of a trade or industry association or on the basis of a concern for consumer relations, which the better business bureaus are already doing; nor, finally, in terms of a commitment to the economic and fiscal policies that are deemed to be in the interests of industry. Instead, it would focus on devising new ethical-behavior codes to which all business would be expected to subscribe. The founding members . . . could be leaders from the business community, but it would draw as well on lawyers, the clergy, statesmen, philosophers and others whose views would represent the moral concerns of society as a whole. This, indeed, would be the very point of the new departure—that it would be, and would be seen to be, operating on behalf of society as a whole. . . ."

Not all businessmen accept the common claim that business cannot be done in many countries without the payment of bribes. As Sen. William Proxmire (D, Wis.) reported to the Senate May 3, 1976, "in recent months, nearly 100 of America's blue chip corporations have admitted to paying corporate bribes overseas. For a large number of companies doing business overseas, bribes to foreign officials was a way of life. In the Senate Banking Committee's investigation of bribery, however, we found that a number of other companies apparently had strict policies of refusing to pay bribes and did not suffer for their greater integrity. The idea that bribes must be paid in certain parts of the world is simply a myth."

Proxmire proposed legislation to "end corporate bribery abroad, first by requiring a systematic program of disclosure to the SEC [Securities & Exchange Commission] of all overseas consultant payments and second, by flatly prohibiting such payments to foreign public officials." "Disclosure," he said "is the heart of this legislation." Proxmire cited a *Wall Street Journal* article in which Lindley H. Clark, Jr. called for "full disclosure" as "a large part of the solution" to the problem of business bribery but simultaneously pointed out that the situation was not a matter of clear-cut "black-and-white cases" because "a distressing number come in various shades of gray." "American multinationals are in a sort of moral-political-economic quandry," Clark declared. As Clark pointed out:

"American businessmen every day are engaged in courting customer good will—and in trying to get along with all of the various branches of government that oversee their operations. Ethical problems can and do arise here as well as overseas. . . . Salesmen take customers to lunch, to a baseball game, to the theater. Manufactur-

ers' representatives, offering the products of several companies,
travel the U.S. making sales on commission. The manufacturers
aren't likely to know what the 'rep' does with the commission. . . . If a salesman entertains a private customer it may be considered perfectly proper; if he does the same thing for the purchasing agent of a city government it may be improper. The public has a
right to expect that its representatives won't profit personally, or
even enjoy hunting-lodge weekends, because of the way they spend
the public's money. . . .

   ". . . SEC Chairman Roderick Hills said that U.S. companies
can continue making payments 'extorted' by foreign tax, customs
and other officials as the price of doing business overseas. Nothing
the SEC has done 'interferes' with such 'grease' payments, Mr.
Hills insisted, provided they are accurately entered on the public's
books and that management knows they are being made. Some of
the questionable payments were channeled through secret funds or
otherwise hidden because company employees knew, or feared, that
top management would not approve. Some such payments were hidden because top management knew, or feared, that the public would
not approve. . . ."

The quandry posed by overseas business bribery is parallelled by
the problems of other types of business corruption that at various
times have provoked public concern. Such forms of corruption include the solicitation and payment of illegal election-campaign contributions, price-fixing and other anti-trust violations, securities
frauds, deceptive advertising and similar consumer deceptions, embezzlement, real estate swindles—the list is almost endless.

This book is designed to serve as a record of the national problem
of corruption in business from the end of the 1960s to the middle
years of the 1970s. It provides details of the disclosures of business
corruption during this period and of the efforts made to correct the
situation. The material in this volume consists largely of the narra-
tive that FACTS ON FILE compiled in its weekly reports on world
events. As in all FACTS ON FILE works, there was a conscientious
effort to keep this book free of bias and to make it a balanced and
accurate reference tool.

LESTER A. SOBEL

New York, N.Y.
January, 1977

Political Entanglements: The ITT & Dairy Cases

ITT Trust Decision Linked To GOP Funds Pledge

The 1972 Presidential election campaign produced an unprecedented number of scandals involving allegations of business-political corruption. Surfacing at a time when the politically motivated burglary of Democratic offices in the Watergate was under investigation, these scandals became inextricable elements of the "Watergate atmosphere." Prominent among them was the charge that the Nixon Administration had granted the International Telephone & Telegraph Corp. (ITT) a favorable antitrust settlement on the understanding that ITT would provide financial aid for the Republican cause in the election campaign.

ITT-Hartford Fire Insurance decree. The trust cases producing the controversial settlement involved ITT's acquisition of the Hartford Fire Insurance Co. in 1970.

The Department of Justice and ITT July 31, 1971 announced their agreement on a consent decree settling three Justice Department antitrust suits against ITT over the corporation's acquisition of Hartford Fire and of two other companies—the Grinnell Corp., a water-sprinkler manufacturer, and the Canteen Corp., a food and vending service company, both in 1969.

The consent decrees, on terms considered favorable to ITT, were approved by two federal judges Sept. 24, 1971. Judge M. Joseph Blumenthal ruled in Hartford, Conn. that the Hartford Fire and Grinnell decrees eliminated "the aspects of the acquisitions which the original complaint alleged to be illegal." Judge Richard B. Austin in Chicago similarly approved the Canteen decree.

Under the settlement, ITT would proceed with its acquisition of Hartford Fire, an action which would produce the largest company in U.S. corporate history, but it would divest itself within two years of the Canteen Corp. and the Fire Protection Division of Grinnell. ITT was given the option of divesting itself within three years of either Hartford Fire or four other holdings—Avis Rent-a-Car, ITT-Levitt and Sons, ITT-Hamilton Life Insurance Co. and ITT Life Insurance Co. Harold S. Geneen, ITT's chairman and president, said in New York July 31 that ITT would retain Hartford Fire rather than the four other companies.

Decree linked to funds pledge. An alleged company memorandum, made public Feb. 29, 1972, linked the antitrust settlement with a purported ITT pledge to underwrite a significant portion of the funds needed to hold the 1972 Republican National Convention in San Diego, Calif.

The memorandum was made public by syndicated columnist Jack Anderson, who embroiled Attorney General-

5

designee Richard G. Kleindienst in the matter March 1, accusing him of having lied about not being involved in the ITT negotiations in 1971. At a Senate Judiciary Committee hearing March 2, scheduled at his request, Kleindienst denied any improper role or knowledge, at the time, of the plans for the convention funding.

Denials of wrongdoing also were issued Feb. 29 by Attorney General John N. Mitchell and ITT. Mitchell denied he had been involved "in any way" in negotiations on the GOP convention site or in settlement of the ITT antitrust case. The company said "there was no deal of any kind to settle our antitrust cases."

The out-of-court settlement of the antitrust cases had been announced eight days prior to the announcement by the Republican National Committee of the selection of San Diego as the site of its party's 1972 presidential convention.

The city's bid for the convention included a pledge by the Sheraton Corp. of America, an ITT subsidiary, to underwrite a major part of the $400,000 needed from private sources to obtain the convention. This did not become known until later.

The memorandum in question, which Anderson released to the press, was attributed to ITT lobbyist Mrs. Dita D. Beard as a "personal and confidential" message to W. R. Merriam, an ITT vice president, dated June 25, 1971 and concluding with a request that the memo be destroyed.

Mrs. Beard referred a number of times in the memo to the ITT "commitment," or "our participation in the convention," and connected it to the antitrust action. The memo referred to the commitment as composed of services or cash, or a combination of the two.

According to the memo: "Other than permitting [Attorney General] John Mitchell, [California Lt. Gov.] Ed Reinecke, [White House aide] Bob Haldeman and Nixon (besides [Rep. Bob] Wilson, of course), no one has known from whom that 400 thousand commitment had come"; ". . . because of several conversations with [former Kentucky Gov.] Louie [Nunn] re Mitchell, that our noble commitment

has gone a long way toward our negotiations on the mergers eventually coming out as Hal [Harold Geneen, ITT president] wants them. Certainly the President has told Mitchell to see that things are worked out fairly. It is still only [Richard W.] McLaren's mickey mouse we are suffering"; "if it [the commitment] gets too much publicity, you can believe our negotiations with Justice will wind up shot down. Mitchell is definitely helping us, but cannot let it be known."

Anderson reported Feb. 29 that Mrs. Beard, in an interview with his associate Brit Hume, had confirmed the authenticity of the memo. She said, according to Anderson, she had discussed the antitrust action with Mitchell for more than an hour during a Kentucky Derby party given by Nunn in 1971 and Mitchell had asked what she wanted and she told him the settlement ITT preferred, which conformed, she said, with the eventual settlement.

In his statement Feb. 29, Mitchell said he had not discussed the ITT antitrust action with anyone in the Justice Department or with ITT "with one exception." Mrs. Beard had approached him, he said, and he had advised her he was not familiar with the matter and "the appropriate people representing ITT should take the matter up with the appropriate people in the [Justice] Department."

Kleindienst role questioned—Kleindienst's name was brought into the case Feb. 29 by Democratic National Chairman Lawrence F. O'Brien, who said Kleindienst had assured him in December 1971, that Mitchell had not been involved in the ITT case. "It is now clear that these are not the facts, and Mr. Kleindienst knew it," O'Brien charged.

In his column March 1, Anderson accused Kleindienst of having lied in his reply to O'Brien denying involvement in the negotiations preceding the antitrust settlement, that the settlement had been "handled and negotiated exclusively" by McLaren and Kleindienst's only role was to concur in McLaren's recommendation for a settlement. Anderson quoted ITT director Felix G. Rohatyn as saying he had discussed the settlement in private with Kleindienst some half-dozen times prior to the settlement.

In his appearance before the Senate Judiciary Committee March 2, Kleindienst told of four private meetings with Rohatyn in 1971 and a meeting he arranged for Rohatyn and other ITT representatives—Kleindienst said he had attended but was silent—to explain the "drastic economic consequences" if the Justice Department pursued and won the antitrust cases against the company.

Kleindienst "categorically and specifically" denied exerting pressure for a settlement favoring ITT or knowing at the time of plans of an ITT subsidiary to secure the financing for the GOP convention site.

"I set in motion a series of events," Kleindienst said, "by which Mr. McLaren became persuaded that he ought to come off his position" against a settlement which would allow ITT to keep the Hartford Fire Insurance Co.

His testimony was supported by McLaren, currently a federal judge, and Rohatyn, who also appeared before the committee March 2.

McLaren and Flanigan—Testimony about the extent of the role played by White House aide Flanigan was amended as the probe proceeded. McLaren had testified March 2 that he did not believe he had talked with Flanigan or anyone in the White House about the ITT case. Asked if he had communicated with anyone in the White House in any way about the case, he had replied, "Not that I recall at this time, and I think that I would recall if I had." When pressed further, he said an analysis on the merit of ITT's economic plea had been recommended either by Flanigan or the Treasury Department.

McLaren amplified this in testimony March 7, conceding he had used Flanigan "simply as a conduit" to have an "independent analysis" made of ITT's claims of "hardship" if it lost its antitrust cases. The study was done by Richard J. Ramsden, 34, who had served as a White House intern for about a year before joining a New York investment management firm.

Ramsden told a New York Times reporter March 3 he had not had any dealings with McLaren but had dealt with Flanigan, who had given him the questions he was to address. He said he had advised Flanigan of his firm's small interest in ITT—control of a pension fund owning $208,890 worth of stock as a small part of the fund's portfolio. Asked at the hearing March 2 whether he had taken the precaution of checking on a Ramsden link to ITT, McLaren said he was sure it had been checked out because that was the policy of his division. He said the study was one of the three things that changed his mind about the ITT situation. The others were the firm's economic presentation arranged through Kleindienst and the Treasury Department's support for the firm's position. The Treasury Department said March 2 that its position, made on the basis of material, which it did not verify, presented by ITT at its economic briefing, concerned only the economics of the issue such as balance of payments.

The Senate committee disclosed March 6 a statement from Solicitor General Erwin N. Griswold that Kleindienst, with McLaren present, had asked him to seek a delay from the Supreme Court in one of the antitrust cases after ITT lawyer Lawrence E. Walsh had requested the government to review its anti-merger policies in general. The delay was granted and the Justice Department never appealed the case, which involved the Grinnell Corp., a part of which ITT was allowed to retain in the eventual settlement.

Walsh told a newsman March 6 Kleindienst had informed him later by telephone of the decision to seek the delay.

The committee March 7 released an April 1971 letter from Walsh conceding to Kleindienst the "high probability" that the government would win if it took its cases before the Supreme Court. McLaren had told the panel the chance of losing before the Supreme Court was another factor for settling the ITT cases without a court decision.

Griswold said March 8 that while he was not an antitrust expert, he believed that the government would have lost all three of the ITT cases before the Supreme Court and that the settlement made was "a very substantial victory for the government."

Flanigan denounced—Sen. Thomas F. Eagleton (D, Mo.) denounced White House aide Peter Flanigan in a Senate speech March 14 as "Mr. Fixit" for big business in the Administration.

It was revealed March 13 that the investment banking firm where Flanigan had been a partner received a $600,-000 fee for helping plan one of the ITT mergers involved in the antitrust suits.

Mitchell denies role—Jack Anderson March 3 quoted Edgar Gillenwaters, an assistant to California Lt. Gov. Ed Reinecke, as saying the two had met with Mitchell in mid-May 1971 and told him of ITT's offer to underwrite the convention in San Diego by as much as $400,000. Reinecke March 3 reported a similar story but said the meeting with Mitchell took place in September 1971. He said he had not mentioned ITT but only the Sheraton Hotel Corp. (a subsidiary). At a news conference March 2, Mitchell said he "did not know as of that time and still don't know what arrangements the Republican party had with San Diego or anyone else."

An ITT statement March 3 said its subsidiary, Sheraton Corporation of America, contributed $100,000, with an additional $100,000 possible later on a matching basis, as a way to attract business to its new hotel in San Diego and that the contribution was "in no sense a political payment." (These were in actual funds. The commitment to underwrite the funding to a range, first of $300,000, later $400,000 reportedly was made by ITT President Harold Geneen.)

Mrs. Beard's involvement—The whereabouts of Mrs. Beard, who had disappeared at the outset of the controversy, became known March 3 when the Justice Department said FBI agents had traced her to the Denver area. The next day it became known that Mrs. Beard, who suffered from a chronic heart ailment, angina pectoris, was in a Denver hospital in serious condition with incipient coronary thrombosis.

Because of her condition, the agents had been unable to serve her with a subpoena from the Judiciary Committee, which sought her for testimony. The subpoena was served March 4 but her doctors said she was too ill to be moved.

The doctor who had been treating Mrs. Beard for about nine years for the heart ailment, Dr. Victor L. Liszka of Arlington, Va., flew to Denver over the weekend and appeared before the Senate committee March 6 to say she had authorized him to testify about her condition. Liszka said she had been suffering from periodic "distorted and irrational" behavior at the time she wrote the controversial memo.

Liszka also volunteered testimony that Mrs. Beard had told him in Denver she never meant to imply in her memo there was any connection between the ITT trust settlement and the contribution to the GOP convention. He said she had telephoned him in 1971 and excitedly related: her meeting at a Kentucky Derby party with then-Attorney General John N. Mitchell; her attempt to argue the merits of the ITT trust case with Mitchell; Mitchell's rebuff to her—"a dressing down such as I never had in my life," as Liszka quoted her; and Mitchell's advice that "I should proceed in proper channels" and refusal to discuss the matter.

Former Kentucky Gov. Louie B. Nunn (R), who held the Derby party Mitchell and Mrs. Beard attended, told the Senate committee March 7: he was with Mitchell the entire time; Mitchell refused to discuss the ITT case with Mrs. Beard; he "heard no offer of no wrongdoing"; Mitchell told Mrs. Beard "he didn't like the approach she was making or the pressures that had been brought"; Mrs. Beard collapsed after the rebuff by Mitchell from exhaustion, her heart ailment and alcohol and "they laid her out on the floor" of the governor's mansion.

White House Involvement Seen

Nixon link denied. The Senate Judiciary Committee was told March 9, 1972 that President Richard Nixon had requested a settlement of the antitrust case instead of an attempt at a Supreme Court decision. The allegations were denied immediately by former Attorney General John N. Mitchell.

Brit Hume testified before the committee that he had interviewed Mrs. Beard

Feb. 24 to verify her controversial memo. He said she told him Mitchell had informed her during a conversation in 1971 that President Nixon had directed him to "lay off" ITT. After he questioned her specifically if she were referring to what the President had said, Hume testified, Mrs. Beard changed the alleged Nixon remark to a request for Mitchell to "make a reasonable settlement" with ITT rather than pursue the antitrust cases to the Supreme Court.

In a statement released later March 9, Mitchell called Hume's testimony about him involving the President "totally false." He said "the President has never, repeat never, made any request to me directly or indirectly concerning the settlement of the ITT case and I took no part in that settlement."

Hume and Anderson testify—During the committee's March 9 session, Hume, in addition to his testimony concerning Nixon, reported other Mrs. Beard statements to him that she had first discussed ITT's financial commitment to the GOP convention with Lt. Gov. Reinecke in January 1971 and that ITT President Geneen had promised to underwrite San Diego's bid to host the convention during a meeting with Rep. Bob Wilson (R, Calif.) May 12, 1971.

Anderson also testified March 9 and involved another White House aide, William Timmons, with the ITT contribution to the convention plus a former White House staff member, Jack Gleason, currently in the public-relations business with, Anderson said, ITT as a client.

Anderson said Gleason had informed him he had discussed, as an ITT public relations consultant, the convention with Timmons in June 1971 to clarify what assistance ITT would give the convention. Anderson said the alleged conversation between the two tended to "corroborate the circumstances mentioned in Mrs. Beard's memo."

Mitchell & Geneen deny decree-funds link. Former Attorney General Mitchell and ITT President Harold S. Geneen testified before the Senate Judiciary Committee March 14–16, 1972 and denied any link between the ITT antitrust decree and any financial aid to the Republican National Convention.

Mitchell testified March 14 he had discussed the department's antitrust policies with Geneen privately in 1970 but that the subject of the department's three antitrust cases against ITT had been ruled out. Mitchell, who had disqualified himself from the ITT cases when attorney general because an ITT subsidiary was a client of his former law firm, disclaimed involvement in any way in the handling or settlement of the suits.

Mitchell, who resigned as attorney general to direct President Nixon's re-election campaign, told the committee March 14 he had taken no part in negotiations selecting San Diego as the site of the convention.

Before hearing Mitchell, the probers heard syndicated columnist Jack Anderson charge March 10 that Mitchell was lying in his denial of knowledge of a financial commitment by an ITT subsidiary to the GOP convention. Anderson referred to California Lt. Gov. Ed Reinecke's statement that he had informed Mitchell of the arrangements in September 1971.

Questioned about Reinecke's report, Mitchell said March 14 he could have forgotten the information because "it made no impression on me, I having no interest in it." He said his first knowledge of the ITT pledge to the convention probably had been gleaned from the newspapers. Later, he said, he learned that "the Republican National Committee, or whatever committee makes these decisions, had picked San Diego" as the convention site.

During Mitchell's second appearance before the committee March 15, Sen. John V. Tunney (D, Calif.) charged that either Mitchell or Reinecke was "not telling the truth" about their discussion.

Other testimony March 14 concerned ITT lobbyist Mrs. Dita D. Beard and her reported meeting with Mitchell at a Kentucky Derby party in 1971. He had met her, Mitchell said, but he did not discuss the ITT trust case with her. When she persisted in raising the subject, he said, he told her to, "in effect, shove off."

In his turn before the committee March 15, Geneen said "there was absolutely no connection" between ITT's pledge of up to $200,000 toward expenses of the GOP convention and the trust settlement with the government.

He corroborated Mitchell's testimony about their meeting, that he had agreed with Mitchell's condition ruling out discussion of the antitrust suits.

Geneen denied knowledge of an alleged company memo by Mrs. Beard about the firm's commitment to the convention in connection with its trust settlement. He conceded that documents in Mrs. Beard's files had been destroyed shortly after publication of her memo, which had touched off the current controversy, but he said he did not know who had ordered the destruction. He added that the move was "probably a reaction that our files were suddenly open to the public" and was not intended "to prevent review of our files by any legitimate agency."

An ITT official reported to the committee March 16 that a day after publication of the Beard memo, ITT employes were ordered to destroy all unneeded or embarrassing papers in company files, that sacks of documents, some pertaining to the GOP convention and others to the antitrust settlement, were fed into a shredder, that a company representative had gone through Mrs. Beard's files with her to select the documents to be destroyed.

As for the ITT commitment to the GOP convention, Geneen said March 15 he personally had pledged the funds for an ITT subsidiary, the Sheraton Corporation of America, as a way to promote the opening of a new Sheraton hotel in San Diego. He said part of the arrangement was that President Nixon's headquarters at the convention would be in the new hotel.

Geneen said the pledge was not for $400,000 in cash and services, as reported, but for $100,000 in cash and another $100,000 on a matching basis if needed. He said smaller amounts had been spent to promote other Sheraton hotels.

(Republican National Chairman Robert Dole said March 10 ITT had offered to underwrite the GOP convention and that the amount was $400,000, which had been offered, he said, as "a guarantee to make up the difference if the other contributors" to a San Diego civic committee did not put up enough funds. He stressed that the arrangement was made by a local civic group and not by the GOP National Committee and there was "no arrangement" between the civic and GOP committees.)

Mrs. Beard disputes version of memo. In a March 17 statement, released by Senate Republican Leader Hugh Scott (Pa.) and her lawyer in Denver, Colo., where she was confined to a hospital with a heart ailment, Mrs. Dita Beard admitted preparing a memo "at about the time indicated"—June 25, 1971—on the convention. But, she said, "it was not the memo Jack Anderson had put in evidence before the Senate."

This allegedly actual Beard memo turned up March 20 when ITT announced it had discovered it "within the past two days" and also found it contained "absolutely no reference to the antitrust cases" and only one paragraph about the San Diego convention. The latter, according to William R. Merriam, head of ITT's Washington office, contained Mrs. Beard's assertions that negotiations for the convention "being held on ITT properties in San Diego have been wholly my responsibility" and "if this possibility becomes fact, it means unbuyable publicity for ITT."

The company submitted its version of the Beard memo to the Senate Judiciary Committee.

The company also produced for the committee at the same time two other affidavits to prove that the Anderson memo was "a fraud." One was signed by Susan Lichtman, Mrs. Beard's temporary secretary at the reputed time the controversial memos were composed, who recalled typing a memo concerning the convention but did not recall typing certain sentences in the Anderson version—one linking ITT's "noble commitment" on the convention to a favorable settlement on its antitrust cases, another claiming President Nixon had told Attorney General John N. Mitchell "to see that things are worked out fairly" in the trust cases, and another saying Mitchell was "definitely helping us but cannot let it be known."

A special Senate Judiciary Committee panel questioned Mrs. Beard at her hospital bedside in Denver March 26 but halted the quiz after $2\frac{1}{2}$ hours when the witness collapsed with severe chest pain. Before her seizure, she denied knowledge of any link between the ITT financial pledge to the Republican National Convention and "a favorable settlement" of its antitrust cases. She denied authorship of the memorandum attributed to her by Anderson and denied a sworn statement by Anderson's associate, Brit Hume, that she had admitted authorship to him.

She conceded she wrote a memo concerning ITT's commitment to the GOP convention and it contained some, but not all, of the material in Anderson's version. She acknowledged in substance a passage cautioning ITT officials to be silent about the commitment with an observation indicating that aside from five persons, including Mitchell and Nixon, "no one has known from whom that $400,000 commitment had come." Under questioning, she said the sentence was "misleading" since it was based on a remark that the five individuals would be informed of the commitment.

Mrs. Beard said she wrote the memo after William R. Merriam, the head of ITT's Washington office, had told her he had received a call from the White House expressing confusion over ITT's commitment, and Merriam had asked her, "Is $600,000 going to Nixon's campaign?"

Sen. John V. Tunney (D, Calif.), one of the panel members, said afterwards the testimony had "raised new and serious questions" and Mrs. Beard's statement "shows a contact between a company involved in a billion-dollar antitrust case and the White House concerning" a political contribution.

Congressional favors cited—Mrs. Susan Lichtman, Mrs. Beard's secretary during the period the alleged memo was written, told a New York Times reporter March 30 that ITT regularly was called upon to do favors for members of Congress, sometimes "favors on a big scale," and she herself had transmitted refusal of a request in 1971 from Sen.

Vance Hartke (D, Ind.) for use of one of ITT's jet planes.

Hartke's office later March 30 issued a denial that Hartke had ever requested use of an ITT plane.

At a press conference in Washington March 31, Mrs. Lichtman told the newsmen she "came to accept anything in the way of corruption" during her sojourn in Washington.

Mrs. Lichtman also reaffirmed her recollection of typing a memo mentioning then-Attorney General John N. Mitchell as keeping discussion of ITT's contribution to the convention on a high plane, a section of the memo Mrs. Beard specifically refuted before the Senate panel.

Nixon on Flanigan & big contributors. At his press conference March 24, 1972, President Nixon was asked for his view of "the proper role" of Presidential aides in dealing with regulatory agencies and law enforcement matters, and in particular the role of Presidential aide Peter M. Flanigan "in some of these matters."

Nixon said Presidential aides "must listen to all who come to the White House, as they do in great numbers on all sides of all cases . . . What is improper is for a Presidential aide to use influence for personal gain and to use influence in any way that would not be in the public interest. As far as Mr. Flanigan is concerned, Mr. [Ronald L.] Ziegler has responded to that charge at considerable length with my total authority . . . and I have nothing further to say."

(White House Press Secretary Ziegler had said March 14 Nixon "has confidence in Mr. Flanigan and feels he has conducted himself properly." "Those who are making partisan attacks on an individual have the responsibility to come forward with concrete evidence that Mr. Flanigan has gained personally in any way from his contacts," Ziegler said.)

Nixon also was asked his view of large political contributions either by business or individuals "in terms of possibly getting something back for it." His reply: "Nobody gets anything back as far as the general contributions are concerned in this Administration." In fact, he added, "some of our major complaints have been that many of our business people have not received the consideration that perhaps they thought that an Administration that was supposed to be business-oriented would provide for it."

As for the persons who received the contributions, Nixon said, "they must be accepted with no understandings, expressed or implied, that anything is to be done, or as a result of those contributions, that would not be done in the ordinary course of events."

As for ITT, Nixon said, his Administration had "moved on" the conglomerate and "required the greatest divestiture in the history of the antitrust law" and barred additional acquisitions that would make it larger. "If we wanted to do a favor for ITT," he said, "we could just continue to do what the two previous Administrations had done, and that is nothing: let ITT continue to grow. But we moved on it and moved effectively."

Wilson & Merriam testimony conflict. Rep. Bob Wilson (R, Calif.) and William R. Merriam, head of ITT's Washington office, testified before the Senate Judiciary Committee April 10, 1972. Both denied any connection between the convention funding and the antitrust settlement.

Merriam told the committee he had ordered the destruction of office files after publication of the Beard memo because "there might be a lot of others in there like that" that might embarrass the firm.

While he "never saw" the memo prior to its publication by Anderson, he said, and he was not even in the office the day it allegedly was typed, he had received a memo from Mrs. Beard dated that same day. As for Wilson's remarks to an interviewer in February that Merriam had told him he had received the Beard memo, Merriam told the committee he had "hedged" on the point in his talk with Wilson.

Merriam said he had deceived Mrs. Beard about receiving an inquiry from the White House concerning details of ITT's commitment to the GOP in San Diego. Actually, he said, he had dealt with the White House through Jack Gleason, a former White House aide, but did not tell Mrs. Beard because he knew she would dislike the source and discredit the information.

Merriam contradicted Mrs. Beard's testimony that he had asked her to write the memo and that he had mentioned a White House inquiry about a possible $600,000 ITT commitment to Nixon's campaign. He also contradicted Mrs. Beard's statements in a television interview that he had instructed her to discuss the firm's desire for an antitrust settlement with then-Attorney General John N. Mitchell at a Kentucky Derby party in 1971.

On the convention funding, Wilson said ITT President Harold S. Geneen, a good friend, had made a "personal commitment" to guarantee up to $400,000 of the convention's cost, but this was not in conflict with Geneen's statement the commitment was only $200,000 because funds could be raised from the San Diego area so that the full $400,000 would not be needed.

ITT sought direct Nixon action. Attorney Lawrence E. Walsh told the Senate Judiciary Committee in testimony April 12 that Geneen had wanted to take his plea for a delay of one of the trust cases directly to Nixon, but had accepted his advice to seek the delay through Kleindienst, who had granted it.

According to Walsh: Kleindienst had been approached through an unplanned "happenstance" by a neighbor, ITT employe John F. Ryan, who spoke of the economic threat to ITT posed by the antitrust action. Kleindienst responded he was accessible to just complaints and agreed to hear a presentation of the firm's "hardship" argument.

Walsh said he was directed to seek a delay until a formal appeal could be prepared for a "high level" review of federal antitrust policy. But the presentation "had gone rather well" and after the "hardship" plea had been made before the federal antitrust staff, nothing more was done about the high-level review.

Flanigan testifies. Peter F. Flanigan, a White House assistant, gave limited testimony April 20, 1972 at the Senate Judiciary Committee's hearings on Kleindienst's nomination to be attorney general.

The six-week hearings, which had centered on the charges of an ITT pledge of financial aid to the Republican National Convention in return for the pro-ITT antitrust settlement, were the longest confirmation hearings in Senate history.

Flanigan's testimony did not shed any new light on the ITT case. Relying on an agreement that he would only be asked questions about certain specific aspects of the ITT affair, Flanigan declined to answer inquiries about contacts he might have had with Kleindienst or with ITT officials.

Flanigan, a White House aide for liaison with big business, testified that he had taken no part in the Justice Department's decision to settle the ITT antitrust suits.

At one point, Flanigan said he had acted only as a "conduit" to obtain for the Justice Department an independent analysis of one aspect of the suits from Richard J. Ramsden, a New York financial analyst.

Flanigan's link to Ramsden was the focus of much of the senators' questioning. Flanigan said that Richard W. McLaren, then chief of the Justice Department's antitrust division, had asked him in May 1971 to contact Ramsden and have him prepare a study of ITT's claim that its divestiture of the Hartford Fire Insurance Co. would severely damage ITT's credit and stock value.

More than two dozen times during the hearing, Republican members objected when Democratic senators attempted to question Flanigan about whether he had discussed the case with ITT officials or other government personnel. Committee Chairman James O. Eastland (D, Miss.) sustained almost every objection.

He did so because of the agreement worked out by the committee and the White House to have Flanigan testify. All but Sen. Edward M. Kennedy (D, Mass.) had endorsed that agreement.

(When the committee first sought to have Flanigan testify, the White House said it would claim executive privilege and he would not appear. But the White House modified its stand April 18 when it learned that Sens. Sam J. Ervin Jr.

[D, N.C.] and Russell B. Long [D, La.], two influential committee members, would vote against reporting out the Kleindienst nomination if Flanigan failed to testify. Faced with that opposition—seen as fatal to the Kleindienst confirmation—the White House agreed to have Flanigan testify, but only about limited aspects of the case.)

Ramsden testimony—Ramsden testified April 17 that the Justice Department had overstated his report on the potentially adverse financial consequences of a successful antitrust action against the ITT mergers. He said his analysis had not implied that the U.S. economy would suffer or ITT stockholders would be disastrously affected. Ramsden said he had been hired by Flanigan and had not conferred with any other government official about the case, and that Flanigan had not tried to influence his findings.

Ramsden said he had requested a document to help with his work and Flanigan had given him one, reluctantly, without mentioning that it was prepared by ITT. However, he had judged the document to be "an advocate report," he said, and it had not influenced his analysis.

SEC injunction. An SEC suit against ITT was settled June 20, 1972 in a consent agreement barring further violations of securities laws. No penalties were involved.

The suit, filed June 15 in federal district court in New York, charged ITT with failing to disclose in a supplement to a prospectus covering the sale of 26,000 shares of ITT stock by its subsidiary, Hartford Fire Insurance Co., the status of private negotiations with the Justice Department which led to the 1971 antitrust settlement.

Two other defendants in the SEC suit, Howard J. Aibel, senior vice president and general counsel at ITT, and John Navin, ITT secretary and counsel for corporate affairs, who were charged with selling ITT stock during the settlement talks with the Justice Department when the terms of the forthcoming antitrust agreement were not available to investors, also agreed to the permanent injunction.

None of the defendants conceded they

had violated securities laws by agreeing to the consent judgment.

In the same suit, Lazard Freres & Co. and an Italian bank were enjoined from distributing unregistered ITT stock, a charge which was unrelated to the antitrust settlement.

Investigators Differ

Reports on Senate hearings. The Senate Judiciary Committee May 5, 1972 released its majority report upholding the nomination of Richard G. Kleindienst as attorney general without the signatures of three members who had voted with the majority to approve the nomination.

The three—Sens. Charles McC. Mathias Jr. (R, Md.), Philip A. Hart (D, Mich.) and Robert C. Byrd (D, W. Va.)—declined to endorse the majority report, which held that Kleindienst had "acted properly" concerning the settlement of the ITT antitrust cases and that the settlement was "not the product of political influence."

The report further held that the settlement "was reached on the merits after arm's length negotiations," that Kleindienst had not lied in testifying the negotiations were handled exclusively by another official or about his contacts with the White House.

In brief statements May 5, Hart said the hearings did not attach to Kleindienst any wrongdoing that might have occurred and Byrd said the entire Senate was entitled to vote on the nomination.

Mathias made a lengthy statement May 5 critical of ITT and the Justice Department but concluding that the ITT settlement was "reasonable" from the government's point of view and that Kleindienst was qualified to be attorney general. Any mistakes he made in the ITT matter resulted from "a highly pressured life," Mathias said, and not from a scheme to help a political contributor.

Other Mathias conclusions: (a) ITT lobbyist Dita D. Beard had written the disputed memorandum linking the antitrust settlement with an ITT pledge of $400,000 for the 1972 Republican convention; (b) ITT had mounted "a massive corporate assault on government" in at-

tempting to get a favorable settlement; (c) the $400,000 pledge was like an "insurance premium; (d) the Justice Department should not have worked through White House aide Peter M. Flanigan to get an analysis of ITT's financial plea on its antitrust cases.

Minority report—The minority report, for which a summary was issued May 9, called the nomination hearings a "whitewash" and said Kleindienst had played "a determinative role" in the ITT settlement. The minority members consisted of Democratic Sens. Birch Bayh (Ind.), Edward M. Kennedy (Mass.), John V. Tunney (Calif.) and Quentin N. Burdick (N.D.), the four who had voted not to approve the Kleindienst nomination.

The report found "an inherent conflict of interest" in the Justice Department's settlement of the ITT antitrust cases at a time when the Republican party was accepting a large monetary pledge for its convention from the company. Taken separately, the report said, the settlement and convention pledge "might each have generated serious questions in the public mind," and "taken together, they reflect a pattern of events which suggests that there was a connection in the minds of most of the parties involved."

The report said "the clearest blame falls upon the White House" in that the hearing testimony showed that several staff members there knew about both the settlement and the pledge. It added, the White House "is where the buck stops and . . . where the bucks should have been stopped."

In another individual view May 8, Hart said that despite an "inevitable shadow" over Kleindienst his nomination should be confirmed and he was convinced the antitrust settlement was not connected to ITT's pledge to the GOP despite an "atmosphere of pressure."

Kleindienst confirmed. Kleindienst's nomination as attorney general was confirmed by 64–19 Senate vote June 8, 1972.

Merger upheld. The Supreme Court Feb. 20, 1973 refused to intervene in the ITT's acquisition of the Hartford Fire

Insurance Co. Consumer advocate Ralph Nader had asked the court to reopen the case, claiming that the Department of Justice, in making the merger settlement, failed to disclose fully its motives for so acting. Justice Douglas dissented.

A federal judge had also rejected Nader's request Sept. 7, 1972, and defended the original settlement made in 1971, saying that the courts did not have to double-check the motives of the Justice Department.

Stockholders' suits against ITT. The Justice Department's controversial antitrust settlements with ITT continued to spawn lawsuits against the company.

Hilda Herbst, a former ITT stockholder, had brought charges in July 1972 in federal district court in New Haven, Conn., alleging that ITT misled investors and the Internal Revenue Service (IRS) in winning approval from stockholders and the government for its merger with the Hartford Fire Insurance Co.

The charges involved a 1969 transaction in which ITT disposed of 1.7 million shares of Hartford Fire stocks previously bought for cash by ITT. Complex tax rules governing the kind of merger planned by ITT demanded that acquisition involve only the exchange of stock, not cash.

Consequently, the IRS ruled that if the merger were to proceed on a tax free basis, ITT would be required to sell its 8% block of stock "unconditionally to an unrelated third party." The 17,000 Hartford Fire stockholders then would be allowed to exchange their shares, valued at more than $1 billion, for ITT stock, without paying immediate capital gains taxes.

ITT eventually disposed of the stock by selling it to Mediobanca Banca di Credito of Milan, Italy, and the stockholders' exchange occurred without objection from the IRS.

Herbst's class action suit contended that "previous understandings" between Mediobanca and ITT's investment banker, Lazard Freres & Co., had preceded the stock sale. According to pretrial documents filed June 15, these "understandings" invalidated IRS-imposed conditions that the sale be unconditional and the buyer be unrelated.

Herbst alleged that Mediobanca was not an independent third party, that instead of actually divesting itself of the Hartford Fire stock, ITT merely "parked" it with Mediobanca and Lazard, and that ITT influenced or controlled Mediobanca's ultimate disposition of the stock and the prices paid for it through its ties to Lazard.

According to the suit: Lazard was not an independent banking house, but a member of the Mediobanca syndicate; Mediobanca was "straw man" for the transaction; Felix Rohatyn, a Lazard partner and ITT director, was intended "to run the entire show"; Lazard retained custody of the shares purchased by Mediobanca and retained the proxy votes on the stock.

A related suit was filed by Benjamin Bernstein, an ITT stockholder, in federal district court in New York, the Wall St. Journal said Aug. 18, 1973. Bernstein claimed that ITT had been despoiled of $11 million by Lazard and its international affiliate, Mediobanca and Les Fils Dreyfus & Cie., a Swiss investment firm, in a scheme that violated U.S. securities laws.

Bernstein challenged Mediobanca's sale of 500,000 shares of ITT stock to Dreyfus and another investment company not named as a defendant. Mediobanca had obtained the ITT stock in an exchange with ITT, which received the Hartford Fire shares it had first owned and had sold to Mediobanca under agreement with the IRS.

Bernstein said the close relationship that existed among the four defendants violated the contract between ITT and Mediobanca calling for an arms length sale to unrelated third parties.

Mediobanca's selling price for the ITT stock was $55 a share. The actual market prices at the time of the sales to Dreyfus and the other investment firm were $73 and $77 a share.

Bernstein had demanded that ITT institute charges against the four defendants. When ITT refused to act, Bernstein brought the suit, naming ITT as a nominal defendant under provisions of a stockholder's derivative action.

The Dairy Case: Fund Pledge Cited in Price & Trust Actions

The dairy industry was accused during 1972 of promising financial contributions for President Nixon's election in return for an increase in federal milk price supports. A federal anti-trust case against a major milk marketing association was also said to involve questionable political contributions.

Milk price rise tied to politics. A consumer suit filed in U.S. district court in Washington Jan. 24 charged that an increase in federal price supports for milk stemmed from "political considerations" and asked the court to rescind the increase. The suit was brought by consumer advocate Ralph Nader and three consumer groups. (Nader and his supporters were also prominently involved in the attack on the ITT's alleged efforts to buy political favors with election campaign money.)

The suit contended that the increase had been granted "illegally" in return for "promises and expectations of campaign contributions for the re-election campaign of the incumbent President [Nixon]."

The suit cited this sequence of events, all in 1971: a decision March 12 by then-Agriculture Secretary Clifford M. Hardin to deny as unjustified a rise in the milk price support level, a $10,000 contribution by milk producers to various GOP fund-raising committees March 22, a meeting of 16 dairy spokesmen with Hardin and President Nixon at the White House March 23 and Hardin's announcement March 25 reversing his decision 13 days earlier and granting an increase of 27¢ a hundredweight in federal price supports for milk.

Other charges in the suit: (1) a total of $322,500 had been donated by dairy producers to GOP committees by the end of 1971; (b) the price support increase, granted on "considerations extraneous" to those provided by law, would cost the government an additional $126.2 million during fiscal 1972; and (c) Hardin had "received no new information or evidence bearing upon dairy farmers' costs, including the costs

of feed," after he denied the increase and up to the time he reversed himself.

The Nader lawsuit was dismissed in March on the grounds that the 1971 milk price support increase had terminated in March 1972, rendering the 1971 legal question moot.

Milk group sued in trust action—One of the main organizations named in the Nader lawsuit—Associated Milk Producers Inc. (AMPI)—was the target of a civil antitrust suit filed by the Justice Department Feb. 1, 1972 in San Antonio, Tex., where the milk marketing cooperative was headquartered. The suit charged the 40,000-member AMPI with violating the Sherman Antitrust Act by numerous anti-competitive practices since 1967 that spanned a 14-state area.

The suit charged that the AMPI illegally (1) manipulated federal milk marketing orders to depress the price of milk sold by independent producers competing with the cooperative's members, (2) forced milk processors who bought milk from the AMPI to agree not to buy milk from AMPI competitors, (3) acquired milk haulers and processors who did business with AMPI competitors, and (4) hindered dairy farmer members from freely withdrawing from the cooperative to market milk as a competitor.

Although the AMPI, formed in 1969 by the merger of 36 diary marketing cooperatives, was organized under the Capper-Volstead Act which granted immunity from antitrust laws for specific marketing activities, the exemption did not extend to the suit's allegations.

The Nader lawsuit Jan. 24 had alleged that the AMPI contributed $2.8 million to a "front" organization, the Trust for Agricultural Political Education (TAPE), for distribution to political candidates.

Letters support price-politics tie. Correspondence uncovered in connection with another lawsuit and published in the Washington Post Aug. 25, 1972, appeared to substantiate claims that the price support increase was politically motivated.

The letters, written by officials of Mid-America Dairymen, Inc, a dairy co-op, stated that the organization contributed $65,000 to the Republican party in 1971.

The money was funneled to GOP finance committees by Murray Chotiner, a longtime Nixon political confidant, and by Marion E. Harrison, Chotiner's law firm partner.

In one letter, written March 29, 1971, Gary Hanman, chairman of Mid-America's political fund, ADEPT, wrote another official, saying, "I can assure you that the TAPE and ADEPT programs, as well as SPACE, played a major role in this administrative decision."

TAPE and SPACE were acronyms for political funds administered by two other dairy organizations, American Milk Producers, Inc. and Dairymen, Inc.

Another letter, written by Mid-America President William A. Powell to a member in 1971 and published by the Post Aug. 25, said:

"The facts of life are that the economic welfare of dairymen does depend a great deal on political action. If dairymen are to receive their fair share of the governmental financial pie that we all pay for, we must have friends in government. I have become increasingly aware that the sincere and soft voice of the dairy farmer is no match for the jingle of hard currencies put in the campaign funds of politicians by the vegetable fat interests, labor, oil, steel, airlines and others.

"We dairymen as a body can be a dominant group. On March 23, 1971, along with nine other dairy farmers, I sat in the Cabinet Room of the White House, across the table from the President of the United States, and heard him compliment the dairymen on their marvelous work in consolidating and unifying our industry and our involvement in politics. He said, 'You people are my friends and I appreciate it.'

"Two days later an order came from the U.S. Department of Agriculture increasing the support price of milk to 85% of parity, which added from 500 to 700 million dollars to dairy farmers' milk checks. We dairymen cannot afford to overlook this kind of economic benefit. Whether we like it or not, this is the way the system works."

The letters, which had been sent to the Justice Department, were obtained by the National Farmers Organization in connection with its suit against major national dairy co-ops.

In an interview, Hanman told the Post that his group had also made contributions to Congressional campaigns after the initial March 12 decision by the USDA barring a milk price support increase.

"That's the hard core of our political action program—to help your friends," Hanman declared. During March, legislation was introduced in the House and Senate to raise milk support prices.

Hanman also revealed that six checks for $2,500 were sent Aug. 19 to Chotiner, who channeled them to campaign committees. The $15,000 was in addition to the $50,000 already pledged by ADEPT to the Administration and paid during March and April. "It's not unusual to bleed you more later," Hanman commented.

Hanman said AMPI had directed him to Harrison and Chotiner.

Nader suit reopened. A federal judge in Washington ruled Oct. 6, 1972, in the case of Nader's dismissed Jan. 24 suit against the milk producers, that Nader and the other plaintiffs, three consumer organizations, Federation of Homemakers, D.C. Consumers Association and the Nader-sponsored Public Citizen, Inc., could begin to take sworn statements from dairy producers and Administration fund raisers.

The appeals court reopened the Nader case, declaring that any "improprieties" in the 1971 decision "were not negated simply by rendition of the 1972 decision," the Washington Post reported Sept. 12.

A pretrial deposition filed in the suit Dec. 16 revealed that a public relations executive established 150 secret fund raising commitees for Nixon so that dairymen could subdivide their contributions in order "to avoid gift taxes."

Robert F. Bennett, son of Sen. Wallace F. Bennett (R, Utah), said nearly every committee received $2,500 each from dairymen with the total sum reaching $232,500 during July-September 1971.

Pretrial testimony filed Jan. 10, 1973 identified President Nixon's personal attorney, Herbert W. Kalmbach, as a solicitor of dairy funds.

The court papers also claimed that Kalmbach withdrew the request when the contributors insisted the gifts be made public.

George L. Mehren, an executive with Associated Milk Producers, Inc. (AMPI) of Texas and treasurer of its political group, TAPE (Trust for Agricultural Political Education), said he met with Kalmbach in Los Angeles in February 1972 when the Nixon spokesman asked "quite unequivocally" for campaign contributions.

Kalmbach ruled out any Administration quid pro quo for the dairymen, Mehren testified. Mehren denied making commitments but said he insisted that any funds he provided must be "explicitly identified and fully reported."

At a later meeting in Washington, Kalmbach withdrew his request without giving specific reasons for the decision, Mehren testified.

AMPI had donated $197,500 to the Nixon campaign during 1971, according to the Washington Post Jan. 11. (Mehren, who had been an assistant secretary of agriculture under the Johnson Administration, claimed that he rejected a second Republican request in October 1972 as well as a perfunctory request from Democratic presidential candidate George McGovern in order not to jeopardize the settlement of an antitrust suit brought against AMPI by the government.)

In a deposition made public Jan. 27, Murray Chotiner insisted that there was no connection between his lobbying activities at the White House as a dairy industry advocate and the Administration's decision to raise the federal support price of milk. He said that the Washington law firm (Reeves & Harrison) he had joined March 9, 1971, after leaving his White House post, represented several dairy cooperatives in addition to directing fund raising for the forthcoming Republican campaign.

Chotiner said he had "personally" spoken with Nixon's principal domestic aide, John D. Ehrlichman, and White House counsel Charles W. Colson and reported telling them that "what was good for the dairy farmers was good for the country, and what was good for the country was good for the dairy farmers."

The Washington Post reported Jan. 30 that Chotiner had been in touch with Administration aides March 9–25, 1971 on behalf of the dairy cooperatives; the Nixon Administration March 25 had reversed an Agriculture Department (USDA) ruling against the requested milk price support increase; dairy farmers, in the company of Chotiner's law partner, Marion Harrison, met with the President March 23 and attended meetings March 24 to discuss political contributions with Chotiner. He later arranged to funnel their donations to various GOP finance committees, according to the deposition.

In the pretrial testimony, Chotiner admitted he had sought out late contributions from the dairymen several months after the March meetings. Chotiner justified his activities saying, "if you don't help the farmer, you don't get his [election] support."

Secret dairy farmers' contribution disclosed. The Lehigh Valley Cooperative Farmers, a Pennsylvania dairy group, made two $25,000 secret contributions (in $100 bills) to the Nixon re-election campaign during 1972, the Washington Post reported June 1, 1973.

The first secret donation was made April 20, 1972, when Agriculture Secretary Earl L. Butz addressed a stockholders meeting in Pennsylvania. (According to the Post, the association had pledged a $100,000 contribution if Vice President Spiro T. Agnew, who was scheduled to appear, addressed the group. When Butz substituted for Agnew, the offer was reduced.) A second Lehigh contribution was made in May 1972.

The General Accounting Office (GAO) May 19 had listed the $50,000 gift as an anonymous contribution which had never been made public, as required by the federal disclosure law, the Post reported.

J. Curtis Herge, a former Nixon campaign aide, told the Post that the $50,000 from the Lehigh group was eventually turned over to former re-election committee aide Frederick C. LaRue in July 1972, "according to the absolute instructions" of former Attorney General John N. Mitchell and Jeb Stuart Magruder, former deputy campaign director. (LaRue had told the GAO that part of the secret money was used to finance the cover-up of Watergate defendants.)

Herge, currently a special assistant to Deputy Attorney General Joseph T. Sneed, said he and campaign scheduling director Herbert L. Porter delivered the $50,000 in cash to former committee treasurer Hugh W. Sloan Jr.

According to the GAO, Sloan, realizing that the anonymous funds had been donated in violation of the federal reporting law, refused to release the money until he could determine its source. When he resigned from the re-election committee in July 1972, the money was transferred to LaRue.

Herge claimed that he was "absolutely certain it [the $50,000] would be properly reported and had no idea what the money might be used for." He said he had informed the FBI of the circumstances surrounding the contribution because of Mitchell's involvement in the transaction.

Other government sources, the Post reported, said the Lehigh lobbyist in Washington, Frank Carroll, delivered the money to the re-election committee.

Pressure for Funds

Funds tied to import quota. Before President Nixon dismissed him as special Watergate prosecutor Oct. 20, 1973, Archibald Cox had obtained a copy of a December 1970 letter from an AMPI representative, it was reported Oct. 23. The letter suggested that if the Administration imposed import quotas on certain dairy products, Nixon could expect up to $2 million in campaign contributions from the group.

Fifteen days after the White House received the letter, dated Dec. 16, 1970, from Patrick J. Hillings, a California attorney, former GOP congressman, long time friend of Nixon and the Washington counsel, with Marion E. Harrison, for AMPI, Nixon ordered that import quotas be set on four dairy products, although at a lower level than desired by the dairy industry.

In his presidential proclamation of Dec. 31, 1970, Nixon sharply curtailed the import of cheese and its substitutes, chocolate containing butterfat, animal feeds containing milk or its derivatives and

ice cream from 25%–90% for the different exporting nations.

Campaign contributions from AMPI and other major dairy cooperatives began to flow to the White House soon after another Administration decision, also sought by the industry, was announced in March 1971.

Hillings' letter complained that a favorable Tariff Commission ruling had been buried in the federal bureaucracy. "This problem is bogged down within the White House. We write you both as advocates and supporters. The time is ripe politically and economically to impose the recommended quotas," Hillings wrote.

"AMPI contributed about $135,000 to Republican candidates in the 1970 election," he continued. "We are . . . working with Tom Evans and Herb Kalmbach in setting up appropriate channels for AMPI to contribute $2 million for your re-election. AMPI is also funding a special project."

Other information related to the dairy industry's ties to the Administration corroborated portions of the 1970 letter: one of the White House memos that had been sought by attorneys for Ralph Nader in connection with his court test of the Administration's increase of federal milk price supports was filed in the court record and published by the Washington Post Oct. 21.

The memo, written for then White House chief of staff H. R. Haldeman by his aide, Gordon Strachan, indicated that the dairy industry's original campaign "commitment" had been reduced to $1 million.

According to the Feb. 1, 1972 memo, "Kalmbach is very concerned about his involvement in the milk producers situation," a statement which prompted Strachan to recommend Kalmbach's dissociation with the milk project "because of the risk of disclosure."

A notation at the end of the document, apparently by Haldeman, added: "I'll dis. w/ AG [Attorney General John N. Mitchell]." Mitchell had testified before the Senate Judiciary committee in March 1972 that he had no party or re-election responsibilities before his selection as President Nixon's campaign manager and would have none until he formally left the Administration.

Kalmbach got $100,000 in 1969.
William Dobrovir took a deposition Nov.
7, 1973 from ex-AMPI lawyer Jake Jacobsen, who said the dairy co-op had paid
Herbert Kalmbach, President Nixon's
personal attorney and chief fund raiser,
$100,000 in cash in August 1969, a year
before Kalmbach had testified he began
soliciting contributions for Nixon.

Jacobsen, who was chairman of the
bank from which AMPI withdrew the
money, testified that before its delivery he
was consulted about the payment by
Herbert Nelson, AMPI's general
manager, and David Parr. "I said it was a
good idea," Jacobsen testified. "I thought
it might produce a more sympathetic
understanding in this Administration to
the problems of the dairy industry."

The cash was delivered by Jacobsen's
Washington law partner, Milton P.
Semer, who was then the chief fund raiser
for Sen. Edmund S. Muskie, a Democratic presidential contender.

Semer testified that he offered Kalmbach checks but was asked for a cash
payment. According to other court
testimony, Attorney General Mitchell had
directed AMPI to Kalmbach, and H. R.
Haldeman, then White House chief of
staff, had cleared the money for receipt
when Kalmbach accepted it.

Jacobsen also testified that he had discussed the price support question with
John B. Connally Jr., then Treasury secretary, "and he said he would do all he
could to help us." Jacobsen said he met
Connally twice—just before Clifford
Hardin rejected the milk price increase
and "shortly before" the Administration
reversed the decision.

Connally told Senate Watergate Committee investigators Nov. 15 that he had
favored higher price supports for the dairy
industry but that he had refused to discuss
their campaign contributions.

Mitchell barred criminal suit. The Justice
Department acknowledged Dec. 26,
1973 that John N. Mitchell, who was
then attorney general, had rejected two
recommendations from the department's
antitrust division that criminal
antitrust action be started against Associated Milk Producers, Inc. (AMPI).

According to Richard McLaren, then
head of the antitrust division, he authorized a civil suit against the dairy
cooperative because of Mitchell's urging.

McLaren's testimony was filed as part
of a government brief in the AMPI case,
asking the court to reject a motion by the
defense to obtain access to all government
documents and tapes relating to a possible
quid pro quo in the relationship between
the price support increase and campaign
contributions.

The defense contended that the
Administration had used extortion in extracting campaign donations from the industry and that the antitrust case had
been initiated after AMPI refused a
second request from Nixon fund raisers
for a subsequent contribution.

Mid-America Dairymen sued. The Justice Department filed a civil antitrust suit
Dec. 27, 1973 against Mid-America Dairymen, Inc.

The Mid-America suit, filed in federal
district court in Kansas City, Mo.,
charged the group with attempting to monopolize milk sales in a 10-state area.

Presidential Explanations

Statements on ITT & dairy cases. President Nixon Jan. 8, 1974 issued two white
papers on the allegations that the International Telephone & Telegraph Corp.
(ITT) and the dairy industry had bargained for federal favors in return for
financial aid in the 1972 GOP election
campaign.

The President denied as "utterly false"
charges that presidential actions were
offered in the matters as a quid pro quo
"either in return for political contributions or the promise of such contributions."

The milk fund—In a 17-page statement,
Nixon defended as "totally proper" his decision to reverse an Agriculture Department ruling and allow an increase in the
federal price support of milk, although he
admitted for the first time that before he
ordered the increase he was aware that the
dairy industry had pledged at least $2
million to his re-election campaign.

However, the statement continued, "he
at no time discussed the contributions

with the dairy industry and the subject was not mentioned in his meeting of March 23, 1971" with dairy representatives. The statement added, "It is also worth noting that the ultimate contributions by the dairy industry to the President's re-election effort (1) were far less than the industry leaders had hoped to raise; (2) were far less than the dairy industry gave to other candidates for the House and Senate, including many prominent Democrats; and (3) represented less than 1% of the total contributions to President Nixon's re-election campaign."

Nixon said his decision to raise the price support was based on three factors:

■ "Intensive Congressional pressure"

■ "The economic merits of the case itself, as presented by the industry leaders in the meeting with the President, and as weighed by the President's advisers [in a meeting later that day]"

■ "Traditional political considerations relating to needs of the farm states."

According to Nixon, dairy lobbyists had mobilized 29 senators and more than 100 congressmen in an effort to raise price supports to levels that were 85%-90% of parity. To bring this about, legislation had been introduced that appeared certain of passage, according to Nixon, and any presidential veto also appeared certain to be overridden.

"Moreover," the statement continued, "if the President were to try to force his will in this matter (i.e., to push parity down to 80%) it could be politically disastrous in some of the Midwestern states, and, in the light of known Congressional intentions, would be both foolish and futile."

During the conference with advisers March 23, 1971, "the political power of the dairy industry lobby was also brought to the President's attention," according to the statement. Treasury "Secretary [John B.] Connally [Jr.] said that their votes would be important in several Midwestern states and he noted that the industry had political funds which would be distributed among House and Senate candidates in the coming election year—although neither the secretary nor anyone else discussed possible contributions to the President's campaign," the statement continued.

"The fundamental themes running through this March 23 meeting were two: (1) the unique and very heavy pressures being placed upon the President by the Democratic majority leadership in the Congress and (2) the political advantages and disadvantages of making a decision regarding a vital political constituency.

"The President himself concluded that the final decision came down to the fact that the Congress was going to pass the higher support legislation, and he could not veto it without alienating the farmers—an essential part of his political constituency."

In claiming that the "economic consequences of the decision [to raise milk price supports] have been beneficial to the entire country," Nixon cited four "results" of his action: the smallest increase in cost of milk to consumers from 1971-72 when compared with previous years; (a .9¢ boost in the average retail cost of a half gallon of milk compared with a 1.5¢ a half gallon increase from 1970-71); a drop in taxpayers' costs of the milk support program (down to $116.6 million in fiscal 1972 from $174.2 million in 1971); an end to the downward trend in milk production; and a decline in government supplies of surplus milk.

Nixon said the dairy industry's lobbying and contribution activities "followed a separate track" and to emphasize this fact, the statement discussed fund-raising and other money matters in a separate context from its justification of the price support increase.

The paper acknowledged that Charles W. Colson, then a White House special counsel, had sent a memo to the President in September 1970 informing him of Associated Milk Producers Inc.'s (AMPI) pledge of $2 million for the re-election campaign; that a letter had been sent in December 1970 to Nixon confirming the pledge, but the President claimed not to have seen it; that AMPI's first Nixon contribution had been given to Herbert Kalmbach, Nixon's personal attorney and chief fund-raiser, in August 1969 (Nixon said he knew nothing of this money although it was deposited by Kalmbach in a trustee bank account used for money left over from the 1968 presidential campaign); that $232,500 in dairy funds had been recorded on a list of secret campaign contributors kept by Rose Mary Woods, Nixon's personal secretary, as "House Account" money. No effort was made to explain why the Administration and the industry took such precautions to conceal the source of the campaign donations.

The ITT case—Nixon claimed that his order to Deputy Attorney General Richard Kleindienst to drop a pending appeal with the Supreme Court on one of the government's antitrust suits against ITT was based entirely on Nixon's personal philosophy that corporations should not be challenged on grounds of "bigness per se." Further, Nixon said in his eight-page statement, he was unaware of ITT's campaign pledge to fund the Republican National Convention when he personally intervened in the case in April 1971.

Nixon limited his role in the case to the phone call to Kleindienst April 19, 1971 and a subsequent call April 21, 1971 reversing his earlier instruction. The order to halt a court appeal of one of three suits pending against ITT was withdrawn, Nixon said, because he feared that Solicitor General Erwin Griswold would resign if the Supreme Court were prevented from considering the case. This warning came from Attorney General John Mitchell who said Nixon's decision to halt court proceedings was "inadvisable," the President said. (In earlier testimony, Kleindienst claimed that it was his threat to resign which prompted Nixon's turnaround.)

According to the statement, Nixon's intercession resulted from his "irritation" with Richard McLaren, head of the Justice Department's antitrust division, who refused to follow Administration policy on the case as it was set down by John Ehrlichman, Nixon's domestic policy adviser.

The ITT case eventually was filed for appeal with the high court but a settlement was reached before arguments were heard. Nixon said he did not "direct the settlement or participate in the settlement negotiations directly or indirectly."

ITT President Harold Geneen tried to discuss the case with Nixon during the summer of 1969, Nixon disclosed, but the meeting was never held because Administration aides considered it "inappro-

priate." However, other White House aides did discuss the case with ITT representatives, the statement added.

According to the statement, ITT did not make its offer to underwrite the Republican National Convention in San Diego until June 1971. "Apparently," its pledge totaled $200,000, of which $100,000 was returned when the site was moved from San Diego to Miami Beach. In any case, the site-selection process was "separate and unrelated" to considerations in the federal antitrust case against ITT, Nixon stated.

Reaction. Nixon's Jan. 8 white papers were compared by observers with previous remarks made on the issues.

At his press conference Oct. 26, 1973, Nixon had declared that throughout his public life he had refused to personally accept campaign contributions, that he had "refused to have any discussion of contributions" and that prior to the 1972 presidential campaign, he had issued orders "that he did not want to have any information from anybody with regard to campaign contributions."

This apparently conflicted with Nixon's admission Jan. 8 that an aide, Charles W. Colson, had sent him a written memo detailing a dairy group's pledge of $2 million.

A White House press spokesman said there was no contradiction in the two remarks. "Occasionally people break rules," the official said, referring to Colson's apparent violation of the President's order about campaign gifts.

Nixon's white paper account also appeared to contradict former Agriculture Secretary Clifford Hardin's sworn testimony that the decision to raise federal milk price supports was based solely "on the basis of statutory criteria," i.e., supply, costs and farm income. President Nixon admitted that "traditional political considerations" in farm states also played a major role in his decision to increase milk supports.

In his official statement, Nixon stated that he had been forced to act because of Congressional pressure in support of the dairy lobby. Sen. William Proxmire (D, Wis.), a supporter of the increase, said Jan. 9 that Nixon's argument was "ridiculous." He and other proponents of higher prices "were consistently unable to persuade our colleagues to enact such legislation over the past 15 years. In any event, it would have been impossible for Congress to override a presidential veto," Proxmire added.

Sen. Edmund S. Muskie (D, Me.), another supporter of the increase, said Jan. 9 that despite his support of the water pollution bill, Nixon had not been deterred from vetoing it. "There is nothing in the President's record to indicate that he is sensitive to the Congress' point of view," Muskie declared.

Lawyers for Ralph Nader introduced into evidence Jan. 11 an extract from a tape recording of Nixon's meeting March 23, 1971 with dairy industry leaders. According to the brief, Nixon's remarks contradicted his assertions in the white paper that campaign contributions were not mentioned.

According to the tape, Nixon told the group:

"I first want to say that I am very grateful for the support that we have had [inaudible word] from this group. I know that in American agriculture you're widely recognized; that it cuts across all the farmer organizations, is represented in all the states.

"I know, too, that you are a group that are politically very conscious, not in any party sense, but you realize that what happens in Washington not only affects your business success but affects the economy; our foreign policy [inaudible word] affects you.

"And you are willing to do something about it. And I must say a lot of businessmen and others I get around this table, they yammer and talk a lot but they don't do anything about it. But you do and I appreciate that. I don't need to spell it out. Friends talk and others keep me posted as to what you do."

Nader's lawyers also contended that a memo prepared for the President by his staff prior to the March 1971 meeting reminded Nixon of the campaign pledge. The memo "briefly noted that the dairy lobby—like organized labor—had decided to spend political money," according to the testimony of a Nixon aide, David Wilson.

Former Solicitor General Erwin

Griswold said Jan. 9 that he disagreed with part of Nixon's statement claiming that on April 19, 1971, he had "authorized the Justice Department to proceed with the [ITT] case in accordance with its own determination." Griswold claimed that he had not received authorization from the White House to file for appeal with the Supreme Court until "about May 15, 16, or 17, 1971."

Observers also noted that in limiting his own involvement in the case to two telephone calls, Nixon failed to mention specifically that ITT officials had met numerous times with key Administration officials.

Nixon also failed to disclose that lawyers for ITT suggested that Deputy Attorney General Richard Kleindienst seek a delay in filing the appeal (a delay that was granted) because the firm feared an adverse Supreme Court ruling and sought time to negotiate an out-of-court settlement with Justice Department officials (a strategy that was successful).

In another major contradiction with previous sworn testimony, Nixon's assertion that he had discussed the case with John Mitchell, then attorney general, and Kleindienst, then deputy attorney general, conflicted with their statements at Senate hearings considering Kleindienst's nomination as attorney general.

Dairy Case Developments

Milk fund defendants plead guilty. David L. Parr and Keifer L. Howard, former officials of Associated Milk Producers Inc.'s (AMPI) Arkansas division, pleaded guilty Jan. 11, 1974 to charges of conspiring to donate $22,000 in corporate funds to the 1968 Democratic presidential campaign.

Harold S. Nelson, a former general manager of the co-op, pleaded innocent March 27 to a three-count perjury indictment in connection with that case. According to the government, Nelson lied to a federal grand jury in September 1973 when he denied authorizing the payment to the 1968 Humphrey campaign.

Parr, who had been Nelson's deputy at AMPA and the co-op's special counsel, entered a plea of guilty July 23 to a charge that he had authorized payment of more than $200,000 in illegal campaign contributions to Humphrey and other candidates of both parties.

Nelson later pleaded guilty July 31 to a charge that he had bribed Former Treasury Secretary John B. Connally Jr. in connection with the effort to secure the increase in milk price supports.

Nelson also admitted that he had conspired to make illegal campaign contributions to a number of Democratic and Republican candidates during the years 1968 through 1972. According to the government, more than $330,000 in illicit AMPI donations were given over the six-year period, including a $100,000 cash payment made in August 1969 to President Nixon's chief fund raiser, Herbert Kalmbach. The money was paid, Nelson stated, "for the purpose of securing access to White House officials."

Nelson and Parr were sentenced Nov. 1 to four months in jail and fined $10,000 each. (The jail sentences actually were three years with all but four months suspended.)

Chief Judge George L. Hart Jr. of federal district court in Washington said he imposed the jail terms to deter other violators. "You pleaded guilty to crimes that hundreds of persons have been guilty of in past years. Nothing was ever done about it," the judge said.

The Arkansas Electric Cooperative Association, its general manager and 15 of its member co-ops had pleaded guilty in September 1973 to charges that they had conspired to funnel AMPI's money to the Democrats.

Lehigh Valley Cooperative Farmers, Allentown, Pa. dairy co-op, pleaded guilty May 6 to charges that it had illegally contributed $50,000 in corporate funds to President Nixon's re-election race.

Federal court in Washington imposed the maximum fine for the criminal offense—$5,000.

Two Lehigh Valley co-op officials entered guilty pleas in federal district court in Washington in connection with the illegal contributions.

Richard L. Allison, who was recently dismissed as president of the co-op be-cause of his role in authorizing the $50,000 contribution, pleaded guilty May 17 and was given a suspended fine of $1,000 for his misdemeanor offense.

Francis X. Carroll, Lehigh's Washington-based attorney and lobbyist who had also been fired by the co-op, pleaded guilty May 28 to a misdemeanor charge of aiding Allison in the transaction. Carroll's fine was also suspended.

Allison disputed the Nixon finance committee's version of the contribution. He said a $35,000 cash honorarium was paid April 20, 1972 when Agriculture Secretary Earl Butz addressed a co-op meeting. Subsequently, Carroll "came back and said it would cost more money," Allison testified. Another $25,000 was then turned over.

A $35,000 fine was imposed on AMPI Aug. 1 after the dairy co-op had pleaded guilty to a six-count criminal information charging conspiracy and illegal campaign giving.

Rejecting pleas for leniency, U.S. District Court Chief Judge George L. Hart Jr. imposed the maximum fine. "The law against corporations giving political contributions has been on the books for a long, long time." Hart said. "It's been completely disregarded by Republicans, Democrats, independents and whatnot for a long, long time. This type of cavalier violation of the law has got to be put to a stop."

AMPI's lawyer had asked Hart to assess a penalty of $15,000 for the felony charges, contending that the co-op "represents a membership of 40,000 hard-working, sincere, honest dairy farmers" whose board of directors was not "sophisticated in this matter" and thereby had delegated operating authority to the co-op's general manager, Harold Nelson.

The co-op's membership had "learned a bitter lesson about giving too much power to a few," the group's lawyer told the court, adding that because of publicity linking the co-op to the "overhanging shadow" of Watergate, AMPI now was finding it awkward to deal with government officials.

Hart replied, "I can't believe the directors of the corporations, even though they are farmers, didn't know what was going on." Hart was also critical of the recipients of these illegal contributions, saying "I find it difficult to believe that these [campaign] organizations are so loose that they know so little about what is going on."

According to the criminal information filed by the Watergate special prosecutor's office, AMPI had made political contributions totaling $280,900 in corporate cash that went to Democratic and Republican candidates from 1968 through 1972.

Politicians who had received the illegal money had denied any knowledge of its corporate source. AMPI President John E. Butterbrodt issued a statement Aug. 1 saying that the co-op was "aware of no evidence whatever" indicating that candidates who had accepted the dairy co-op's funds "had any knowledge whatsoever of the actions taken in their apparent behalf."

Stuart Russell, a lawyer for Associated Milk Producers Inc., was sentenced Aug. 14 to serve three concurrent two-year prison terms for helping the dairy cooperative illegally funnel corporate money to two candidates for federal office.

Russell had been convicted July 11 on one count of conspiracy involving a $100,000 contribution given to Nixon fundraiser Herbert Kalmbach, and two counts of aiding and abetting the donation of $8,400 to Sen. Edmund S. Muskie (D, Me.) in 1970–1971.

Milk funds reported 'laundered.' The Senate Watergate investigators had come across evidence that at least $200,000 in contributions from the dairy lobby was donated to two Republican Congressional campaign committees in 1972 in a scheme to conceal and "launder" money actually intended for President Nixon's re-election campaign, the New York Times reported Feb. 15, 1974.

According to Congressional sources, Senate committee members informed their Republican colleagues in Congress that an investigation showed that of $300,000 given to the Republican Senatorial Campaign Committee and the Republican Congressional Campaign Committee, $200,000 was diverted to the Finance Committee to Re-elect the President.

The Congressional donations had been made public earlier, but the transfer to Nixon's campaign had remained secret. Until this report, it was believed that the dairy group's total contributions to the presidential race had been $422,500.

According to the Times, in mid-October 1972 presidential fund raiser Lee Nunn visited George Mehren, general manager of AMPI, and asked Mehren for additional contributions from the industry.

Mehren reportedly told Nunn he feared further negative reaction if more contributions were offered. Nunn then proposed that AMPI funnel the money through Congressional committees, the Times reported. On Oct. 27, 1972 AMPI donated $150,000 to each Republican Senate and House committee; between Oct. 31 and Nov. 7, 1972, the Congressional campaign committees transferred $221,000 to the Republican National Finance Committee. They in turn sent $200,000 to the Nixon finance committee from Nov. 7 to Nov. 13, 1972. Former Commerce Secretary Maurice Stans was chairman of both committees.

Because the Congressional transactions were reported March 10, 1973 as required by law, no illegality was involved, but because the money was received just prior to the pre-election deadline for revealing campaign donations, no publicity was given the contributions until after the election.

Report lists AMPI irregularities. A report commissioned by the board of directors of the nation's largest milk cooperative, Associated Milk Producers, Inc. (AMPI), revealed that AMPI had engaged in a broad pattern of irregularities involving campaign contributions to Democrats as well as Republicans since 1968.

The report, prepared by the Little Rock, Ark. law firm of Wright, Lindsey and Jennings, with an audit by the accounting firm of Haskins & Sells, was made public March 14, 1974 after being submitted to U.S. District Court in Kansas City, Mo. for use in an antitrust suit against AMPI. (The principal author of the report was Edward L. Wright, a former president of the American Bar Association.)

Items uncovered in the Wright report surfaced in the press throughout March:

■ It was reported March 14 that AMPI paid $104,521.62 to print and distribute copies of a book of President Lyndon Johnson's speeches during the 1968 presidential race in order to help the Democratic presidential candidate, Hubert H. Humphrey.

Records indicated that the book's printer was referred to the dairymen by a White House letter. If regarded as an indirect political contribution, the payment was in violation of a federal law barring donations from corporate funds.

■ According to a report March 27, AMPI donated at least $91,691 in corporate funds to Humphrey's 1968 presidential race and $34,500 to his 1970 senatorial campaign in Minnesota.

Other information in the Wright report indicated that after Humphrey's defeat in 1968, the dairymen made plans to donate money to President Nixon while continuing to back Humphrey and other Democrats in later elections.

■ According to reports March 26, Harold S. Nelson, former AMPI general manager, had arranged to deliver a $100,000 cash contribution to Herbert Kalmbach, then Nixon's chief fund raiser, in August 1969.

AMPI records showed that the money, intended to "make peace" with Nixon after the co-op's prior support of Humphrey, was withdrawn from the account of AMPI's political unit, Trust for Agriculture Political Education (TAPE), and delivered to Kalmbach by Milton P. Semer. (His law partner, Jake Jacobsen, had been indicted for perjury regarding an alleged $10,000 payoff to the Nixon Administration. Jacobsen pleaded not guilty March 15.)

"Several days later," according to the Wright report, AMPI's treasurer Robert O. Isham realized that the donation was in violation of the Federal Corrupt Practices Act because it violated the $5,000 limit to any campaign organization and had not been reported to the clerk of the House of Representatives.

Subsequently, Nelson and Isham met in December 1969 with W. De Veir Pierson, a former assistant to President Johnson, and at that time one of AMPI's lawyers in Washington, to discuss an elaborate scheme to cover up the illegal contribution by using dummy payments to prominent Democrats.

The Wright report stated that these AMPI officials decided to conceal their donation to Nixon by borrowing another $100,000 from an Austin, Texas bank to replace the money withdrawn and given to Kalmbach. According to the "payback plan" detailed in the report, "this loan would then be repaid through money solicited and obtained by Mr. [Bob A.] Lilly [Nelson's assistant and a TAPE official] from lawyers and public relations consultants employed by AMPI." These persons, many of them prominent Democrats, were compensated for their donations to Lilly with increased fees (and taxes paid on the additional income) paid by AMPI. All denied knowledge of the cover-up scheme of the original $100,000 contribution to Nixon.

Among those named in the report as conduits for Lilly were Pierson; Richard Maguire, former treasurer of the Democratic National Committee and later an AMPI lawyer in Washington; Ted Van Dyk and Kirby Jones, public relations consultants who became high ranking aides in Sen. George McGovern's presidential race in 1972; James R. Jones, former White House aide to President Johnson, former AMPI lawyer in Tulsa, Okla. and editor of a dairy industry publication, and currently a Democratic congressman elected in 1972 from Oklahoma; the late Clifton C. Carter, a former executive director of the Democratic National Committee and Washington lawyer for AMPI.

Van Dyk said March 26 he was asked to give Lilly $10,000 for use as a "bonus outside of the regular AMPI channels. I had no reason to think there was anything under the table about this at all," Van Dyk declared. "These [AMPI] people were essentially country people and they operated in an extremely erratic, harum-scarum way. I had no reason to suspect anything untoward."

Lilly eventually raised $142,500 by 1971 to pay off the $100,000 loan and others, the Wright report stated.

(AMPI officials had sought return of what the company termed its "illegal" $100,000 contribution from Nixon campaign committee lawyer, Kenneth Parkinson.)

Another AMPI lawyer who funneled money to Lilly, it was disclosed March 26, was Stuart H. Russell. Between 1968 and 1973, Russell was paid more than $1 million by the co-op. Payments to Lilly, for which Russell subsequently was reimbursed, went to Humphrey and Rep. Wilbur D. Mills (D, Ark.). AMPI paid the salaries and Washington living expenses for two Mills campaign workers in late 1971 and early 1972 when Mills was preparing to declare his candidacy for the Democratic presidential nomination, according to the Wright report.

■ It was reported March 24 that AMPI also spent $137,000 in 1971 on a computer mailing list for campaign use by Humphrey; Sen. James Abourezk (D, S.D.); Gov. David Hall (D, Okla.); Gov. Robert Docking (D, Kan.); and the Iowa Democratic Party. (Sen. Harold Hughes of Iowa said he refused an AMPI offer.)

The Minneapolis-based computer mail firm that compiled the list, Valentine, Sherman and Associates, admitted receiving the money and falsifying invoices to conceal the source of payments, according to the Wright report.

■ It was revealed March 24 that the Wright report also quoted Lilly as saying he made contributions in 1969 to Texas state legislators through another "conduit for political funds"—an official in the Texas Agriculture Commission.

Plan to kill antitrust suit disclosed— Also included in the Wright report was a statement from Dwight L. Morris, a former AMPI executive, that the dairymen made arrangements with Herbert Kalmbach to buy their way out of the antitrust suit. The plan fell through before the money could be paid when the Nixon Administration's controversial handling of the ITT antitrust suit was revealed, Morris asserted.

Morris also testified privately March 6 before the Senate Watergate committee and a Watergate grand jury in Washington.

Morris said he was told of the settlement plan by AMPI President John E. Butterbrodt. According to Morris' statement filed with the court March 12, he was told in April 1972 that Butterbrodt and George Mehren, Harold Nelson's successor as general manager of AMPI,

had "gone to Washington in an attempt to settle the suit in February 1972." (The suit had been filed Feb. 1, 1972.)

"No one in Washington would talk to them about this—not the Justice Department, FTC [Federal Trade Commission] or the White House," Morris testified. "A suggestion was finally made to them that they should see Kalmbach." Butterbrodt told Morris that [after a meeting on the West Coast] "they had agreed with Kalmbach to pay $300,000 to Kalmbach and the antitrust suit against AMPI would die a natural death," Morris said.

"Kalmbach was to direct them where [to which committees, etc.] the money should be sent. Before this could be accomplished the ITT thing hit the press and Kalmbach sent word that he didn't want their money," Morris added.

Another document entered as evidence in a related milk fund suit and made public Feb. 9 was a memo dated Sept. 24, 1971 from Charles Colson, then White House special counsel, to H. R. Haldeman, then White House chief of staff. Colson, who had been identified in other court records as the "point of contact with the dairy people within the White House," warned Haldeman that "there is underway in the Justice Department at the moment an Antitrust Division investigation of the milk producer cooperatives. . . . If this goes too far, there will be a number of very serious adverse consequences which I would be glad to elaborate on in detail."

Colson had informed President Nixon in September 1970 that the dairymen were prepared to contribute $2 million to his 1972 campaign.

The Colson memo was entered as evidence in consumer advocate Ralph Nader's suit seeking to overturn a 1971 increase in the federal price support for milk.

According to a pretrial deposition filed Jan. 21 in the Kansas City antitrust suit, AMPI's former lawyer David Parr said the co-op's aim was "to manage or control the total supply of milk in the U.S. including imports and exports."

Court documents made public May 4 alleged that Mehrens had also offered **$150,000 to President Nixon's re-election campaign in an effort to secure Administration efforts that would "slow down the** antitrust action" and then "reduce it to just a wrist slap."

The charges were made by former AMPI lobbyist Robert Lilly in a statement to Edward Wright.

Lilly claimed that 30 checks for $5,000 each, with the payee unspecified, were drawn up and signed by Mehren April 4–5, 1972, but were later voided. Mehren was reported to have told Senate investigators that he "had no recollection" of the checks, according to the Washington Post May 4.

Lilly said the decision to make the contribution grew out of a Washington meeting held March 16, 1972 between Treasury Secretary John B. Connally Jr. and AMPI officials. According to Mehren, "Connally called Attorney General [John] Mitchell and said rather harshly, 'Get off your [expletive deleted]. You're losing votes in the Midwest.'" Connally then suggested that AMPI delay making any more contributions "until near the end of the election,'" Mehren told Senate investigators.

The deal to quash the antitrust suit was never carried out, according to Mehren, because Herbert Kalmbach had called off the request for more AMPI contributions at another Washington meeting April 24, 1972. No reason was given, Mehren said.

The former executive director of another major dairy co-op, Dairymen Inc., told Senate investigators that he was asked at a predawn meeting March 24, 1971 with officials of two other dairy co-ops to raise $300,000 immediately for use in Nixon's campaign, the Post reported May 11.

D. Paul Alagia said he was unable to raise $300,000, $200,000 or $100,000 as requested by executives from AMPI and Mid-America Dairymen, Inc. Instead, $25,000 was quickly put up and sent by messenger to Washington.

Kalmbach had testified that Nixon's aides sought to confirm dairy industry campaign pledges in a meeting March 24, 1971 with co-op leaders one day after President Nixon decided to increase federal price supports. After securing the commitment and receiving a token contribution, the Administration announced the price decision March 25, 1971, according to Senate investigators.

Lilly admits funds-price tie. According to court papers filed in the government's antitrust suit against AMPI, AMPI lobbyist Robert Lilly said AMPI had made a "commitment" of campaign funds to President Nixon's re-election race "in conjunction with the 1971 price support" increase authorized by Nixon.

Lilly's statement, reported in the press May 2, 1974, was made to Edward L. Wright, who had investigated the alleged payoff for AMPI's directors. Wright's notes of his interview with Lilly had been subpoenaed for the antitrust trial.

Lilly said he was told of the arrangement April 4, 1972 during a meeting with AMPI's general manager, George L. Mehren, and Mehren's predecessor, Harold S. Nelson. "The commitment [of a campaign contribution] was made in March of 1971 by Nelson, [David] Parr, Marion Harrison, and [Jake] Jacobsen," Lilly told Wright.

"There was a big argument over how much money had been committed," Lilly said. "The figures ranged from $500,000 to $1 million. Jacobsen contacted Connally in March of 1971 about the contribution. Connally said there had to be new money or additional money."

Mehren disputed President Nixon's defense of his controversial price support decision made in an Administration white paper on the milk fund controversy, the Washington Post reported May 5.

Nixon had claimed that he had been pressured to authorize the price increase because of overwhelming Congressional backing for the legislative proposal. Mehren contested that assertion in statements made to Congressional investigators. "We had lined up quite a bit of support [in Congress]," Mehren said, "but not in my opinion sufficient to override a presidential veto."

When he and other industry officials met with Nixon March 23, 1971, Mehren said, they were not hopeful about their chances to win White House support for the increase. However, the Nixon campaign received a check for $25,000 from the political arm of Dairymen Inc. the next day, and on March 25, 1971, the Agriculture Department announced that it had reversed a previous ruling and would allow an increase in the support price of milk.

Herbert Kalmbach, the President's personal attorney and chief fund-raiser, also gave an account of the circumstances surrounding the dairy industry's pledge of campaign funds, it was reported May 6.

Kalmbach told the Senate Watergate Committee staff that a secret midnight meeting was held March 24, 1971 in his Washington hotel room for the purpose of asking dairymen to reconfirm their offer (made in 1970) to contribute $2 million to Nixon's campaign. Murray Chotiner, a Nixon confidant who had left the Administration three weeks earlier and set up private law practice, conveyed the message to Harold Nelson. (Chotiner had also just been retained by AMPI as its Washington counsel.) Nelson reaffirmed the pledge, Kalmbach testified.

The information was passed on to the House Judiciary Committee, according to the Washington Post, and formed the basis of the committee's request for White House tapes and other documents relating to the milk fund controversy. Sources close to the Senate Watergate Committee said testimony from Kalmbach and others caused the committee to conclude that the efforts to seek reconfirmation of the $2 million pledge were launched with Nixon's approval by John Ehrlichman, his top domestic affairs aide. Ehrlichman telephoned White House Special Counsel Charles Colson, who then met with Chotiner, investigators said. The arrangements were concluded March 23, 1971, immediately after Nixon had met with Ehrlichman and other aides and decided to authorize the milk price increase. (Nixon had met earlier that day with the dairy representatives.) Later that night, the dairymen agreed to make an immediate donation of $25,000—Dairymen Inc. met the deadline with its contribution March 24, 1971, according to Congressional investigators. Public announcement of the price increase was not made until March 25, 1971 when the White House was certain it would receive additional campaign funds, investigators charged.

Johnson & Mills also involved. Court documents filed in the antitrust case also yielded evidence supporting charges that dairy industry payoffs involved the late President Lyndon B. Johnson and Rep. Wilbur D. Mills (D, Ark.), it was reported May 7 and 9, 1974.

According to subpoenaed interview notes, AMPI comptroller Robert O. Isham told Edward Wright that "phony bonuses" paid to AMPI employes were subsequently used to make contributions to Johnson's "$1,000 Club," a group comprising big campaign contributors. The payments were later restored to the co-op when the corporation set up a legitimate political spending arm, TAPE (Trust for Agricultural Political Education).

Another court document quoted George Mehren as saying that AMPI leased a plane from a holding company for the Johnson financial interests for $94,000 a year. The lease, which Mehren termed "lush" and Johnson family spokesmen labeled "a bargain," was signed by Mehren's predecessor, Harold Nelson, despite opposition from AMPI's board of directors, the document stated. When he became general manager, Mehren said, he tried to cancel the agreement but was unable to win Johnson's approval. He agreed to cosign the lease, Mehren stated, when "it became plain to me that AMPI was in no position to charge the immediate past president of the U.S. with being party to a fraudulent transaction."

He also told Wright that Johnson welcomed the payments on the plane as a "supplement" to his "retirement income." Mehren also claimed that Johnson had told him in 1972 that "the dairy people in his last campaign had agreed to give $250,000 but had not done so and he had forgotten it."

It was reported May 5 that David Parr, an Arkansas attorney for AMPI and at one time the dairy co-op's second ranking official, hoped to raise $2 million in cash for Rep. Mills' race for the Democratic presidential nomination. (Mills, who was chairman of the House Ways and Means Committee, had been one of the chief backers of legislation mandating an increase in the federal support price of milk.)

Parr ordered five to seven paid employes of AMPI to work for the Mills campaign, according to statements from

Lilly and Isham. The assistance was ended in early 1972 when Mehren was named general manager in a corporate shakeup.

Watergate staff report. The staff of the Senate Watergate committee concluded that campaign pledges made by major dairy cooperatives (totaling $2 million) "apparently [were] directly linked to a favorable milk price support decision by the President worth hundreds of millions of dollars to the industry—and costing the same amount to the government and consumers."

The staff draft, published May 31, 1974, was submitted to the Senate panel chaired by Sen. Sam Ervin (D, N.C.). White House Press Secretary Ronald Ziegler immediately denounced the paper as "one of the crudest and most obvious political reports I've yet seen come from the Ervin committee."

In analyzing the President's decision to overturn an Agriculture Department ruling and raise milk price supports, the report said, Nixon "ignored the opinion of every agriculture expert in his Administration and the criteria of the government statute."

Staff disputes about Nixon's defense of his action centered on three points:

■ Nixon had said he acted largely because legislation that would also have raised milk price supports was pending in Congress in early 1971 and had such backing that a presidential veto would likely have been overridden. This claim was "overstated," according to the staff.

"At the very least," the report declared, "the President's decision was an act of political one-upmanship calculated to outdo the Democratic members of Congress who supported milk price support legislation." Nixon had claimed in his White Paper that during the period he considered the decision, 30 separate bills authorizing the increase were introduced in the House and that legislation in the Senate had the backing of 29 senators. According to the report, eight of the 30 House bills were not introduced until after Nixon acted and 27 of the 29 cosponsors of a Senate bill were not added until April 5, 1971. (The Administration had announced its approval of the increase March 25, 1971.)

Only one Republican senator, and 29 GOP House members co-sponsored milk price legislation in early 1971, the report stated, observing that Republican support needed to override any presidential veto would not have been forthcoming.

■ In another disputed point, the report claimed that Nixon understated the cost of his decision to consumers. The higher price support level backed by Nixon was $4.93 per hundredweight, "a level 1¢ higher than that called for in virtually every bill introduced [in Congress] in 1971," the report asserted. Total costs of Nixon's action were said to be at least $300 million, or "$10 million more than 34 of the 36 bills introduced in Congress," according to the staff paper.

By making the decision in the spring when milk production and supply were high, the report added, Nixon's "decision raised the support level just in time to have the maximum impact on milk prices."

■ The committee staff also accused Nixon of misrepresenting the significance of the co-ops' campaign pledges in his re-election race. Nixon had admitted he was aware that major dairy co-ops had pledged $2 million but said this information had not influenced his decision. The White Paper had also emphasized that the dairymen eventually contributed an estimated $427,500, or "less than 1% of the total" received by the Nixon campaign.

In rebuttal, the staff report charged that Nixon and his fund raisers had no reason "not to expect the full amount of the pledge," which, "even by the standards of the 1972 presidential campaign" was "enormous." It "represented one of the three largest pledges of his campaign and a full 1/20th of this entire projected campaign budget of $40 million," the report stated.

The dairy donations were important for other reasons, according to the staff paper: the money, which was pledged in 1970, "represented the 'early money' which is critical to every campaign;" the commitments also represented a "potential loss of $2 million" to the Democratic campaign which had benefitted from dairy industry donations in the past. Hence, the pledge could have been worth $4 million to Nixon, the report concluded.

No limit set on AMPI contributions.
Former AMPI general manager Harold
Nelson testified before the Senate Watergate Committee that the co-op had set no
ceiling on its proposed contributions to
the Nixon re-election campaign, but that
the President's fund raisers "bungled"
plans for collecting the money and
thereby limited the dairy lobby's potential
for donations.

The testimony was reported by the
Washington Post July 17, 1974. According
to Nelson's reported admissions, the total
amount of donations from AMPI would
have far surpassed the actual amount
given (more than $500,000) if Nixon aides
had not been so slow in setting up dummy
committees to receive (and conceal) the
subdivided contributions. "Even when
they gave us the committees, they bungled
it," he said. "For instance, one of the
committee's address was a ballroom. . . .
Another one, the chairman was a Washington lawyer whose name I cannot tell
you. He had not even been consulted. . . ,
and it made him so mad that he blew his
stack and called the clerk of the House."

Although he urged the White House to
set up the conduits for donation early in
1971, Nelson said, the Administration was
slow to act until many weeks after the decision was made to increase federal milk
price supports. This tardiness worried
him, Nelson added. "It was a constant
thing in the back of my mind that if we
didn't get the names of these committees,
we might be read off just because of some
inept—for want of a better term, I will say
'bureaucrat'—within the party hierarchy
not coming forth and giving us the names
of the committees."

"We told them [Nixon fund raisers]
from the word go that we would make
large contributions," he said. "At various
times, $1 million, $2 million or even more
money was discussed. And had they given
us the names of the committees, they
could have gotten much more money
from us," he testified.

Government & AMPI settle trust suit.
Associated Milk Producers, Inc. Aug.
13, 1974 accepted the terms of a consent
decree filed that day by the Justice Department in federal district court in
Kansas City, Mo. The proposed consent
agreement ended the civil antitrust suit
filed against AMPI in 1972.

The settlement was approved by a federal judge in Kansas City April 30, 1975.

The 37,000 member co-op had been accused of illegally trying to monopolize the
production and sale of milk in 14 midwest,
southern and southwestern states and
using coercion to force farmers to join the
organization. As was standard in the settlement of other civil antitrust suits,
AMPI agreed not to engage in the future
in these allegedly illegal practices, but the
co-op made no admission of wrongdoing.
The dairy group also was prohibited from
buying any new milk plants for 10 years
without the Justice Department's prior
consent, an unusual restriction that
government lawyers acknowledged was
rarely used outside of bank merger cases.

AMPI also agreed to refrain from
selling cheap milk in selected areas to
punish nonmembers by driving down their
prices; to give members at least one year
to withdraw from the co-op; and to file
reports with the Justice Department for
the next 10 years and allow government
agents to inspect its records on request.

Connally acquitted. Former Treasury
Secretary John B. Connally Jr. was acquitted April 17, 1975 of charges of accepting $10,000 in illegal gratuities
from AMPI as a "thank you" gift for
his 1971 recommendation that the Nixon
Administration raise federal milk price
supports.

At the request of the Watergate special
prosecutor's office, Chief Judge George L.
Hart Jr. April 18 also dismissed the two-
count perjury charge and one-count
charge of conspiracy to obstruct justice
that remained pending against Connally in
connection with the bribery case.

The bribery charge brought against
Connally by the Watergate special
prosecutor's office was based on the
testimony of Jake Jacobsen, AMPI's
former lawyer and one-time Connally
friend, who claimed he had delivered two
$5,000 cash payments to Connally in ap-
preciation for his role in winning the price-
support increase.

Jacobsen also claimed that when the
prosecutor's office began examining the
dairymen's large contributions to the
Nixon re-election campaign, he and Connally attempted to cover up the alleged
payoff by agreeing to tell investigators

that Jacobsen offered him $10,000 in cash for use by political candidates of his choosing, but that Connally twice refused the offer and that Jacobsen then stored the untouched money in a Texas safe deposit box.

Early in the case Jacobsen agreed to cooperate with the prosecution. Under a plea bargain arranged with the government, Jacobsen agreed to plead guilty to a single bribery charge if felony charges pending against him in Texas involving misapplication of bank funds were dropped.

The defense charged that Jacobsen was a liar and embezzler who framed Connally to save himself. According to Connally's lawyer, Edward Bennett Williams, Jacobsen told investigators six times—four under oath—that Connally had never accepted an illegal gratuity, and only changed his story when he faced up to 40 years in jail on the perjury and bank fraud charges. In pleading guilty to the single bribe-giving count involving Connally, Williams noted, Jacobsen faced only up to two years in jail. Williams also charged that Jacobsen converted the AMPI money intended for Connally to his own use.

Jacobsen testified April 13 that Connally had solicited the alleged payoff and that $10,000 was obtained from AMPI official Bob A. Lilly for that purpose. The first installment was delivered to Connally May 14, 1971 and the second was turned over Sept. 24, 1971, Jacobsen said. Both payoffs occurred at Connally's Treasury Department office in Washington, according to Jacobsen.

The prosecution alleged that the coverup was concocted when Jacobsen told Connally in October 1973 that Lilly was believed to be cooperating with federal investigators probing AMPI's massive illegal political contributions.

After agreeing on the cover-up story, the prosecution alleged that Connally delivered the replacement money to Jacobsen in a cigar box Oct. 29, 1973 at a meeting in Connally's Houston law firm. Jacobsen subsequently deposited the money as arranged in an Austin bank box.

Several days later, the prosecution contended, Connally asked Jacobsen to substitute another $10,000 for the money in the safe deposit box when it was dis-covered that the first replacement cash bore Treasury Secretary George P. Shultz's signature, and hence, could not have been circulation in May 1971. (Shultz succeeded Connally in May 1972.) According to Jacobsen, the exchange took place at the Austin home of a mutual friend, George Christian, former President Lyndon B. Johnson's press secretary.

The prosecution claimed that despite the exchange, 16 bills in the second batch "just were too new to have been put" in circulation in May 1971 as Connally and Jacobsen had said.

The prosecution rested April 11 after Jacobsen and 35 other witnesses, including officials of all 12 Federal Reserve regional banks, testified in support of the charges. Although considerable circumstantial evidence was introduced corroborating Jacobsen's accounts of meetings with Connally and bank dealings, the prosecution was unable to produce a witness to the alleged payoff and the case hinged entirely on Jacobsen's testimony.

Unlike other Watergate-related trials, the prosecution produced no incriminating tapes or documents that tied the defendant to illegal activities.

The prosecution also introduced no evidence that Connally banked or spent the alleged payoff and failed to document Connally's source of the $20,000 in replacement cash he allegedly gave Jacobsen.

Lilly testified under a grant of immunity April 8 that he had given Jacobsen $10,000 in May and September 1971 and another $5,000 in December of that year after Jacobsen claimed AMPI was "obligated" to Connally for his help in the price-support increase. Under questioning by Williams, Jacobsen said he could not recall having given the additional $5,000 to Connally, but said he "must have" if Lilly turned the cash over to him.

The defense emphasized Jacobsen's financial difficulties—he had filed for bankruptcy in 1972. During the summer of 1971 when it was alleged he made the payoff to Connally, Williams said Jacobsen had paid off $10,000 in bank debt. On the same day that Lilly gave Jacobsen the third $5,000 installment, Williams said Jacobsen paid another $5,000 debt.

Connally took the stand in his own defense April 14 to deny that he had ever sought or accepted a payoff from Jacobsen on behalf of dairy interests. Seven character witnesses, including Mrs. Lyndon B. Johnson, evangelist Billy Graham, and Rep. Barbara Jordan (D, Tex.), also testified that day on Connally's behalf.

In other testimony April 14, George Christian refuted Jacobsen's story that Connally had passed the second replacement cash to him in a car outside Christian's house.

In cross examination April 15, Connally admitted that he had made several mistakes or omitted information in his testimony under oath before the Senate Watergate Committee and the grand jury examining the bribery allegations. However, he attributed the errors to a faulty memory, misunderstood questions and his lack of preparation for the investigation, which he thought would not amount to a "hill of beans."

ITT Case Developments

No ITT antitrust crime seen. Special Watergate prosecutor Leon Jaworski said May 30, 1974 that his staff had found no evidence that International Telephone & Telegraph Corp. (ITT) officials had committed any criminal offenses in connection with the 1971 settlement of the government's antitrust suits against ITT.

Jaworski's comments were contained in a letter to Rep. J. J. Pickle (Tex.), the ranking Democrat on the Special Investigations Subcommittee of the House Commerce Committee, one of several Congressional panels examining various aspects of ITT's links to the Administration. However, Jaworski said the case against ITT "was not closed." Allegations that ITT officials had improperly influenced the Internal Revenue Service (IRS) and the Securities and Exchange Commission (SEC) would be "vigorously pursued," he said.

IRS rescinds ITT tax break. ITT announced March 6, 1974 that the Internal Revenue Service (IRS) had re-voked its 1969 ruling that had enabled ITT to acquire the Hartford Fire Insurance Co.

The IRS ruling was integral to ITT's take-over plans: the 17,000 Hartford shareholders, whose approval of the merger was required, were allowed by the government to exchange their stock for ITT stock without immediately paying capital gains taxes.

With retroactive revocation of that favorable tax ruling, the former Hartford shareholders could be liable for up to $50 million in back taxes, according to the Wall Street Journal.

The IRS confirmed that its 1969 order had been rescinded but refused to disclose the basis for its decision. ITT officials said March 7 that the action stemmed from the government's investigation of another aspect of the tax arrangements involving ITT's sale of a separate block of Hartford shares to Mediobanca, a Milan bank.

A class action suit brought by a former Hartford shareholder had also challenged this preliminary aspect of the merger which was a basis for the tax break given the Hartford group and ultimately for actual take-over approved by the Hartford shareholders.

The suit, brought by Hilda Herbst, alleged that ITT had obtained the IRS ruling by providing the government with false information. Under an agreement concluded by ITT with the IRS, the Hartford shareholders' tax-free arrangement depended upon ITT's pledge to sell a block of Hartford stock obtained earlier in 1969 "unconditionally to an unrelated third part"—Mediobanca. (ITT had bought the Hartford stock for cash, which violated an IRS requirement that the Hartford acquisition be completed only through an exchange of stock.) The Herbst suit charged that the Mediobanca purchase was not unconditional and that the Italian bank was not as "unrelated" as ITT had claimed.

Suspended sentence for Kleindienst. Former Attorney General Richard Kleindienst pleaded guilty May 16, 1974 to a misdemeanor charge of failing to testify "accurately" at a Senate hearing. He received a suspended sentence for his criminal offense June 7.

Chief U.S. District Court Judge George L. Hart Jr. imposed the minimum sentence under law—a $100 fine and one month jail term—and suspended both penalties. Kleindienst, who wept openly in court, was placed on one month unsupervised probation.

Hart praised Kleindienst as a man who had exhibited the "highest integrity throughout his personal and official life." The crime to which he had pleaded guilty was a "technical violation" of the law, Hart said in announcing the sentence. It "is not the type of violation that reflects a mind bent on deception.... Rather, it reflects a heart that is too loyal and considerate of the feelings of others."

Had Kleindienst testified "accurately and fully," Hart said, "it would have reflected great credit on this defendant—but would have reflected discredit upon another individual," an apparent allusion to President Nixon.

The minor criminal offense related to Kleindienst's testimony in March and April 1972 before the Senate Judiciary Committee, which was considering his nomination to succeed John Mitchell as attorney general. As part of the hearing, the committee was inquiring into the ITT antitrust settlement.

Kleindienst was the first person who had served as the nation's top law enforcement officer to be convicted of criminal misconduct. At the time of the hearings, Kleindienst was serving as acting attorney general. While supervising the Justice Department's ITT cases, he was deputy attorney general, the department's second ranking post. Kleindienst resigned as attorney general in April 1973 as a consequence of the widening Watergate affair.

Kleindienst pleaded guilty to concealing from the committee his communication about ITT with President Nixon and John Mitchell and circumstances surrounding the Justice Department's decision to appeal one of the antitrust cases against ITT to the Supreme Court. In sworn committee testimony, Kleindienst had said, "I was not interfered with by anybody at the White House. I was not importuned. I was not pressured. I was not directed."

Later statements issued by Kleindienst and White House documents released recently contradicted this testimony.

Watergate, Agnew & Related Scandals

Watergate Probes Reveal Illegal Election Gifts

The various investigations of the Watergate scandal turned up a mass of evidence that corporations throughout the U.S. had provided illegal contributions—sometimes in large sums—for election campaigns. In several instances, the companies offered the gifts on their own initiative, presumably in expectation of some political payoff. In a great many other cases, the donations were solicited by political figures, sometimes, it was suggested, with a degree of insistence bordering on coercion.

American Airlines' illegal gift. George A. Spater, chairman of American Airlines, said July 6, 1973 that he had arranged for the illegal contribution of $55,000 in corporate funds to the Finance Committee to Re-elect the President in early 1972.

Spater said the money, with another $20,000 from individual contributors, had been given after he was approached in late 1971 by Herbert W. Kalmbach, former personal counsel to President Nixon.

"I knew Mr. Kalmbach to be both the President's personal counsel and counsel for our major competitor. I concluded that a substantial response was called for," Spater said in a statement issued by the airline.

At the time of the contribution, Kalmbach was attorney for United Airlines, the largest U.S. carrier. Further, the Civil Aeronautics Board (CAB) then had before it a plan for American's merger with Western Airlines, a move strongly opposed by United. (The CAB rejected the merger July 28, 1972.)

American acknowledged July 9 it had asked the Nixon re-election committee to return the $55,000. The finance committee said July 11 it had sent American a check for $55,000. In an accompanying cover letter, the finance committee denied being aware of the illegal nature of the gift.

Federal laws prohibited corporate campaign contributions and stated that corporations and their officers, as well as campaign committees and their officials, were liable to criminal prosecution.

The American Airlines contribution was initially revealed by special Watergate prosecutor Archibald Cox.

In his statement, Spater said his admission had been made to mitigate possible penalties against those involved and to "focus attention on the evils of the present political fund-raising system."

"Under existing laws a large part of the money raised from the business community for political purposes is given in fear of what would happen if it were not given. A fair and honest law is one that

35

would remove the need of any candidate to exert such pressures, as well as the need for any businessman to respond," Spater said. (Spater resigned from American Airlines in September.)

The total of $75,000, given in five cash installments, did not have to be reported if given by individuals while the campaign fund disclosure act of 1926 remained in effect. The most recent federal campaign contribution reporting law—effective April 7, 1972—ruled out all secret cash contributions.

The Washington Post reported July 7 that some of the corporate money had been "laundered" through a broker in Lebanon. The $55,000 was raised through phony invoices for which payments were reflected on the airline's books, the Post said.

James H. O'Connor, attorney for Kalmbach, said in Phoenix his client had asked Spater for $100,000 but no mention of cash was made. Kalmbach denied that he knew American planned to make an illegal contribution, O'Connor said.

Eastern Airlines said July 6 that Kalmbach had approached the company for a contribution but had been turned down.

Ashland Oil admits illegal gift. Orin E. Atkins, chairman of the Ashland Oil Co. of Kentucky, revealed July 20 that he had illegally contributed $100,000 in corporate funds to the Finance Committee to Re-elect the President in April 1972.

Atkins released a statement saying he had voluntarily informed special Watergate prosecutor Archibald Cox of the contribution and intended to "fully cooperate" with Cox in any investigation.

Cox said the contribution "was solicited by and delivered to Maurice H. Stans," former chairman of the finance committee.

Atkins said the Nixon committee "was not told that corporate funds were involved. When advised of this fact, the finance committee returned the contribution to the company." Atkins said the contribution was given by "a subsidiary" identified as the Ashland Petroleum Gabon Corp.

Ashland Petroleum Gabon pleaded guilty Nov. 13 in federal district court in Cat-

lettsburg, Ky. to charges of donating $100,000 in corporate funds to Nixon's re-election committee. Atkins pleaded no contest and was fined $1,000. The corporation was fined $5,000.

Gulf & Goodyear disclose gifts. The Gulf Oil Corp. and the Goodyear Tire & Rubber Co. admitted Aug. 10, 1973 that they had made large, illegal campaign contributions to President Nixon's reelection committee. Both companies had notified the office of special Watergate prosecutor Archibald Cox of their actions and the subsequent refund of their money by the Finance Committee to Re-elect the President.

Gulf's $100,000 had been given in response to "intense" and "irresistible" requests for money by unidentified representatives of the Nixon finance committee, according to B. R. Dorsey, chairman of Gulf's board. Two separate contributions of $50,000 were made in 1971 and early 1972 before the federal election law requiring disclosure of all campaign funds became law April 7, 1972.

Goodyear revealed that it had made two cash contributions of $20,000 each in March 1972. The money had been given to Maurice Stans, chairman of the finance committee.

Both companies said the finance committee had not been informed that the money derived from corporate funds.

A total of $900,000 had been refunded to individual and corporate campaign donors, according to a spokesman for the finance committee. He added that the Gulf and Goodyear contributions had been returned July 26.

Gulf Oil Corp. and its vice president, Claude C. Wild Jr., entered guilty pleas Nov. 13 in the federal district court in Washington. The court fined Gulf $5,000 and Wild $1,000 for contributing $100,000 to President Nixon's campaign committee, $15,000 to the presidential campaign of Rep. Wilbur D. Mills (D, Ark.) and $10,000 to Sen. Henry M. Jackson (D, Wash.), another unsuccessful contender for the Democratic presidential nomination.

The Mills and Jackson donations were the first known evidence that Democratic contenders for the presidency had accepted illegal contributions. Neither had joined in the voluntary disclosures of campaign funds made in early 1972 by their rivals in the Democratic race.

Jackson, who denied knowledge that Gulf's contribution had come from corporate funds, said he was "preparing to return the money." Mills was "seeking information from the company as to whether the company feels a refund is in order," a spokesman said.

Braniff admits donation. Braniff Airways announced Aug. 23, 1973 that it had made a "voluntary disclosure" to the office of special Watergate prosecutor Archibald Cox of two contributions made in 1972 to the Nixon re-election committee.

The first donation, totaling $10,000, was made by the firm's chairman, Harding L. Lawrence, and another unidentified officer out of their personal funds. When Maurice Stans, chairman of the Nixon finance committee, solicited a "substantial further contribution," another $40,000 donation was made out of corporate funds by Braniff officers and other individuals. The company claimed that the donors subsequently had reimbursed Braniff for the $40,000 gift.

Braniff and Lawrence pleaded guilty in Washington to violating the federal campaign finance law. Braniff was fined $5,000, and Lawrence was fined $1,000. Defense attorneys told the court that although Lawrence had made a substantial personal contribution, estimated at $10,000, to the Nixon committee, he had been "under some pressure to make this [illegal corporate] contribution" because Nixon campaign officials had expressed dissatisfaction with the original amount.

Corporations fined for gifts. Special Watergate prosecutor Archibald Cox announced Oct. 17 that criminal charges had been brought against Goodyear Tire & Rubber Co. and its chairman, Russell DeYoung; Minnesota Mining and Manufacturing Co. (3M) and its chairman, Harry Heltzer; and American Airlines. They were accused of making illegal contributions to President Nixon's re-election campaign.

After entering guilty pleas the same day, the defendants were fined but received no prison sentences. (The maximum penalty for corporations was a $5,000 fine. Individuals faced a $1,000 penalty and one year in jail.) Goodyear and DeYoung were fined $5,000 and $1,000 each by federal district court in Cleveland. 3M and Heltzer paid $3,000 and $500 each in Minneapolis federal court decision. American was fined $5,000 by federal district court in Washington.

All three companies had voluntarily admitted donating a total of $125,000 to the Finance Committee to Re-elect the President, which later returned the money.

Cox's office had urged corporations to make public disclosures of their wrongdoing after investigations uncovered evidence that a large amount of campaign funds had originated with corporate contributors. George A. Spater, former chairman of American Airlines, had been the first business official to reveal an illegal contribution, a factor which Cox said caused him to seek more lenient treatment for Spater.

"I believe that the example of American Airlines had something to do with prompting others to come forward with voluntary disclosures of corporate contributions," he said.

"The general policy of this office," Cox said, "will be to charge the primarily responsible corporate officer with [a] misdemeanor violation." Legal action against the corporation alone would have "little deterrent effect," he added.

Cox also warned that felony charges could be brought under certain circumstances: if investigations showed evidence of criminal actions but violators refused to make a voluntary confession; if evidence showed that the contribution was offered to influence government action; and if there was an effort to conceal or withhold evidence of other federal crimes by persons under investigation.

According to Cox, all three companies charged had used "secret and clandestine" methods to hide their contributions. Goodyear and American had employed overseas channels to conceal the source of the money.

The defendants also had made "much smaller" contributions to other Democratic and Republican political campaigns but no charges were filed for these violations, he said.

Cox said the investigation showed no evidence that the firms sought a tangible return for their contributions in government actions, but merely wished to "be known as supportive" of the Nixon Administration.

Favors for political gifts? A Midwest businessman was quoted in July 1973 as saying a GOP official had told him the White House would listen to his "problem[s]" if he contributed enough money to the election campaign fund.

Currier Holman, chairman of Iowa Beef Processors Inc. of Nebraska, was approached by a Nixon campaign aide who discussed quid pro quo arrangements for large contributors, the New York Times reported July 19.

Holman and his company were under federal investigation in 1971 and 1972. In March 1973, Holman was indicted by federal and state grand juries in New York, charged with conspiring to bribe union and supermarket officials to sell company products in New York. The company also was party to the state charges.

Holman donated $2,000 to the Nixon campaign in October 1972.

Holman said Clayton Yeutter, who had resigned from the Agriculture Department to work for the campaign, had solicited the money in March or April 1972. Yeutter currently was assistant secretary of agriculture. Yeutter recalled the discussion but said the rewards he promised potential contributors were "purely a public relations kind of thing," such as invitations to White House functions or luncheons with Cabinet officials.

According to Holman, Yeutter told him:

"If you gave $25,000, if you had a problem, you could talk to someone in the White House. I think I said, 'What if I gave more?' And he said maybe the yardstick would be for $25,000 you get to talk to somebody in the White House, a Cabinet officer or someone like that. For $50,000 you get to talk to the President. I can't remember the exact amounts, really, but I remember something to the effect that with a very large contribution you can talk to the President—if you had

a serious problem."

Truckers donated, bill died. The Nixon re-election committee received its largest single industry gift—more than $600,000—from the trucking industry, according to Senate Watergate Committee investigators. The contributions were offered while the industry was opposing an Administration-sponsored bill in Congress that would have lowered trucking rates and increased shipping competition, the New York Times reported Nov. 6, 1973.

John Ruan, an official of the Washington-based lobbying group, the American Trucking Association, was identified as the organizer of the fund-raising drive. He denied that truckers, whose rates and routes were regulated by the government, had contributed the money in order to obtain favorable Administration rulings.

The Nixon re-election committee made public disclosures of the truckers' donations in the fall of 1972, but did not identify the funds as comprising an industry-wide money package. The bill which was opposed by the truckers died in Congress during the same period.

Testimony on corporate gifts. The Senate Watergate Committee heard testimony Nov. 13–15, 1973 from officers of six big corporations, who admitted engaging in schemes to circumvent federal campaign laws barring corporate gifts to political campaigns.

Among highlights of the testimony:

Nov. 13—Two officials of the American Ship Building Co. told the committee that they and six other "loyal" employes had been used as conduits through which the company's president, George M. Steinbrenner 3rd, had channeled $25,000 in contributions to the President's re-election fund.

The two witnesses, Robert E. Bartlome, company secretary, and Matthew E. Clark Jr., director of purchasing, also said Steinbrenner had induced them to lie to agents of the Federal Bureau of Investigation (FBI) when questioned about the contributions.

The two witnesses testified that in 1972 Steinbrenner arranged to have bonuses paid to the eight employes, totaling $26,000 after taxes. Each recipient of a bonus then wrote personal checks totaling the amount of his bonus, and the checks were forwarded to Herbert W. Kalmbach, the President's personal attorney, at the Washington headquarters of the Committee to Re-elect the President. According to Clark, the transactions occurred April 6, 1972, the day before a new campaign contribution law took effect.

While the witnesses indicated that they had received other bonuses in 1970 and 1971, their testimony failed to make clear the amounts or the disposition of the money.

"I knew from those conversations" with Bartlome in 1970, Clark testified, "that the bonuses I was to receive were for political contributions and weren't bonuses at all."

Bartlome testified that the company began a cover-up of the contributions in January 1973. The company granted real bonuses to legitimize the bogus ones, Bartlome said. In April, a false memo, backdated a year, was placed in the files for "cosmetic" purposes. However, the cover-up lasted only until August, when the eight employes, subpoenaed to testify before a grand jury, decided against perjuring themselves, Bartlome said.

When informed of the decision by his employes to tell the truth, Steinbrenner, Bartlome testified, "laid his head on his desk" and cried that both he and the company would be "ruined."

The Wall Street Journal reported Nov. 15 that records of the Committee to Re-elect the President showed that Steinbrenner, who in 1970 received company bonuses totaling $75,000, had made his own $75,000 contribution to the 1972 Nixon re-election campaign. Committee sources, the Journal said, indicated they had no evidence showing Steinbrenner had been reimbursed for his contribution, merely implications of a pattern.

Nov. 14—Two oil company executives testified that they had both been approached for $100,000 contributions to the 1972 Nixon re-election campaign.

Orin E. Atkins, chairman of Ashland Oil Inc., and Claude C. Wild Jr., vice president for governmental affairs for Gulf Oil Corp., said they had arranged for the contributions to be paid to Maurice Stans, director of the Finance Committee to Re-elect the President.

Atkins said he obtained the money from an Ashland subsidiary in Gabon, Africa. Wild said he chose to withdraw cash from a Gulf subsidiary in the Bahamas.

In neither case, both witnesses testified, did Stans or Lee Nunn, a re-election committee official who helped solicit Gulf, ask for contributions directly from the corporations. But both men used company funds because, as Atkins put it, "in my mind it could have only come from one place, the corporation ... because $100,-000 is an awful lot of money."

Atkins also testified that Stans, afraid the Nixon re-election committee would be forced to make its campaign contribution lists public, called him sometime in 1973 and asked him to reconstruct a list of individual contributors. Atkins said he refused.

Nov. 15—The Watergate committee took testimony from the chairman of the Goodyear Tire & Rubber Co., the former chairman of American Airlines and two officials from Braniff International Airways, Inc.

Russell DeYoung of Goodyear admitted that his company had used a Swiss bank account as a secret source of funds for the Nixon re-election committee. The money, which for accounting purposes was disguised as rebates given by Goodyear to European suppliers, was given to Stans in two $20,000 payments, and DeYoung claimed that he added $5,000 of his own money. Unlike other executives who claimed to have been pressured into contributing, DeYoung said he agreed to the gift "solely because we thought the re-election of the President was in the best interest of the country."

George A. Spater, formerly of American Airlines, related information he had divulged in July, when he became the first corporate executive to voluntarily admit illegal corporate gifts to the Nixon campaign.

Spater reiterated that it had been his "fear" that his company would suffer competitively if a contribution were not made.

He told the committee that such abuses could be discouraged by a law barring certain persons with obvious control over government decisions from soliciting campaign gifts.

Camilio Fazrega, an official for Braniff, said he had been asked by a company vice president to raise $40,000 and did so through a family-owned company in his native Panama. The cash was forwarded to Braniff and then to the Committee to Re-elect the President, Fazrega testified.

Phillips pleads guilty. Phillips Petroleum Corp. and William W. Keeler, retired chairman, pleaded guilty Dec. 4, 1973 in federal district court in Washington to charges of making an illegal $100,000 cash contribution to President Nixon's re-election campaign.

The firm, one of the nation's 10 largest oil companies, was fined the maximum $5,000 for the misdemeanor.

Keeler was fined $1,000 for authorizing the gift. (He had invoked Fifth Amendment rights and refused to testify before the Senate Watergate Committee Nov. 22 regarding the Phillips contribution to the Nixon campaign and those of other oil companies. Keeler was believed to have coordinated President Nixon's fundraising efforts within the oil industry.)

The prosecutor's office also revealed that Phillips had admitted making other gifts to the campaigns of House and Senate candidates in 1970 and 1972.

Keeler resigned as chief executive of Phillips Petroleum in January 1974 and as chairman in April.

Carnation convicted re political gifts. Carnation Co. and H. Everett Olson, its chairman, pleaded guilty Dec. 19, 1973 in federal district court in Washington to charges that $7,900 had been contributed to President Nixon's re-election campaign and $1,000 to a fund for Senate Republican candidates. The donations, made from corporate funds, violated the federal campaign spending law.

The firm was fined $5,000 and Olson $1,000 (for authorizing a $5,000 contribution to Nixon officials).

According to the Watergate special prosecutor's office, Carnation had made a voluntary admission to the federal prosecutors, but the information had not been made public.

'Laundered' checks traced. The Washington Post June 3, 1973 provided a chronological account of "laundered" Mexican checks used to finance the political office break-in that triggered the Watergate scandal.

April 3, 1972: Gulf Resources and Chemical Corp. of Houston allegedly contributed $100,000 to the Nixon re-election campaign, in violation of federal campaign laws which prohibited political donations from corporations.

The money was routed from a Mexican subsidiary of Gulf Resources to the personal bank account of Mexico City lawyer Manuel Ogarrio, 82.

Ogarrio converted the money to four bank drafts totaling $89,000 plus $11,000 in cash and passed the funds to Houston where they were transported in an oil executive's suitcase to Washington April 6, 1972.

According to Maurice Stans, chairman of the Finance Committee to Re-elect the President, and committee treasurer Hugh W. Sloan Jr., the checks, which were received one day before the new federal reporting law for campaign funds took effect, were given to convicted Watergate conspirator G. Gordon Liddy, then counsel to the finance committee.

Liddy gave the checks to Bernard Barker, also convicted in the Watergate break-in. Barker returned the cash to Washington, but the checks were traced by the FBI in a routine investigation to Barker's Miami bank account.

July 10, 1972: FBI agents interviewed Ogarrio who revealed the Houston source.

Northrop admits violation. Northrop Corporation, a Los Angeles-based aerospace company and major Defense Department contractor, and two of its executives pleaded guilty May 1, 1974 to charges of making illegal contributions totaling $150,000 to President Nixon's 1972 re-election campaign.

A federal district court in Los Angeles imposed maximum fines; Northrop and Thomas V. Jones, chairman and chief executive, were each fined $5,000. Jones could have received up to five years in prison. The Watergate special prosecutor's office, which brought the case, said it was the first such action under a 1940 statute prohibiting political contributions by government contractors. Previous illegal campaign financing charges had been filed under provisions prohibiting corporate campaign contributions in general.

At the same hearing, Northrop Vice President James Allen pleaded guilty to the corporation-contribution statute and received the maximum $1,000 fine. Both executives were charged with "nonwillful" misdemeanor violations.

The special prosecutor's charges said that on Jan. 25, 1973, Jones substituted $100,000 in personal money for corporate funds and then had documents backdated to show falsely that all contributions were made from personal, rather than corporate money. The charges stated that Allen partially reimbursed other Northrop officers for contributions they had made to the 1972 election campaign.

Herbert Kalmbach, President Nixon's attorney, had told the Senate Watergate committee in 1973 he had received $75,000 from Jones.

Ashland Oil admits more violations. Ashland Oil Inc., which had pleaded guilty in 1973 to illegally donating $100,000 in corporate funds to the Nixon re-election campaign, said Dec. 30, 1974 that an additional $169,364 in campaign funds had also been donated illegally to politicians of both parties.

Ashland admitted the illegal donations in pleading guilty to five new charges brought by the Watergate special prosecutor's office. Chief Judge George L. Hart Jr. of U.S. district court in Washington imposed the maximum fine of $25,000.

A spokesman for the firm said Ashland's chairman, Orin E. Atkins, would personally pay the fine "out of pocket," although he was not accused of wrongdoing.

According to the special prosecutor's office, Atkins had denied that the firm had made donations to Congressional candidates when he had been interviewed during the summer of 1973 about the Nixon contribution.

However, the special prosecutor's office charged that Atkins had been "aware that Ashland, in fact, [had] made such contributions." After pleading no contest in November 1973, Atkins had ordered a "full audit of corporate cash transactions," according to court documents. Evidence about the previously undisclosed contributions was discovered at this time and turned over to the special prosecutor's office by an Ashland lawyer. (An Internal Revenue Service investigation of the firm's records had also uncovered the illegal donations.)

The illegal contributions listed in the new charges:

■ A $50,000 cash donation made to the Democratic National Committee for use in 1972 elections. The money was delivered from June 1970 to January 1972 to Robert S. Strauss, then committee treasurer and currently its chairman.

■ $100,000 in cash to unidentified Senate and House candidates. The money was channeled through oil and gas lobbyist Carl F. Arnold, then a fund raiser for Rep. Wilbur D. Mills (Ark.), who was seeking the Democratic presidential nomination.

■ A $10,000 cash contribution to Louie B. Nunn, former Republican governor of Kentucky who was defeated in his bid for a Senate seat in 1972.

■ $6,864.65 spent to reimburse Ashland employes for their contributions to committees supporting Sen. Hubert H. Humphrey's (D, Minn.) presidential bid in 1972 and his senatorial campaign in 1970.

■ $2,500 spent to reimburse Ashland employes who had supported Sen. John Tower's (R, Tex.) re-election race in 1972.

Ashland also admitted donating $50,000 to the Democratic presidential campaign in 1968 and another $100,000 to the Republican campaign that year. Because the statute of limitations for prosecuting these offenses had expired, no charges were brought concerning the illegal use of corporate funds for 1968.

None of the recipients of the Ashland contributions was charged by the special prosecutor's office with knowing that the donations were illegal.

Ashland, Goodyear revise total donations. Ashland Oil Inc. and Goodyear Tire & Rubber Co., firms that had been convicted of making illegal contributions to the Nixon re-election campaign, revealed in 1975 that they had also made other illegal political contributions.

Ashland, which previously had admitted giving $320,000 in political donations, disclosed Jan. 30 that its actual contributions totaled $533,000. The figure did not include the $100,000 returned to Ashland by the Nixon campaign committee after charges were filed against the firm by the Watergate special prosecutor's office.

The contributions, given from 1967–1972, "went to candidates of both major political parties," an Ashland spokesman said, but their identities were not revealed.

Ashland's announcement was made at its annual shareholders' meeting by chairman Orin E. Atkins.

Goodyear's announcement was made March 4 in a proxy statement. Officials disclosed that Goodyear's political donations from 1964–1972 may have totaled $242,000.

According to the proxy statement, $260,000 was transferred from a foreign bank account to Goodyear for use in political campaigns and was not entered on company books. (Apparently, $18,000 was not spent.)

Senate panel accuses 13 companies. The Senate Select Committee on Presidential Campaign Activities, known as the "Watergate Committee" or "Ervin Committee," released its final report July 13, 1974 on its investigation of the Watergate and other scandals related to the 1972 presidential campaign.

The committee reported that "at least 13 corporations made [political] contributions totaling over $780,000 in corporate funds," donations that were in violation of a federal statute prohibiting campaign contributions from corporations and unions.

Of this total, an estimated $749,000 was given to President Nixon's re-election campaign. (The donations Nixon received from the dairy industry were not included in this figure).

"While there is no evidence that any fund raiser for President Nixon directly solicited a corporate contribution," the report said, "there is evidence that a number of them were indifferent to the source of the money or, at the very least, made no effort whatsoever to see to it that the source of the funds was private rather than corporate. In any event, there is no evidence that any fund raiser who was involved in these contributions sought or obtained assurances that the contribution was legal at the time it was made."

The committee concluded that there was "no clear pattern to the solicitations." Sources of the corporate money also varied but "the most utilized source" of the illegal contributions was foreign subsidiaries. "In the great majority of cases, the contributions were in the form of cash," the report stated, and "the bulk" of the donations were made prior to April 7, 1972—the date on which a new federal reporting law took effect—in order to cloak the contributions.

There was no disclosure of any of the donations until July 6, 1973—15 months after most of the money was received. "The main impetus" for these disclosures, the report said, was a suit brought by Common Cause to compel the Finance Committee to Re-elect the President to name its secret donors and the amounts of their gifts.

When the finance committee, realizing it might be forced by the courts to reveal the sources of its contributions, sent letters to corporations seeking the names of individuals who had actually made the donations, responses from the corporations varied, the committee report declared.

Some corporate officials prepared false lists of individual employe donors, some made voluntary disclosures, "and in at least one case, an elaborate scheme to conceal the corporate nature of a contribution was indulged in, and involved lying to the FBI," according to the committee.

Corporations cited for illegal contributions:

American Airlines, Inc.—$55,000 was given in March 1972 to the Nixon campaign. The gift, given in cash, was laundered through the Swiss bank account of the firm's Lebanese agent.

American Ship Building Co.—$100,000 in cash was given April 6, 1972, of which $25,000 originated from corporate funds. The remaining amount was credited to the firm's chairman, George M. Steinbrenner, but the source of that money has not been determined, according to the committee.

Evidence obtained by the committee indicated that Steinbrenner attempted to conceal the source of the donation in August 1973, when he instructed company officials to "arrange a 'legitimate bonus payment plan' to camouflage" the transaction. The committee said that eight persons who participated in the deception, including Steinbrenner, signed false FBI statements about it. Steinbrenner and the company were indicted on charges related to the donation and both pleaded not guilty.

Ashland Oil Co., Inc.—$100,000 in cash was given April 3, 1972 after the money was laundered through a Gabon subsidiary.

Braniff Airways, Inc.—$40,000 in cash was given between March 28, 1972 and April 7, 1972. Officials conceded that the gift was made from corporate funds but contended they had intended to reimburse the company. No steps were taken, however, until July 1973, when informed by the finance committee that public disclosure of their contribution might be required.

Carnation Co.—A total of $7,900 in two contributions was made to the Nixon campaign.

Diamond International Corp.—$5,000 was given to the Nixon campaign and $1,000 to Sen. Edmund S. Muskie's (D, Me.) campaign for the Democratic presidential nomination.

Goodyear Tire & Rubber Co.—$40,000 in cash was given to the Nixon campaign.

Gulf Oil Corp.—$100,000 in cash was given to the Nixon campaign, $10,000 to Sen. Henry M. Jackson's (D, Wash.) campaign for the Democratic presidential nomination and $15,000 to Rep. Wilbur D. Mills (D, Ark.) in the same race.

Hertz Corp.—An estimated $8,000–$9,000 in car rentals were provided the Muskie campaign in 1971 and 1972. More than half was written off and the remainder that was billed, $4,103.29, was actually paid by Hertz. Officials were authorized "to provide funds to outside lawyers to enable them to make contributions to the Muskie campaign in the total amount of the outstanding bills," according to committee evidence. (The lawyers were also paid an extra 25%–30% more than the donation "for the purpose of reimbursing them for their income tax obligation," the report stated.)

Lehigh Valley Cooperative Farmers, Inc.—$50,000 in cash was given to the Nixon campaign and was used to pay hush money to the original Watergate defendants.

Minnesota Mining & Manufacturing Co.—A total of $36,000 in two contributions was given to the Nixon campaign, and two Democratic contenders for the nomination, Rep. Mills and Sen. Hubert Humphrey, each received $1,000 in cash. According to the committee, 3M had maintained a secret slush fund since the 1950s. The money had been obtained by overstating prepaid insurance and was then transferred to a Swiss bank account. In 1967 this procedure was changed—a Swiss attorney was paid for fictitious services and he returned the money in cash to a 3M official.

Northrop Corp.—$150,000, laundered through Luxembourg, was given to the Nixon finance committee in several transactions. Two deliveries of $50,000 each were made in March 1972 and on April 5, 1972. Another $50,000 in cash, was given secretly to Herbert Kalmbach in July 1972. Northrop officials later pleaded guilty to violations of the federal campaign law, but, the committee declared, "the information contained in the indictments, to which the defendants pleaded guilty, is in direct contradiction with the information supplied . . . to the committee during the fall of 1973." Northrop Chairman Thomas V. Jones, "among others, also represented to the General Accounting Office, the FBI, and the [Watergate] grand jury that the $100,000 contribution was part of a personal commitment unrelated to the corporation," the report stated. "Jones represented that a post-April 7 contribution of $50,000 came from a personal cash fund which he kept," the report added.

Phillips Petroleum Co.—$100,000 in cash was given to the Nixon campaign.

The report also traced the course of five checks, totaling $114,000, that originated from the corporate funds of Gulf Resources and Chemical Corp. of Texas. The money had been laundered in Mexico and Miami and the cash was found in the possession of Watergate burglar Bernard Barker during the break-in.

The committee report described fund raising attempts by the National Hispanic Finance Committee, involving Miami contractor John Priestes, and his efforts to obtain a quid pro quo from the Administration in return for making a secret cash contribution.

Two fund raising programs, organized by the Nixon campaign and aimed at business groups, were described—the Corporate Conduit Program, and the Industry-by-Industry Campaign.

Part of the committee's report was based on information obtained from questionnaires sent to 700 individual contributors, corporate officers and union executives in the fall of 1973.

Responses were received from officials of every corporation and union and from about 80% of the unaffiliated individuals.

The milk fund—The thrust of the committee's report on its investigation of the circumstances surrounding the dairy industry's large campaign fund pledges and contributions to the Nixon re-election campaign differed considerably from the draft report prepared by the committee staff and published in May.

The staff report's accusatory tone was tempered in the report issued by the committee, which concluded that the "dual role played by many Nixon officials of both policy maker and fund raiser gave at the very least, the appearance of impropriety and provided circumstances that were ripe for abuse. Whether or not these two roles were directly tied, they *appeared* [committee emphasis] to be linked, and this had a significant impact on the approach taken by the dairymen. [Harold] Nelson [general manager of Associated Milk Producers, Inc.] said they gave the first $100,000 in 1969 because 'it appeared we were not going to get any place if we did not.' And when called upon in March 1971 to re-affirm the $2 million pledge [made the previous September], Nelson explained that he felt he had no choice. . . ."

Nixon's decision, announced in March 1971, to raise federal price supports for milk, "was worth at least tens of millions of dollars to the milk producers and they spared no effort in seeking that favorable action," the report stated.

However, the report continued, "price supports were just one item on the dairymen agenda. In fact, the milk producers, representing one of the wealthiest political funds in America and one of the largest groups of contributors to the 1972 campaign, had actively sought favorable action from the Nixon Administration throughout its first term on a number of matters of great financial importance to dairy farmers at the same time that they were pledging hundreds of thousands, and even millions to President Nixon's re-election campaign—with the knowledge of the President himself and with the encouragement of top presidential aides and fund raisers."

(Some of these matters of importance to dairy farmers "included dairy import quotas, government cheese purchases and school milk programs, and the approach taken by the Antitrust Division of the Justice Department toward certain practices of the dairy co-ops," the report said.)

The committee focused on charges that Nixon's decision to raise milk price supports was directly related to the dairy co-ops' promised campaign contributions. The committee noted that the President, his key advisers and dairy representatives denied that any quid pro quo was involved. It was also declared in the report that "much of what the President says [in defense of his decision to authorize the increase] is supported by the surrounding events," especially, the report added, Nixon's assertion that "his action was influenced primarily by Democratic Congressional pressure (generated by the dairymen) coupled with his fear of losing dairymen support in his 1972 re-election bid if he opposed them."

But, the report also stated that the committee had uncovered other "key facts" that "shed light on the type of potential 'support' the dairymen represented" to Nixon. "The crux of the committee's investigation was, thus, not whether it was the correct decision but whether the President made that decision for the 'wrong' reason," the report stated.

Over a hundred persons were interviewed in the course of the committee investigation, the report noted, but it added that its inquiries were limited by the White House's withholding of key documents and tapes. Nixon also refused to permit the committee to take testimony from his former agriculture secretary, citing executive privilege.

Despite these limitations, the report said, the committee discovered that "a presidential aide was instructed [March 23,

1971] to 'alert' the dairymen of the decision" reached that day in a meeting of the President and his top aides. Earlier that day, Nixon had met with the dairy representatives at the White House.

The message received by the dairymen before a public announcement was made "carried an additional twist," the report stated. "The co-op leaders were informed that an increase was a good possibility but not certain. . . . A key dairy leader (Harold Nelson) was expected to re-affirm the $2 million pledge at a late night meeting prior to the public announcement. . . . At the pre-arranged meeting [arranged by John Ehrlichman], [Herbert] Kalmbach, [Nixon's chief fund raiser, and Nixon associate Murray Chotiner were] . . . informed of the re-affirmation 'in view of' the price support increase which had been set for the next day."

According to the report, the dairymen began meeting their promised campaign obligations within one week after the price decision was announced. By early September 1971, the report stated, nearly all of the entire $250,000 [promised] was in fact contributed—and at the same time, AMPI "accomplished one of its long sought after objectives. The President attended and addressed an AMPI annual convention."

According to the report, an additional contribution was made during the convention "at the special request of Charles Colson. Colson testified before a state grand jury that [$5,000 in] milk money was used to pay for the break-in of the office of Daniel Ellsberg's psychiatrist."

"Even before these contributions were made, the milk producers made at least one, and perhaps two, payments to [AMPI lawyer] Jake Jacobsen for [Treasury] Secretary [John] Connally's use," the report charged. Separate payments of $10,000 and $5,000 were cited.

"Both Connally and Jacobsen deny that Connally ever took or used $10,000," the report stated. "Jacobsen has testified that the $10,000 remained in his safe deposit box untouched for over 2½ years," the report continued. "However, the committee has obtained documentation from the Bureau of Engraving and the Federal Reserve System indicating that some of the bills of the $10,000 were not even placed into circulation until almost two years

after Jacobsen says he placed them in his box. Jacobsen denies even requesting, much less receiving, the $5,000 payment, and Connally denies any knowledge of the $5,000 matter."

The dairymen also sought Connally's assistance in terminating an antitrust suit brought by the Justice Department against AMPI. Furthermore, the dairy industry also sought the aid of other high level White House officials, such as H. R. Haldeman and John Mitchell, in halting the antitrust suit, but most of their efforts were directed at Herbert Kalmbach, who was offered a "substantial and secret pre-April 7, 1972 contribution" in exchange for help on the antitrust matter, according to the report.

Humphrey under criticism—"It should be noted," the report declared, "that improprieties in campaign financing were not limited to any particular candidate or party." Sen. Hubert Humphrey was cited for several apparent violations of campaign financing laws, but the committee's investigation was hampered by his refusal to be interviewed by the committee staff, and by his campaign manager's refusal to testify under oath. Humphrey also did not fully comply with the committee's request for campaign records, the report stated.

The committee's investigation centered on four general areas:

■ Humphrey's relationship to the dairy lobby: According to the report, Humphrey received services worth $25,000 from a Minneapolis firm specializing in computerized political services, Valentine, Sherman and Associates (VSA). The bill was paid by AMPI, the report stated, adding, "there is evidence that . . . [Jack Chestnut, Humphrey's campaign manager] was aware of and promoted this payment." The report also charged that under terms of a "covert arrangement" set up in 1970, Chestnut was paid a monthly retainer by AMPI and it was concealed as payment to another lawyer.

The report alleged that AMPI funded a number of other political services performed by VSA for Humphrey and other Democratic candidates and party groups in Iowa, South Dakota, Kansas and Oklahoma in 1971. The total amount AMPI paid VSA in 1971 for the benefit of Humphrey and other Democratic officials was $137,000, according to the report.

In addition to the $25,000 payment from AMPI, the report stated, Humphrey also received $17,225 for his presidential campaign from dairy producers' trusts (which, like political committees established by the unions, could legally dispense funds to candidates and parties if the money was contributed voluntarily by members of the dairy cooperatives. Contributions originating from the personal funds of corporate officials and employes also were allowed under law.)

The committee noted that Humphrey, a supporter of dairy industry legislation since 1949, had introduced legislation in March 1971 that would have raised the federal price support for milk. Humphrey had stated that there was "no relationship between his receipt of dairy contributions and his support of the price increase legislation," the report said.

■ Large individual contributions: Under the law in effect until April 7, 1972, the report noted, it was illegal for any individual to donate more than $5,000 in any calendar year to a presidential candidate or to any national campaign committee operating in his behalf, yet "more than $500,000 was contributed to the Humphrey presidential campaign in 1971 and 1972 (up to April 7) in the form of donations in excess of $5,000."

Unlike other presidential candidates, Humphrey made no effort to circumvent this rule by establishing dummy committees to receive subdivided, hence legal, contributions.

Evidence gathered by the committee showed that Humphrey received four contributions of stock, each worth at least $86,000 channeled through a limited partnership, Jackson & Co., which sold the stock and distributed the proceeds to a Humphrey committee.

A "purported personal loan" of $100,-000 also was made by Paul Thatcher, an official in the Humphrey campaign, to Humphrey through a trust account maintained by Chestnut, the report said.

One of Humphrey's principal backers, Dwayne O. Andreas, was said to have served as trustee for a "blind trust" maintained for Humphrey's benefit. (Andreas, and three others had donated more the than 10,000 shares of stock in Archer-Daniels-Midland Co., the nation's largest soybean processing firm, to Jackson & Co. Andreas was chairman of the firm.)

■ Corporate funds received from 3M: A Humphrey aide, the report declared, solicited a contribution from an official of Minnesota Mining and Manufacturing Co. in February 1972. The campaign received a total of $1,000 in April 1972 from 10 of the firm's executives, who were later reimbursed for the contributions from 3M's secret cash reserves used for political activities.

■ The Loeb contribution: Humphrey personally solicited a contribution from John L. Loeb Sr., a partner in a prominent Wall Street investment banking house, according to the report. A violation of campaign financing laws was committed when Loeb tried to conceal that he was the source of the $50,000 donation. It was also a violation of federal statutes for a campaign committee to accept a contribution by one person in the name of another, but it was not clear from the committee's report whether Humphrey's fund raisers were aware of the deception practiced by Loeb.

Mills campaign abuses—Alleged campaign abuses also occurred in Rep. Wilbur D. Mills' brief race for the Democratic presidential nomination.

The committee said it was unable to make a complete study of Mills' campaign practices, however, because Mills ignored repeated requests from the committee for an interview and his campaign manager, like Humphrey's, refused to testify, citing his 5th Amendment rights against self-incrimination.

The committee's probe centered on Mills' relationship to the dairy industry, principally Associated Milk Producers, Inc. (AMPI). Evidence obtained by the committee showed that Mills received $185,000, or 38% of his total campaign revenues, from dairy industry sources. Of that total, TAPE and the group which replaced it in 1972, CTAPE, contributed $26,500, SPACE donated $12,500, ADEPT contributed $16,000 and members, employes and officers of AMPI gave $40,000.* In addition to these sums, Mills also re-

―――――――――
*The dairy cooperatives' political trusts: AMPI's political arm was TAPE (Trust for Agricultural Political Education). It was replaced in 1972 by CTAPE (Committee for Thorough Agricultural Political Education). The political arm of Dairymen, Inc. was SPACE (Trust for Special Political Agricultural Community Education). Mid-America Dairymen, Inc.'s political group was ADEPT (Agricultural and Dairy Educational Political Trust).

ceived $15,000 from the corporate funds of Mid-America Dairymen Inc. and "up to $75,000 in money, goods and services from AMPI corporate assets."

"This limited investigation has not uncovered any direct evidence that ... Mills' support of the March 1971 dairy legislation constituted a specific quid pro quo for the money, goods and services given to him," the committee declared.

Joseph Johnson, Mills' campaign manager, had been on AMPI's payroll while working on the Mills campaign in 1971, the report said, and he refused to testify under oath before the committee.

The committee also cited evidence that Mills' fund raisers solicited corporate contributions from Gulf Oil Corp. and from 3M. The $15,000 comprising Gulf's donation, laundered through a subsidiary in the Bahamas, was delivered in cash prior to April 7, 1972. A 3M executive contributed $1,000 in July 1972, the report stated, and was reimbursed from 3M's slush fund.

Hughes official: gift sought from Hughes. Richard G. Danner, an official in President Nixon's 1968 campaign and currently an employe of billionaire industrialist Howard R. Hughes, told the Senate Watergate Committee that he attended a meeting in 1968 with Nixon and Charles G. Rebozo, a friend of Nixon, during which a campaign gift was solicited from Hughes.

"We have denied that the President discussed a possible contribution of any amount from Hughes," a White House spokesman said Jan. 16, 1974.

The New York Times reported the testimony Jan. 16, the Washington Post Jan. 17.

The Times reported Danner told committee investigators that Nixon personally suggested he attempt to solicit a campaign contribution from Hughes. The Post reported that Nixon was present at the meeting when the request was made.

According to the accounts:

Danner subsequently raised the issue of a gift with Edward P. Morgan, a lawyer for Hughes, who then relayed the request to Hughes aide Robert Maheu.

In a sworn deposition by Danner in a suit filed by Maheu against Hughes, Danner said Rebozo at one point had almost decided that the gift would best be forgotten, as he had been told that Hughes aide John Meier and Nixon's brother, F. Donald Nixon, would be involved in delivering the gift.

A few months later, Danner said in his deposition, Maheu, accompanied by Paul Laxalt, a former Nevada governor, attempted to deliver a $50,000 cash contribution to President Nixon, who was staying at the Palm Springs, Calif. home of Walter Annenberg, later named U.S. ambassador to Great Britain. The two couriers were turned away with the explanation that Nixon was too busy to see them.

Danner, hired by the Hughes organization in February 1969, finally delivered a $50,000 cash payment to Rebozo in July 1970 and followed it with another $50,000 cash contribution in August of that year.

Maheu testified in a deposition given in his suit against Hughes that the first $50,000 was intended for Nixon's 1968 campaign. The second $50,000, Maheu said, related to an antitrust problem Hughes was having concerning his attempts to acquire a Las Vegas, Nev. hotel. After the second gift was received, Maheu testified, John N. Mitchell, then attorney general, granted Hughes an antitrust exemption over objections of the Justice Department's antitrust division. However, the transaction was never consummated, Maheu said.

(The Washington Post had reported Oct. 10, 1973 that Rebozo had kept the $100,000 in safe deposit boxes in Florida for nearly three years before refunding it.)

Mitchell & Hughes—A Senate Watergate Committee staff report was said June 25, 1974 to have charged that Mitchell had bypassed his Antitrust Division and had approved Hughes' 1970 plan to buy the Dunes Hotel in Las Vegas.

Made without analysis by the Justice Department's antitrust lawyers, Mitchell's "secret, ad hoc" decision was "clothed with the appearance of impropriety" and was a "classic case of government decision-making for friends" of the Nixon Administration, the report asserted.

The report also said the $100,000 cash campaign contribution by Hughes to

Charles G. Rebozo, President Nixon's personal friend, might have been connected with Mitchell's decision.

According to the report, the Hughes organization had been warned by the antitrust division in 1968 that further additions to its Las Vegas holdings—four casino-hotels—would violate merger guidelines set forth in the Clayton Antitrust Act. However, Hughes was later allowed to purchase a fifth casino-hotel under the so-called "failing company doctrine," which provided for antitrust exemption in cases where the only alternative was financial failure.

When the Dunes became available in late 1969, the staff report said, Richard G. Danner, the Hughes aide who also delivered the $100,000 to Rebozo, was dispatched to Washington to deal directly with Mitchell, whom Danner knew from the 1968 presidential campaign.

Three meetings between Mitchell and Danner in January, February and March 1970 followed, the report stated. Mitchell testified to committee investigators that he recollected only one such meeting, but Danner, buttressed by Justice Department appointment logs, asserted there had been three, the report said.

The argument put to Mitchell by Danner entailed changing the definition of the relevant market. Instead of considering the impact of the purchase of the Dunes on Las Vegas alone, Danner suggested, the Justice Department should view the acquisition in terms of the whole state market.

At their February meeting, Danner supplied Mitchell with statistics on concentrations of hotel rooms in Las Vegas. A third meeting, requested by Mitchell, followed March 19. According to Danner, Mitchell said, "From our review of these figures, we see no problem. Why don't you go ahead with the negotiations" [for the Dunes.] (Negotiations for purchase of the Dunes by Hughes later fell through for unrelated financial reasons.)

Richard McLaren, head of the antitrust division at the time, told Watergate committee investigators that he first learned of the proposed acquisition March 12, 1970, two months after Danner broached the idea with Mitchell. He informed Mitchell that the purchase would violate merger guidelines, McLaren testified, but Mitchell ended their discussion without indicating his final position. One week later, the report said, Mitchell approved the purchase.

Disclosures & Convictions

The conclusion of the major Watergate inquiries did not end the revelations that the scandal had provoked. Watergate-related investigations and trials continued to provide new details of Watergate-era events.

3M settles SEC case. Minnesota Mining & Manufacturing Co. and three top corporate officials consented to a federal court order enjoining them from further violations of securities laws in connection with illegal political contributions, (reported Feb. 3, 1975). The SEC had filed civil charges against the firm Jan. 30, charging that about $489,000 in corporate funds was given to political candidates from a secret 3M slush fund.

The consent settlement followed 3M's disclosure to the SEC that a $634,000 slush fund had existed from which illegal corporate contributions were made to political campaigns.

Under the settlement, 3M agreed to name a special master to investigate disbursements from the secret fund and the officials, Harry Heltzer, Bert S. Cross and Irwin R. Hansen, agreed to reimburse 3M at least $425,000 for the donations.

A federal judge July 27, 1976 dismissed a federal tax-fraud indictment filed against 3M, Cross and Hansen.

The defendants were accused of conspiring to file false corporate income-tax returns in 1963–69 to cover up illegal corporate gifts from the slush fund.

In agreeing to the defense motion for dismissal, Judge Donald D. Alsop of U.S. District Court in St. Paul ruled that the indictment violated a prior agreement with the Watergate special prosecutor's office.

The defendants had won the agreement in 1973 against further prosecution after 3M voluntarily disclosed making an illegal $30,000 contribution to the Nixon re-election campaign in 1972.

Northrop accused of big slush fund.
The SEC April 16, 1975 accused Northrop Corp., a Los Angeles-based aerospace firm, of maintaining a $30 million slush fund for "unlawful political contributions and other unlawful purposes." Northrop, with assets estimated at $410 million, was a major defense contractor and a leading exporter of U.S. warplanes.

The SEC charges, contained in a complaint filed with U.S. District Court in New York, also named Thomas V. Jones, Northrop president and chairman, and James Allen, a Northrop vice president and director from 1951 until 1974.

Northrop, Jones and Allen had pleaded guilty in 1974 to making an illegal $150,-000 contribution to the Nixon re-election campaign. Later, in a settlement of a stockholder suit stemming from this disclosure, Northrop officials admitted making illegal contributions to Sen. Hubert H. Humphrey's (D, Minn.) 1968 presidential campaign and to Democratic and Republican candidates for senatorial and gubernatorial races in California.

According to the SEC complaint, Northrop's involvement in illegal campaign funding activities was far larger than previously indicated. The SEC charged that beginning in 1961, Northrop, Jones and Allen caused "in excess of $76,-000 in corporate funds to be paid for political contributions and related expenses, a substantial portion of which was unlawful."

The money was laundered through over-payments made to William Savy, a Paris-based Northrop consultant, who converted the disbursements to cash and returned the money to an agent in New York, the complaint stated. Allen then picked up the cash from this agent, according to the SEC.

The Northrop slush fund was greatly expanded from 1971 through 1973, according to the SEC, until "approximately $30 million in Northrop corporate monies was or would be disbursed." However, the agency did not identify the recipients of the $30 million or specify how the money was used.

Northrop settled the SEC suit April 17 without admitting or denying the charges. The defendants accepted a permanent decree barring them from making false entries in corporate books and from maintaining any secret or unrecorded fund of corporate monies or assets.

In a statement issued with the settlement announcement, Northrop said that the $30 million fund "consists of fees and sales commissions that have been or will be paid over a number of years in relation to sales of company products and services abroad totaling $777.4 million."

Political payments detailed—In addition to the illegal $150,000 contribution to the Nixon re-election campaign, Northrop had illegally given $250,000 to Democratic and Republican political figures during 1962–73, according to documents filed with the SEC.

The payments were made from a $1.1 million political slush fund established in 1961 by Northrop Chairman Jones and ex-Vice President Allen.

Disclosure of Northrop's additional political payments was made to the SEC in 1974 in a special audit report prepared by Ernst & Ernst, an accounting firm hired by the company to investigate its secret slush fund transactions. Northrop had agreed early in 1975 to make the disclosures as part settlement of a stockholder's suit, filed in connection with the illegal Nixon gift.

A breakdown of the political payments, based on the Ernst & Ernst report filed with the SEC, was published May 6 by the Washington Post and May 6 and 8 by the New York Times. According to the Post, the accounting firm was advised by a Washington law firm that of the $338,000 in donations made through the slush fund and uncovered in the audit, some $250,000 in contributions were believed to violate the 1971 federal campaign law. No determination was made whether Northrop's political contributions may have violated other federal or state laws, the Post reported.

Among the candidates for federal office who received the Northrop payments:

Sen. Alan Cranston (D, Calif.), a total of $26,200 for the years 1966, 1968, 1972, and 1973; former President Richard M. Nixon, $10,000 for his 1968 campaign; former Sen. George Murphy (R, Calif.), $8,000 for 1970; Sen. Hubert H. Humphrey (D, Minn.), $6,175 for 1966 and 1968; Rep. Charles H. Wilson (D, Calif.), a member of the House Armed Services Committee, $2,350 for 1966, 1971, and

1973; Sen. John V. Tunney (D, Calif.), $2,000 in 1970; the late Sen. Richard Russell (D, Ga.), former chairman of the Senate Armed Services Committee, $1,000 in 1966; Sen. Henry M. Jackson (D, Wash.), $1,000 for his presidential bid in 1972; Sen. Mike Mansfield (D, Mont.), $250 in 1964; and former Sen. Thomas H. Kuchel (R, Calif.), $250 in 1964.

Eugene Wyman, a prominent Democratic fund raiser in California, was given $20,000 for the years 1962–1973 and Holmes Tuttle, a Republican fund raiser in the state, received $30,000 over those years.

Candidates for state office in California who received Northrop payments: former Gov. Ronald Reagan (R), $6,000 in 1970; former Gov. Edmund G. Brown (D), $5,000 in 1966; Treasurer Jess Unruh, $1,085 in 1970; Gov. Edmund G. Brown Jr. (D), $800 in 1970 when he ran for secretary of state; and Mayor Thomas Bradley (D, Los Angeles) $100 for his unsuccessful 1969 mayoralty bid.

1972 Nixon contributors plead guilty. A Baltimore construction company, Ratrie, Robbins & Schweitzer Inc., and two of its officers, pleaded guilty Jan. 28, 1975 to donating $5,000 in corporate funds to the Nixon re-election campaign in 1972.

Chief Judge George L. Hart Jr. of U.S. District Court in Washington fined the firm $2,500 — half the maximum penalty. Harry Ratrie and Augustus Robbins 3rd were placed on unsupervised probation for one month.

Singer Co. & 2 aides plead guilty. The Singer Co., a defense contractor, pleaded guilty June 11, 1975 to a misdemeanor charge that it had illegally contributed $10,000 in corporate funds to the 1972 Nixon-Agnew campaign with expectations of receiving favorable treatment in the awarding of federal contracts.

The firm was fined $2,500, half the maximum amount, by a U.S. District Court judge in Baltimore after the defense argued that no high corporate officials authorized the donation. In return for the guilty plea, the government agreed to drop felony charges alleging the firm conspired to funnel the donation through J. Walter Jones Jr., a wealthy friend of Agnew. If Singer had been convicted of felony charges, federal contracts could have been denied the firm.

Arthur M. Carter Jr., a former official of one of Singer's Maryland offices, entered a guilty plea in the campaign fund case, federal prosecutors disclosed June 10. Carter was accused of using a bogus invoice from Lester Matz, an engineering consultant and witness against Agnew, to launder the campaign gift.

Martin A. Leader, another former Singer official, pleaded guilty July 10 to a misdemeanor offense regarding the donation. He had been indicted June 14.

The government dropped charges June 10 against another defendant in the case, Raymond A. Long. Two others named with him in a March indictment, James F. Fanseen and John W. Steffey, pleaded no contest, it was reported June 10.

The campaign contribution charges were part of a 2½-year federal investigation of political corruption in Maryland that led to Agnew's resignation as Vice President.

Stans pleads guilty. Former Commerce Secretary Maurice Stans, who had been President Nixon's chief campaign fund raiser, pleaded guilty March 12, 1975 to misdemeanor violations of the federal campaign finance law.

Stans admitted he had "nonwillfully" accepted two illegal contributions totaling $70,000 and had failed to report three other cash transactions totaling $150,000.

In a statement to reporters after the guilty plea was entered in U.S. District Court in Washington, Stans claimed that disposition of the misdemeanor charges "established once and for all that I had no guilty involvement in the Watergate burglary, the Watergate cover-up, the Segretti sabotage, the ITT case, the White House plumbers affair, or the 1971 dairy industry dealings."

The five counts to which Stans pleaded guilty included:

■ Secretly accepting a $30,000 contribution from Minnesota Mining & Manufacturing Co. in March 1972.

■ Secretly accepting an illegal $40,000 contribution from Goodyear Tire & Rubber Co. in March 1972.

■ Failing to report a $39,000 contribution given by former Montana Gov. Tim Babcock on behalf of Armand Hammer, chairman of Occidental Petroleum Corp.

Stans was fined $5,000 by U.S. District Judge John Lewis Smith Jr. May 14.

No prison term was set, Judge Smith explained, because "it is not alleged that Mr. Stans profited personally, that money went into his own pocket." Another factor in his sentencing decison, the judge added, was Stans' "long public and private career."

Stans had been acquitted in 1974 with former Attorney General John Mitchell of conspiracy, obstruction of justice and perjury charges involving a secret campaign contribution from fugitive financier Robert Vesco.

Steinbrenner to repay firm. A special committee set up at the urging of the Securities and Exchange Commission to review the political gift practices of American Ship Building Co., recommended May 7, 1975 that company chairman George M. Steinbrenner III be required to repay the firm $42,325.17 for illegal campaign contributions made to the Nixon re-election campaign that he had authorized or permitted.

Steinbrenner said he would "honor" the recommendations, but he insisted that the contributions were "made in the full belief that they were legal."

The review committee had been created in October 1974 following settlement of an SEC complaint filed against American Ship Building and Steinbrenner regarding the firm's practice of paying bonuses to employes, who were then instructed to make contributions to various political parties and candidates.

Although the panel concluded that "everything was in order as to the overwhelming majority of bonuses paid by the company" during 1970–1972, the group stated that bonuses paid and contributions made on April 6, 1972—the day before a new and more stringent disclosure law regarding federal campaign contributions took effect—appeared "to have been a questionable corporate expenditure."

Steinbrenner was urged to repay the company for the gross amount of those bonuses. (A total of $25,000 was donated to the Nixon finance committee; the remainder of the bonus payments went toward payment of the employes' additional income tax.)

It was not recommended that Steinbrenner repay the firm for $55,000 given as bonuses in the 1970–1972 period, although according to the Watergate special prosecutor's office, these funds represented illegal contributions. (Felony charges against Steinbrenner related to these donations were dropped under a plea bargaining arrangement in which he agreed to plead guilty to two lesser charges.)

The review committee also had been instructed to search for expenditure irregularities in American Ship Building's books, but the report stated that all of the expenses "appear to be proper and legitimate." The sole exception, the report added, was a "single $500 item in petty cash," apparently donated to Sen. Daniel K. Inouye's (D, Hawaii) campaign.

Hammer & associates plead guilty. Tim M. Babcock, former governor of Montana, pleaded guilty Dec. 10, 1974 to aiding and abetting Armand Hammer, chairman of Occidental Petroleum Corp., in illegally donating $54,000 to President Nixon's re-election campaign. The misdemeanor charges filed by the Watergate special prosecutor's office, accused Babcock of violating a federal law that prohibited campaign donations given in the name of another person.

According to the prosecutor's office, Babcock delivered the cash to the Committee to Re-elect the President between September 1972 and January 1973, while serving as executive vice president of a Washington-based Occidental subsidiary. (He had been governor of Montana from 1962–68.) In May 1973, he told the committee that the money had been given in his name.

Two other Hammer associates, James B. Patton and John Tigrett, had been granted immunity from prosecution by the special prosecutor's office as part of its continuing investigation, according to the Washington Post Dec. 11.

Babcock was sentenced Jan. 31, 1975 to serve four months in jail and was fined $1,000. Before sentencing, Chief Judge

George L. Hart Jr. of U.S. District Court in Washington told Babcock, "You could have told Hammer you had no intention of assisting him in breaking the law." Hart sentenced Babcock to the maximum one-year jail sentence but said he was required to serve only four months and then would be put on probation for two years.

Hammer himself pleaded guilty Oct. 1, 1975 to three misdemeanor charges.

According to court documents, Hammer pledged $100,000 to the Nixon finance committee with the stipulation that the contribution be made anonymously. However, Hammer provided only $46,000 to the committee before April 7, 1972, when a new federal campaign law took effect requiring the disclosure of donors' identities. The remaining $54,000 was channeled secretly to the committee through Babcock, who arranged to have the gift made in installments in the names of friends.

U.S. District Court Judge William B. Jones threw out Hammer's guilty plea Dec. 12 and ordered him to stand trial.

Jones said he believed the guilty plea had no factual basis, a legal condition that was required before a plea could be accepted. Jones based his opinion on a letter, dated Oct. 27, Hammer sent to a probation officer.

In the letter, Hammer claimed he was pressured by the Nixon re-election committee to increase his contributions, and was duped by Babcock.

The U.S. Court of Appeals in Washington then ruled Jan. 20, 1976 that Hammer could withdraw the controversial letter and enter a new guilty plea to the original misdemeanor counts.

The case was transferred to Los Angeles Feb. 5 after court-appointed physicians said Hammer, hospitalized in Los Angeles with a heart condition, was too ill to travel.

Hammer pleaded guilty again March 4.

Judge Lawrence T. Lydick March 23 sentenced Hammer in U.S. District Court, Los Angeles, to one year's probation and fined him $3,000.

Hammer, 77, appeared in court in a wheelchair. The judge, who could have sentenced Hammer to up to three years in prison, said the sentence was reduced because of Hammer's age and ill health.

Hart June 4 set aside Babcock's jail term since Hammer and Maurice Stans, chairman of Nixon's finance committee

and the recipient of the illegal donation, had been ordered only to pay fines. Hart upheld a $1,000 fine for Babcock.

Former Postmaster General W. Marvin Watson pleaded guilty in Washington Sept. 23 to helping Hammer cover up the illegal 1972 contributions. Watson was fined the $500 maximum. Watson had become an Occidental Petroleum official after leaving the government.

Chestnut convicted in milk fund gift. Jack L. Chestnut, 42, Sen. Hubert H. Humphrey's campaign manager during his 1970 senatorial race, was convicted May 8, 1975 of soliciting and accepting an illegal $12,000 campaign contribution from Associated Milk Producers, Inc.

Chestnut was the first aide to a prominent Democratic politician to be convicted after a trial stemming from an investigation by the Watergate special prosecutor's office, which had obtained his indictment. The jury verdict was returned in U.S. District Court in New York, where the case had been transferred in December 1974.

Chestnut, and members of the jury who were questioned after the trial, said his case would have fared better in Minnesota, where he maintained a law practice. "People there would have understood the dairy business," Chestnut said.

The prosecution charged that Chestnut had attempted to conceal the illegal AMPI donation by making the co-op's checks payable to a New York advertising firm, Lennen & Newell, now bankrupt, that had handled the Humphrey campaign's publicity in 1968 and 1970.

The government's case was based on the testimony of two men involved in the campaign transaction, Bob A. Lilly, an aide to Harold S. Nelson, then the dairy co-op's general manager, and Barry Nova, a former executive with Lennen & Newell.

Lilly, who admitted he knew the contribution to be illegal, testified that he had personally delivered two AMPI checks for $6,000 each to Chestnut for forwarding to the advertising firm. The arrangements were made on Chestnut's instructions, Lilly testified.

Nova said that he had sent Lennen & Newell's bill to AMPI on Chestnut's instruction. Eventually, Nova said, he had received payment from the co-op.

Lilly also testified that he had made three other contributions totaling nearly $24,000, two as personal checks and one as cash, to the Minnesota Democratic Campaign Committee through Chestnut in 1970. (Nelson and AMPI's then second-ranking official, David L. Parr, had pleaded guilty to making these illegal contributions. Lilly had been granted immunity from prosecution in return for testifying as a government witness in various milk-fund cases.)

Lilly described the means by which these illegal contributions were concealed: he took out a personal loan, made the donation with a personal check, the co-op was billed by a law firm for double the amount of the contribution; the bill for the fictitious legal services was paid; and Lilly received funds to retire the loan.

The prosecution contended that Chestnut must have realized that Lilly's personal checks, which were referred to as "AMPI funds," did not represent a legitimate contribution from C-TAPE, the dairy co-op's political committee, and that this knowledge must have carried over to the donations received on Humphrey's behalf in 1970 that were funneled through the advertising firm.

Chestnut testified that he could not recall having made the arrangements with Lilly, nor could he recall having signed and sent letters to AMPI regarding Lennen & Newell's bill.

Humphrey appeared as the prosecution's first witness on May 5 when the trial opened. He said he had personally solicited a contribution from AMPI, but had no "personal knowledge" of the actual financial transaction, which was left to the "campaign committee and Mr. Chestnut."

Chestnut was sentenced June 26 to four months in prison and fined $5,000.

Corruption Charges Force Vice President Agnew's Resignation

Faced with corruption charges that he obviously could not defend successfully, Spiro T. Agnew resigned as Vice President of the U.S. Oct. 10, 1973 and pleaded no contest to a single count of income-tax evasion. He thus avoided trial on an indictment that included charges of exacting bribes from engineering firms doing business with the state of Maryland at a time when he was governor of the state.

Agnew deal blocks prosecution. Agnew resigned as Vice President Oct. 10 and pleaded nolo contendere (no contest) to the tax-evasion charge as the price of the Justice Department's agreement to drop all pending charges against him and to request lenience in the tax case.

In a dramatic courtroom hearing in Baltimore shortly after he submitted his letter of resignation, Agnew avoided imprisonment by pleading no contest to a federal charge that he had failed to report $29,500 of income he received in 1967, when he was governor of Maryland. Such a plea, while not an admission of guilt, was tantamount to a plea of guilty on the charge. Agnew had faced federal indictment for violation of bribery, conspiracy and tax laws.

As required by law, Agnew's formal instrument of resignation was a statement transmitted to Secretary of State Henry A. Kissinger.

Agnew also formally notified President Nixon by letter, saying "the accusations against me cannot be resolved without a long, divisive and debilitating struggle in the Congress and in the courts." Agnew had concluded that it was "in the best interest of the nation" that he relinquish the office.

Almost simultaneously with the delivery of his resignation letter to Kissinger, Agnew appeared before U.S. District Court Judge Walter E. Hoffman in Baltimore to plead no contest to the charge of filing a "false and fraudulent" income tax return for the year 1967 and attempting to evade payment of $13,551.47 in federal taxes. According to the charge, Agnew had understated his and Mrs. Agnew's joint income by $29,500.

Hoffman asked Agnew if he understood the implications of waiving indictment and entering a plea of no contest, which, Hoffman noted, was "the full equivalent of a plea of guilty" and would protect Agnew only in that it could not be used in a civil suit as evidence that Agnew had actually committed the offense. As Hoffman pointed out in a formal statement, a no contest plea used in tax evasion cases "merely permits the parties to further litigate the amount due without regard to the conviction following such a plea."

Hoffman cited the provisions of Agnew's agreement with the Justice Department: that Agnew resign; that the department would not prosecute on other charges while reserving the right to use Agnew's name in proceedings against others; and that Agnew might still be subject to action by the State of Maryland "or some private organization."

"Do you understand and ratify the agreement as I have stated it?" Hoffman asked.

"I do so understand it," Agnew said.

Agnew was sentenced to a fine of $10,-000 and three years' unsupervised probation. Hoffman said that without the recommendation for leniency by Attorney General Elliot L. Richardson, he would have been inclined to follow his usual procedure in tax evasion cases of imposing a fine and prison sentence of two to five months. But, Hoffman added, "I am persuaded that the national interests in the present case are so great and so compelling . . . that the ends of justice would be better served by making an exception to the general rule."

In a statement read to the court, Richardson said no agreement could have been reached without a provision that he appeal for leniency. Mindful of the "historic magnitude of the penalties inherent in the vice president's resignation from his high office and his acceptance of a judgment of conviction of a felony," Richardson said that a prison sentence was more than he could "recommend or wish."

Richardson emphasized that a central element of the agreement was that the department be allowed to present the details of its other evidence against Agnew while agreeing to waive prosecution based on it.

Richardson said that for the people to "fairly judge the outcome" of the Agnew case, he would offer "for the permanent record" an "exposition of evidence" which "establishes a pattern of substantial cash payments to the defendant during the period when he served as governor of Maryland in return for engineering contracts with the State of Maryland." Richardson added that none of the government's major witnesses had been promised immunity from prosecution and that each who would have testified to making direct payments to Agnew had signed a sworn statement "subject to the penalties of perjury."

According to the "exposition of evidence," Agnew—shortly after becoming governor in 1967—established a system of taking payments from engineering firms. I.H. Hammerman 2d, a Baltimore investment banker, acted as "collector" from companies designated by Jerome B. Wolff, then chairman of the Maryland State Roads Commission. After initial disagreements about division of the payments, the three agreed—on Agnew's order—that the payments would be divided 50% for Agnew and 25% each for Hammerman and Wolff. The three would then discuss which firms should be awarded contracts, but "the governor always exercised the final decision-making authority."

The evidence also detailed the relationship between Agnew and the presidents of two engineering firms who made direct cash payments. Agnew allegedly complained to Allen Green of Green Associates, Inc. about the "financial burdens" of the office of governor, and Green began making payments which continued until the beginning of the Maryland grand jury investigation in January 1973.

A similar relationship existed with Lester Matz of Matz, Childs and Associates who also continued making "corrupt payments" to Agnew after he became vice president. In addition to payments "still owed" for contracts awarded to Matz while Agnew was Maryland governor, Matz allegedly paid $2,500 in April 1971 in return for the awarding of a federal contract to a Matz company.

According to the evidence, Agnew received payments totaling about $100,-000.

In acknowledging to the court that he had received taxable payments in 1967, Agnew conceded that such payments had been made by companies receiving state contract awards in 1967 "and other years," but he denied that the payments had "in any way" influenced his official actions. He stressed that no contracts were awarded to "contractors who were not competent to perform the work and in most instances state contracts were awarded without any arrangement for the payment of money by the contractor."

Charges against Agnew. The "full exposition" of the federal grand jury's charges against Agnew follow:

I. The relationship of Mr. Agnew, I. H. Hammerman 2d and Jerome B. Wolff.

I. H. Hammerman 2d is a highly successful real estate developer and mortgage banker. He has entered into a formal written agreement with the government, pursuant to which he has tendered his complete cooperation to the government with respect to the present investigation. Under the terms of this agreement, Hammerman will plead guilty to a charge of violating a felony provision of the Internal Revenue Code. As a result of that plea, Mr. Hammerman will be exposed to a maximum sentence of three years in prison. In return, the government has agreed not to charge Mr. Hammerman with any other crime relating to the subject matter of this investigation and to bring his cooperation to the attention of the court at the time of his sentencing. The government has not agreed to make any specific recommendation with respect to the period of incarceration, if any, to which the government believes it would be appropriate for Mr. Hammerman to be sentenced, and, in particular, the government has made no representation to Mr. Hammerman that it will recommend to the court that he be placed on probation.

Jerome B. Wolff is an engineer and also an attorney. He is the president of Greiner Environmental Systems, Inc. Wolff has tendered his complete cooperation to the government in the present investigation. The government has not entered into any agreement with Wolff as to what consideration, if any, he may expect in return for his cooperation, other than the assurance that his own truthful disclosures to the government will not be used against him in any criminal prosecution.

At the government's request, both Hammerman and Wolff have executed sworn written statements that recount their relationships with Mr. Agnew. Their testimony, the corroborative testimony of other witnesses, and various corroborative documents, would prove the following:

Hammerman has known Spiro T. Agnew for many years. When Mr. Agnew ran for Baltimore County executive in 1962, however, Hammerman actively supported his opponent. The day after the election, Hammerman called to congratulate Mr. Agnew and asked to see him. They met in Hammerman's office and again Hammerman congratulated Mr. Agnew on his victory. Hammerman told Mr. Agnew that he knew all campaigns had deficits, and he offered Mr. Agnew a post-election contribution of $10,000. Mr. Agnew refused, but he told Hammerman that he would expect a contribution three times as large when he ran for office again.

Between 1963 and 1966, while Mr. Agnew was the Baltimore County executive, he and Hammerman developed a close, personal friendship. During the period and continuing up until early 1973, they often discussed Mr. Agnew's personal financial situation. Mr. Agnew complained about it, and told Hammerman

that he had not accumulated any wealth before he assumed public office, had no inheritance, and as a public official received what he considered a small salary. Mr. Agnew believed, moreover, that his public position required him to adopt a standard of living beyond his means and that his political ambitions required him to build a financially strong political organization. During the period when he was county executive, Hammerman entertained him, introduced him to substantial political contributors, and gave him substantial gifts.

At the outset of the 1966 Maryland gubernatorial campaign, Hammerman found himself in a difficult situation. Some of his closest business associates were involved in the Democratic candidates' campaign, but Mr. Agnew insisted that Hammerman choose between them and him. Hammerman decided actively to support Mr. Agnew, contributed $25,000 and raised an even larger amount in campaign funds for Mr. Agnew. Hammerman was one of Mr. Agnew's financial chairmen and devoted considerable time, energy and money to his campaign. After he became governor and later vice president, Hammerman continued to entertain him, travel with him and provide him with other financial benefits. These benefits were not related to the monies discussed below.

In the late nineteen fifties, while Wolff was deputy chief engineer and later assistant director of public works for Baltimore County, Mr. Agnew became a member of the Baltimore County Board of Zoning Appeals. Mr. Agnew and Wolff became acquainted as a result of Wolff's appearances as a witness before the board.

Wolff left employment with the county approximately six months after Mr. Agnew took office as county executive. Mr. Agnew and he became good friends between 1963 and 1967 while Wolff was in business as a consulting engineer, and Wolff became an unofficial adviser to him. Mr. Agnew arranged for him to receive contracts from the county. Wolff greatly admired Mr. Agnew and believed that Mr. Agnew was sincerely attempting, with considerable success, to do a good job as county executive.

Friends in the consulting business asked Wolff, while Mr. Agnew was county executive, how much Wolff was paying for the engineering work that he was receiving from Baltimore County. They seemed to assume that he was paying, as it was well known in the business community that engineers generally, and the smaller engineering firms in particular, had to pay in order to obtain contracts from the county in those days. Only a few of the larger and well established firms were generally considered to be immune from this requirement.

It is Wolff's belief, based upon his experience and his understanding of the experience of others, that engineering firms generally have to struggle for 10 to 15 years in order to become established. During this period, and for some time thereafter, they generally make payments—sometimes through middlemen—to public officials at various levels of government throughout Maryland in order to receive public work. Sometimes they reach a point where they are sufficiently established as qualified engineers that they do not generally have to make illegal payments in order to obtain a fair share of the public work.

It was Wolff's belief that a certain close associate of Mr. Agnew's (referred to hereafter as "the close associate" or "the middleman") was his principal middleman in Baltimore County. The close associate courted engineers, developers and others and bragged a great deal about his relationship with Mr. Agnew.

Although Wolff was in a favored position with Mr. Agnew, on two or more occasions while Mr. Agnew was county executive, the close associates requested money from Wolff in return for contracts Wolff wanted or had obtained from the county. Wolff paid him $1,250 in cash in April 1966, and in addition made a payment to another associate of Mr. Agnew's, ostensibly as legal fees. Wolff's present recollection is that he also made one or two other payments to the close associate.

It was Wolff's belief that another individual also acted as a middleman for Mr. Agnew. Wolff learned from others that a certain Baltimore engineer was paying for work through that other individual. It is Wolff's recollection that in his office, Mr. Agnew once remarked to Wolff that the engineer in question was paying 10 per cent for the work that he received from the county. Wolff inferred from Mr. Agnew's comment that Mr. Agnew was surprised that that engineer was paying as much as 10 per cent, in view of the fact that the going rate was generally 5 per cent. Through conversations with still another engineer, Wolff learned that he also was making payments for county work.

During Mr. Agnew's 1966 campaign for governor, Wolff gave him $1,000 in cash as a campaign contribution. Wolff also worked in Mr. Agnew's campaign. Wolff knew that he had a potential personal stake in Mr. Agnew's candidacy, as Mr. Agnew had sometime earlier indicated to him the possibility that he might appoint Wolff as chairman-director of the State Roads Commission if Mr. Agnew were elected governor.

Wolff had first become acquainted with Hammerman during the period when Wolff had been an assistant engineer employed by the Baltimore County Public Works Department. Hammerman considered Wolff to be a brilliant engineer, and Wolff had handled in an efficient manner various problems that Hammerman had had with county agencies in connection with Hammerman's building ventures. A close personal friendship had developed between them. Hammerman had been so impressed with Wolff that he had advised him that if he ever decided to leave county government, Hammerman would retain him as the engineer for his building projects. After Wolff had left county government in 1963 and established his own engineering business, he had done virtually all of Hammerman's engineering work.

After his election as governor, Mr. Agnew told Hammerman that he intended to appoint Wolff chairman-director of the Maryland State Roads Commission. Hammerman objected strenuously because he wanted to retain Wolff's engineering services. Mr. Agnew responded, however, that Hammerman should not be too upset about Wolff's appointment because, Mr. Agnew told Hammerman, "You won't lose by it."

On or about March 1, 1967, Wolff took office as Governor Agnew's appointee as the chairman-director of the State Roads Commission. Governor Agnew had Wolff monitor every consulting engineering and construction contract that came through the state. It became obvious to Wolff that, in view of the provisions of the states road commission legislation, he would in effect control the selection of engineers and architects for contracts to be awarded by the State Roads Commission, subject only to the ultimate decision-making authority of Governor Agnew.

Shortly after Wolff took office, Governor Agnew asked Hammerman to come to his office in Annapolis, Md. At this meeting, Governor Agnew advised Hammerman that there was in Maryland a long-standing "system," as he called it, under which engineers made substantial "cash contributions" in return for state contracts awarded through the State Roads Commission. Governor Agnew referred to the substantial political financial demands that would be made on both himself and Hammerman, and said, in effect, that those who would be benefitting (the engineers) should do their share. Governor Agnew said that Hammerman could help him by collecting cash payments from the engineers, and told him to meet with Wolff to set things up.

Hammerman subsequently met with Wolff and told him of the discussion he had had with Governor Agnew. Wolff readily agreed to participate and suggested that the payments be equally divided among the governor, Hammerman and Wolff. Hammerman then met again with the governor and told him of the suggested division of the payments. Governor Agnew at first replied that he did not see why Wolff should receive any share of the money, but he agreed to the division as long as he received 50 per cent of the total payment. He told Hammerman that he didn't care what Hammerman did with his share.

Hammerman went back to Wolff and told him that Mr. Agnew insisted on 50 per cent of the money, and that Hammerman and Wolff should equally divide the rest between themselves. Wolff agreed.

Over the course of the subsequent 18 or 20 months that Mr. Agnew served as governor of Maryland, the scheme agreed to by Mr. Agnew, Hammerman, and Wolff was fully implemented. Wolff kept Hammerman informed as to which engineers were to receive state contracts and Hammerman kept Wolff informed as to which engineers were making cash payments. It was soon generally understood among engineers that Hammerman was the person to see in connection with state roads engineering contracts. As a result Hammerman soon found himself meeting with individual representatives of certain engineering firms. They would inform Hammerman of their interest in obtaining state work, and Hammerman would reply he would see what he could do. In some cases an engineer would specify the particular work in which he was interested; in most cases, the engineers would not specify any particular job.

There was no need for Hammerman to make coarse demands or to issue threats because the engineers clearly indicated that they knew what was expected of them. The discussions were generally about "political contributions," but the conversations left no doubt that the engineers understood exactly how the system worked—that is, that cash payments to the governor through Hammerman were necessary in order for their companies to receive substantial state contracts. The "contributions" were almost always in cash, and many of them were made when there was no campaign in progress.

Although Wolff had told Hammerman that "contributions" should average between 3 per cent and 5 per cent of the contract amount, Hammerman did not specify any exact amount to be paid, and accepted any reasonable sum. Sometimes the "contribution" was made in one payment, sometimes in several. When a contract was about to be awarded to one of the engineers who was known to be willing to make payments, Wolff would advise Hammerman that the engineer had been selected for a certain job. Hammerman would then contact the engineer and congratulate him. His congratulations were intended as signals that a cash "contribution" was due, and the engineer would then meet Hammerman and bring him the money.

Pursuant to his understanding with Mr. Agnew and Wolff, Hammerman retained 25 per cent of the payment and delivered to Wolff his 25 per cent share. Hammerman generally held Mr. Agnew's 50 per cent share in a safe deposit box until Mr. Agnew called for it. From time to time Mr. Agnew would call Hammerman and ask how many "papers" Hammerman had for him. It was understood between Mr. Agnew and Hammerman that the term "paper" referred to $1,000 in cash. Hammerman would tell Mr. Agnew how many "papers" he had and Mr. Agnew would ask Hammerman to bring the "papers" to him. Hammerman would then collect the cash from the safe deposit box and personally deliver it to Mr. Agnew to his office in Annapolis or in Baltimore or wherever else Mr. Agnew would designate.

The cash which Wolff received from Hammerman was initially kept in Wolff's home. It was then transferred to two, and later, three safe deposit boxes, two in Baltimore and one in Washington. Most of the money was spent on ordinary personal expenses over a period of more than four years. A small portion of it was used by Wolff to make payments to other public officials in order to obtain work for the two consulting firms which he had sold before he had become chairman of the State Roads Commission, but in which he still had a financial interest. Wolff kept detailed contemporaneous documents on which he recorded the dates, amounts, and engineering firm sources of the monies that he received from Hammerman as his share of the proceeds of the scheme. These records are among a large volume of corroborative documents that Wolff has turned over to the United States attorney's office.

The selection process for the state roads contracts generally worked in the following manner: Usually, based upon previous discussions with Governor Agnew, Wolff would make preliminary decisions with regard to the consulting engineering and architectural firms to be awarded contracts. He would then obtain the approval of the State Roads Commission. Governor Agnew would then make the final decision.

During Mr. Agnew's tenure as governor of Maryland, Wolff met with him from time to time to discuss the status of various projects and the decisions which had to be made with respect to engineering, management and sometimes architectural contracts. Wolff generally prepared agendas for these meetings in advance. Governor Agnew appeared to have confidence in Wolff's technical ability and generally accorded substantial weight to Wolff's preliminary decisions as to which consulting firms should be awarded contracts, generally concurring with Wolff's selection. Where important or unique projects were involved, Wolff would present Governor Agnew with a list of several possible firms from which Governor Agnew would select the firm to be awarded the contract.

Governor Agnew always had and from time to time exercised the power to make all final decisions.

Several factors influenced Wolff in his own decision-making in the selection process outlined above:

1. It was the basic premise of Wolff's selection process that an engineering firm had to be competent to do the work before it could even be considered for a contract. Any engineering firm which, in Wolff's judgment, was competent to perform a certain assignment might be given consideration.

2. Both Governor Agnew and Hammerman would from time to time ask Wolff to give special consideration to a particular engineering firm, which might or might not be making cash payments, and he would then try to do so. He remembers, for example, that the governor on one or more occasions asked him to give work to two specific engineering firms. Hammerman also recommended to Wolff, presumably because of Hammerman's friendship with one or more particular engineers, that work be given to at least one company that, according to Wolff's understanding, had not made any cash payments.

3. Wolff's decision-making (and he recalls that this was a matter that he discussed with Hammerman in particular) was intended to avoid substantial and noticeable deviations from general fairness—that is, he tried to avoid a situation in which any firm received more or less work than could be justified on a purely legitimate basis. Wolff always viewed the process as one of accomplishing competent public work for the State of Maryland, very similar to that which would have been accomplished if all the selections had been made strictly on their merits, while at the same time serving the mutual ends of Mr. Agnew, Hammerman, and himself.

Wolff believed it was important not to deviate too obviously from the appearance of fairness and even-handedness in the selection of engineers. For example, he became aware—he believes initially as a result of a conversation he had with Governor Agnew—that Hammerman had apparently approached a certain engineer to solicit cash payments in connection with potential state work, and that the engineer had complained to Governor Agnew that state contracts should not be awarded on this basis.

The governor was very upset, as Wolff understood it, because Hammerman had apparently been especially heavy-handed with the engineer, and apparently because the governor felt that the engineer might make his complaint public. For these reasons, Wolff continued thereafter to give the engineer's firm some work.

The investigation also established that the same engineer also complained to his attorney, a close personal friend of Mr. Agnew's, about Hammerman's solicitation. Shortly after the engineer complained to his attorney, and several months before the engineer complained directly to Mr. Agnew, the attorney met with Mr. Agnew and gave him a detailed account of Hammerman's solicitation and of his client's outrage. He warned Mr. Agnew that Hammerman's activities could undermine all the attorney believed Governor Agnew was attempting to accomplish.

Although he indicated that he would look into the matter, Mr. Agnew never reported back to the attorney. He did several months later meet personally with the engineer, at the attorney's insistence, but the investigation has established Mr. Agnew did nothing whatever to stop Mr. Hammerman's continuing solicitations of cash payments from engineers in return for state work and that he (Mr. Agnew) continued for several years thereafter to accept his 50 per cent share of these cash payments.

4. The fact that a certain firm was making cash payments was a definite factor in the firm's favor. It was, therefore, accorded special consideration in the decision-making process. Wolff believes that a comparison of the amount of work given to certain firms before, during and after Governor Agnew's administration would confirm this.

On the other hand, there were times when a firm was selected for a specific job without regard to whether or not the firm was making cash payments. Some local Maryland firms had outstanding expertise in certain fields of engineering. This made them obvious choices for certain jobs, whether or not they were making cash payments. Even such firms, however, can never be completely sure that such considerations would be decisive in the decision-making process, so that even some of those companies were vulnerable to solicitations for cash payments.

5. Various other factors worked for or against particular firms or individuals in the selection process. For example, Wolff definitely favored Lester Matz and Allen Green, and their companies, not only because he understood they were making cash payments directly to the governor, but also because Wolff was receiving money from certain illegal dealings that he had with Matz and Green that did not involve Governor Agnew. Conversely, one engineering firm was disfavored by Wolff because in his view that firm had taken positions contrary to the best interests of the commission.

The evidence accumulated to date, both testimonial and documentary, establishes that Hammerman obtained, and split with Mr. Agnew and Wolff, cash payments from seven different engineering firms in return for state engineering contracts, and from one financial institution in return for a lucrative arrangement with the state involving the financing of certain state bonds. Those seven engineering firms and the one financial institution will not be named in this statement in order to avoid possible prejudice to several presently anticipated prosecutions.

It is worth noting, however, that Hammerman specifically recalls discussing with Mr. Agnew whether or nor the particular financial institution would be awarded the lucrative state bond business, and that during that discussion Mr. Agnew commented that the principals at the particular financial institution in question were "a cheap bunch" who "don't give you any money." Mr. Agnew informed Hammerman that he did not intend to award that institution the bond business in question unless a substantial "contribution" were made. Hammerman carried that message to the appropriate person; a substantial cash "contribution" was made; the institution got the bond business.

Hammerman also remembers that, while Mr. Agnew was governor, Hammerman observed that Allen Green and Lester Matz, two engineers whom he had known for some time, were receiving very substantial amounts of state bonds work. Hammerman mentioned that fact to Wolff and, since he had not received any money from Green and Matz, asked Wolff if he should approach them. Both Green and Matz had indicated to Wolff that they were making their payments directly to the governor. Wolff therefore told Hammerman that both Green and Matz were making "contributions" and that Hammerman should "stay away." Hammerman did so.

It is Wolff's understanding and belief that both Green and Matz continued to make cash payments directly to Mr. Agnew after he had become vice president. Wolff bases this conclusion on conversations that he has had with both Green and Matz since January 1969, in which each of them has indicated to Wolff that he had made payments directly to the vice president.

At a certain point, which Wolff believes was after Mr. Agnew's election as vice president in November 1968, but prior to his inauguration as vice president on January 20, 1969, Mr. Agnew asked Wolff to determine the details of payments that had been made by the State Roads Commission under his administration to the engineering company owned and operated by Allen Green. Wolff then discussed this request with Green, who subsequently prepared a list that he submitted to Wolff. Wolff then prepared a final list, a copy or duplicate of which he gave to Mr. Agnew.

When Wolff handed Mr. Agnew the list, they did not discuss it to any extent, according to Wolff's present recollection. Mr. Agnew just put it away.

Wolff would testify that much of his understanding concerning Mr. Agnew's actions and reactions to specific situations was inferential, since he and Mr. Agnew did not discuss Wolff's relationship with Hammerman or others or the fact that he and Mr. Agnew were acting, either jointly or individually, in a corrupt manner. Wolff believes his relationship with Mr. Agnew flourished because of their mutual sensitivity to their own positions and their mutual respect for one another. He does recall, however, an occasion on which he was in the governor's office in the State House. Governor Agnew and he were standing in front of the fireplace after a meeting, and the governor said to Wolff in substance: "Look after yourself but be careful."

II. The relationship between Mr. Agnew and Allen Green.

Allen Green is the president and one of the principal owners of Green Associates, Inc., a Maryland engineering company which has, over the years, performed various types of engineering work.

Green has signed a formal written agreement with the government under which he has agreed to plead guilty to a criminal felony violation of the Internal Revenue Code that will expose him to a maximum sentence of three years in prison. He has given the government his complete cooperation in this investigation. In return, the government has promised him that he will not be prosecuted for any offense related to this investigation other than the one to which he will plead guilty, and that at his sentencing the government will bring his cooperation to the attention of the court. The government has expressly refused to promise Green that it will recommend to the court at his sentencing that he be placed on probation.

At the government's request, Green has executed a sworn written statement detailing his relationship with Mr. Agnew. Green's testimony, the corroborative testimony of other witness, and various corroborative documents would prove the following:

Green has been an engineer in Maryland for 21 years. During this period, he has often made cash payments on behalf of his company in return for various state and local consulting contracts and in order to remain eligible for further contracts. He used cash for the simple reason that checks could have been traced and might have led to the discovery of these illegal payments. These payments formed a pattern over the years and reflected his understanding, based upon experience, of the system in which a firm such as his had to participate in order to insure its survival and growth in the State of Maryland. This system had developed long ago in Maryland and in other states as well.

Engineering contracts have not been awarded on the basis of public bids in Maryland. Instead, the selection of engineers for state roads contracts has rested exclusively in the discretion of public officials—in Maryland, the governor and the members of the State Roads Commission. They have had virtually absolute control. There are many engineering companies which seek contracts, but price competition was not allowed under the ethical standards of this profession until October of 1971. Therefore, engineers are very vulnerable to pressure from public officials for both legal and illegal payments. An engineer who refuses to pay can be deprived of substantial public work without effective recourse, and one who pays can safely expect that he will be rewarded.

A few companies developed in time a size, expertise, and stature that insulated them to some extent from this system. One or two developed an expertise, for example, in large bridge design, that other local companies could not match. One or two grew so large and had been awarded so many substantial contracts that the state could not do without their services unless out-of-state consultants were employed. In these ways, a few companies in effect "graduated" in time from the system to a position of lesser vulnerability, and they could afford to resist and perhaps in some instances, refuse to participate. In fact, Green believed that his own company was in recent years in the process of moving into this class.

It was seldom necessary, in Green's experience, for there to be any express prior agreement between an engineer and a public official in Maryland. Under this system, which each state administration perpetuated, the connection between payments and contracts rested on a largely tacit understanding under which engineers knew that if they did not pay, they would not receive very many contracts and that if they did pay, they would receive favored treatment. Therefore, when a politician requested a payment or when an engineer offered one, it was not necessary for anyone expressly to refer to the connection between payments and contracts because everyone understood the system, and could rely upon it without actually talking about it.

Green came to know Spiro T. Agnew in mid-1963, when Mr. Agnew was the county executive for Baltimore County, Maryland. Although his company received some engineering contracts from the county, Green does not recall making any cash payments to Mr. Agnew or to anyone in his administration during these years. Green cultivated his relationship with Mr. Agnew and occasionally had lunch with him. By 1966, they had developed a close relationship.

In connection with Mr. Agnew's successful 1966 campaign for governor, Green gave him approximately $8,000 to $10,000 in campaign contributions. He did so in part because he genuinely admired Mr. Agnew and believed that he would make an excellent governor. He also knew, however, that Mr. Agnew would be grateful for his support, and he anticipated that Mr. Agnew would express his gratitude by giving the Green company state work if he were elected.

After the inauguration, Green met with Governor Agnew on several occasions in his new offices, usually in Baltimore, but sometimes in Annapolis. At one of these meetings Governor Agnew expressed his concern about the substantial financial obligations and requirements imposed upon him by virtue of his new position. He told Green that, as the titular leader of the Republican party in Maryland, he would need substantial funds in order to support his own political organization. In addition, he believed that he would be called upon to provide financial assistance to other Republican candidates around the state.

Furthermore, he complained that it was extremely difficult for a person in his limited financial situation to bear the personal expenses of high public office, in the sense that his new position would require him, he believed, to adopt and maintain a life style that was beyond his means. He said that he had served as county executive at substantial financial sacrifice because of the small salary and that, although the governor's salary represented an increase in income, it would still be insufficient to meet the additional demands that he believed his new position would impose upon him.

This was neither the first nor the last occasion upon which Mr. Agnew mentioned to Green his concern about his personal financial difficulties. He had voiced similar complaints while county executive, and he continued from time to time to mention his personal financial difficulties thereafter.

Green inferred from what Mr. Agnew said, the manner in which he said it, and their respective positions that he was being invited in a subtle but clear way to make payments. He, therefore, replied that he recognized Mr. Agnew's financial problems and realized he was not a wealthy man. Green told him that his company had experienced successful growth and would probably continue to benefit from public work under the Agnew administration. He, therefore, offered to make periodic cash payments to Governor Agnew, who replied that he would appreciate such assistance very much.

On the basis of Green's experience, he had developed a policy that, where required, he would make payments in amounts that did not exceed an average of 1 per cent of the fees that his company received on public engineering contracts. This informal calculation included legitimate political contributions as well as cash payments. He knew that many politicians believed that engineers were wealthy and often demanded payments in much greater amounts, frequently 5 per cent and sometimes higher. Although he believed that some engineers made payments in these amounts he knew that such percentages were unrealistic, given the economics of the engineering industry. An engineering firm could not, in his judgment, make a profit on public work if payments in these excessive percentages were made. He had come to the conclusion that his company could not afford to pay more than 1 per cent and, in areas where more was demanded, he had simply refused to pay and had sought work elsewhere.

Therefore, Green calculated, largely in his head, that it would be appropriate for him to make approximately six payments a year to Mr. Agnew in amounts of $2,000, $2,500 or $3,000 each.

The exact amount of each payment to Mr. Agnew depended upon the amount of cash available to Green for such purposes at the time of the payment.

After the meeting at which this subject had first been discussed, Green scheduled appointments with Governor Agnew approximately six times a year. At the first such meeting, he handed an envelope to Governor Agnew that contained between $2,000 and $3,000 in cash. Green told the governor that he was aware of his financial problems and wished to be of assistance to him. Governor Agnew accepted the envelope, placed it in either his desk drawer or his coat pocket, and expressed his gratitude. Over the next two years, they gradually said less and less to each other about each payment; Green would merely hand him an envelope and Governor Agnew would place it in either his desk drawer or his coat pocket with little or no discussion about it.

During these meetings, Green and Governor Agnew would discuss a number of matters, but Green almost always made it a point to discuss state roads contracts with him. Indeed, Green's principal purpose in meeting with him was always to increase the amount of work that his company received from the state. They would discuss state contracts in general, and frequently, specific upcoming road and bridge contracts in particular. Green would express his desire that his company receive consideration for proposed work and would occasionally ask for specific contracts that he knew were scheduled to be awarded by the State Roads Commission. Green knew from experience and from what he learned from Wolff that Governor Agnew played a substantial role in the selection of engineers for State Roads Commission work. Governor Agnew would often tell him in these meetings that his company could expect to receive substantial work generally, and on occasion, he promised Green specific contracts. On other occasions, however, Governor Agnew would tell Green that a contract had already been or was to be committed to another company.

Green admits that his principal purpose in making payments to Governor Agnew was to influence him to select the Green company for as many state roads contracts as possible. Based upon his many years of experience, it was his belief that such payments would probably be necessary and certainly helpful in obtaining substantial amounts of State Roads Commission work.

With one exception (to be related later in this statement), Mr. Agnew never expressly stated to Green that there was any connection between the payments and the selection of the Green company for state contracts. According to Green, the understanding was a tacit one, based upon their respective positions and their mutual recognition of the realities of the system; their relationship was such that it was unnecessary for them to discuss openly the understanding under which these payments were given and received. The circumstances were that Green gave Governor Agnew cash payments in substantial amounts and asked for contracts, and from time to time, Governor Agnew told him that contracts would be awarded to the Green company.

Green paid Governor Agnew approximately $11,-000 in each of the years he served as governor of Maryland (1967 and 1968). Green generated the necessary cash to make these payments through his company by various means that violated the Internal Revenue Code and that were designed to obscure the purpose for which the cash was used.

Green also recalls that during the early part of the Agnew administration, the governor occasionally asked him to evaluate the competency of certain engineering companies which he was considering for State Roads Commission work. On at least one occasion, the governor also asked him if certain companies could be counted upon to provide financial assistance if state work were received.

Under the Agnew administration, the Green company received substantial work from the Maryland State Roads Commission. It was awarded approximately 10 contracts, with fees approximating $3,-000,000 to $4,000,000.

On a few occasions during these years Green was asked by Wolff if he was taking care of his "obligations" with respect to the substantial state work that the Green company was receiving and Green replied that he was.

Green saw little or nothing of Governor Agnew between his nomination as the Republican candidate for vice president in the summer of 1968 and the election in November. He made some campaign contributions by check to the Nixon-Agnew ticket in the 1968 election.

In November or December, 1968, after Mr. Agnew was elected vice president but before his inauguration, Wolff came to Green with a list that he had prepared of the contracts that the Green company had received

from the State Roads Commission under the Agnew administration. Wolff told Green that Governor Agnew had asked him to prepare the list, and Green concluded that the list had been requested and could possibly be used as a means of assessing what he owed to Governor Agnew in return for those contracts.

Wolff and Green discussed the contracts and fees and, in effect, bargained about the matter. Green argued that some of the contracts that appeared on the list had in fact been awarded to his company under the J. Millard Tawes administration and that the Agnew administration was simply implementing a contract for which the selection had been made previously. Wolff, however, reminded him that the Agnew administration could have canceled at least some of the contracts, or could have awarded portions of the contracts to other firms. Subsequently, Green prepared a revised list of his own and submitted it to Wolff.

Some time thereafter, but still before the inauguration, Green met with the vice president-elect in his Baltimore governor's office. He gave Mr. Agnew a payment during the meeting. Mr. Agnew began the conversation by making some reference to the list and indicated that the Green company had received a lot of work from the State Roads Commission. Mr. Agnew said that he was glad that things had worked out that way.

He then reiterated that he had been unable to improve his financial situation during his two years as governor and that, although his salary as vice president would be higher than his salary as governor, he expected that the social and other demands of the office would substantially increase his personal expenses. For these reasons, he said he hoped that Green would be able to continue the financial assistance that he had been providing to him over the preceding two years, and, Mr. Agnew continued, he hoped he could be helpful to Green with respect to federal work.

This was the only occasion upon which Green can now recall that Mr. Agnew made any such express statement to him about the connection between payments and favors. Green did not believe that it was necessary expressly to refer to specific favors in return for payments. Indeed, throughout Mr. Agnew's gubernatorial tenure, it had never been necessary to state expressly that Green would receive anything in return for the payments that he had made, because a tacit understanding on this matter was more than sufficient to satisfy Green and to accomplish his purposes.

Green replied by telling Mr. Agnew that he would be willing to continue to be of financial assistance, but that he was not certain that he could continue to make payments in amounts as great as those he had made during the previous two years. Green knew that contracts awarded by the Agnew administration would generate income to his company over the next several years, and that therefore he could continue to make payments for several years. Green also hoped that his company's federal work might increase in amount as a result of Vice President Agnew's efforts on his behalf.

He did tell Mr. Agnew of one important concern: that the new administration in Annapolis might take credit for, and possibly demand payments in connection with, projects that had actually been awarded to the Green company by the Agnew administration. Mr. Agnew, however, confidently indicated that he did not believe that would happen.

Green continued to make cash payments to Mr. Agnew after he became vice president. Payments were made three or four times a year and were personally delivered to Mr. Agnew by Green either in the vice president's office in the Executive Office Building in Washington or at his apartment in the Sheraton Park Hotel in Washington. Green made his last payment during the Christmas season in December of 1972.

As Green recalls it, these payments invariably amounted to $2,000 each. As before, the money was always in a plain envelope, and the two men were always alone when the payment was made.

Green particularly recalls the first occasion upon which he paid money to Mr. Agnew in his offices in the Executive Office Building. Green was quite impressed with Mr. Agnew's office and position and felt very uncomfortable about the transaction that was about to occur. In addition, Green had some concern that the conversation between him and Vice President Agnew might be overheard or even taped. For all of these reasons, Green did not believe that it was appropriate or wise to continue to speak of personal financial assistance. Therefore, he stated to the vice president that this money was part of his continuing and unfulfilled commitment to Mr. Agnew with respect to "political contributions." Thereafter, Green usually made a similar statement when he delivered money to Mr. Agnew to his Executive Office Building offices. Green recalls that on the first occasion he made such a statement to Mr. Agnew. Green raised his eyes to the ceiling in order silently to suggest to Mr. Agnew the reason for the unusual and inaccurate statement.

In 1969 and 1970, Green paid Mr. Agnew $8,000 a year, four payments of $2,000 each in both years. In 1971 and 1972, he paid Mr. Agnew $6,000 a year, three payments of $2,000 each in both years.

In Green's meetings with Vice President Agnew, he frequently asked about federal engineering contracts for his company, and Mr. Agnew generally indicated to him that he was attempting to be as helpful as he could. Green soon realized, however, that the vice president did not exercise any substantial control over federal work, and, in fact, the Green company received only one federal job during this period.

The payments were discontinued after December 1972, because of the investigation conducted by the United States attorney's office into corruption in Baltimore County, Maryland.

Over the six-year period between 1966 and 1972, Green's cash payments to Mr. Agnew totaled approximately $50,000.

III. The relationship between Mr. Agnew and Lester Matz.

Lester Matz has been an engineer in Maryland for approximately 24 years. He is the president of Matz, Childs and Associates, Inc., and Matz, Childs and Associates of Rockville, Inc., two Maryland engineering companies. John C. Childs is his principal business associate in these two companies. Matz has tendered his complete cooperation to the government in this investigation. The government has not entered into any agreement with him as to what consideration, if any, he may expect in return for his cooperation, other than the assurance that his own truthful disclosures to the government will not be used against him in any criminal prosecution. At the government's request, Matz has executed a sworn written statement that recounts his relationship with Mr. Agnew. His testimony, the corroborative testimony of Childs and other witnesses, and various corroborative documents, would prove the following:

Between 1956 and 1963, Matz and Childs supplied various engineering services to private developers, principally in the metropolitan Baltimore area. Although they wanted to do as much public work as possible for the Baltimore County government, they found it extremely difficult to receive any substantial amount of county work. They observed that a relatively small number of engineering companies received most of the substantial county engineering work during these years, and that most, if not all, of these companies were closely associated with county administration or public officials. They simply could not break into this group, despite their repeated efforts to do so.

They, therefore, welcomed Mr. Agnew's candidacy for Baltimore County executive in 1962 because they believed that his election would present their company with an opportunity to be one of the few engineering companies that, they believed, would inevitably form around his administration and receive most of the substantial county engineering work. Matz had known Mr. Agnew casually for possibly two years, and during the 1962 campaign, he and Childs made a $500 cash contribution directly to Mr. Agnew.

Prior to the 1962 election, Matz had also worked professionally with one of Mr. Agnew's close associates. Indeed, by this time the three of them (Mr. Agnew, Matz and the close associate) had already begun to develop what would in the next four years become a close personal friendship. Very shortly after Mr. Agnew assumed office as county executive for Baltimore County, Matz was contacted by the close associate. During this conversation the close associate told Matz that the two of them were going to make a lot of money under the Agnew administration. Although he did not elaborate on this comment, Matz inferred from what he said during the conversation that under the Agnew administration, the two of them could expect substantial favors from the Baltimore County government.

Shortly thereafter, Matz was invited by the close associate to meet with Mr. Agnew. At this meeting there was no specific discussion about payments for county work, but Mr. Agnew told Matz that he had a lot of "confidence" in his close associate. Matz inferred from what Mr. Agnew said during this meeting that he should work through the close associate and make any payments through him.

After Mr. Agnew became county executive, the close associate contacted Matz and asked him to prepare a chart which would set forth the amounts of money that could be reasonably be expected from engineers on the various kinds and sizes of consulting contracts that the county generally awarded. Matz calculated the profits that could generally be anticipated under the various types of contracts and he determined that, on the average, 5 per cent of the fee was not unreasonable, although the percentage varied depending on the size and nature of the contract. He gave a copy of the chart to the close associate.

The chart showed the expected profit on each type of contract and the percentage that engineers could reasonably afford to pay on it. Matz later showed his retained copy of this schedule to Mr. Agnew in his office and told him that he had given a copy to the close associate. Mr. Agnew looked at the chart and thanked Matz for his effort on the matter. Matz cannot recall today whether Mr. Agnew returned the copy to him.

When Matz gave a copy of this schedule to the close associate, he was told that he would be expected to make payments to the close associate for county contracts. The close associate said that as Matz's company received fees from the county, payments were to be made to him in the appropriate percentages, 5 per cent on engineering contracts and $2\frac{1}{2}$ per cent on surveying contracts. He led Matz to believe that this money would be given to Mr. Agnew. These payments were not described by the close associate as "political contributions;" they were payments made in return for contracts.

Thereafter, Matz discussed this proposition with Childs. They were not surprised that payments would be necessary because it was generally understood that engineers had been making such payments for consulting work in a number of Maryland jurisdictions. They agreed that this would be a satisfactory arrangement. In fact, they were delighted that they would be among the small group of engineers who would be close to the Agnew administration and that they would, therefore, receive their share of the substantial county engineering consulting work. Although the 5 percent payments were not insubstantial, the company could afford to make them, and Matz and Childs both believed that the payments would make a substantial difference in the amount of work that their company would receive from the county.

During the balance of Mr. Agnew's tenure as county executive, Matz and Childs would find out what contracts were coming up in the county, and Matz would then contact the close associate and ask him for as many of these contracts as possible. The close associate always seemed well aware of the work to be let, and from time to time, he would advise Matz that his company had been awarded a particular contract. Matz then knew that, under their arrangement, the necessary payments were due, and he would therefore deliver the required cash payments personally to the close associate in the latter's office.

On most occasions, Matz placed the necessary cash in plain white envelopes. Usually he paid in installments rather than in one total payment in advance. Matz and Childs believed that even if they had refused to make these payments, their company would have received some county contracts, but that, as before, the company would not have received any substantial amount of work. In short, they believed that the payments made a great difference in the amount of work they received.

At first Matz and Childs personally generated the necessary cash to make these payments. As the size of the various cash payments they were making increased, however, they found it necessary to employ other methods by which to generate these cash funds in their company. These methods violated the Internal Revenue Code and were designed to obscure the purpose for which the cash was used.

During the first year or two of the Agnew administration in Baltimore County, the company's county work increased. Matz, however, was not satisfied because he believed that his company was entitled to an even larger share of the county's work, due to his reliability in making payments. He told the close associate that he was dissatisfied, and the close associate arranged a meeting with Mr. Agnew.

The three men met at Mr. Agnew's house. At this meeting, Matz complained that his company had not received enough county work. Both Mr. Agnew and the close associate promised that they would help the company to receive more county work, and in particular, Mr. Agnew told him that he would speak on Matz's behalf to the appointed county officials who were nominally responsible for the selection of engineers for county consulting contracts.

In the 1966 gubernatorial campaign, Matz and Childs made campaign contributions to Mr. Agnew, in part because they believed that Mr. Agnew would make an excellent governor. They also, however, had another substantial reason for supporting Mr. Agnew. Under Governor Tawes's administration, their company had not received any substantial amount of work from the Maryland State Roads Commission. They realized that their inability to secure any substantial amount of state work was the result of the fact that they were not among the small group of engineering firms that were closely associated with the Tawes administration and that had received most of the state work awarded by the administration. Both men were therefore excited about Mr. Agnew's candidacy because they believed that if he were to be elected governor, their company could begin to receive substantial amounts of work from the State Roads Commission by continuing to make payments to Mr. Agnew through his agents.

Several months after the Agnew administration took office, the State Roads Commission began to generate new projects and to award new contracts, and Matz's company began to receive substantial amounts of state work. On several occasions during the spring and summer of 1967, the close associate called Matz and attempted to perpetuate the arrangement under which payments had been made for contracts in the past. Matz was reluctant, however, to continue this arrangment, for several reasons.

First, he knew that if he paid Governor Agnew through any middleman, the credit to which he was entitled by virtue of these payments would be somewhat diluted because the middleman himself would receive a substantial portion of the credit. Second, he suspected that the close associate had, without Mr. Agnew's knowledge, retained for himself some of the money that had been paid to him by Matz between 1963 and 1966. Third, he knew that Mr. Agnew believed that the close associate had given him poor advice on certain matters that had resulted in bad publicity and embarrassment to Mr. Agnew.

Sometime early in Governor Agnew's administration, Matz met with Governor Agnew alone in his offices. During this conversation Matz told Mr. Agnew that he believed that the close associate lacked the discretion necessary safely to represent Mr. Agnew's interests and that sooner or late he would lead the two of them into trouble. Therefore, rather than continuing to pay through the close associate, Matz suggested that his company establish a savings account into which he would deposit the money that he owed on state contracts. After Mr. Agnew left office, Matz could pay him the money accumulated in this account, perhaps under the guise of legal fees. Governor Agnew liked the idea, and at a later meeting he referred to the idea again with approval.

These factors and, in particular, these conversations with Mr. Agnew, led Matz to conclude that he could dispense with the close associate and pay Mr. Agnew directly. He therefore told the close associate that he would take care of his obligations directly. Subsequently, however, he abandoned the savings account idea because he feared that it would involve too many records of payments and thereby lead to the disclosures of the scheme. Instead, he decided to make his cash payments to Mr. Agnew directly.

The amount of work that Matz's company received from the State Bonds Commission continued to increase substantially, and, on at least one occasion. Matz was asked by Wolff if he was taking care of his "obligations" with respect to his contracts. Matz told Wolff that he was taking care of his obligations "directly."

Although Matz's company received several substantial state contracts in 1967, he made no payments that year. On the basis of his experience, he assumed that he would have to pay 5 per cent of the fees that his company received from the state on these contracts. The contracts and fees that their company was receiving from the State Roads Commission were much more substantial than those it had ever received before, and Matz and Childs therefore decided that they would defer payments until after they had received fees from the state.

No payment was made until the summer of 1968, by which time Matz knew that he was behind in his obligations. He was anxious to fulfill them because he wanted to maintain his reputation as a man who could be trusted to fulfill his obligations, in order to insure that he would continue to receive substantial amounts of work from the State Roads Commission. Although his company was in a financial position to make the large payment that was due, he knew that it would be extremely difficult to generate safely the substantial amount of necessary cash, particularly if he continued to rely exclusively upon his usual methods for generating the money with which to make cash payments.

Sometime in late June or early July, 1968, Matz calculated that he owed Governor Agnew approximately $20,000 on the basis of 5 per cent of the fees that his company had already received from the state. He reviewed this calculation with Childs, who agreed with it. They did not believe that they could safely generate this amount of cash from within the company and, therefore, decided to go outside the company.

Matz approached an old client and friend of his who was in a business in which he customarily dealt in large sums of cash. Since Matz knew that he would be receiving substantial fees from the state within the next several months, on which he would owe Governor Agnew approximately an additional $10,000 he told his friend that he needed $30,000 in cash in the very near future. He did not disclose to his friend why he needed this money.

They agreed upon the following scheme: Matz's company would by corporate check "lend" his friend $30,000; his friend would then generate $30,000 in cash through his own company which he would return to Matz. The "loan" would be repaid to Matz's company by $1,700 quarterly checks for principal and Matz would return these "loan payments" to his friend in cash. This scheme was satisfactory to Matz because his regular procedures were adequate to generate $1,700 in cash on a quarterly basis.

The friend reluctantly agreed to assist Matz in this manner. He immediately generated $20,000 in cash, which he delivered to Matz. Matz showed this $20,000 in cash to Childs before he delivered it to Governor Agnew. The friend promised that he would supply Matz with the additional $10,000 in cash as soon as he could generate it, and he did so within the following several months. Thereafter, the "loan" repayment scheme was implemented.

Matz then called Governor Agnew's office and set up an appointment with the governor. The meeting

occured in mid-July, 1968. Matz met with the Governor alone in his office and handed him a manila envelope that contained $20,000 in cash. Matz expressed his appreciation for the substantial state contracts that his company had received and told the governor that the envelope contained the money that his company "owed" in connection with these contracts. The meeting was a very short one and very little else was said.

To the best of Matz's present recollection, he made no further payments for state work to Mr. Agnew while he was governor of Maryland. During the 1968 national campaign, however, Matz's firm contributed to Mr. Agnew's campaign. He also acted as a fund raiser for Mr. Agnew in 1968. Matz also recalls that at some point in 1967, Governor Agnew called him and asked him to contribute $5,000 to Nelson Rockefeller's campaign for the Republican Presidential nomination, a campaign which Mr. Agnew was then publicly supporting. Matz asked if he wanted cash or a check, and Mr. Agnew asked for a check which Matz subsequently sent to him. When Rockefeller later withdrew, Mr. Agnew returned the money to Matz with a letter.

A couple of months after Mr. Agnew had assumed the office of vice president, Matz decided that it was time for his company to make another payment in connection with contracts that had been awarded by the State of Maryland under the Agnew administration. He was willing to make this payment, even though Mr. Agnew no longer controlled the contracts awarded by the Maryland State Roads Commission, because he wanted to maintain his reputation as a man who would meet his obligations in order to influence Vice President Agnew to assist him in securing federal engineering contracts for his company.

Matz called the vice president's office in Washington and set up an appointment to meet with Mr. Agnew. On a piece of yellow legal-size paper, Matz calculated the sum then owed to Mr. Agnew for work received by Matz's company from the State of Maryland. He took this piece of paper with him when he went to the vice president's office. He met with Mr. Agnew, showed him the calculations, and briefly reviewed them for him. He then handed him an envelope, containing approximately $10,000 in cash. Matz told him that the envelope contained the money that his company "owed" in connection with the State Roads Commission contracts that he had been awarded under Mr. Agnew's administration in Annapolis. Mr. Agnew placed this envelope in his desk drawer.

Matz also told the vice president that the company might "owe" him more money in the future as these contracts continued to generate fees, and that he would fulfill these obligations. They agreed that Matz was to call Mr. Agnew's secretary when he was ready to make the next payment and to tell her that he had more "Information" for Mr. Agnew. This was to be a signal to Mr. Agnew that Matz had more money for him. After this meeting, Matz returned to Baltimore and told Childs of the payment. He also told Childs that he was shaken by his own actions because he had just made a payoff to the vice president of the United States. Matz also told Wolff, who was then working or about to begin working on the vice president's staff, that he had made a direct payment to the vice president.

Although Matz believes that he made several additional cash payments totaling approximately $5,000 to the vice president, he never completely fulfilled his obligations to Mr. Agnew with respect to the State Roads Commission contracts, in part because Mr. Agnew had very little, if any, influence with respect to Federal engineering contracts.

Sometime in late 1970 or early 1971, Matz received a telephone call from the close associate who told him that there was an upcoming Federal project and that some or all of the engineering contracts could be controlled by the vice president. He told Matz that, as usual, he would be expected to make a payment in order to receive a contract. At first, Matz resisted on the ground that he was entitled to this job without a payment by virtue of his prior payments, but the close associate insisted, and Matz agreed to a payment of $2,500. Matz asked that the contract be awarded to a certain small company in which Matz, Childs and Associates had an interest, and that small company was later awarded the contract. Thereafter, Matz received another telephone call from the close associate, during which they agreed that the payment would be made in the vice president's office.

Matz contacted the president of the small company and explained that a payment was necessary in connection with the contract. The man at first balked and refused to make any such payment, but he subsequently agreed to participate. An appointment was then made for Matz to meet with Vice President Agnew in the latter's office in Washington. This meeting occurred in the spring of 1971. The evidence is somewhat contradictory as to whether or not the close associate was present at the meeting. Matz placed an envelope containing the $2,500 cash on the vice president's desk and stated that the envelope contained the money required for the contract. When he left the meeting, the envelope had not been removed from the desk, but moments later Matz re-entered the office and noticed that the envelope was gone. Matz received $1,000 from the president of the small company as his contribution to this payment.

In the spring of 1972, the close associate called Matz and asked him for $10,000 for the 1972 Nixon-Agnew campaign. Matz declined. When the close associate continued to press him, Matz complained about these solicitations to Mr. Agnew, who told Matz to say that he gave at the office.

Agnew associates given jail terms. A three-judge federal court Nov. 25, 1974 rejected recommendations of leniency and gave prison sentences to businessmen I.H. Hammerman 2nd and Allen I. Green, who had participated in kickbacks to Agnew.

Hammerman and Green had pleaded guilty Nov. 11 to obstructing tax laws by delivering cash kickbacks to Agnew while he was governor of Maryland. In return for the pleas, the U.S. attorney for Maryland, Glenn Beall, had agreed to recommend against prison sentences for the defendants.

Despite the recommendations, the panel of judges ordered Hammerman to serve a two-year jail term. Green received a sentence of 12 months in prison. Both men were fined $5,000, the maximum allowed by law.

Anderson convicted. N. Dale Anderson, successor to Agnew as Baltimore County executive was sentenced May 1, 1974 to five years in prison. The county officer, convicted on 32 counts of conspiracy, extortion and income tax evasion, had resigned his office April 23.

Anderson was charged with having received $46,420 in cash and $1,375 in checks in some 33 payments from 1968 to 1972 from eight companies doing business with the county on sewer, water, road and courthouse projects.

Named as a co-conspirator but not a defendant in the indictment was William E. Fornoff, former top aide in Baltimore County under both Agnew and Anderson. Fornoff resigned in June, pleading guilty to a tax violation and admitting he had acted as a conduit for cash payments between architects and engineers and a county official. Fortunoff was fined $5,000 and given a two-year suspended sentence.

Ex-Maryland official enters guilty plea—Joseph W. Alton Jr., who resigned as Anne Arundel County (Md.) executive Dec. 2, pleaded guilty in Baltimore federal court Dec. 6 to a charge that he participated in a scheme to extort cash kickbacks from architects and engineers seeking county contracts.

Gov. Mandel, 5 others indicted. Gov. Marvin Mandel (D, Md.) and five of his friends and associates were indicted by a federal grand jury in Baltimore Nov. 24, 1975 on charges of mail fraud and "a pattern of rocketeering activity." Mandel was also charged with bribery and with falsifying his federal income tax returns.

Mandel denied the charges. While regretting the indictment, he said it would have "a positive effect" since he would have the opportunity to prove his innocence in a court of law. The lengthy federal probe had been accompanied by an intensive press investigation and accounts of the progress of the federal investigation in Baltimore and Washington newspapers.

The indictment grew out of the same investigation that led to the resignation of Vice President Spiro Agnew. Mandel had succeeded Agnew as governor of Maryland.

Those indicted with Mandel, on charges of mail fraud and "a pattern of racketeering," were W. Dale Hess, 45, a real estate developer, insurance executive and former majority leader of the Maryland House of Delegates; Harry W. Rodgers 3rd, 48, and his brother, William A. Rodgers, 49, insurance executives; Irwin Kovens, 57, a financier; and Ernest N. Cory Jr., 61, an attorney.

The indictment charged a "scheme and artifice" to "defraud" the state's citizens of their right to government in the public interest.

The central charge, according to U.S. Attorney Jervis S. Finney, involved a race track. Mandel was said to have vetoed legislation authorizing profitable additional racing days for the track and, after his associates had obtained a concealed interest in the track, to have persuaded the Democratic legislature to override the veto.

Mandel was alleged to have received in return financial interests in two real estate investment ventures. The bribery charges were related to this activity. Payments allegedly flowing from the concealed gift of an interest in the investment firm were the basis for the income tax charges. The indictment said the payments were disguised as legal fees for work attributed to Mandel before assuming the governorship in January 1969.

Politics & Government

Federal Aid to GOP Supporters

Federal officials and Republican Party aides were accused of using government influence to help businessmen from whom they expected (or had received) political campaign contributions.

Life accuses Administration. Life magazine made public March 19, 1972 an article in its March 24 issue charging that the Nixon Administration had "seriously tampered with justice" in San Diego by squelching investigations and delaying prosecutions "in an effort to protect certain of its important friends."

The article, entitled "How the Nixon Administration Blocked Justice," said the Administration "has in several instances taken steps to neutralize and frustrate its own law enforcement officials."

Among the article's statements and charges:

■ U.S. Attorney Harry Steward, appointed to the Southern District of California by Nixon in 1969 on the recommendation of San Diego millionaire C. Arnholt Smith, a close friend and long-time Nixon supporter, "squelched" an investigation of Smith and several other San Diego residents in 1970 at the time a federally-organized crime strike force was "putting together a case" against them "for conspiring to violate federal tax laws and the Corrupt Practices Act." A key item was a $2,068 contribution allegedly channeled illegally to Nixon's 1968 campaign fund through the Barnes, Champ Advertising Agency. Despite protests from federal investigators, Steward canceled a subpoena for Frank Thornton, the agency's vice president, Smith's "political lieutenant" and Nixon's campaign chairman in San Diego.

Steward also was accused of ordering special Internal Revenue Service investigator David Stutz "to lay off" an investigation of allegations that the $2,068 was "part of a much larger scheme to illegally funnel thousands of dollars into political campaigns" from companies controlled by Smith. The FBI looked into the case for "possible obstruction of justice" by Steward but then-Deputy Attorney General Richard G. Kleindienst (Nixon's current nominee for attorney general), after an evaluation by the Justice Department, announced that Steward had been cleared.

■ Former San Diego Mayor Frank Curran was indicted in 1970 on charges of taking a bribe from a taxi cab firm

67

and acquitted after what was considered key prosecution testimony from Stutz was blocked on a ruling from IRS Commissioner Randolph Thrower. Life quoted a statement from Curran that Nixon had telephoned and congratulated him after the trial.

■ During a criminal investigation of John Alessio, a wealthy financier, for tax evasion, Smith, a close friend, "went to Washington to plead Alessio's cause in person to President Nixon." The federal grand jury investigation was suspended but later resumed on FBI Director J. Edgar Hoover's recommendation. Alessio was indicted, convicted and sentenced to a three-year prison term.

Before the trial, White House aide Jack Caulfield sought from Stutz direct information about Smith, Alessio and Steward without notification to FBI superiors, which Stutz refused. He later refused another request to go to San Clemente to discuss the case with "an Administration representative."

Denials, corroborations—Life also reported an interview with Smith in which he denied that he talked to Nixon about Alessio's case or that any of his companies had illegally channeled money to political campaigns.

The Associated Press (AP) reported March 20 from Thornton that $2,068 had been donated by the cab company in San Diego to the 1968 Nixon campaign but it was later returned to the donor and "never used in the campaign." The AP also reported from Curran that everything in the Life article "pertaining to me is untrue."

A Steward statement denying Life's charges was issued March 20.

Stutz called a news conference March 21 to say "those facts set forth in the article relating to my personal involvement are true."

Other portions of the article relating to Steward were called accurate March 21 by Richard Huffman, a former special assistant to Steward and currently chief deputy district attorney of San Diego County. He told the San Diego Evening Tribune that Steward had refused to have the subpoena served on Thornton and that he, Huffman, had informed the FBI about Steward's "interference with a federal grand jury investigation of Alessio."

GOP aide fired. Douglas W. Inglish Jr., special assistant to Republican National Committee Co-chairman Thomas B. Evans, was fired Aug. 5, 1972 from his $25,000-a-year job for his role in arranging a bank loan for Washington builder Dr. Cyrus Katzen.

Newspaper reports had disclosed that Katzen had paid Inglish $5,000 Aug. 3 for his services. Inglish had enlisted U.S. Postal Service banking director James T. Blair, who contacted the vice president for government banking at First National City Bank of New York, which later granted the loan.

Katzen said the payment was "perfectly routine and normal," and that he was unaware of Blair's role. Blair said he made the call as a personal favor to Inglish, and was unaware of the $5,000 fee. Evans said he was "opposed to anyone using his connection with the Republican party for an economic gain," and that Inglish had not been candid with him on the matter.

Carpet industry gift charges. Sen. Warren G. Magnuson (D, Wash.) charged Oct. 6, 1972 that GOP fund-raiser Maurice Stans had arranged to postpone flammability regulations for carpet manufacturers at a meeting held in Washington July 27 in order to obtain $94,850 in campaign gifts from Martin B. Seretean, chairman of Coronet Industries, Inc. of Dalton, Ga.

Magnuson alleged that Seretean acted "on behalf of the industry." Coronet, one of many carpet companies in the Dalton area, was a subsidiary of RCA Corp., of which Seretean was one of the three largest stockholders. Contributions from him in the form of 30 separate checks were received by the Finance Committee to Re-elect the President, which Stans headed, between Aug. 11 and Aug. 16.

Magnuson had been one of the principal sponsors of the Flammable Fabric Amendment of 1967, according to the Washington Post Oct. 6.

Implementation of testing and enforcement standards was being delayed by the Nixon Administration, Magnuson charged. He claimed Stans called the meeting to "appease the fears" of carpet manufacturers regarding enactment of more stringent federal regulations.

Stans said Oct. 6 that the meeting was limited to "technical industry matters that had no political purpose." Seretean was not among the industry representatives who attended. Stans, Charles W. Colson, a White House aide who had been linked with Stans to the raid on the Democrats' Watergate office, and an Office of Consumer Affairs spokesman represented the Administration at the gathering.

Panel probes SBA, White House pressure. The House Banking and Currency Committee's Small Business Subcommittee began public hearings Nov. 27, 1973 on charges of corruption and mismanagement in the Small Business Administration (SBA) and allegations that the White House had pressured the agency both to grant loans to Nixon supporters and halt investigations of some loan recipients.

While testimony focused on charges of misconduct in the Richmond, Va. district office of the SBA, chief subcommittee investigator Curtis Prins said he had evidence of political pressure, bribery and kickbacks and faulty loan practices in 21 other offices.

In appearances Nov. 27 and Nov. 29, Prins said the Richmond office had granted $11.7 million in direct and indirect loans to Joseph C. Palumbo, brother-in-law of Thomas F. Regan, who had been suspended as director of the Richmond office earlier in November.

Regan appeared Nov. 29 to defend his loan policies, denying conflict of interest. Nor was there any conflict, he maintained, in his incurring almost $500,000 in personal financial obligations from banks doing business with the SBA.

Prins also told the panel that the SBA's Office of Minority Business Enterprise was heavily politicized and had been misused in many parts of the country.

A prime example, Prins said in testimony Nov. 29 and Dec. 10, was the case of Dr. Thomas W. Matthew, an advocate of black capitalism and strong Nixon supporter.

Prins said that Nixon had once personally ordered that "all assistance possible" be given to Matthew. When Matthew later began defaulting on SBA loans and other federal assistance, the White House attempted to thwart investigations of Matthew by the SBA and local authorities in New York City. The SBA had continued to make loans to Matthew, Prins charged, even after Matthew had defaulted on some loans and had come under criminal investigation.

Asked Dec. 10 why the assistance to Matthew had continued, SBA Administrator Thomas S. Kleppe said "aside from the pressure that existed," Matthew was "trying to help reach people having trouble—drug addicts, prostitutes and criminals. This appealed to me."

Kleppe had first appeared before the subcommittee Dec. 4, reading a statement defending his agency and accusing Prins of "innuendo and smear." He denied that the minority aid program was politicized but said that it was inherently "controversial and difficult to manage." He defended the quality of the loan guarantee program and argued that the proportion of defaults was relatively small.

3 officials fired—Three SBA officials who had been involved in allegations of corruption and political pressure within the agency were dismissed Dec. 21.

Cited for "failure to adhere to agency regulations" were: Thomas F. Regan, former director of the Richmond, Va. district office; Russell Hamilton Jr., Philadelphia regional director and Regan's superior; and Joseph T. Clark, Hamilton's deputy.

Regan was sentenced June 25, 1976 to 19 years in prison for fraud and bribery in connection with a scheme to defraud the government agency and Virginia banks of more than $800,000.

Ten years of the sentence on one count of fraud and one of conspiracy were suspended. He was placed on five years' probation on each of the remaining 11 counts, most of them charging Regan with racketeering and accepting gratuities. A U.S. District Court jury had convicted Regan June 5.

Federal prosecutors claimed that in 1973 dummy corporations had been set up solely to receive SBA-guaranteed loans which Regan approved. Four men had already pleaded guilty to participating in the fraud scheme and had received sentences ranging from 17 months to seven years.

Corporations & Political Funds

1972 campaign violators fined. Greyhound Corp. Oct. 30, 1974 was fined $5,000, the maximum allowed under law, for violating a federal campaign finance statute prohibiting corporate political donations. Greyhound had pleaded guilty Oct. 2 to the charge, filed by the Watergate special prosecutor's office with the federal district court in Washington.

The firm admitted using a double bonus system for its employes to conceal payments totaling $16,040 made to the 1972 presidential campaigns of Richard Nixon and George McGovern. Greyhound officials had been encouraged to make personal donations to the candidates, and then were awarded bonuses twice the amount of their contributions, according to a Greyhound spokesman.

In a separate action, Norman Sherman and Jack Valentine were each fined $500 for "aiding and abetting" the illegal use of $82,000 in corporate funds donated by Associated Milk Producers Inc. to several Democratic candidates for federal office in 1972. Sentence was imposed Oct. 10.

Sherman, a former press secretary to Sen. Hubert H. Humphrey (D, Minn.), and Valentine were partners in a Minneapolis computerized mail service firm which had been hired to prepare voter surveys. They had pleaded guilty to a misdemeanor. The $1,000 maximum fine was not imposed, the court stated, because there was "substantial factual basis" to their claim that they had been assured by an AMPI attorney that the transaction was legal.

Time Oil pleads guilty. Time Oil Co. and its president, Raymond Abendroth, pleaded guilty Oct. 23, 1974 to charges they made illegal corporate campaign donations.

Chief Judge George L. Hart Jr. of federal district court in Washington fined the firm $2,500—half the maximum amount—for each of two counts involving a contribution totaling $6,600 to President Nixon's re-election campaign, and purchase of tickets worth $1,000 to a fund-raising dinner for Sen. Henry M. Jackson (D, Wash.), a contender for the Democratic presidential nomination.

Abendroth was fined the maximum amount, $1,000, for each of the two counts. According to his lawyer, Abendroth made the contributions at the request of the Seattle oil firm's chief stockholder, G. Edward Miller.

Ex-Rep. Wendell Wyatt (R, Ore.) was fined $750 July 18, 1975 for not reporting expenditures from a secret $5,000 cash fund he controlled while heading the Oregon campaign for former President Nixon in 1972.

Wyatt, a five-term congressman, pleaded guilty to the misdemeanor charge June 11 in U.S. District Court in Washington. He could have been sentenced to one year in jail and a $1,000 fine. According to the Watergate special prosecutor's office, money from the secret fund was given by Time Oil Co.

Phillips Petroleum accused. The SEC March 6, 1975 accused the Phillips Petroleum Corp. and four of its current and former officers of illegally diverting more than $2.8 million in corporate money since 1963 to a secret political fund from which it made illegal political donations.

Named as defendants, accused of falsifying company financial records to conceal the slush fund, were Phillips chairman William F. Martin, vice president Carstens Slack, and two former chairman, William W. Keeler and John M. Houchin.

Phillips and the four men consented to a court order enjoining them from further securities law violations, but the defendants neither admitted nor denied the SEC charges.

According to the SEC complaint, filed in U.S. District Court in Washington, Phillips channeled more than $2.8 million in corporate funds to two Swiss corporations which returned $1.3 million in cash to the U.S. The remainder "was distributed overseas in cash," according to the SEC. (Disposition of the money abroad was not revealed.) Of the $1.3 million returned to the U.S., "$600,000 was expended for political contributions and related expenses, a substantial portion of which was unlawful," the SEC charged.

Phillips Petroleum and Keeler had been convicted in 1973 of illegally giving corporate funds to the Nixon reelection campaign. In a disclosure made subsequently, Phillips admitted that secret contributions totaling $585,000 also had been made to other political candidates from a secret fund. In making the disclosure, the firm also said that more than $700,000 remaining in the slush fund had been discovered in a company safe and had been returned to the corporate treasury.

In a special report to stockholders, Phillips Petroleum revealed that Martin, Houchin, Keller and two other former chief executives, K. S. Adams and Stanley Learned, had paid $150,000 to the company to release claims Phillips Petroleum might have against it in connection with funds used to make apparently illegal political contributions.

According to the special report, about $585,000 in corporate funds was contributed from 1964 through 1973. (That was about $100,000 less than Phillips originally reported in an earlier statement to shareholders.) $90,000 was contributed to candidates in states that permitted corporate donations, the report stated.

Of the $495,000 in apparently illegal contributions, a $100,000 contribution to the Nixon re-election campaign was recovered, leaving a $395,000 balance.

According to the Phillips report, the only disbursements from the cash fund, which was generated from foreign operations, were for political contributions.

The special investigating committee that prepared the report recommended that no further action be taken against chairman Martin because his actions related to the cash fund "amounted for the most part to acquiesence in a program which had been earlier instituted by his superiors." The investigating committee also recommended that no action be taken against Carstens Slack, Phillips' Washington-based vice president, because, although he distributed some of the political contributions, he "had no

knowledge that the funds belonged to the company."

Illegal funds recipients listed—In a report filed with the SEC Sept. 26, Phillips Petroleum listed the recipients of $585,000 in largely illegal campaign contributions from the company's $1.35 million slush fund during 1964–72.

Among the candidates that Phillips supported were President Gerald Ford and former Presidents Richard Nixon and Lyndon Johnson. Johnson received $25,000 for his 1964 presidential campaign. Nixon got $50,000 for his 1968 race and another $100,000 in 1972. Phillips admitted giving a total of $125,000 to Congressional candidates, including President Ford, who received $2,000 in both 1970 and 1972 when he ran for reelection to the House from Michigan.

In its report, Phillips also said it spent about $70,000 on tickets for political dinners and contributed $215,000 to candidates for state office, chiefly in Texas, Oklahoma and Alaska where the oil company had business interests. Phillips was based in Bartlesville, Okla.

All but $90,000 of the $585,000 in campaign contributions were made illegally. (Candidates for federal and most state offices were barred from accepting corporate contributions.) Most of the legal contributions were made to Oklahoma candidates for state office.

Phillips said there was no evidence that candidates who accepted the donations knew the money was contributed illegally. The funds, which were donated in the name of "friends at Phillips," were handled in such a manner as to avoid disclosure under reporting requirements of campaign finance laws.

Phillips said that since no written records were kept on the contributions, they had been unable to reconstruct a complete list. In preparing the report for the SEC, Phillips relied on the memories of such company officials as former president William W. Keeler, convicted of making the illegal $100,000 donation to the Nixon campaign, and Carstens Slack, vice president in charge of Phillips' Washington office, who was named with Keeler in the SEC complaint:

Details of the Phillips list:

Receiving $1,900 each in 1972 were Sen. Howard H. Baker Jr. (R, Tenn.); Sen. Robert P. Griffin (R, Mich.); Sen. James A. McClure (R, Idaho); Sen. Sam

Nunn (D, Ga.); and Wesley Powell, who ran unsuccessfully for the Senate seat from New Hampshire.

Ten successful senatorial candidates received $1,000 each in 1972; former Sen. Gordon Allott (R, Colo.); Sen. Carl Curtis (R, Neb.); Sen. Clifford P. Hansen (R, Wyo.); Sen. Mark O. Hatfield (R, Ore.); former Sen. B. Everett Jordan (D, N.C.); former Sen. Jack Miller (R, Iowa); Sen. James B. Pearson (R, Kan.); Sen. Jennings Randolph (D, W. Va.); Sen. Strom Thurmond (R, S.C.); and Sen. John G. Tower (R, Tex.). Another $1,000 contribution went to a congressional committee, earmarked for Sen. Ted Stevens (R, Alaska).

Receiving smaller amounts in 1970, generally $200–500 were Sen. Hiram Fong (R, Hawaii); Sen. Henry M. Jackson (D, Wash.); former Rep. William C. Cramer (R, Fla.); Rep. Clark MacGregor (R, Minn.); Sen. Frank E. Moss (D, Utah); former Sen. George Murphy (R, Calif.); and Sen. Hugh Scott (R, Pa.).

Politicians receiving the largest contributions were generally candidates for federal office from Oklahoma: Ed Edmondson, who ran unsuccessfully for the Senate, got $11,000 in 1972; former Republican Rep. Page Belcher got $3,000 in 1970; House Speaker Carl Albert received $2,500 in 1970 and $500 in 1972; Rep. John Jarman, a Democrat who recently turned Republican, got $3,000 in both 1970 and 1972; Democratic Rep. Tom Steed received $2,000 in both 1970 and 1972.

Other Congressional candidates who received illegal contributions from Phillips included former Rep. Leslie C. Arends (Ill.), who was Republican whip; and Democratic majority leader Thomas P. O'Neill Jr. (Mass.).

In its report to the SEC, Phillips stated that it did not pay "any bribe, commission, contributions or another political payment to any government official, politicians or political party" abroad.

Tax fraud charge—Phillips Petroleum, William Martin, Stanley Learned and William Keeler were indicted by a federal grand jury in Tulsa, Okla. Sept. 2, 1976 on tax-fraud charges related to the allegedly illegal political contributions. The four defendants were accused of conspiring to conceal from the Internal Revenue Service nearly $3 million in assets that were deposited in Swiss bank accounts or held as cash at the firm's Bartlesville headquarters.

According to the indictment, the money was generated through "confidential transactions" involving agreements made by Phillips and its Panamanian subsidiary with an Illinois construction firm and its French subsidiary, a New York ship broker and a refinery in India.

The indictment said that Phillips used "international couriers, code names, misleading [bookkeeping] entries, and false invoices and billings" to conceal the company's true expenses and incomes from the IRS. The income from the secret transactions was not reported on corporate tax returns for 1963–71, according to the indictment. The company also was accused of filing false returns for 1969–71. Martin was accused of assisting in their preparation.

Secret Gulf political fund charged. The Securities and Exchange Commission March 11, 1975 accused Gulf Oil Corp. and its former vice president, Claude C. Wild Jr., of funneling more than $10 million through a wholly owned Gulf subsidiary, Bahamas Exploration Co., Ltd., from which secret political contributions were made beginning in 1960.

Gulf signed a consent agreement without admitting or denying the charges but Wild chose to contest the charges.

According to the SEC, at least $5.4 million was returned to the U.S. from the now-defunct Bahamiam firm. Most of the money was disbursed as illegal campaign contributions, the SEC charged. The remainder of the fund was distributed abroad by Gulf and unidentified "others."

According to testimony taken by the Senate Watergate Committee, Wild, who had headed Gulf's Washington office, decided which political candidates should receive donations from Gulf. He then ordered William C. Viglia, comptroller of the Bahamas firm, to send him the desired amount of cash for disbursal as contributions.

Company records showed that the board of directors of the Bahamas firm voted Aug. 7, 1973 to cease operations of the company. That date was three days before Gulf voluntarily disclosed to the Watergate special prosecutor's office that an illegal $100,000 contribution had been made to the Nixon re-election campaign and contributions totaling $25,000 had been given to two Democratic candidates for the presidential nomination. Gulf and Wild later pleaded guilty to violating the federal campaign finance law.

The SEC named Viglia as disburser of the $5.4 million and also claimed that Royce H. Savage, former general counsel and director of the Bahamas company, also had known of the contributions. Neither man was charged in the SEC complaint. Savage currently was serving as court-appointed trustee of the bankrupt Home Stake Production Co.

In accepting the consent judgment, filed with U.S. District Court in Washington, Gulf revealed that a special committee, headed by John J. McCloy, former U.S. high commissioner in Germany and former chairman of Chase Manhattan Bank, had been established to review the company's investigation of its corporate contributions.

Wild acquitted—Claude C. Wild Jr. was acquitted July 27, 1976 on charges of making an illegal political contribution in 1973 to Sen. Daniel K. Inouye (D, Hawaii). The court ruled that in Wild's case the three-year statute of limitations governing campaign contributions had expired.

Federal Judge Joseph C. Waddy of U.S. District Court in Washington, who heard the case without a jury at the defense's request, ruled that the Watergate special prosecutor's office had failed to prove that Wild made the contribution in the three years prior to his indictment March 12.

(Waddy June 24 dismissed another count against Wild involving an illegal contribution made to Sen. Sam Nunn's [D, Ga.] 1972 campaign. Waddy ruled that Wild's statute of limitations waiver on the Nunn donation was ineffective.)

During the two-day trial, Wild admitted that he had acted illegally in giving $5,000 in cash on Gulf's behalf to Inouye's 1974 re-election campaign on the condition that the money not be reported, as required by federal law. Wild testified, however, that the money was turned over to Inouye's administrative assistant, Henry Giugni, before Feb. 7, 1973.

The Senate Watergate Committee was established on that date. Inouye was a member of the committee. Speaking of the donation, Wild testified, "I just thought it would be too sensitive a matter to get involved in after Feb. 7."

Giugni, who said he had solicited the money from Wild in December 1972, testified that he had received the cash in March or April 1973, a period that fell within the statute of limitations.

In ending the trial, Waddy said he "found the evidence of the defendant worthy of greater credence than that of Mr. Giugni."

Giugni admitted during the trial that he had committed perjury in September 1975 before a federal grand jury investigating his handling of the Gulf contribution.

Giugni said he had discussed the Wild donation with Inouye for the first time after Giugni's grand jury appearance. (Inouye, who also took the stand during the Wild trial, testified that he had received $1,200 in cash from Giugni for campaign expenses in April, May and June 1973, but never asked the source of the cash.)

Giugni said that after his talk with Inouye and with the prosecutor's office, he had returned to the grand jury with immunity and testified truthfully about the Wild donation.

After months of negotiations, with the prosecutor's office, Wild appeared before the grand jury in January 1976 and testified with immunity on all 1973 contributions he had made on Gulf's behalf, except the Inouye donation.

During his trial, Wild said he had told the prosecutor's office of eight senators and representatives who had received up to $5,000 from him in 1973. Only one member of Congress had been indicted as a result of Wild's alleged testimony—Rep. James R. Jones (D, Okla.), who pleaded guilty in January.

While the special prosecutor's office was investigating illegal corporate contributions to legislators, Congress had passed a new campaign fund law that reduced the statute of limitations on illegal donations from five years to three years.

Viglia sentenced—A federal court in Tulsa Aug. 4, 1976 sentenced William C. Viglia, 71, a former Gulf official, to a year in jail for his part in making illegal corporate contributions.

Viglia, who the SEC said had acted as Wild's courier in handling the cash contributions, was the only Gulf official to receive a jail sentence in connection with the payments.

Federal probe of Bell units. In 1975, federal officials investigated charges the Southwestern Bell Telephone Co. and Southern Bell Telephone Co. used corporate funds for illegal political contributions and maintained improper ties to state officials charged with overseeing the companies.

The allegations were made by former Bell employes. The charges against

Southwestern Bell were first raised by T. O. Gravitt who had headed the company's Texas operations. Gravitt committed suicide in October 1974 and in a suicide note accused the company of making illegal campaign contributions and engaging in improper business practices including illegal wiretapping.

James H. Ashley, another Southwestern Bell employe who was dismissed after he corroborated Gravitt's charges, claimed that at least 40 Bell executives based in Missouri had been required to contribute $50 a month to political candidates selected by the company and were reimbursed through a salary kickback plan. Ashley claimed that since 1966, executive employes had been given pay increases that included $1,000 a year to cover the alleged monthly political contributions. (Ashley's charges were reported in the New York Times March 1.)

Ashley had joined Gravitt's widow and sons in filing a $29 million libel suit against Southwestern Bell. In a deposition given in connection with that suit, Southwestern Bell's chief lobbyist in Texas, Ward. K. Wilkinson, admitted that he had managed a political slush fund collected from top Bell officials. Wilkinson said that about $14,500 was collected every year, the Washington Post reported Feb. 22.

Existence of the slush fund was corroborated by another former Bell employee, David L. Forbis, who resigned in 1973 as Southwestern Bell's general staff manager. In a deposition given Feb. 13, Forbis said that he had collected $50 a month from the 10 most senior Bell officials in Dallas and turned the money over in cash to Wilkinson.

Some of the money from the slush fund—$1,000 in cash—was delivered to Sen. John Tower (R, Tex.) in the spring of 1972, Wilkinson said. City council members in San Antonio, Austin, Fort Worth, and Dallas also acknowledged receiving contributions from Southwestern Bell employes, the Post reported.

John J. Ryan, former general manager of Southern Bell, told the Charlotte (N.C.) Observer Jan. 15 that he had administered a political slush fund during his nine year tenure as manager of Southern Bell's North Carolina opera-

tions. About $10,000 was paid into the secret fund annually by Southern Bell's top officials, Ryan charged.

Ryan cited slush fund payments he made to each of the four candidates in North Carolina's 1972 gubernatorial election. Bell considered it to be a vital political race, Ryan said, because the governor had the power to make appointments to the Public Utilities Commission.

It was also revealed that the Bell System sought political favors by other means. According to the New York Times March 1, William R. Clark resigned from the Missouri Public Service Commission after it was disclosed that he had been the guest of Southwestern Bell on a three day hunting trip in Texas in 1969. Clark, who had served on the commission for 10 years, resigned while the agency was considering Bell's request for a $52.3 million rate increase. The company subsequently accepted a compromise increase totaling $32.5 million.

In Kansas, the Times reported, two members of the state regulatory commission revealed that they had received two free phone credit cards from Southwestern Bell and also had been guests of the firm in 1974 on a trip with a Las Vegas stopover.

A Southern Bell spokesman confirmed a report in the Atlanta Constitution that the speaker of the Georgia legislature, a Georgia Democratic Congressman (Rep. Phillip M. Landrum) and others had been guests of the phone company on a hunting trip to Mexico. Maryland Gov. Marvin Mandel also admitted that he had regularly accepted deep sea fishing trips from the chief lobbyist of the Chesapeake and Potomac Telephone Co., a Bell unit serving Washington, Maryland, and Virginia. (Both reports were printed in the Times Feb. 8.)

Airlines accused. The Civil Aeronautics Board's enforcement bureau, in a complaint filed with the CAB March 13, 1975, charged that Braniff Airways maintained a political slush fund that was financed by the sale of "at least 3,262 unaccounted-for" flight tickets to the public. "Off-the-book" income from these sales totaling at least $641,285 and as much as $926,955 was diverted to a secret fund "for the use of Braniff management ... at least in part for unlawful purposes," the enforcement bureau charged. Some of the money allegedly was laundered through Panama.

With the exception of an illegal $40,000 contribution to the Nixon campaign, none of the revenue from the slush fund was reflected in Braniff's books, the bureau charged. Braniff and Harding L. Lawrence, the airline's chairman, had pleaded guilty in 1973 to making the unlawful donations and were fined.

The enforcement bureau charged that Lawrence and C. Edward Acker, Braniff's president, had access to the secret fund. Five other airline officials also were accused of participating in or having knowledge of the ticket scheme.

American Airlines agreed May 19 to pay a $150,000 fine under a settlement with the CAB, which had accused the airline of building up a political slush fund to make illegal campaign contributions. The CAB accepted the proposed settlement May 27.

The agency's enforcement bureau filed a complaint with the board March 13 against the airline and eight of its current and former officers. According to the complaint, between 1964 and 1973, American maintained a secret fund totaling "at least $275,000" that was used in part to make illegal corporate donations to political candidates. Some of the money was funneled through Mexico; other funds were paid as a commission to a Lebanese agent.

American had pleaded guilty in 1973 to unlawfully donating $55,000 to the Nixon re-election campaign and was fined for the violation.

The CAB claimed that $119,546 in donations paid out of the slush fund later was returned to the airline, $117,479 could not be traced, and $57,975 in contributions was not returned. In addition to the Nixon contribution, which was returned in 1973, American donated money to at least 132 other candidates for federal and state office or their campaign committees received money from the airline, the CAB stated. Among the recipients were the Senate Democratic Campaign Committee and the Democrats for Nixon Committee, according to the complaint.

By concealing the slush fund, the CAB charged, American violated federal cam-

paign laws and the agency's regulations dealing with airline accounting and financial reporting requirements. Agency officials said that the civil penalty, the largest fine ever collected by the CAB, would have been larger if American had not voluntarily disclosed the Nixon contribution and cooperated with the agency. Several airline officials also reimbursed American for $125,000, a CAB spokesman added.

The enforcement bureau's separate actions against American and Braniff ended a year of investigations into their campaign contribution practices. Controversy over the scope of the CAB's investigation had surfaced after the death of the bureau's chief, William M. Gingery, who committed suicide Feb. 17.

Gingery left a note charging that his predecessor as head of the enforcement bureau, acting CAB chairman Richard J. O'Melia, had terminated several investigations into illegal political contributions and ordered the files "impounded," according to the New York Times March 4.

Testifying for the Senate Judiciary Committee's Administrative Practice & Procedure Subcommittee, O'Melia said March 21 that in November 1973 when he had headed the bureau, then-CAB chairman Robert D. Timm ordered an abrupt end to the investigations of political gift-giving by airlines. O'Melia testified that he had received the order in a memo from Timm, but said he refused to accept a copy of it.

Timm, who remained a member of the CAB after President Ford refused to reappoint him chairman because of alleged improper ties to the airline industry, denied the existence of the memo. Timm testified March 21, however, that he had strictly limited the scope of questioning the enforcement board could pursue when investigations were initiated in July 1973.

O'Melia admitted he had ordered all "politically sensitive" material related to the investigations placed in a safe, but denied he had blocked the bureau's probe of unlawful campaign contributions.

Federal Housing Programs

HUD concedes subsidy abuses. An audit by the Department of Housing and Urban Development (HUD) of federal mortgage subsidy programs, released by HUD Secretary George Romney, confirmed earlier reports of widespread financial and construction abuses.

The report was made public in February 1972. The report alleged wholesale cheating by businessmen dealing with the federal housing program.

According to the audit, cost per unit in the "section 236" program of the 1968 Housing Act had run substantially higher than in privately financed housing because of excessive fees and land markups and other fraudulent practices inadequately policed by the Federal Housing Administration (FHA). Rents under the program, which subsidized apartment house mortgages, were consequently higher then for comparable apartments on the private market.

High vacancy rates, resulting partly from locations near junkyards, factories, power lines and former lake beds, were high enough to cause or threaten frequent defaulting of section 236 mortgages. HUD had fired seven employes for "wrongdoing" under the program, Romney reported, and referred 27 alleged violations to the Justice Department. Grand jury probes with HUD cooperation were investigating projects in Philadelphia, New York, Newark, N.J., and Detroit.

In the "section 235" program, which subsidized new and used private home mortgages for moderate income families, some 26% of a sample of 700 new houses and 43% of a sample of used homes contained serious property, safety, health or "livability" deficiencies. HUD referred 362 alleged section 235 violations for Justice Department investigation, including false applications and fraudulent repair certificates.

Dun & Bradstreet in FHA fraud case. Forty persons and 10 corporations, among them the credit investigating firm of Dun and Bradstreet, were named March 29, 1972 in indictments in U.S. district court in New York charging them with participating in a scheme to defraud the Federal Housing Administration (FHA).

The indictments had been returned by a federal grand jury March 28 after an 11-month investigation.

According to the indictments, the defendants procured false credit records and false appraisals which were used to obtain FHA insurance for excessively high mortgages on houses in the boroughs of Brooklyn and Queens. The houses were then said to have been sold to low-income families.

Specifically, the defendants were charged with bribery, conspiracy and filing false statements. In all, the indictments charged 500 counts of wrongdoing.

One of the other firms indicted was Eastern Service Corp., one of the largest mortgage-lending concerns in the East. Both the chairman of Eastern Service and his wife were named in the indictment. The other eight corporations were all local real estate firms.

Of the 40 persons named, eight were present or former FHA employes. The indictments alleged that they had been bribed to participate in the housing fraud.

The other 32 defendants were mostly real estate speculators, brokers, lawyers and appraisers. All were from the New York area.

Dun & Bradstreet was charged with 24 counts of making false statements to the FHA. Arthur Prescott, identified in the indictment as a vice president of Dun & Bradstreet, was indicted on the same 24 counts. But Charles F. G. Raikes, Dun & Bradstreet general counsel, denied March 29 that Prescott was a vice president of the firm. Raikes declared that the charges against the firm were "groundless."

The Department of Housing & Urban Development (HUD) ordered its 87 regional offices April 2 not to do business with Dun & Bradstreet.

An HUD spokesman said that the regional offices had been instructed not to use credit ratings prepared by Dun & Bradstreet and the firm had been informed its contract was canceled.

But United Press International reported April 29 that HUD had resumed most of its suspended contract with Dun & Bradstreet. At the time it picked up the existing contract, HUD sent a warning to its employes to avoid "petty chiseling and . . . outright bribery."

HUD said that although it was resuming the contract with Dun & Bradstreet, it was not continuing that part of the contract with the office involved in the New York case.

Dun & Bradstreet wins acquittal—Dun & Bradstreet Cos. and one of its employes, Arthur Prescott, were acquitted in federal court in New York Nov. 11, 1974 of charges that they had participated in a scheme to defraud the FHA. U.S. District Court Judge Anthony J. Travia granted the dismissal on the urging of the company's lawyers.

Earlier, a mistrial had been declared by Travia July 5.

The jury, which had been sitting in the case since Oct. 1, 1973, had previously found five other defendants guilty of taking part in the alleged conspiracy to misuse federal funds. Its failure to agree on a verdict with regard to Dun & Bradstreet, Prescott and two former FHA officials resulted in the mistrial.

Detroit scandal. A Detroit housing scandal involving the FHA was discussed by HUD Secretary George M. Romney in a speech in Detroit March 27, 1972.

The pattern of the Detroit scheme followed closely to the trickery used by the defendants in the New York case.

In the Detroit case, real estate speculators bought run-down houses in poor neighborhoods for a few thousand dollars and then had them valued by FHA appraisers at sometimes quadruple the original purchase prices. The speculators then sold the houses to the poor who could not keep them up.

The dilapidated houses had with time deteriorated further, blighting entire blocks and neighborhoods in Detroit's inner city.

Speaking to the Economic Club of Detroit, Romney conceded that FHA units in the central cities had not been adequately prepared to deal with "speculators and fast-buck artists." "And there is no city where there are more of them than in Detroit," Romney said.

(Similar scandals were reported in the FHA programs in other cities, including Chicago, Philadelphia, St. Louis, Los Angeles, Newark, N.J., Miami, Fla. and Hempstead, N.Y.)

50 convictions in Los Angeles FHA & VA home frauds. A two-year inquiry by a federal task force in Los Angeles had led to over 50 convictions of persons for defrauding the Federal Housing Administration (FHA) and the Veteran's Administration (VA), the Wall Street Journal reported Aug. 15, 1975. The Journal said the VA fraud was found in its home-loan-guarantee program. The FHA corruption was uncovered mostly in its property rehabilitation and resale programs, the Journal reported July 17.

Among those sentenced were Michael J. Whelan, a former FHA area management broker, and William Radich, a contractor, who together set up six fictitious contracting companies to defraud the FHA. In addition, the companies received kickbacks from various contractors. Whelan was sentenced to five years probation and fined $2,500 and Radich received a six-month prison term, it was reported July 17.

Congressional Involvement

Congress members, Congressional employes and even their close friends often have access to powers that can be of considerable aid to business enterprises. It is not surprising, therefore that many have been accused—and in some cases convicted—of misusing these powers, of "influence peddling," of soliciting and/or accepting bribes and of other corrupt deals with the business community.

House Speaker's top aide under fire. House Speaker John W. McCormack (D, Mass.) suspended his top aide, Martin Sweig, Oct. 16, 1969 after a civil suit was filed in New York by the Securities and Exchange Commission (SEC) naming Sweig as an intervenor in a stock case.

(The case finally ended in 1971 with Sweig's imprisonment for perjury.)

The case concerned the Parvin-Dohrmann Co., manufacturer of restaurant equipment and owner of three casino-hotels in Las Vegas, Nev. The suit also involved Nathan Voloshen, a friend of McCormack, who was retained by Parvin-Dohrmann. A meeting was arranged "through Sweig," the SEC charged, at which Voloshen and a company attorney attempted to persuade the SEC to lift its May 6 ban against trading in the firm's stock. The SEC suit said Voloshen received $50,000 for his effort. (The suspension was lifted May 12 after the firm released some financial reports.)

In the Oct. 16 suit, in which the SEC sought a court order barring "fraud and deceit" in the trading of Parvin-Dohrmann stock, Voloshen was named a codefendant along with company officers. Sweig was not a defendant in the suit.

A similar Voloshen-Sweig intervention was reported with the Labor Department in a case involving Jack McCarthy, a New York labor official and an alleged racketeer, who was sentenced June 14 on a conviction of filing false financial reports with the Labor Department. At the time of the sentencing, the federal prosecutor referred to "a blatant attempt at influence peddling" to protect McCarthy. At a meeting, brought up during McCarthy's trial by Labor Department officials, McCarthy, accompanied by Voloshen, attempted to convince Labor Department officials that his income reports were in order. At the trial, the department said the meeting was held only because it had been requested by "a congressman." Officials confirmed Oct. 22 that the meeting had been requested by Rep. Adam Clayton Powell (D, N.Y.) and by Sweig invoking the name of McCormack.

Other allegations of "influence peddling" based on McCormack's prestige were attributed to Voloshen and Sweig by newspapers and magazines.

Life magazine charged in its Oct. 31 issue that Voloshen, sitting in McCormack's office chair at a time when McCormack was absent, accepted a $5,000 fee for an attempt (unsuccessful) to "fix" a case of income tax evasion. The magazine article, written by William Lambert, said Voloshen was known as "the man from the Speaker's office." It also said: "Precisely how much action this has evoked is unknown, as is the precise involvement of Speaker McCormack

himself in Voloshen's manipulations. The fact is that Voloshen has made free use of the official prestige. . . . In this he had the full compliance of Dr. Sweig. . . ."

McCormack told reporters Oct. 16 he was "just as clean as the first day I entered public life in 1917." At a formal news conference Oct. 20, McCormack said he had suspended Sweig, who had worked for him for 24 years, for an "error of judgment"—intervention in the Parvin-Dohrmann case. "I've always told those associated with me I did not want them to make appointments with anyone in any sensitive department," McCormack said. He said Sweig "denied emphatically" receiving any money in the matter and he (McCormack) had no evidence of more serious wrongdoing on Sweig's part.

McCormack said he had known Voloshen for "at least 10 years" but as a "public" friend "as distinguished from a personal or private friendship." He had "never had any business or financial relationship" with Voloshen "nor was my office, with my knowledge or consent, ever used for his personal or private business," McCormack said. When he learned "several weeks ago" of investigation concerning Voloshen, he said, "I told him that I did not want him to come into my office any more."

McCormack received personal support Oct. 20—a standing ovation when he entered the House and a series of speeches from both sides of the aisle acclaiming his integrity. Joining in the tributes were Rep. Carl B. Albert (D, Okla.), majority leader, and Rep. Gerald R. Ford (R, Mich.), minority leader, who called McCormack "a puritan in the highest tradition."

Sweig and Voloshen were indicted by a federal grand jury in New York Jan. 12, 1970 on charges of conspiracy to exert pressure on federal agencies from an operating base in McCormack's office. Both were also accused of perjury. No charges were made against McCormack, who gave a deposition on the case to federal investigators.

Pressure was exerted, according to the indictment, on behalf of at least 11 Voloshen clients on the Justice, Treasury, Defense, Labor and Post Office departments, the Selective Service System and the SEC.

Among the activities cited—including alleged concessions to businesses and favors for federal prisoners and soldiers —were telephone calls from McCormack's office "to express the interest" of that office in the matter involved, personal visits to government officials and a pretense by Voloshen to be a member of McCormack's staff. Among those named as intended recipients of the favors were convicted stock swindler Edward Gilbert and Salvatore "Sally Burns" Granello, a convicted tax evader and reputed Cosa Nostra leader.

Voloshen pleaded guilty June 17.

Judge Marvin E. Frankel said Voloshen "affirmed every allegation" of the indictment except one, that of having impersonated a member of McCormack's staff. The guilty plea covered charges of conspiracy to defraud the U.S. and deprive its agencies of the right to be free of "improper and undue influence" and of perjury before a grand jury. The plea was made as trial was about to begin of Voloshen and Dr. Martin Sweig, suspended as McCormack's administrative assistant. Voloshen and Sweig had pleaded innocent in January.

Frankel Nov. 24 fined Voloshen $10,000 but withheld imposition of a jail sentence because Voloshen was cooperating in new investigations of possible influence peddling in Washington.

Voloshen contended in a statement read by his lawyer that other lobbyists and businessmen had used McCormack's office on behalf of clients.

A federal jury in New York July 9 convicted Sweig on one perjury count but acquitted him on five other perjury charges and on charges of conspiring with Voloshen to use McCormack's office to defraud the government. Frankel sentenced Sweig Sept. 3 to 2½ years in prison and fined him $2,000. Sweig began serving his sentence July 22, 1971 in Lewisburg, Pa.

Fong aide convicted. Robert T. Carson, the suspended administrative aide to Sen. Hiram L. Fong (R, Hawaii), was convicted in New York Nov. 20, 1971 of a role in a million-dollar conspiracy.

Carson had been suspended by Fong in January.

The former Fong aide was found guilty on two counts of conspiracy and perjury. He was acquitted on two counts of using interstate travel to promote bribery.

Two co-conspirators in the case, Edward Adams and Joseph Bald, pleaded guilty Nov. 8.

The alleged scheme centered around a $100,000 bribe to stop a stock fraud prosecution. During Carson's trial, Deputy Attorney General Richard G. Kleindienst testified that Carson had told him of an offer to pay up to $100,000 as a political contribution for President Nixon if something could be done to halt a stock fraud prosecution involving several figures tied to organized crime.

Carson was sentenced Jan. 4, 1972 to 18 months in prison and fined $5,000.

Judge Marvin E. Frankel sentenced Carson to 18 months for conspiracy and 18 months for perjury with the sentences to run concurrently.

Dowdy convicted. Rep. John Dowdy (D, Tex.) was convicted by a jury in Baltimore Dec. 30, 1971 of taking a $25,000 bribe, of conspiracy to obstruct justice and of perjury. Dowdy, 59, a member of the House Committee on the District of Columbia, was accused of having intervened with various federal and district agencies to thwart investigation of a home improvement company.

The conspiracy and bribery convictions were reversed by the 4th Circuit Court of Appeals March 13, 1973. The court held that the acts Dowdy was accused of on these counts "might be interpreted as preparation" for a legislative hearing and therefore protected under the free speech and debate clause of the U.S. Constitution.

The court left standing Dowdy's conviction on three counts of perjury. Dowdy had been sentenced to 18 months in prison and fined $25,000.

The firm involved was the defunct Monarch Construction Corp. The indictment had been handed down March 31, 1970.

Also named in the indictment were Myrvin C. Clark, former sales manager of Monarch, as a co-defendant, and Monarch's president, Nathan H. Cohen, as a co-conspirator but not a defendant. (Clark and Cohen had pleaded guilty in U.S. district court in Washington earlier in March to charges of defrauding Monarch customers.)

A separate indictment was returned March 31 against Washington lawyer Hugh J. McGee, who was charged with joining Dowdy and Cohen in a conspiracy to "corruptly influence . . . the proper administration of law."

Brewster convicted. Former Sen. Daniel B. Brewster (D, Md.) was convicted Nov. 17, 1972 on charges of accepting an unlawful gratuity to influence his vote on postal rate legislation.

Also found guilty by the federal jury in Washington was Cyrus T. Anderson, the lobbyist who offered money to Brewster.

Though Brewster had orginally been charged with bribery, the jury convicted him on the lesser offense of accepting an unlawful gratuity. That in effect meant he had taken the money without corrupt intent.

At issue in the case were Anderson's attempts to influence Brewster's vote on postal rate legislation while Brewster was a member of the Senate Committee on Post Office and Civil Service. Anderson represented Spiegel Inc., a Chicago mail order house.

During the trial, Spiegel was separated from the case when its lawyers decided to plead guilty to a lesser charge of payment of an unlawful gratuity. The company was fined $25,000.

Brewster was sentenced Feb. 2, 1973 to two to six years in prison and was fined $30,000. Anderson received a sentence of 18 to 54 months in jail and was also fined $30,000.

But the U.S. Circuit Court of Appeals in Washington voided the conviction Aug. 2, 1974 and ordered a new trial. The appellate court said district court trial Judge George L. Hart Jr. had failed in his instructions to the jury to make a sufficient distinction between accepting a bribe and accepting illegal gratuities.

Brasco convicted in bribery case. Rep. Frank J. Brasco (D, N.Y.) was found guilty by a federal jury in New York July 18, 1974 of bribery and conspiracy in connection with a scheme to obtain mail-hauling contracts for a trucking firm allegedly run by an organized crime figure.

Prosecution of Brasco on the same charges had ended in a mistrial March 19 when jurors were unable to reach a verdict.

A four-term congressman, Brasco was accused of accepting a $27,500 payoff in exchange for helping John Masiello, an alleged Mafia member, obtain Post Office contracts for hauling mail. Masiello, who was currently serving a prison term for other offenses, testified against Brasco in return for a favorable letter to his parole board.

The indictment, handed down Oct. 23, 1973, named as unindicted co-conspirators Masiello and Joseph P. Doherty, a former Post Office official who pleaded guilty in 1970 to charges he helped a Baltimore contractor obtain federal contracts.

A federal grand jury in Baltimore had recommended a similar indictment in 1971, but the Justice Department quashed the case, citing lack of corroborative evidence.

According to the indictment, Masiello submitted a bid for hauling mail in New York City in 1967. Although he was underbid by six other firms, Masiello won the contract after Brasco, a member of the House Post Office and Civil Service Committee, and Doherty interceded on his behalf. In return, Masiello allegedly delivered $10,000 to Joseph Brasco, ex-Rep. Brasco's uncle, who also was indicted.

The indictment also charged that the Brascos helped dummy corporations owned by Masiello obtain Post Office hauling contracts from June 1968 to May 1969, after Masiello had lost his original contract when his criminal background was discovered.

The Brascos also agreed to assist Masiello obtain a loan to buy trucks in return for a payment of $17,500, the indictment charged.

Brasco was sentenced Oct. 22, 1974 to three months in jail and was fined $10,000.

Podell pleads guilty to conspiracy. Rep. Bertram L. Podell (D, N.Y.) pleaded guilty in federal district court in New York Oct. 1, 1974 to charges of conspiracy and conflict of interest in connection with $41,350 payment he received from a small Florida airline seeking government approval of a route to the Bahamas. Podell, whose surprise plea ended his nine-day bribery-conspiracy trial, admitted accepting the money from co-defendant Martin Miller to appear before federal agencies on behalf of Florida Atlantic Airlines. This act, Podell conceded, constituted a conflict of interest for a congressman. The plea by Podell was not an admittance that he had accepted any bribes.

Miller, head of the parent firm of the now defunct airline, also changed his plea to guilty on a charge of conspiracy to pay Podell in violation of the conflict-of-interest law.

The indictment, handed down July 12, 1973, had also accused Podell of bribery and perjury.

Also indicted were Podell's brother and law partner, Herbert S. Podell, and Martin Miller, former president of Leasing Consultants Inc., the parent company of the now bankrupt Florida Atlantic Airlines.

The indictment alleged that Podell, in violation of the Congressional conflict of interest law, represented Florida Atlantic before the Civil Aeronautics Board (CAB) and the State Department. The Podells were also charged with accepting a bribe in the form of a $12,430 legal fee and a $29,000 donation to the Citizen's Committee for B. L. Podell. The three were also charged with lying to the Federal Bureau of Investigation (FBI) and perjuring themselves before a federal grand jury.

Ex-Sen. Gurney acquitted. Former Sen. Edward J. Gurney (R, Fla.) was acquitted Oct. 27, 1976 of the last of seven felony charges brought by the Justice Department before he resigned his Senate seat in 1974.

A jury in U.S. District Court, Orlando, Fla. found Gurney innocent of a perjury charge related to a political shakedown scheme that had involved members of his staff. The trial began Oct. 12. The prosecution claimed that Gurney had lied to a federal grand jury when he said he did not know until the summer of 1973 that $400,000 that had been paid by Florida builders in return for promised favors

from the Federal Housing Administration was used to pay expenses of Gurney's Florida field offices. Larry E. Williams, Gurney's fund-raiser, had collected the money.

Gurney had been acquitted in August 1975 on five other charges connected with the shakedown scheme, but the jury had been unable to reach a decision on the two remaining charges of perjury and conspiracy. The Justice Department Sept. 1 had dropped the conspiracy count but announced it would retry Gurney on the perjury count.

U.S. District Judge George C. Young, who presided over Gurney's trial in Orlando, Oct. 25 dismissed a portion of the perjury count against him. Young ruled that the government had not introduced sufficient evidence to prove its contention that Gurney had lied to the grand jury when he denied knowing before June 7, 1972 that Williams was raising funds on his behalf.

Williams, 32, served a five-month prison term after pleading guilty to felony charges stemming from the shakedown case. Williams, who was the chief prosecution witness at the Orlando trial, claimed that he had told Gurney about his activities since being hired as a fund raiser in 1971.

The Federal Bureau of Investigation (FBI) had investigated charges brought in November 1971 by a Gainesville, Fla. builder, Philip I. Emmer. He said he had been "shaken down" in February 1971 by Williams, who had demanded a $5,000 "contribution" for winning federal approval of two FHA-funded apartment projects.

Williams was sentenced to a year in jail Feb. 21, 1974 after he had pleaded guilty to charges of attempting to evade federal income taxes totaling $19,000 in 1971 and helping a government official collect a bribe.

Williams had been indicted Jan. 17 by a federal grand jury for channeling a $10,-000 bribe from Miami builder John J. Priestes to William F. Pelski, former director of FHA's insuring office in Coral Gables and the former mayor of Pompano Beach.

Priestes received 20 FHA contracts to build subsidized housing in return for his illegal payment, according to the indictment. (He was serving a one-year jail term, the Miami Herald reported Jan. 18, 1974.)

Pelski pleaded guilty March 19, 1974 to conspiring to defraud the government by promising FHA financing to Gurney's political contributors. He was sentenced to 18 months in prison. Williams and James L. Groot, Gurney's former administrative assistant, were named as unindicted co-conspirators in the criminal information filed against Pelski. According to the government, Pelski gave Williams the names of persons seeking FHA insuring commitments for mortgages and loans. Williams used the list to solicit contributions for Gurney and turned the kickback money over to Groot, who used it to pay office expenses incurred by Gurney and his staff. Williams subsequently instructed Pelski to authorize the insuring commitments to the donors.

Gurney himself was charged by a federal grand jury July 10, 1974 with bribery, conspiracy, and lying to the grand jury in connection with an influence-peddling and extortion scheme to raise campaign funds.

Gurney and six others also indicted were accused of having conspired since December 1970 to demand money from Florida contractors and developers "who had matters pending before" the Department of Housing and Urban Development (HUD). "In return for the contributions and payments, pressure and influence would be exerted on HUD to give favored treatment to the contributors in awarding contracts for HUD housing projects and mortgage insurance," the indictment charged.

Gurney was alleged to have extorted $223,160 over a 3½-year period for use as "personal, political and travel expenses" and for use in the operation of his Washington and Florida offices. Gurney also was accused of having "corruptly solicited and accepted a bribe on Aug. 15, 1971 from the owner of a Vero Beach, Fla. condominium apartment in return for Gurney's assistance." The bribe, according to the government, was a "fifth floor, ocean-front apartment," valued at $67,000.

Indicted with Gurney were James L. Groot; Joseph Bastien, Gurney's executive assistant in his Winter Park, Fla.

office; Earl M. Crittenden, an Orlando, Fla. citrus grower and former state Republican chairman; George Anderson, an Orlando banker and former state GOP treasurer; Wayne Swiger, director of HUD's Tampa, Fla. insurance office; and Ralph Koontz, special assistant to the Florida area director for HUD. Forty-two persons, including 39 real estate developers, were named as unindicted co-conspirators. Another unindicted co-conspirator, Larry E. Williams, had been hired to "demand" and collect the payments, according to the government.

The indictment cited 115 overt acts in the conspiracy, including some that occurred while Gurney was serving as a member of the Senate Watergate Committee. He was charged with one count of bribery, one count of conspiracy, one count of receiving unlawful compensation and four counts of making false statements to a grand jury in May 1973.

Gurney was acquitted Aug. 6, 1975 of five felony charges in his bribery-conspiracy trial in Tampa, Fla. On two other charges, including a key conspiracy count, the jurors announced they had been unable to reach a verdict during 10 days of deliberations. Gurney was declared innocent of a bribery count, accepting unlawful compensation, and three perjury counts relating to his grand jury testimony.

Two co-defendants in the case, Ralph M. Koontz and K. Wayne Swiger, were found innocent of conspiracy charges. They had been suspended as Florida officials of the FHA. A fourth defendant, former Gurney aide Joseph Bastien, was acquitted on a charge of receiving unlawful compensation, but a mistrial was declared on a conspiracy charge.

Six other men had pleaded guilty to felony charges stemming from the case against Gurney. Larry E. Williams admitted collecting nearly $400,000 from builders in exchange for favors from FHA officials for subsidized housing contracts.

James L. Groot and Earl M. Crittendon entered pleas of guilty during the nearly 24-week trial. Both admitted complicity in the shakedown of Florida contractors to raise an illegal $233,000 slush fund for Gurney's 1974 re-election race.

George F. Anderson, a Florida banker and former treasurer of the party, also pleaded guilty to a conspiracy charge. William Pelski, a former FHA administrator in Florida, admitted he had awarded federal contracts to home builders who had made contributions to the Gurney fund and said he had received a kickback for his services. The Miami builder who paid the kickback at Williams' behest, John Priestes, also had pleaded guilty.

The prosecution had contended that Gurney had known "all along" of the illegal fund-raising scheme, and that he developed a policy of "deniability" about the shakedown by insulating himself from Williams' pressure tactics and Groot's handling of the cash.

Williams' testimony was the core of the government's case against Gurney. Williams testified, and two other witnesses corroborated, that Gurney had hired him as a fund-raiser in January 1971. Williams said he received his instructions from Groot, who accepted the cash for Gurney to pay office and personal expenses.

Groot claimed Gurney had been aware as early as June 1972 of Williams' efforts to shakedown FHA contractors. Groot also admitted he had accepted $50,000 from Williams in July 1972 and had deposited the money in Gurney's Washington office safe.

(In testimony June 12, Groot also charged that immediately before the 1972 election, he had given $10,000 in cash from the safe to L. A. Bafalis, who was subsequently elected to Congress from Florida's 10th district. Bafalis never reported the secret campaign contribution, Groot testified. Bafalis denied the charge in testimony June 23.)

Gurney testified in his own defense during July, claiming that he had been unaware of the slush fund's existence until the summer of 1973 when the Senate Watergate hearings were underway. He defended his failure to release information on the illegal fund-raising, contending his "effectiveness on the Watergate committee would have been totally destroyed." He added that the information also would have proved an embarrassment to former President Nixon and the Republican Party.

The three other defendants in the bribery-conspiracy case also took the stand to deny participating in the shakedown scheme.

New York Cases

Marcus admits kickbacks. Ex-New York City Water Commissioner James L. Marcus pleaded guilty in federal district court in New York June 3, 1968 to charges of sharing a $40,000 kickback in return for awarding an $840,000 city contract. Marcus had been arrested and indicted Dec. 18, 1967 on a federal charge of conspiracy; indicted with him were Herbert Itkin, 41, a lawyer; Antonio (Tony Ducks) Corallo, 54, described by the FBI as a Mafia leader; Daniel J. Motto, 57, president of Local 350 of the Bakery & Confectionery Workers Union; Henry Fried, 69, owner of S. T. Grand, Inc., a construction company; S. T. Grand, Inc., and Charles Rappaport, 30, Itkin's ex-law partner.

The indictment charged that Fried, whose company had received the contract in 1966, had paid 5% of the total contract price to Marcus, Corallo, Motto and Itkin. The federal government contended that by arranging for the alleged bribe through interstate New York-to-Connecticut phone calls, the defendants had violated the federal anti-racketeering statute. (Normally, bribery is a state, not a federal, crime.)

As a witness for the government, Marcus testified against the men indicted with him. (His trial was severed since he had pleaded guilty to the charges against him.) Marcus indicated in testimony June 7 that he expected a N.Y. County grand jury to indict him in connection with an alleged $20 million conspiracy involving Consolidated Edison contracts. He said he would plead guilty to that charge, to 2 other felony charges (including a charge of grand larceny) and to a misdemeanor charge.

The jury June 19 convicted, as co-conspirators with Marcus: Fried, S. T. Grand, Inc., Corallo and Motto. Rappaport, an FBI informer, was acquitted. The case of Itkin, also charged as a co-conspirator, was severed from the trial after he disclosed that he had been an FBI and CIA informer.

Testimony at the trial rocked the city government. Witnesses mentioned, often in an accusatory manner, many prominent New York businessmen, firms, union leaders and lawyers. Among those named were Consolidated Edison, ex-Tammany Hall leader Carmine Gerard De Sapio, N.Y. County Republican Chrmn. Vincent F. Albano Jr. and N.Y. County Republican Law Chrmn. Joseph E. Ruggiero. Itkin caused a stir June 11 when he said that another N.Y. City commissioner had shared a payoff that "was very close to a bribe," but he did not name the commissioner.

Fried testified June 11 that the late Joseph Pizzo, an alleged Cosa Nostra "muscleman," had forced him to pay the $40,000 as a "further fee" after he had originally refused a demand for the money by Carl D'Angelo, to whom he paid a $7,500 annual retainer as his lawyer. (D'Angelo's father, Armand D'Angelo, had been water commissioner in the previous city administration.)

Judge Edward Weinfeld July 26 sentenced Corallo to 3 years in prison and Fried and Motto to 2-year prison terms. Marcus was sentenced Sept. 9 to 15 months in prison, but his sentence was imposed under a federal code that allowed his parole board to free him at any time.

Shortly after the federal indictment in Dec. 1967, Marcus and Itkin had been arrested again and charged Jan. 18 under N.Y. State laws with bribery, conspiracy and accepting $10,000 of illegal fees. A N.Y. County grand jury indicted the 2 men June 27, and Marcus, surprisingly, pleaded not guilty to the 2 indictments against him. Gus Spatafora, a salesman, also indicted, was accused of being a go-between in a proposed preferential treatment deal. Itkin and Spatafora also pleaded not guilty.

In N.Y. County Supreme Court Sept. 5 Marcus changed his plea to guilty on the 2 indictments.

Marcus pleaded not guilty Nov. 27 on a 3d state indictment charging that he had accepted a $20,000 bribe in the Con Edison case.

Fried, also charged with conspiracy in the Con Edison case, pleaded not guilty at his arraignment Sept. 7 in state Supreme Court.

As the implications of the Marcus case and testimony spread, Carmine De Sapio, 59, was indicted by a federal grand jury in New York Dec. 20 on charges of conspiring to bribe Marcus and shake down Consolidated Edison Co. for construction contracts. He pleaded not guilty and was released without bail. Carallo and Fried, indicted with De Sapio, pleaded not guilty Dec. 23 and were freed on bail. In this case, as in the earlier federal case, federal jurisdiction was based on interstate phone calls; in addition, the alleged conspiracy involved the interstate transmission of electricity. Marcus and Itkin, both of whom had discussed the Con Ed case in the previous trial, were named as co-conspirators in the indictment.

DeSapio found guilty—Carmine G. DeSapio, once the most influential Democratic leader in New York politics, was found guilty in a New York federal court Dec. 13, 1969 of conspiracy to bribe James L. Marcus and extract inflated contracts from the Consolidated Edison company that would result in illicit profits.

DeSapio was found guilty on three counts of bribery. A co-defendant, Antonio Corallo, was found guilty on one count of conspiracy and acquitted on another.

(Federal jurisdiction in the case was based on interstate telephone calls made by DeSapio and Corallo, and the charge that DeSapio had conspired to violate federal laws by plotting for Marcus to withhold from Con Ed a permit as part of a plan to extort from the utility company inflated contracts.)

Marcus guilty in Con Ed case—James L. Marcus entered a plea of guilty Jan. 12, 1970 to a charge of having solicited and received a bribe in exchange for approving Consolidated Edison Co.'s request to rebuild its transmission lines in Westchester, N.Y. Marcus admitted that he had agreed to accept $20,000 in return for a work permit to allow the work over lands owned by New York City.

Rep. Roncallo acquitted. Rep. Angelo D. Roncallo (R, N.Y.) was acquitted of charges of extortion and conspiracy by a federal jury in Westbury, N.Y. May 17, 1974.

Diane Zaslowsky, one of the jurors said, "We acquitted them [Roncallo and a co-defendant] because of a lack of evidence and the government just never proved its case."

Roncallo had been indicted by a federal grand jury in New York Feb. 21 on charges that he extorted money from a contractor in 1970 when he was controller of Nassau County, N.Y.

According to the two-count indictment, Roncallo, a first-term congressman, conspired with two officials of the Town of Oyster Bay, N.Y. to extort money from a contractor who was modernizing the town's incinerator. After repeated threats by Roncallo's associates to ruin his business, the indictment charged, the contractor paid money to Roncallo, who subsequently assured him that "everything would be all right."

Goldman indictment dismissed. A fraud indictment against New York City's former Cultural Affairs Commissioner Irving Goldman was dismissed by State Supreme Court Justice John M. Murtagh Nov. 10, 1975. Murtagh ruled that Maurice Nadjari, special presecutor, had neither the evidence or the authority to call a special grand jury in the case.

Goldman had been charged in March with defrauding the New York Transit Authority during his stewardship of vending machines for the N.Y. subway system. But Justice Murtagh decided that the indictment did not fall into Nadjari's jurisdiction. As special prosecutor, Nadjari was empowered only to prosecute corruption within the criminal justice system. Traditionally, the office investigated police, prosecutors and the judiciary. From the outset of the Goldman case in 1974 questions as to Nadjari's jurisdiction had been raised.

Murtagh's Nov. 10 action was not directed at a second indictment brought by Nadjari's office Oct. 7 charging Goldman with bilking the Shubert Foundation, which managed many of New York's theaters, of $100,000. Goldman was suspended from his post as president of the Shubert Foundation Oct. 8.

An April indictment in federal district court in New York had accused Goldman on similar charges of conspiracy (one count) as well as on 43 counts of mail fraud. The indictment was in connection with his stewardship of two companies, the Interborough News Co., which operated the more than 6,000 vending machines in N.Y. subways, and the Jola Candy Corp.

The federal indictment charged Goldman and Jack Zander, an unindicted co-conspirator and former president of Interborough, with entering into a "three-pronged conspiracy" which centered on an alleged scheme by the pair to defraud the company of over $200,000 by using Jola as a front to bill Interborough "at inflated and excessive prices" for vending machine candy. In addition, the two were charged with offering a $5,000 bribe in 1970 to the director of concessions at a time when their company was seeking the exclusive rights to sell candy from subway vending machines. The third "prong" of the alleged conspiracy charged Goldman with filing false corporate income tax returns from 1971–73 based on false entries in Jola's records.

The state indictment charged that Goldman, through Jola, siphoned $250,000 from Interborough as well as defrauded the city by getting a rent reduction of $500,000 by paying a transit authority official $6,250. He was also charged with lying to a grand jury, misusing political connections and trying to bribe transit authority patrolmen to get better vending machine protection.

Blumenthal case dismissed. New York State Supreme Court Justice Aloysius J. Melia April 13, 1976 dismissed all charges in a perjury and bribery indictment against Albert H. Blumenthal, New York State Assembly majority leader.

Melia was critical of the case brought against Blumenthal by special state prosecutor Charles J. Hynes. The judge said that Hynes utilized "gross speculation" and "inference upon inference" that had "unduly coerced" the grand jury.

The case involved Blumenthal's relationship with indicted nursing-home promoter Bernard Bergman.

New Jersey Cases

8 New Jersey officials convicted. A federal jury in Newark, N.J. convicted Jersey City Mayor Thomas J. Whelan and seven other Hudson County public officials July 5, 1971 of conspiring to extort millions of dollars from local contracting firms.

In addition to Whelan, 48, those found guilty by the jury of nine women and three men were Philip Kunz, Jersey City business administrator; Thomas A. Flaherty, president of the Jersey City council; Bernard Murphy, purchasing agent for Jersey City; Walter W. Wolfe, Hudson County Democratic chairman; Fred J. Kropke, Hudson County police chief; Joseph Stapleton, Hudson County treasurer; and William A. Sternkopf, New Jersey commissioner of the Port of New York Authority.

Only Kunz was found not guilty of some counts of the indictment. The jury acquitted him of 12 counts of the 29-count charge. The other defendants were convicted on all 29 counts.

During the trial, which opened May 17, the government charged that the conspiracy netted the eight defendants more than $182,000. It was estimated that over an eight-year period the defendants received about $3.3 million in kickbacks from contractors doing business with Jersey City and Hudson County.

Presiding Judge Robert Shaw granted a motion for personal recognizance bonds for $25,000 to be continued for all the defendants. He set no date for sentencing.

The maximum punishment under federal law was 20 years imprisonment for 28 counts of the indictment and five years in prison for the other count. Fines for the eight could total more than $290,000.

Among those indicted in the original charge—handed down in November 1970 —was John V. Kenny, 78, the former Hudson County Democratic boss. Kenny went on trial with the eight other defendants but had his case severed June 10 because of illness. During the trial, Herbert Stern, the U.S. attorney for New Jersey who prosecuted the case, called Kenny the "master-mind" of the conspiracy.

Also indicted in the 1970 charge but later severed from the trial in exchange for their testimony under immunity were John J. Kenney, 52, former Hudson County freeholder, and Frank G. Manning, 60, a Hudson County engineer.

A 12th defendant, James R. Corrado, a Jersey City hospital official, pleaded guilty May 20 to one of the counts of the indictment and was awaiting sentencing.

Whelan, Flaherty and Murphy were sentenced Aug. 10 to 15-year terms, the top penalty imposed by Federal Judge Robert Shaw. Sternkopf was sentenced to 10 years in prison and was fined $20,000. Kropke was given a five-year term. Stapleton was sentenced to six months and ordered to stop all political activity. Kunz received a six-month sentence.

John V. Kenny was fined $30,000 May 24, 1972 on six income-tax evasion counts.

In handing down the sentences, Shaw denounced the defendants and the Hudson County Democratic Organization as a "rotten system whose sole function was to enrich itself."

Kenny had been in a hospital for 14 months contending that he was too ill to stand trial on three U.S. indictments.

But Kenny had appeared in a Newark courthouse in a wheelchair May 18 to plead guilty to the tax charges.

In sentencing Kenny, U.S. District Court Judge Robert Shaw committed him to three months at the U.S. prison hospital center at Springfield, Mo. for a study of his physical condition.

Kenny ultimately was granted parole, effective March 1, 1973. Originally sentenced to 18 years in prison, he had his sentence reduced to 18 months in 1972, after a judicial review. The Parole Board, in its Feb. 6 announcement, said Kenny still had to pay the $30,000 fine originally imposed before he could be paroled.

Burkhardt guilty of bribery. Robert J. Burkhardt, former New Jersey secretary of state with influence in the inner circles of the national Democratic Party, pleaded guilty May 12, 1972 in federal court in Newark to charges of bribery and extortion.

Burkhardt admitted to U.S. Judge John J. Kitchen that he had shaken down a New York City construction company, J. Rich Steers, Inc., that had sought a contract for construction work on the Delaware Memorial Bridge.

According to the charges, Burkhardt had demanded and received $20,000 in campaign contributions from the Steers concern for his influence in awarding Steers the contract in 1964. At that time, Burkhardt was secretary of state in the administration of Gov. Richard J. Hughes.

In addition, Burkhardt had been accused of taking $10,000 in "political contributions" in 1965 when he was organizing Gov. Hughes's re-election campaign.

Burkhardt was fined $5,000 June 29 and put on three years' probation.

Judge Kitchen said he had received a "very good" pre-sentencing report and a number of supporting letters from "very prominent" friends of the former New Jersey official.

Burkhardt had been indicted by a federal grand jury in Newark Aug. 11, 1971. The same jury simultaneously indicted State Sen. William B. Knowlton on 34 counts of extorting $181,000 from the same company as his price for helping the construction firm obtain contracts from the New Jersey Turnpike Authority and the Delaware River Port Authority in 1968 and 1969.

A federal official said the charges against the two were unrelated and the alleged conspiracies were conducted separately.

Named in both indictments as a co-conspirator was Eugene Rau, president of the Steers company.

Sherwin & 2 others guilty. Paul J. Sherwin, New Jersey secretary of state, and two other men were convicted Oct. 28, 1972 by a Freehold jury of conspiracy to fix a road contract bid in return for a $10,000 political contribution.

Convicted with Sherwin were Michael J. Manzo, a contractor, and William C. Loughran, a prominent state Republican fund raiser. Each was found guilty on conspiracy and bribery counts and sentenced Nov. 22 to two years in jail and fined $2000.

Sherwin, a close political adviser to Gov. William T. Cahill, had been on leave of absence from his post since his indictment. In that indictment, Sherwin and the others were charged with rigging a $600,000 highway contract for Manzo's firm in return for a $10,000 contribution to New Jersey's Republican finance committee.

The firm did not get the contract despite the alleged kickback and Manzo, angered at the officials, revealed the incident during courtroom testimony on another matter earlier this year.

Kervick confesses guilt. John A. Kervick, former New Jersey state treasurer, pleaded guilty June 12, 1973 in U.S. District Court in Trenton, N.J. to a charge that he accepted a $27,000 bribe to fix a highway contract.

Kervick was fined $10,000 and put on three years' probation by a federal judge in Trenton June 17, 1974.

Somers found guilty. William T. Somers, former mayor of Atlantic City, N.J., was found guilty March 8, 1973 by a federal jury in Camden, N.J. of participating in a scheme to extort money from contractors who did business with the city. Seven former and present Atlantic City officials had been indicted in the scheme.

McCrane guilty. Joseph M. McCrane Jr., former New Jersey state treasurer, was convicted by a federal court jury in Scranton, Pa. Dec. 11, 1974 of four counts of assisting corporations in filing fraudulent income tax returns. McCrane was accused of providing the corporations with phony business vouchers enabling them to disguise contributions to the 1969 election campaign of former N. J. Gov. William T. Cahill (R) as tax-deductible business expenses. McCrane's trial was shifted to Scranton after two mistrials and a subsequent court decision that extensive pretrial publicity made a fair trial in New Jersey impossible.

McCrane and Nelson G. Gross, former state chairman of the New Jersey Republican Party, had been indicted by state and federal grand juries in May 1973.

McCrane was indicted by a state grand jury May 15 on charges of bribery and misconduct. He was alleged to have used the power of his office to have more than $6 million deposited in three New Jersey banks, which in turn used the money to purchase securities through McCrane's brother Kevin, a New York City stockbroker.

A federal indictment handed down May 24 alleged that McCrane helped mastermind an income tax fraud scheme during the 1969 gubernatorial campaign of Gov. Cahill. He was charged with aiding Cahill contributors in forging documents so they could deduct a total of $46,710 from their federal income taxes.

McCrane and Gross were named in the federal charges as unindicted co-conspirators in each other's case.

Federal indictments handed down May 29 and 31 charged four companies with taking part in schemes to make campaign contributions made in 1969 appear as business expenses for the purpose of income taxes.

Gross was found guilty by a federal jury in Newark, N.J. March 29, 1974 of five counts of tax fraud and perjury. Gross was sentenced to two years in prison and fined $10,000 June 16.

Chairman of the 1969 gubernatorial campaign of former Gov. William T. Cahill, Gross had been charged with advising trading stamp executive William H. Preis to disguise a $5,000 campaign contribution as a tax-deductible business expense and with subsequently urging Preis to lie to a grand jury investigating the contribution.

Crabiel acquitted. New Jersey Secretary of State J. Edward Crabiel was acquitted in a nonjury trial April 23, 1975 of charges that he had conspired to rig bids and fix prices on public road construction contracts. Franklin Contracting, the firm Crabiel headed before entering the N.J. cabinet in 1974, was also found not guilty. In its decision, the court said it could not find instances of overt conspiratorial acts after August 1969. The state had claimed that Crabiel and Franklin had conspired with other firms to rig public contracts in New Jersey between 1957 and 1970 but it was required, by a statute of limitations, to show a conspiracy in a five-year period before July 1974 when the indictment was issued.

Ft. Lee bribe convictions. Seven defendants were convicted March 28, 1975 on bribery and conspiracy charges stemming from an attempt to win zoning approval for a $250 million shopping mall in Fort Lee, N.J. They were given maximum prison terms and heavily fined June 3 by federal Judge Frederick B. Lacey in U.S. District Court in Newark, N.J.

Sentenced to five-year prison terms were Norman Dansker, president and board chairman of the bankrupt Investors Funding Corp.; Stephen Haymes and Donald Orenstein, Investors Funding executives; Andrew Valentine and Joseph Diaco, president and vice president of Valentine Electric Co.; Nathan L. Serota, former Fort Lee official and builder, and Arthur Sutton, a land developer. Sutton, who had pleaded guilty and subsequently testified against the other defendants, had 4½ years of his sentence suspended June 4.

West Virginia Cases

Ex-Gov. Barron admits guilt. William Wallace Barron, former governor of West Virginia, pleaded guilty in federal district court in Charleston March 29, 1971 to charges of paying a bribe of $25,000 to influence the vote of a foreman of a jury that acquitted him of other bribery charges in 1968.

Barron was sentenced July 16 to 12 years in prison and was fined $50,000.

In the indictment, which was returned Feb. 20 by a federal grand jury, Barron's wife was also named as a defendent. She was accused of delivering a $25,000 bribe to the wife of the jury foreman, Ralph Buckalew. At the request of the federal prosecutor, all charges against Mrs. Barron were dropped.

Buckalew pleaded guilty Feb. 20 to two counts of the indictment and was sentenced by a federal judge in Charleston to 20 years in prison.

The 1968 indictment, handed down Feb. 14, had named Barron and five others on charges of conspiring to "carry out bribery activities in state government." Named with Barron were 3 state officials who were suspended the same day: Road Commissioner Burl A. Sawyers, Deputy Road Commissioner Vincent

J. Johnkoski and Finance & Administration Commissioner Truman E. Gore. Bonn Brown, a lawyer, and Alfred W. Schroath, an auto dealer, were also indicted.

The 6 were charged with taking part in a conspiracy, beginning in Jan. 1961, for Barron to appoint the 3 commissioners, who were then to award state contracts to firms that would be asked to make payments to several concerns set up by Schroath. It was charged that Brown and Schroath had notified the companies that such payments could be made and that the defendants had shared equally in the payments. The 6 were charged with conspiring to use interstate facilities to aid racketeering enterprises.

Barron was acquitted Aug. 30, 1968 by the Buckalew jury, which simultaneously convicted four of the other defendants: Sawyers, Johnkoski, Brown and Schroath. A mistrial had been declared in the case of Gore.

Ex-treasurer & others guilty. John H. Kelly resigned as West Virginia state treasurer July 3, 1975 and pleaded guilty July 7 to federal charges of fraud, extortion and misuse of bank funds. He pleaded no contest to a charge that he had accepted a $1,000 bribe from an investment advisory company.

Kelly was sentenced in September to a five-year prison term and fined $7,500 for extorting bribes from executives of banks that were depositories of state funds. Joseph F. RyKoskey, Kelly's former assistant, who also pleaded guilty, received a two-year prison term.

Convicted of misapplying bank funds in supplying the bribes were Theodore J. S. Caldwell and Bernard C. McGinnis, former bank executives. A jury had convicted Caldwell; McGinnis pleaded guilty.

Chief among the charges was the alleged extortion by state officials of $40,000 in bribes by the use of "fear and economic harm and under the color of official rights."

The money and gifts allegedly came from three West Virginia banks and a New York investment firm. The banks, designated as state depositories, were threatened by Kelley and Rykoskey with financial harm unless the bribes were paid,

according to the indictment. The investment counseling firm, Calvin Bullock Ltd., which had been an advisor to the West Virginia Board of Investors, allegedly had been threatened with losing that contract. According to the indictment, the counseling firm gave Kelley $4,000 during 1972, purportedly as a campaign contribution.

Gov. Moore acquitted. West Virginia Gov. Arch A. Moore Jr. was acquitted by a federal jury in Charleston May 5, 1976 of charges that he had conspired to extort $25,000 from a banker during his 1972 election campaign. Moore's fellow defendant, William H. Loy, his 1972 campaign manager, was also acquitted.

The two men were indicted on charges of extorting the $25,000 from Theodore Price, former president of the defunct Diversified Mountaineer Corp., formerly a chain of savings and loan institutions in West Virginia, Tennessee and Kentucky.

The indictment said Price, who pleaded guilty May 1, 1975 to securities fraud charges, had applied for a state bank charter in September 1972 on behalf of Diversified Mountaineer and had secretly handed cash to Moore on three occasions in order to obtain approval of the pending application. The application was ultimately rejected in 1973.

The grand jury named two other West Virginia officials, George B. Jordon Jr., state banking commissioner, and Nowlan Hamric, a member of the state building commission, as unindicted co-conspirators.

Illinois Cases

Judge Kerner convicted. Otto Kerner, 64, judge of the U.S. Circuit Court of Appeals (7th Circuit), was convicted Feb. 19, 1973 on 17 counts of conspiracy, fraud, perjury, bribery, and income tax evasion in connection with the purchase and sale of race track stock when he was governor of Illinois (1961 to 1968). Theodore J. Isaacs, 62, former state revenue director under Kerner, was convicted of all the same counts except perjury.

Also indicted were William S. Miller, appointed head of the Illinois Racing Board by Kerner in 1961; Faith McInturf, Miller's secretary; and Joseph E. Knight, a horse breeder and former treasurer of the Illinois Democratic party. Charges were dropped against Miller and Ms. McInturf when they agreed to become state's witnesses. Knight's trial was severed because of his ill health.

In bringing in a conviction, the jury accepted the prosecution's contention that Kerner and Isaacs agreed to a lucrative stock offer which netted them over $400,000 for an investment of $70,000. The tax evasion charges stemmed from Kerner and Isaacs' declaration that their profits from the stock sales were long term capital gains when in fact the proceeds should have been taxed as ordinary income. The charge of perjury stemmed from testimony that Kerner gave to the grand jury that indicted him.

The trial judge was Robert L. Taylor, who was brought in from Tennessee's eastern district because of Kerner's friendships with judges in the Illinois area.

After his indictment, Kerner took a leave of absence from the bench with pay. He was appointed for life and could not be removed unless impeachment proceedings were brought.

Kerner and Isaacs were sentenced April 19 to three years in prison and were fined $50,000 each.

According to the indictments, Kerner and Isaacs bought $356,000 worth of race track stock for $70,158. In return, the indictments alleged, race track owners' were given favorable treatment in the assignment of dates for races. The grand jury said the stock transaction constituted a bribe.

Kerner was also charged with lying to a U.S. grand jury when he testified that he had never talked to members of the Illinois Racing Commission about setting racing dates. In addition, the grand jury charged that Kerner had made a false statement to the Internal Revenue Service (IRS) in 1967 when he insisted that an entry in his tax return was the name of a Chicago company and not a listing for Illinois racetrack stock. The indictment against him further charged that he failed to pay $147,000 in taxes in 1966 and lied to IRS agents about his ownership of race-track stock.

Chicago aldermen guilty. Alderman Thomas E. Keane, floor leader for Mayor Richard J. Daley in the Chicago City Council, was convicted by a U.S. district jury Oct. 9, 1974 of 18 counts of mail fraud and conspiracy. He was accused of secretly buying up tax delinquent properties on the city's South Side, influencing council decisions to obtain reductions in tax liens and then prodding city and other local government agencies into purchasing the land.

According to the indictment, Keane held land in secret trusts and later sold it to city and county agencies at a profit. Using his knowledge of pending city and county development projects, the indictment alleged, Keane shepherded measures through the City Council that enabled his real estate group to buy tax-delinquent properties at bargain rates.

Keane was sentenced Nov. 18 to five years in prison and was fined $27,000.

Keane had been acquitted Dec. 11, 1973 of state charges of official misconduct and conflict of interest.

Cook County Circuit Judge Daniel J. Ryan dismissed the charges against Keane and Alderman Edwin P. Fifielski after ruling that the prosecution had failed to prove its case.

Keane and Fifielski were accused of approving deposit of city funds in a bank in which they held substantial interest.

Alderman Paul T. Wigoda, another political ally of Daley, was convicted in federal court Oct. 10, 1974 of income-tax fraud. He had been charged with failure to report as income $50,000 he allegedly received as a bribe to obtain favorable council action on a rezoning request.

In another case involving a Daley political ally, Earl Bush, longtime press secretary to the mayor, was found guilty by a Chicago federal court jury Oct. 13 of 11 counts of mail fraud. The charges stemmed from Bush's failure to disclose ownership in a company that had exclusive contracts for display advertising in the Chicago airports.

The U.S. Supreme Court Dec. 8, 1975 upheld, by refusing to review, the conviction (under the federal law banning extortion in interstate commerce) of Alderman Frank J. Kuta, who had been found guilty of accepting $1,500 from a realtor in return for a favorable vote on a zoning change.

Oklahoma Cases

Ex-Gov. Hall guilty of bribery. A federal jury in Oklahoma City, Okla. March 14, 1975 found former Gov. David Hall (D, Okla.) guilty of four counts of bribery and extortion. At the same time, Texas financier W. W. Taylor was found guilty of three bribery charges. The former governor was sentenced April 25 to three years in prison on each of the four counts, to run concurrently. Taylor received 18 months on each of the three counts against him, also to run concurrently.

The government had contended, in an indictment handed up Jan. 16, three days after Hall left office as governor, that the men had conspired to bribe Secretary · of State John Rogers Jr., who was then chairman of the board that administered retirement funds for the state, to vote to invest $10 million in such funds in one of Taylor's companies, Guaranteed Investors Corp. (The investment was eventually approved by the board but the indictments were handed up before the money was turned over.)

In addition to the bribery charge, Hall was convicted of extorting $50,000 from Taylor and his associate, R. Kevin Mooney, to take part in the scheme. During the trial Mooney pleaded guilty to a single conspiracy charge and two other charges against him were dropped in return for his testimony as a Government witness. The trial, which began Feb. 24, included the presentation of taped conversations made with the conspirators by Rogers who acted as an undercover agent for the Federal Bureau of Investigation. Hall, who lost a reelection bid in the wake of a corruption scandal in 1974, had accused U.S. Attorney General William R. Burkett of prosecuting him for political reasons.

State treasurer cleared. Oklahoma State Treasurer Leo Winters, accused of four counts of mail fraud, was found not guilty in Oklahoma City federal court, it was reported May 19, 1975. Winters had been indicted May 31, 1973 on charges of de-positing state funds in various banks in return for political contributions. He had been acquitted in 1974 on extortion charges stemming from the same bribery indictment.

Other State & Local Cases

Alioto, 2 others cleared. San Francisco Mayor Joseph L. Alioto and two former Washington state officials were cleared March 26, 1972 by a county jury in Vancouver, Wash. of civil charges based on their splitting of $2.3 million in legal fees.

A jury of six men and six women decided in favor of Alioto, John J. O'Connell, a former Washington state attorney general, and George K. Faler, a former Washington state assistant attorney general, after deliberating $10\frac{1}{2}$ hours.

Washington State and 12 publicly owned utilities had sought to recover $2.3 million in legal fees paid to Alioto for antitrust work he did for them when he was a practicing attorney. The suit alleged that Alioto had improperly split the fee with O'Connell and Faler.

Federal District Judge Ray McNichols in Tacoma, Wash. announced June 19 a directed order of acquittal for the same three defendants on federal charges of bribery, conspiracy and mail fraud.

Massachusetts judge disbarred. Judge Edward J. DeSaulnier Jr., a judge of the Massachusetts Superior Court, was disbarred Jan. 11, 1972 by the state Supreme Judicial Court for his alleged implication in a plot to let a convicted stock swindler go free.

Another superior court judge who was implicated in the case, Vincent R. Brogna, was censured by the high court.

The state supreme court found that DeSaulnier was "unfit to continue either as a judge or as a member of the bar."

No criminal charges had been brought against the two judges because the six-year statute of limitations had expired.

DeSaulnier and Brogna had been named by Michael J. Raymond after he had become an informer for the Federal

Bureau of Investigation. Raymond had testified that he paid $35,000 to get a suspended sentence from Brogna in a 1962 stock fraud case. DeSaulnier was accused by Raymond of arranging the bribe.

Texas Speaker, other sentenced. A judge in Abilene sentenced Gus Mutscher, speaker of the Texas House, and two of his top aides to five-year suspended prison terms March 16, 1972 for their roles in a stock-fraud scheme.

Mutscher, State Rep. Tommy Shannon and Rush McGinty, a Mutscher aide, had been convicted March 15 of conspiracy to accept a bribe in the stock fraud case.

During the trial, Texas prosecutors and lawyers representing the Securities and Exchange Commission (SEC) charged that the defendants had accepted unsecured bank loans from a Houston financier, Frank Sharp, and used them to buy stock in Sharp's National Bankers Life Insurance Co. According to the prosecution, the defendants made large profits when that company's stock went up because of manipulation.

Sharp had pleaded guilty earlier to two federal felony charges in connection with the case. He was fined $5,000 and sentenced to three years' probation on the federal charges.

Arizona legislators lose posts. Two Republican members of the Arizona House of Representatives were stripped of their committee chairmanships Oct. 19, 1973 following disclosures that they had set up a private insurance company to take advantage of insurance legislation they had successfully co-sponsored.

House Speaker Stan Akers (R), who removed Reps. Ray Everett and Jay Stuckey from their posts, said he had sent information concerning possible criminal charges to the State Department of Public Safety and to the Maricopa County prosecutor's office.

East Chicago bank fined. William J. Riley, chairman of the First National Bank of East Chicago (Ind.), pleaded no contest May 8, 1974 to 10 counts of violating a 1948 law prohibiting campaign contributions from a national bank or any corporation organized by authority of Congress. Riley was fined $10,000 and the bank was fined an additional $15,000 on the same counts.

The donations totaling $14,200 were made from 1970-72 to Gov. Otis R. Bowen (R), a former governor, Sen. Vance Hartke (D) and Rep. Ray Madden (D), all of Indiana.

3M guilty in Minnesota. Minnesota Mining & Manufacturing Co. pleaded guilty Jan. 22, 1975 to five counts of making illegal campaign contributions in 1972 to candidates for state and local elections in Minnesota. The firm was fined $5,000 for violating the state election law, which barred the use of corporate funds as campaign contributions.

Irwin Hansen, a 3M director who had resigned recently as the firm's chief financial officer, also pleaded guilty to three counts of aiding and abetting the illegal contributions and was fined $3,000.

3M and its president, Harry Heltzer, had pleaded guilty in 1973 to illegally donating $36,000 to the Nixon re-election campaign and $1,000 each to Humphrey and Rep. Wilbur Mills (D, Ark.), both contenders for the 1972 Democratic presidential nomination.

In a disclosure to the Securities and Exchange Commission Dec. 31, 1974, 3M had admitted using bogus bookkeeping procedures to maintain a $634,000 secret political fund. Only $167,000 remained in the fund, officials said.

The disclosures came in response to a shareholder's suit, filed after 3M and Heltzer pleaded guilty to the initial campaign violation. In a settlement of that suit, announced Jan. 1, five former and current 3M officials agreed to reimburse the company for $475,000.

William L. McKnight, who was chairman from 1949 to 1966 during the period when the slush fund was established, agreed to pay $300,000; Heltzer and Cross would pay $70,000 each; Hansen, $34,000 and William M. Bennett, director of civic affairs, $1,000.

3M, Heltzer, Cross and Hansen consented to a federal court order against further violations of securities laws in connection with illegal political contributions, it was reported Feb. 3. The SEC had filed civil charges against the firm Jan. 30, charging that about $489,000 in corporate funds was given to political candidates from a secret 3M slush fund.

Under the settlement, 3M agreed to name a special master to investigate disbursements from the secret fund and the three officials agreed to reimburse at least $425,000 to the company.

Albuquerque bank pleads guilty. First National Bank of Albuquerque, N.M. pleaded guilty March 21, 1975 to making illegal campaign contributions of $8,000 during 1972. The bank, which had faced maximum penalties of $25,000 in fines, was fined $15,000. The five-count criminal information was filed that day by the Justice Department with U.S. District Court in Albuquerque.

According to the government, the bank donated $3,000 to the Congressional election campaign of Rep. Manuel Lujan Jr. (R); $2,000 to the unsuccessful U.S. Senate campaign of Democrat Jack Daniels; $1,000 to the Nixon re-election campaign; $1,000 to Democrat Jesse D. Kornegay's unsuccessful U.S. Senate primary race; and $1,000 to the unsuccessful U.S. Senate primary campaign of Roberto A. Mondragon, a Democrat.

David G. Livingston, former chairman of the Albuquerque bank, pleaded guilty April 7 to charges that he had concealed about $35,000 in illegal contributions made to 15 politicians between 1970 and 1972 by maintaining a "special travel expense account." Two other bank officials also were named unindicted co-conspirators in connection with the slush fund.

Alabama PSC official guilty of bribery. Kenneth J. Hammond, president of the Alabama Public Service Commission, was convicted in Montgomery, Ala. on a charge of soliciting a bribe to get vending machines placed in telephone company service buildings (reported Dec. 13, 1975). Hammond was sentenced to three years in prison and removed from office as required by state law.

Christopher Whatley, a former staff member of the commission, was im-

mediately appointed by Gov. George C. Wallace as Hammond's successor.

Hammond's conviction was largely based on the testimonies of Rex Moore, an Alabama businessman, and Charles Price, a vice president of the South Central Bell Co.

Hammond, according to Moore, had helped arrange for Moore's company to get its vending machines into the telephone company's properties through the efforts of Price. Price said that he agreed to intercede because he thought that if he did not do so Hammond would vote against a pending increase for the telephone company. (An increase, lower than that requested, was subsequently approved by the commission.)

Testimony further revealed that Moore went to Alabama Attorney General William J. Baxley following a demand by Hammond for $10,000, which Moore said he could not afford.

The attorney general's office arranged to record Moore's conversation with Hammond at which the payoff was discussed.

Moore and Price were not indicted and the attorney general indicated that they were granted immunity in return for their testimony as state witnesses.

Pennsylvania cases. The Pennsylvania state treasurer of the Democratic Party, William Casper, was sentenced Oct. 24, 1975 to one to two years in prison and fined $11,500 on state charges of extortion and conspiracy.

Casper, who was also the Butler County Democratic chairman and chief fund raiser for the 1974 reelection campaign of Gov. Milton Shapp (D, Pa.), was found guilty in March of coercing Pennsylvania Department of Transportation employes and contractors who leased equipment to the department into making political contributions.

The U.S. Supreme Court Dec. 8, 1975 upheld, by refusing to review, the federal extortion conviction of former Pennsylvania State Sen. Frank Mazzei. Mazzei said that his acceptance of payments in connection with the awarding of leases was not extortion because he was not in an official position to affect the awards.

Tennessee firm guilty. The Builders Transportation Corp. of Memphis, Tenn. entered a guilty plea Dec. 4, 1975 to federal charges of making illegal contributions to Gov. Ray Blanton's (D, Tenn.) 1972 unsuccessful Senate campaign. The firm was placed on one year's probation.

Politics cost bank $232,300. Politically-related transactions involving bond deals and trust funds cost Missouri's largest bank, Mercantile Trust Co., $232,300 from 1964 through 1970, according to the report of a special review commission Feb. 27, 1976.

The audit committee was established by the board of Mercantile Bancorp Inc., a holding company created in 1971 with Mercantile Trust as its lead bank, to investigate charges of improper political activity.

A federal grand jury in Kansas City was investigating possible wrongdoing by the administration of former Missouri Gov. Warren E. Hearnes (D). Attention was focused on the bank's dealings with the late J. V. Conran, a Democratic boss of southeastern Missouri and political ally of Hearnes.

Donald E. Lasater, chairman and chief executive officer of both the holding company and the bank, was indicted in 1975 on four counts of perjury before the grand jury. He was acquitted.

The audit committee concluded that Lasater "acted in the best interest of the company at all times," but determined that the late Kenton R. Cravens, former chairman of the bank, had initiated the bond deals with Conran and set up a private political trust fund that cost the bank money.

Bailey cleared in Connecticut. A report made public Jan. 17, 1976 cleared the late John M. Bailey of accepting a $250,000 influence-peddling fee in Connecticut's jai alai scandal.

The report was released in Hartford by Superior Court Judge Harold M. Mulvey, who sat as a special one-man grand jury investigating the charges. Mulvey made no recommendation for criminal prosecution but he criticized many figures in the scandal, which involved allegations of corruption, fraud, tax evasion and organized-crime influence.

The scandal broke in the fall of 1975 when David Friend, who headed a company that had built a jai alai fronton in Bridgeport, allegedly approached state police investigators in Florida and told them that he had "bought" Bailey, the former state and national Democratic Party chairman.

After hearing secret grand jury testimony on the charges, Mulvey found that "there is no evidence approaching even a minimal standard of credibility that John Bailey ever received any money or any valuable thing whatsoever from David Friend or from anyone else on his behalf."

Also cleared of any wrongdoing were nine members of the State Gaming Commission, four state legislators who met with Bailey to discuss the fronton, and J. Brian Gaffney, the former Republican state chairman.

Those criticized by Mulvey included John L. Sullivan, the 77-year-old former state tax commissioner, who testified at public hearings that he had accepted $7,000 in return for introducing Friend to Bailey. Mulvey urged all state officials to avoid dealing with Sullivan.

Paul Manafort, a former state public works commissioner, also came under attack in the Mulvey report. Manafort, whose family demolition company was contracted to clear the fronton's building site, had arranged a meeting between fronton officials and officials of the State Department of Environmental Protection that resulted in a waiver of a state air-pollution permit requirement, which Mulvey said had been fraudulently obtained.

Hinshaw convicted. Rep. Andrew J. Hinshaw (R, Calif.) was found guilty Jan. 26, 1976 on two counts of taking bribes while serving as the assessor for Orange County, Calif. The bribes—a payment of $1,000 and stereo equipment—were received from Tandy Corp. in 1972. He was acquitted of a charge of soliciting a bribe from a lawyer of another corporation.

Hinshaw was sentenced Feb. 24 to serve one to four years in prison.

The U.S. House of Representatives Oct. 1 killed a move to expel Hinshaw.

The ouster bid, which was tabled by voice vote, had been brought before the full House by Rep. Charles E. Wiggins (R, Calif.) after the House Committee on Standards of Official Conduct had rejected it, 10–2, on Sept. 2.

Defense Inquiries

Officials censured for accepting corporation hospitality. Defense Secretary Donald Rumsfeld March 16, 1976 reprimanded the department's chief of research and engineering, Malcolm R. Currie, and admonished Navy Secretary J. William Middendorf 2nd for visiting fishing and hunting lodges operated by Rockwell International Corp., a major defense contractor.

Currie, the 4th ranking official at the Pentagon, also was ordered to forfeit about four weeks pay, totaling $3,200, and reimburse Rockwell for all expenses incurred during a two-day stay at a fishing lodge on Bimini Island in the Bahamas.

The Pentagon said Currie, his daughter and an unidentified friend spent the 1975 Labor Day weekend at the lodge with Rockwell chairman Robert B. Anderson, his wife and two daughters. According to the Pentagon, "at no time was any official or corporate business or either the department or Rockwell discussed." Anderson was said to be a long-time personal and business friend.

Middendorf received a "letter of admonition" from Rumsfeld, a less serious form of reproof than Currie received. Middendorf was admonished for accepting an invitation from Ardeshir Zahedi, the Iranian ambassador to Washington, to spend a day at a hunting lodge in Maryland. According to the Pentagon, Middendorf was unaware until recently that Rockwell leased the lodge.

Rockwell was the principal contractor for the Air Force's new B-1 bomber. Because it was still in the development stage, the project was within Currie's purview as director of research. Currie had been expected to participate in the Pentagon's decision later in 1976 whether to put the plane into production.

The Currie-Middendorf case was embarrassing to the Pentagon because Deputy Defense Secretary William P. Clements Jr. had declared in October 1975 that the department's civilian and military employes "must be above reproach" and "avoid even the appearance of a conflict of interest" by not accepting hospitality, gratuities, or favors from defense contractors. (Middendorf's visit to the Maryland lodge reportedly occurred the same day Clements issued a "standards of conduct" memo to service secretaries.)

At a news conference in February, Rumsfeld reiterated Clements' warning and said he would "land all over individuals" who violated the department's rules. Rumsfeld reportedly considered firing Currie to emphasize the department's displeasure over the incident.

Rockwell March 17 informed Sen. William Proxmire (D, Wis.), a critic of the Pentagon's close ties to contractors, that the chairman of the Joint Chiefs of Staff and director of the Defense Intelligence Agency were among 41 military and civilian employes of the Pentagon who had been guests of the company at its Maryland hunting lodge between 1973 and 1975.

Named were Adm. Thomas H. Moorer, who retired as chairman in June 1974, and Vice Adm. Vincent de Poix, former director of the DIA.

Rockwell's list of 39 Pentagon guests was in addition to another list that Proxmire provided the department Feb. 3 after Clements contended the Pentagon had been unable to determine who had been entertained at the Rockwell lodge. Proxmire's list, culled from hunting licenses and other records, named 55 high-ranking Pentagon employes.

Northrop case—The Defense Department Nov. 11, 1975 had sent letters of reprimand to 22 employes who had visited a Maryland hunting lodge as guests of the Northrop Corp. The 22 military personnel were among a group of 170, which included members of Congress, who had used a goose-hunting lodge provided by the defense contractor.

A Pentagon spokesman said the 22 government employes also had been reprimanded privately for their "severe error of judgment in conflict with the existing rules of the department."

The Pentagon notified Sen. William Proxmire that it had taken formal action against Pentagon personnel.

Proxmire had sharply criticized an earlier finding by the Pentagon's acting general counsel that more than 40 high-ranking military officers and civilians who had accepted Northrop's hospitality between October 1971 and January 1974 "weren't necessarily in technical violation" of the Pentagon's rules barring officials from accepting any gift, gratuity, entertainment or favor from government contractors.

Most were personal friends of Northrop employes and accepted the invitation "on a social basis," the counsel said in a letter Oct. 3 to three congressional committees.

Proxmire termed the finding an "obvious whitewash" and an "absurdity."

With congressional criticism mounting, James R. Schlesinger, then defense secretary, Oct. 6 ordered a "broad inquiry" into the gratuity issue.

Newsday reported Nov. 1 that Schlesinger had reversed the counsel's ruling and formally reprimanded a top aide, Erich F. von Marbod, for violating the "spirit" of the department's code-of-conduct rules. Newsday also reported that von Marbod had been reassigned recently to Iran as the Pentagon's representative for arms sales made there by U.S. firms, including Northrop.

The Pentagon announced Nov. 25 that it had tightened its policy against acceptance of gratuities offered by defense contractors, and had expanded the number of military officers required to submit financial statements.

According to Proxmire's investigative subcommittee Oct. 22, Northrop was not the only defense contractor that had entertained Pentagon officials at hunting lodges. Lockheed Aircraft Corp., Rockwell International, Raytheon Co. and Martin Marietta Corp. also were cited. General Dynamics Corp. was added to the list Oct. 24.

Proxmire charged Oct. 18 that Rockwell also had entertained employes of the National Aeronautics and Space Administration. The company held a $6.4 billion NASA contract to develop a space shuttle.

Meat-purchasing abuses. A Senate subcommittee heard testimony May 10, 1976 that two New England companies had charged the Defense Department top prices for inferior cuts of beef, using payoffs, gifts and prostitutes to persuade Army meat inspectors to go along with the fraud. One witness testified that in some cases knuckle meat (priced at $1.85 a lb.) had been substituted for sirloin ($3.85 a lb.) that was specified in government contracts.

The Senate Government Operations Committee's subcommittee on federal spending practices, efficiencies and open government had conducted a nine-month investigation of military meat-purchasing. The companies that came under fire at the hearings were the G & G Packing Co. of Roxbury, Mass. and the Blue Ribbon Frozen Food Corp. of Hamden, Conn. The companies—both co-owned by Harry Goldberg and David Goldberg (not related)—went out of business in July 1975.

In the year that ended June 30, 1975, the two companies together had sold the Pentagon 15.3 million pounds of beef for $21.9 million. (The Pentagon had been spending about $110 million annually on domestic beef.)

Edward Kehl, the witness who told of the substitution of knuckle meat for sirloin, was a former employee of G & G Packing Co. He said the company had made up to $960,000 a week in illegal profits. Manuel Pacheco, a civilian inspector, testified May 10 that he had received between $100 and $200 a week from Harry Goldberg to "refrain from hassling the employes." Pacheco admitted, in response to a question, that he had known about the inferior meat being substituted for expensive cuts. Two army meat inspectors—one no longer connected with the service—also testified May 10. Charles Reidinger, a former sergeant, said he had received payments and the free services of prostitutes. Sp. 4 Nadja Hoyer-Boots admitted that she had received free clothes, plane tickets and weekend trips from G & G officials while she was assigned to their plant.

Sen. Lawton Chiles (D, Fla.), the subcommittee chairman cited two factors May 7 that he said contributed to the "breakdown" in military beef procurement. One, he said, was the rigid and burdensome contract specifications that the Pentagon imposed on beef items. Since most meat packers would not go to the trouble of trying to meet the specifications, the standards, in effect, stifled competition, Chiles said.

(Chiles noted a Pentagon requirement that steaks be nearly identical in size. He said that this forced manufacturers to process the steaks through special machines. "The housewife," Chiles said, had "a much better chance of getting her money's worth at any store.")

The other factor Chiles cited was what he called the Army's laxness about selecting and training personnel to inspect meat. The subcommittee, Chiles said, "found that young kids recruited into the system were inadequately trained, unsupervised, and encouraged to steal meat." Chiles added that "the kids also quickly learned to accept gratuities from the meat vendors they were supposed to be monitoring."

A Justice Department spokesman, quoted in the May 8 Washington Post, said that the department was looking into "numerous allegations involving the meat industry" in New England and elsewhere. A federal grand jury in New Haven, Conn. was also looking into the charges made by the subcommittee.

Lawyers for the Goldbergs charged May 12 that the subcommittee's public reports on its investigations had smeared the reputations of their clients and violated their rights to a fair trial.

Overseas Bribery & Corruption

Extensive Corruption

Congressional and Securities & Exchange Commission investigations during 1975–76 disclosed an extensive and long-standing pattern of bribery and political corruption by American companies doing business abroad.

Ford orders probe of overseas practices. Reacting to mounting disclosures of bribes and questionable payments made abroad by U.S. businesses, President Ford Feb. 10, 1976 ordered a high-level investigation of the overseas practices of U.S. corporations.

In announcing the President's decision, Ron Nessen, White House press secretary, said that although the format of the inquiry had not been decided, Ford was "leaning toward" a cabinet-level study of the bribery issue.

Nessen said Ford "condemns in the strongest terms" any illegal activities practiced by U.S. businesses. "Any American company or individual making unlawful payments to officials or foreign governments will not receive protection from the State Department against legitimate law enforcement actions by either responsible officials in foreign countries or responsible officials in the U.S.," Nessen said.

Nessen claimed this view reflected a State Department policy adopted in May 1975. However, in court papers filed in December 1975 in connection with efforts to force the disclosure of identities of those who had accepted Lockheed payoffs, Secretary of State Henry Kissinger said the publicity could "cause damage to the foreign policy of the U.S."

In a related development, Treasury Secretary William E. Simon Feb. 10 directed the Internal Revenue Service to "intensify and broaden" its ongoing investigation of U.S. companies that violated federal tax laws by writing off bribes and other illegal payments as legitimate business expenses.

Two actions would be taken to comply with Simon's order, IRS officials said. IRS agents would be instructed to interview all corporate officers when conducting the agency's annual audit of corporate books and the IRS international operations office would be brought in to all corporate suit procedures.

Sen. Church on situation. Sen. Frank Church (D, Ida.) told the Senate May 5, 1976 that "over the past year, the [Senate] Subcommittee on Multinational Corporations has held extensive hearings on the subject of political contributions and agents' fees, questionable payments and outright bribes paid by U.S.-based corporations to persons in other countries. The results of our investigations, unfortunately, have been very fruitful."

Church continued: "Lockheed Aircraft Corp. alone spent hundreds of millions of dollars attempting to sell planes around the world. Bribes were paid high government officials in Italy and in the Netherlands; over a hundred million dollars were spent in the Middle East on agents who may very well have passed the money on to those in influential positions. In Japan millions were paid to the prime supporter of the ultra-rightwing militarists in Japanese political life. Obviously, we are not talking about a little 'grease' to some petty clerk to speed documents through a bureaucracy. Further, as we all know, the Lockheed affair has been indicative of the behavior of many other U.S.-based corporations. The Multinational Subcommittee alone held hearings on overseas payments by such companies as Northrop, Exxon, Gulf, and Mobil. The Senate Banking Committee has also produced days of testimony in this area. Scores of corporations have voluntarily disclosed such payments to the Securities and Exchange Commission; others have done so under duress of court order. The record is replete with examples of these practices."

Church denied that bribery "is . . . just a way of doing business abroad. In fact, James Akins, previously ambassador to Saudi Arabia, stated in sworn testimony before the Multinational Subcommittee that bribery was unnecessary, and in fact, detrimental to good business relations in Saudi Arabia." Church warned that corrupt business "practices have extremely serious consequences both for the conduct of U.S. foreign policy and the reception U.S. business receives abroad."

Church also said:

"U.S.-based corporations should not be allowed to weaken a friendly government through bribery and corruption while the United States is relying on that government as a stable sure friend supporting our policies. U.S.-based corporations should not be supporting political factions antithetical to those supported by the U.S. government. Nor do we want, as was revealed in Multinational Subcommittee hearings, the defense priorities of our allies distorted by corporate bribery. Further, when these payments become known, and they will and do, whether it be through revelations by Senate subcommittees or through the common

knowledge that leads to revolution and the downfall of such governments as the Idris regime in Libya, the repercussions are often international and the foreign policy implications for the United States severe. Payments by Lockheed alone may very well advance the Communists in Italy. In Japan, a mainstay of our foreign policy in the Far East, the government is reeling as a consequence of payments by Lockheed. Inquiries have begun in many other countries. The Communist bloc chortles with glee at the sight of corrupt capitalism. . . .

"This is not to say that only the corporations are at fault. For every giver there is a taker. And often the initiative comes from the foreign government official. Indeed, in some cases, this initiative amounts to extortion. But too often the corporate response has been passive acquiescence, a shrug of the shoulders, passing the added cost on to the consumer. Moreover, our government has initiated no real concern with this problem. Rather, aside from some statements of a cosmetic nature, it prefers to stick its head in the sand and hear no evil, see no evil, and pretend there is no problem. But there is a problem, a problem of cancerous dimensions which is eating away at the vitals of democratic society. . . ."

Proxmire on corruption's effects. Sen. William Proxmire (D, Wis.) also was concerned with the effects of overseas bribery. He told the Senate Sept. 14, 1976:

". . .There have been bribes paid by large American companies that have embarrassed foreign countries, that have resulted in great danger to governments in foreign countries, the danger that they may fall, and it has been a source of embarrassment and humiliation to many Americans who believe so strongly in our free enterprise system.

". . .There is a broad consensus that the payment of bribes to influence business decisions corrodes the free enterprise system. Bribery short circuits the marketplace. Where bribes are paid, business is directed not to the most efficient producer but to the most corrupt. This misallocates resources and reduces economic efficiency. . . .

"More importantly, bribery is simply unethical. It is counter to the moral expectations and values of the American public. It erodes public confidence in the integrity of the free market system. Bribery of foreign officials by some U.S. companies casts a shadow on all U.S. companies. It makes it harder for any American company to sell abroad when some of our most prominent and successful companies have engaged in that kind of activity.

"It puts pressure on ethical enterprises to lower their standards and match corrupt payments, or risk losing business.

"When bribery is exposed, it usually leads to sanctions both by the host government and the marketplace, against the offending company. The results have included cancellation of contracts, expropriations fines, lawsuits, and a loss of confidence in the company by investors.

"Bribery of foreign officials by U.S. corporations also creates severe foreign policy problems. The revelations of improper payments invariably tends to embarrass friendly regimes and lowers the esteem for the United States among the foreign public. It lends credence to the worse suspicions sown by extreme nationalists or Marxists that American businesses operating in their country have a corrupting influence on their political systems. It increases the likelihood that when an angry citizenry demands reform, the target will be not only the corrupt local officials, but also the United States and U.S.-owned business.

"Bribery by U.S. companies also undermines the foreign policy objective of the United States to promote democratically accountable governments and professionalized civil services in developing countries.

The Lockheed Case

Lockheed admits payoff. After months of denials, the Lockheed Aircraft Corp. admitted Aug. 1, 1975 that since 1970 it had paid at least $22 million to "foreign officials and foreign political organizations" to win lucrative aerospace contracts.

Lockheed defended its payoff practice, saying the payments "were necessary in consummating certain foreign sales."

"The company also believes that such payments are consistent with practices engaged in by numerous other companies abroad, including many of its competitors, and are in keeping with business practices in many foreign countries," Lockheed said in its statement disclosing the payoffs. Officials also admitted the payments were made with the full knowledge and consent of its management. (No corporate political payments were made in the U.S., spokesmen added.)

The $22 million paid to officials abroad represented 15% of the $147 million in "commissions and other payments to consultants and others" over the five-year period in connection with foreign sales, the company stated. Another $55 million had been committed under existing consulting agreements, Lockheed added.

Officials also admitted that the company paid $290,000 in commissions and other payments out of a secret $750,000 fund that was "maintained outside the normal channels of financial responsibility." Use of the fund had been discontinued and the balance transferred to a bank checking account, according to the statement.

Lockheed refused to publicize details about its foreign payments, contending disclosure would have a "material adverse impact" on its future operations. The admission about foreign payoffs was contained in Lockheed's quarterly earnings report.

Lockheed's admission about its foreign payments elicited strong responses from the Securities and Exchange Commission, a Senate committee and subcommittee, and spokesmen for the Ford Administration.

An SEC investigation into charges that Lockheed paid bribes to foreign officials had been underway since the Northrop Corp., another major defense contractor that had admitted paying bribes abroad, accused its competitors for foreign aerospace contracts of engaging in the same practices. Northrop also said that one of its groups set up to secretly channel the bribes to foreign leaders, the Economic and Development Corp., had been patterned after a Lockheed payoff program.

The SEC had not yet filed a formal complaint against Lockheed, charging the firm with violating financial reporting laws, but Lockheed conceded Aug. 1 that negotiations were being held to devise a consent agreement that would settle the expected charges.

The SEC, which earlier had forced Ashland Oil Inc. to make a public disclosure to its investors about payments to U.S. and foreign politicians, was seeking a similar disclosure from Lockheed.

Lockheed initially resisted the SEC demand for disclosure, but after pressure mounted from other groups within the government, agreed to cease making its foreign payoffs and accept SEC guidelines on the issue.

Lockheed contended that publication of a list of its recipients would effectively force an end to the practice, which officials insisted was necessary to win contracts. The "future refusal or inability of Lockheed to conform to local competitive business practices could seriously prejudice the company's ability to compete effectively in certain foreign markets," the company said.

Commenting on this statement, an SEC official told the Wall Street Journal Aug. 6, "We haven't run into the argument before that disclosures of this nature are going to wipe the company out."

According to the Journal Aug. 4, Lockheed remained in "precarious" financial health after its near collapse in 1971, despite having won $195 million in U.S. government-backed loan guarantees.

Lockheed's Senate and Administration critics focused on the possible relationship between the government's assistance to the aerospace firm—aid which remained a controversial subject—and foreign payoffs.

Noting continuing government aid for Lockheed, Sen. Frank Church (D, Ida.), chairman of the multinationals subcommittee, asked "whether the taxpayers were putting up the money for Lockheed to buy the orders it needed to survive." Church Aug. 1 attacked the payoffs, calling them "bribes," and said his subcommittee was preparing to hold hearings on the issue.

In hearings held Aug. 25 by the Senate Banking Committee, Treasury Secretary William E. Simon strongly condemned Lockheed's payoff practices, saying the "bribes" were "deplorable."

"We are disturbed," Simon told the committee, "that Lockheed's apparent long-standing practice of resorting to bribery to sell its products in foreign markets has escaped detection by the [Emergency Loan Guarantee] Board and others monitoring the company's activities."

(Simon was chairman of the board, which was established in 1971 to oversee the loan-guarantee program. Other members were Federal Reserve Chairman Arthur C. Burns and SEC Chairman Ray Garrett Jr.)

"We are distressed," Simon added, "that Lockheed's management has apparently not been forthright with the board and with Congress."

The board "does not, and will not, condone illegal or unethical activities by American business, here or abroad," Simon said. "Practices such as bribes made to secure foreign business can only increase the distrust and suspicion that is straining our national institutions," he said.

Shortly after Simon testified, a spokesman for the loan guarantee board said it would "require that Lockheed not make any future improper payments, directly or indirectly, to foreign governmental officials, or political organizations, including any such payments presently committed." If Lockheed failed to comply with the ruling, he added, it risked losing the government loan-guarantees.

Simon told the banking committee that Lockheed officials had assured him that, in connection with promoting foreign sales, "all payments including commissions, have ceased right now." Lockheed's board would meet in September to adopt a policy prohibiting future bribes and would resume payment of legitimate commissions after that date, Simon added.

Lockheed Chairman Daniel J. Haughton also testified Aug. 25. He refused to characterize the foreign payments as bribes, saying his lawyer "preferred to refer to it as a kickback." Lockheed was represented by the New York law firm Rogers & Wells, whose senior partner was former Secretary of State William P. Rogers.

Haughton claimed that the federally-backed bank loans had not been used to make foreign payoffs. He said the money had come from advances from sales received by the company. Haughton told the committee Lockheed would comply with any new law or SEC guideline governing foreign payments.

Sen. William Proxmire (D, Wis.), a long-time critic of the government's rescue of Lockheed, was chairman of the banking committee. In response to a query from Proxmire, Treasury Undersecretary Edward C. Schmults said Aug. 25 that Lockheed admitted "certain" payoffs had been used to promote foreign sales of the L-1011 Tri-Star jetliner. Cost overruns incurred in developing the giant jet had been a chief cause of Lockheed's near collapse; government aid was voted to allow Lockheed to build and sell the planes.

Payoffs in Mideast & Asia. Lockheed Chairman Haughton told the Senate Subcommittee on Multinational Corporations Sept. 12, 1975 that Lockheed had paid or promised commissions totaling $106 million to Saudi Arabian businessman and arms broker Adnan M. Khashoggi.

A portion of the money was intended for use as bribes for officials of the Saudi government, Haughton testified. He added that Lockheed also had paid bribes directly to Saudi officials and to Indonesian military officers.

These payoffs were deposited in number bank accounts in Liechtenstein and Geneva, Haughton said.

Through a spokesman, Khashoggi expressed "surprise" at Haughton's testimony, which he said was based on "misunderstanding, confusion and hearsay."

Haughton testified that Khashoggi had told him the bribes were necessary to win arms contracts from the Saudi government. Haughton also said that government officials had made this same point to other Lockheed representatives in Paris and Geneva.

Haughton told the subcommittee that the commissions and bribes had had no adverse financial impact on the company because the payments were included in the purchase price established in contracts with foreign governments.

Haughton said he was not condemning or condoning Lockheed's action. "We only say that the practice exists and that in many countries it appeared, as a matter

of business judgment, necessary in order to compete against both U.S. and foreign competitors."

When asked for evidence that foreign arms makers also paid bribes to secure contracts, Haughton could only cite a London newspaper article and business "gossip." This response provoked an outburst from Sen. Joseph Biden (D, Del.), who told Haughton his answers were "phony."

When Lockheed first revealed the extent of its bribes and other foreign payments, corporate officials had strongly defended the practice and said competitive considerations required that the secret payments be continued.

However, Lockheed reversed its stand Sept. 9 and said overseas payments would not be made unless they were legal under all applicable U.S. and foreign regulations. The only payments deemed permissible under the new policy, Lockheed said, would be business expenses deductible from federal income taxes.

(According to the Wall Street Journal Sept. 10, it was a violation of the Internal Revenue Service code to deduct concealed bribes as business expenses, even if paid through a third party and made in a nation where such payments were not illegal. It was a violation of federal securities laws for companies to fail to report that certain "expenses" actually were bribes.)

Lockheed said the "new policy is subject to future revisions to reflect evolving national policy and laws." Four government investigations currently were underway into Lockheed's foreign payments. Probing the payoff issue were the IRS, the SEC, the Senate subcommittee, and the Emergency Loan Guarantee Board, a group which administered the federal loan guarantee program voted in 1971 to save Lockheed from bankruptcy.

The board had threatened to withdraw government backing for the loans unless Lockheed altered its stand on foreign payoffs.

The subcommittee Sept. 11 released more than 200 pages of previously secret Lockheed documents that showed the company had paid millions of dollars to officials and/or military officers in four foreign countries: Saudi Arabia, Indonesia, Iran, and the Philippines.

Highlights of the documents:

Saudi Arabia—Lockheed deliberately violated a 1969 Saudi government decree that required foreign contractors to declare they would not pay agents' fees in making government sales. A memo showed that the government intended to sign the contracts with the required assurances, "but with the full intention of paying our representative his usual fee."

Lockheed agreed to pay Khashoggi commissions of 12% of the selling price of the L-1011 commercial jet, plus 5% for spare parts and materials costs, and 5% for training and logistics support needed for the L-1011.

The documents also showed Lockheed officials knew the payments funneled through Khashoggi were for the express purpose of making "so-called 'under-the-table' compensation to Saudi officials in order to get the contract signed." Payments were made out of Lockheed's "market contingency fund," according to the documents.

In one memo, a Lockheed sales representative cabled his superior in Paris when contract negotiations were slowing down: "Strongly suspect machinery stall for lack of grease."

Iran—In memos written early in 1975, Lockheed officials expressed concern about the Iranian government's new policy forbidding U.S. firms to deal through agents. A literal interpretation of the decree suggested that any company employing an Iranian agent "runs a considerable risk of being barred from doing business in Iran," a Lockheed official wrote.

Soon thereafter, Lockheed's agent met in Teheran with officials of the Iranian government and the U.S. embassy and negotiated a "new interpretation" of the government ruling that would permit the continuation of Lockheed's payments to agents.

Indonesia—Following the Indonesian coup in 1965 when President Sukarno was deposed, Lockheed officials worried about the status of their agent there because he had been close to the ousted Sukarno.

Company officials asked the U.S. embassy in Jakarta to evaluate the agent's relationship with the new government, headed by Gen. Suharto. According to the documents, "embassy CIA personnel"

checked out the matter and reported that the agent "was definitely well connected with the Suharto regime."

Documents showed that bribes paid in Indonesia could have reached as high as Sukarno and Suharto.

Bribes paid to Indonesian military officers caused concern to Lockheed officials for two reasons. The first worry was that disclosure of the bribes "could be damaging to Lockheed's name and reputation," a company officials wrote in May 1971.

The second consideration involved a U.S. tax angle. Bribes, unlike commissions, could not be written off as legitimate tax deductions and thus were costly to the company, officials noted. However, they added, if Lockheed refused to pay the bribes, the company could lose $300,000 in annual sales of spare parts and a $40 million contract for the sale of eight planes.

The memos show that Lockheed officials tried to convince the military officers of the need for making the bribes through agents because of the "significant protection provided for them as well as for us."

Philippines—Lockheed made payoffs to government officials, army officers, and journalists. "As you know, moving around in the local circles for this kind of objective [sales of planes] involves financial requirements," Lockheed's agent wrote in one memo.

Prince Bernhard & German leaders allegedly were paid. According to charges made public late in 1975, Prince Bernhard of Holland and other prominent figures abroad took money to aid Lockheed.

The Senate's multinationals subcommittee was investigating charges that "regular payoffs" were made to high officials in the Netherlands and West Germany to promote the sale of Lockheed's F-104 jet fighter in the early 1960s, the Wall Street Journal reported Dec. 4.

The allegations were raised by former Lockheed employe Ernest F. Hauser, a sales representative in the company's Koblenz, West Germany office from 1961–1964. Hauser charged that secret payments were made to Prince Bernhard, husband of Queen Juliana of the Netherlands; to the Christian Social Union, a West Germany political party headed by Franz Josef Straus, and to Col. Guenther Rall, formerly of the West German air force.

According to Hauser, Prince Bernhard was bribed to increase Lockheed's revenues on the F-104, particularly by winning government approval for Lockheed to make costly engineering changes on planes already purchased by the Netherlands. Bernhard, who then had been and was still inspector general of the Dutch armed forces, said through a spokesman he had never received Lockheed payoffs.

Hauser claimed that payoffs were made for the same reason to the Christian Social Union. At the time of the alleged bribe, Strauss was both head of the party and defense minister, a post he no longer held. Strauss told reporters he had "no knowledge" of such payments. A spokesman for the party denied it had received Lockheed bribes.

Hauser said that he personally delivered cash to Rall, who at the time was head of the F-104 planning staff for the West German air force. Rall denied the charges. According to the Journal Dec. 4, Rall was forced to resign in September 1974 as West Germany's military representative to NATO and quit the air force after it was revealed he had accepted gratuities. Lockheed was not involved in that incident, the Journal reported.

Lockheed ordered to produce papers. U.S. District Court Judge John H. Pratt Dec. 15, 1975 ordered Lockheed Aircraft Corp. to comply with a Securities and Exchange Commission subpoena for documents on secret payments made abroad in connection with arms sales to foreign governments.

Lockheed had resisted honoring the SEC subpoena, issued in June, contending that disclosure of the names of recipients of the secret payments could jeopardize its lucrative weapons contracts with foreign governments and cause diplomatic problems for the U.S.

Lockheed's concern over public disclosure was shared by Secretary of State Henry A. Kissinger, who told the court Dec. 11 that "premature disclosure to third parties of certain of the names and

nationalities of foreign officials at this preliminary stage [of the SEC's investigation] . . . would cause damage to United States foreign relations."

Kissinger's views were made known in a "suggestion of interest" statement given to Attorney General Edward H. Levi. The legally unusual document was relayed to the court by the Justice Department.

In filing the suggestion, Kissinger acceded to a request by Lockheed's lawyers, who included William P. Rogers, Kissinger's predecessor as secretary of state. Lockheed chairman Daniel J. Haughton had testified earlier before the Senate Subcommittee on Multinational Corporations, which was also investigating corporate payoffs abroad, that Rogers had discussed Lockheed's case with State Department officials. Haughton did not name the officials.

Based on Kissinger's assertion, the Justice Department asked the court to retain jurisdiction over the Lockheed documents, a step which lawyers for the company believed would protect the information from disclosure under the Freedom of Information Act.

In his ruling Dec. 15, Judge Pratt denied this request and gave the SEC custody of the documents. However, he accepted another Kissinger proposal, also supported by the Justice Department, that agencies of the U.S. government give 10 days notice of their intent to release the material to interested parties petitioning under the information act, thereby giving Lockheed the opportunity to challenge the release in court. Pratt's order marked the first court decision supporting the SEC's right to obtain corporate documents on secret foreign payoffs.

However, Pratt significantly modified that ruling Dec. 18. His amended order gave the court custody of the documents and authority to rule on the release of the material to third parties, such as Congressional committees, journalists or historians.

Judge Pratt had stated earlier that the SEC had the right to obtain the documents, but he also expressed sympathy for Lockheed's claim that disclosure would be "embarrassing" to the company and to the individuals involved.

To balance these considerations, Judge Pratt Oct. 21 had proposed a plan designed to sidestep the Freedom of Information

Act. Under the compromise proposal, Lockheed would deliver the documents to the SEC, but delete the names of recipients and identify them only in code. The key to the code would be left with the court, which would provide the SEC with the identities upon request.

The SEC rejected the plan Oct. 28 saying the arrangement could set a bad precedent for compliance with other SEC subpoenas and possibly hamper full prosecution of the agency's case against Lockheed.

During hearings on the judge's proposal Oct. 21, lawyers for Lockheed admitted the aerospace firm had made under-the-table payments to government officials in 15 foreign countries.

Japan, Italy, Holland, Germany & Turkey involved. Lockheed Aircraft Corp. secretly paid $7.1 million to a rightwing Japanese militarist, ostensibly to promote the sale of its L-1011 commercial jetliner to Japan, according to company documents released Feb. 4, 1976 by the Senate Subcommittee on Multinational Corporations.

The documents had been subpoenaed from Lockheed in connection with the subcommittee's continuing probe of illegal payments made abroad by U.S. companies.

The $7.1 million, paid in yen as cash and sometimes delivered in packing crates, was turned over to Yoshio Kodama, a senior war criminal who had served three years in prison following World War II.

Subcommittee chairman Sen. Frank Church (D, Idaho) described Kodama as a "prominent leader of the ultra right-wing militarist faction in Japan."

Church charged that by underwriting Kodama's group, which supported Japanese rearmament, Lockheed was pursuing a foreign policy contrary to that of the U.S. government. "In effect," Church said, "we have had a foreign policy which has vigorously opposed this political line and a Lockheed foreign policy which has helped to keep it alive through large financial subsidies in support of the company's sales efforts" in Japan.

The sole witness at the day's hearing was William Findley, a partner in Arthur Young & Co., Lockheed's auditor. Findley testified that Kodama had been paid be-cause he was "an influential figure . . . with access to important people [and] a very powerful lobbyist." Kodama, who was chairman of the right-wing "Seishi Kai" group, or Youth Ideology Society, had been instrumental in the founding of Japan's ruling Liberal Democratic Party. According to the New York Times Feb. 4, Kodama "has had a hand in naming several prime ministers [and] also has strong influence over underworld figures in that country."

Kodama's consulting arrangement with Lockheed began in 1958, Findley said. Kodama's influence had been used to win the sale of Lockheed's F-104 Starfighter jets to the Japanese air force in the 1960s, and six L-1011 jumbo jets, worth $130 million, to Japan's commercial airlines in 1972 and 1973, according to testimony.

The Lockheed documents also showed that apart from payoffs to Kodama, $3.2 million was paid to an agent identified only as Marubeni, and $2.15 million was paid to an agent described as the Hong Kong-based I-D Corp., chiefly for public relations payments "and possibly including payments for stories in Japanese press." Findley testified that Lockheed executives had told him a portion of the I-D payment was destined for officials in Japan's government and commercial airlines.

Other Lockheed documents released by the subcommittee revealed corporate payoffs in Italy, West Germany, Turkey and Europe.

In Italy, the subpoenaed documents showed that Lockheed had made payoffs totaling about $2 million to high officials of the Italian government in order to sell 14 C-130 cargo-carrying transport planes to the Italian air force in 1970. The payoffs were disguised as fees paid through consulting firms registered in Panama and Switzerland. (A portion of Kodama's payoff also was made through a Swiss account.)

No names were revealed during the hearing, but the corporate documents listed $1.48 million as "contributions to minister's party," $224,000 as "payment for [defense] minister," $78,000 as "payment to previous minister," and $50,000 reportedly also paid a defense minister.

Regarding one of the payoff arrangements, a document stated: "The minister is suspicious that perhaps the reason for our lack of action is that we are merely waiting for a government change so no payment to his party will be necessary."

Subcommittee member Sen. Charles H. Percy (R, Ill.) charged that Lockheed's payoffs threatened national security. "We can't have the defense priorities of our allies being perverted by corrupt practices, especially practices perpetrated by American corporations," Percy said.

The subpoenaed documents showed that in West Germany, Lockheed divided an $8,000 payoff between two major political parties as a "preprocurement hedge toward the sale of a fourth Jetstar" to the ministry of defense.

On another occasion, records showed, Lockheed knowingly violated West German law by making secret payments out of a Swiss account to a West German consultant who had not registered, as required, with the government as a corporate agent. The consultant was hired to promote the sale of Lockheed's S-3A patrol crafts to the West German navy.

In Turkey, gifts to political parties totaled $876,000, according to company records. Another $30,000 was spent to obtain "competitive data intelligence" in connection with the sale of jet planes to the Turkish air force. One company memo spoke of the need to provide Lockheed's Turkish agent with a "thoroughly adequate amount with which to buy real influence, not just intelligence."

The documents also revealed the existence in 1973 of a $600,000 cash account, maintained in a safe-deposit box in Lockheed's Paris office but not recorded on company books. According to Church, $265,000 from this fund was spent "buying business intelligence and paying officials from European airlines, including West Germany's Lufthansa, Swissair, and SAS, the Scandanavian airline.

Testifying Feb. 6, A. Carl Kotchian, Lockheed vice chairman and chief operating officer, confirmed many of the previous day's disclosures. He did not dispute the $7.1 million figure that company documents stated was paid Kodama. Kotchian added that Kodama still was receiving $60,000 for each L-1011 commercial jetliner delivered to Japan.

Kotchian said "approximately $2 million" was funneled through intermediaries to Japanese government officials. I-D Corp. was one of the firms that "provided

a cover" for the payoff arrangements, Kotchian testified.

Kotchian also acknowledged an earlier report that Lockheed had paid $1 million to a "high official" in the Dutch government from 1961–1962 to "establish a climate of goodwill, a climate in which our products would receive favorable consideration."

Kotchian said the same Dutch official later was paid an additional $100,000. (Kotchian added that the official initially had asked to be provided with a Jetstar, but perhaps because of the "difficulty of transferring title" to the plane, was given money.)

When asked if he termed the cash payment a "bribe," Kotchian replied, "I would categorize this more as a gift, but I don't want to quibble with you."

Kotchian conceded that $2 million was paid to Italian politicians and political parties but said he regarded the payment as a "reasonable sales expense for a $60 million order."

Regarding the committee's estimate that $876,000 in commissions was paid in Turkey, Kotchian said that figure "seems to be in the ballpark," but added he did know whether the money went to government officials.

Kotchian also claimed no knowledge of payoffs to a Swedish general or to West German political parties, but testified Lockheed had paid $10,000 to a London firm to provide the company with "intelligence" on its competitors' pricing practices in Europe.

Kotchian echoed the view, expressed in earlier testimony by Lockheed chairman Daniel J. Haughton, that payoffs were made out of competitive considerations. "We don't condone this" practice, Kotchian said. "In our judgment, this was the only way we could sell our product."

Haughton, Kotchian resign—Lockheed's two top executives—chairman and chief executive Daniel J. Haughton, and vice chairman and chief operating officer A. Carl Kotchian—resigned Feb. 13 in the wake of the international furor caused by disclosures that the company had paid millions of dollars to foreign government officials to promote arms sales.

Robert W. Haack, 58, former president of the New York Stock Exchange and a member of Lockheed's board, was named interim chairman. He would share day-to-day operations of the company with Roy A. Anderson, vice chairman for finance and administration, and Lawrence O. Kitchen, president.

Haack announced the shake-up after emerging from a lengthy board meeting at Lockheed's Burbank, Calif. headquarters. "The board had a very difficult meeting this morning at which Mr. Haughton and Mr. Kotchian saw fit to resign," Haack told reporters.

Explaining the resignations of the company's top officials, Haack said the board felt "the company, employes, and shareholders would perhaps be better protected if they [Haughton and Kotchian] excused themselves from the process."

The payoff disclosures and related developments had aggravated problems for the financially troubled aerospace firm. Because Lockheed had refused to comply with the Securities and Exchange Commission's demands regarding full disclosure of the identities of payoff recipients, the company had been unable to hold its annual meeting and schedule a vote on a crucial refinancing plan.

The company had $600 million in outstanding bank loans, including a $195 million bank loan guaranteed by the federal government after Lockheed was threatened with bankruptcy in 1971. Bankers and government officials were pressing the company to resolve the payoff issue so that financial restructuring of the company could begin.

One of the immediate consequences of the payoff disclosures was the loss of a $130 million contract in Japan and the threatened loss of another in the Netherlands.

Prior to the departure of Haughton and Kotchian, Lockheed Feb. 5 announced the appointment of a special commission of outside directors to "supervise and audit an investigation of commissions and payments on sales contracts."

Japanese developments. Japanese Premier Takeo Miki told the Diet (parliament) Feb. 6, 1976 that he would "make it a point of honor" to investigate the burgeoning reports of the involvement of officials, politicians and business executives in an estimated $12.6 million in payoffs made by the Lockheed Aircraft

Corp. since 1958 to secure Japanese aircraft contracts.

Miki's Liberal Democratic Party (LDP) had been deeply implicated in the Lockheed bribery revelations, with suspicion directed toward two former LDP premiers, Nobusuke Kishi, who left office in 1960, and Kakuei Tanaka, who resigned in 1974 over charges of financial irregularities. Both currently held Diet seats.

The charges stemmed from their alleged ties to Yoshio Kodama, who reportedly received $7.1 million from Lockheed between 1958 and 1975 for his lobbying activities on behalf of the corporation.

A New York Times article Feb. 6 reported that a book written by Kodama recounted that, by interceding with the Kishi government, he had "straightened out" a pending 1958 deal in which Lockheed and the U.S. Grumman Corp. vied for a jet fighter contract. The government ultimately chose the Lockheed aircraft.

Additionally, it was revealed Feb. 6 in Senate subcommittee testimony that Kenji Osano, a confidant and financial supporter of Tanaka, had allegedly been enlisted by Lockheed vice chairman A. Carl Kotchian to promote aircraft sales in the country. The 1972 meeting reportedly had been arranged through Kodama. Osano, at that time, was also the single largest shareholder in All-Nippon Airways, which bought 21 Lockheed Tristar airbuses for its domestic service.

(The presidents of All-Nippon Airways and the Marubeni Corp., a leading trading company and Lockheed agent, which assertedly figured prominently in the Lockheed payoffs, Feb. 5 issued separate denials of illegality in the Lockheed affair.)

The Miki move followed Feb. 5–6 demands by the opposition Socialist, Communist, Democratic Socialist and Komeito ("Clean Government") Parties that a Diet inquiry be conducted. By Feb. 7 each of the parties, including the LDP, had announced it had formed an investigative unit to look into allegations of impropriety and said it would send a research team to the U.S. to examine Senate subcommittee documents. The LDP investigative committee was headed by a former justice minister.

The New York Times Feb. 7 reported that among the government agencies enlisted in the payoffs probe were the National Police Agency, akin to the U.S. FBI; the Board of Audit, a government accounting body; and the National Tax Agency, the internal revenue service.

One immediate casualty of the scandal was a pending Lockheed deal with the defense ministry. Defense officials announced Feb. 10 that they were cancelling a $1.3 million order for 100 P-3C Orion antisubmarine aircraft. The New York Times Feb. 11 said that, according to defense sources, the anti-American fallout following the disclosures, had jeopardized other U.S. aircraft companies' sales worth approximately $2 billion.

The Times article also reported that, under pressure from the Socialists, the LDP agreed to a parliamentary ruling that those called to testify before the Diet would appear as "witnesses" and not "references." Under parliamentary procedure "witnesses" could be compelled to talk and faced perjury charges for false testimony. "References" did not.

The public prosecutor's office Feb. 10 announced it had begun a probe into possible criminal violations of the tax and political contributions laws, while the ministry of international trade and industry said it found nothing illegal in the reported $2 million to $3 million in commissions the Marubeni Corp. had received from Lockheed. Marubeni officials, however, continued to face charges of illegally advising Lockheed to bribe others.

Marubeni Feb. 13 said it was severing all ties with Lockheed.

Japanese government officials Feb. 12 appealed to the U.S. Senate subcommittee to release the names of individuals implicated in alleged Lockheed bribes.

In Los Angeles, Japanese Socialist Party members Feb. 13 met with Lockheed vice chairman Kotchian. Kotchian reportedly told the fact-finding group that former premier Tanaka had held Jan. 1972 discussions with him. Tanaka that day issued a statement confirming the meeting, but indicated that the talks had been limited to questions of the feasibility of a joint project to manufacture passenger liners.

In other developments, the Diet Feb. 16–17 held two days of hearings, during which Kenji Osano, representatives of All-Nippon Airways and two Marubeni Corp. officials testified. Osano Feb. 16 denied all

charges of influence-peddling and corruption. He reportedly threatened to sue Kotchian for his "deplorable" testimony in Washington. The two Marubeni officials Feb. 17 similarly denied any wrongdoing, but submitted their resignations to the trading organization after the hearings. Yoshio Kodama was excused from testifying due to "ill health."

Premier Miki Feb. 19 announced the creation of a cabinet-level committee to monitor the multi-faceted probe into the Lockheed charges. Ichitaro Ido, the chief cabinet secretary, and Takeo Fukuda, the deputy premier, were among the 10 ministers appointed to the new body.

Miki also reasserted previous demands that the U.S. release the names of those business and governmental officials accused of accepting over $12 million in illegal contributions from Lockheed since 1958 to secure national aircraft contracts for the corporation. The Diet (parliament) Feb. 23 unanimously adopted a resolution to that effect and the new ambassador to the U.S., Fumihiko Togo. Feb. 24 delivered Miki's formal request to the State Department on his arrival to assume his new duties.

(The U.S. position had been that premature disclosure of the findings of the Senate Subcommittee on Multinational Corporations, which was investigating the Lockheed scandal, could jeopardize national security and violate Senate rules of confidentiality.)

Police and tax officials Feb. 24 launched raids in the Tokyo area to uncover information about possible violations of the bribery, tax evasion and foreign exchange laws in connection with the Lockheed payments issue. More than 25 homes and offices of executives of Lockheed and the Marubeni Corp., its national trading agent, were entered and more than 600 boxes of documents impounded. Also searched were the homes of Toshiyoshi Oni, Lockheed's Asian representative, and Shig Katayama, president of the I.D. Corporation, allegedly a dummy organization set up to siphon Lockheed funds to political officials.

Hiro Hiyama, board chairman of the Marubeni Corp., Lockheed's national agent, resigned March 3 "to take responsibility" for the impaired image of the company. Hiyama asserted, however, that his departure signified no admission of

Marubeni involvement in the scandal. Toshiharu Okubo and Hiroshi Itoh had submitted their resignations Feb. 17 after testifying before the Diet.

(Reuters March 3 reported that Hiyama would be retained by Marubeni as a director. UPI Feb. 20 said that Okubo and Itoh had rejoined Marubeni as counselors.)

The repercussions of the Lockheed scandal on Marubeni were beginning to be felt. The city council of Sapporo, the capital of the northern island of Hokkaido, told company officials it wished to end a Marubeni commission to build a subway for the city, it was reported March 4. The Asahi Evening News March 6 said that several prefectural and municipal governments had suspended all contract talks with Marubeni pending clarification of its role with Lockheed. Boycotts were reported in the cities of Yokosuka and Hakodate and in the Osaka and Hyogo prefectures.

It was reported March 10 that opposition parties in the Diet were boycotting legislative sessions until the government agreed to make a full disclosure of information relating to the Lockheed scandal.

Meanwhile, Shigejiro Inoh, former chief of the Self-Defense Agency, the national military body, said in an interview published March 9 that the Lockheed F-104 jetfighter had been selected over a competing U.S. Grumman Corp. model in 1959 in order to help then Premier Nobusuke Kishi retain power. Kishi allegedly needed the backing of Ichiro Kono, an important Liberal Democratic Party factional leader who advocated purchasing the Lockheed aircraft, Inoh said.

U.S. offers Japan secret Lockheed data— In a letter March 11, President Ford offered to give Japan's Premier Takeo Miki all available information on Lockheed Aircraft Corp.'s alleged payoffs in Japan, on condition that the data remain secret while an investigation into the matter by the Securities and Exchange Commission was underway.

The Japanese government, which made public Ford's letter March 12, reportedly accepted the U.S. condition.

Robert W. Ingersoll, deputy secretary of state, earlier had outlined the Administration's position regarding the limited disclosure of information gathered by U.S. agencies on the widening foreign payoff scandal.

Ingersoll said the U.S. also had proposed "a multilateral agreement within the United Nations system to help deter and punish such activities."

Ingersoll outlined the Administration's proposal for the bilateral exchange of evidence on corporate payoffs and bribery in testimony March 5 before a subcommittee of the Joint Economic Committee of Congress. He said the Justice Department would give the material to "responsible" foreign law enforcement agencies if they agreed to keep the information confidential unless it were used in a criminal prosecution.

Ingersoll also restated the State Department's view that "premature public disclosure of unsubstantiated charges against foreign officials might seriously damage the rights of individuals and cause serious problems in U.S. relations with other countries."

Ingersoll charged that "unsubstantiated allegations against foreign officials" already had inflicted "grievous damage" on U.S. foreign relations. "Serious political crises in friendly countries, possible cancellation of major overseas orders for U.S. industries and the risk of general cooling toward U.S. firms abroad" had resulted from recent disclosures about the payoffs, Ingersoll said.

Ingersoll's statements echoed the view expressed by Secretary of State Henry A. Kissinger in a court suit brought by Lockheed to prevent the disclosure of names of alleged payoff recipients.

Regarding the "multilateral agreement on corrupt practices," Ingersoll said the U.S. proposal had been submitted to the United Nations Permanent Commission on Transnational Corporations, currently meeting in Lima, Peru.

Ingersoll said the pact, which covered government procurement and other governmental actions affecting international trade and investment, would apply to those who solicited or accepted payments, as well as to those who made them.

Importing countries would establish guidelines concerning the use of business agents for foreign companies and set "appropriate penalties for bribery and extortion," Ingersoll said.

The pact also would include uniform provisions for disclosure by companies, agents and officials of political contributions, gifts and payments made in connection with the transactions covered.

Ingersoll defended the need for an international pact, saying unilateral actions by the U.S. against corporate payoffs "would put U.S. companies at a serious disadvantage in the export trade."

Sen. William Proxmire (D, Wis.), who presided at the subcommittee hearing, termed the Administration's disclosure plan a "mighty cumbersome procedure." Under questioning, Ingersoll conceded that negotiations between the Justice Department and foreign law enforcement agencies for release of data could take six months.

Proxmire said the proposed international agreement was "very welcome and very intriguing," but he was skeptical about the U.N.'s effectiveness as an enforcement agency for the pact.

Japan arrests eight in scandal—Tokyo police June 22 arrested four persons in connection with the Lockheed Aircraft scandal in Japan.

Arrested were Toshiharu Okubo, former managing director of the Marubeni Trading Corp., Lockheed's national trading agent in Japan, and three executives of the All Nippon Airways—Yuji Sawa, the managing director, Hisayori Aoki, chief of the accounting department, and Tadao Ueki, head of the airline's international department and business operations.

Okubo was held under suspicion of perjury in connection with testimony under oath before a parliamentary budget committee in February. He was accused of having lied to the committee by claiming that he signed receipts dealing with the payoffs without knowing what they were for. The three others were accused of having conspired in June–July 1974 to accept $170,000 in illegal commissions from A. H. Elliott, Lockheed's former representative in Tokyo, as payment for the sale of the firm's 21 Tristars to All Nippon.

Two more arrests were made July 2.

Tsuneo Tachikawa, personal secretary to Yoshio Kodama, Japanese lobbyist for Lockheed, was charged with threatening a housing company executive to force his resignation in 1975 in another case involving tax evasion. Although the incident had

no apparent connection with the Lockheed scandal, police made it clear that they intended to use it to pressure Tachikawa about any knowledge he might have of the Lockheed affair.

The second man arrested, Hiroshi Itoh, was charged with having committed perjury in testimony before a parliamentary committee in February and March. Itoh had been managing director of Marubeni Corp. at the time it was an agent for Lockheed in Japan.

Two officials of All Nippon Airways, the firm cited in the Lockheed case, were arrested July 7 and 8. Koichi Fujiwara, management director, was taken into custody July 7 on charges of currency law violations. Tokuji Wakasa, All Nippon president, was detained July 8, also accused of having violated the foreign exchange law by accepting large sums of Lockheed money, which entered Japan without the proper registration procedure.

Wakasa was charged, in addition, with having committed perjury in testimony before a parliamentary committee in February and March by saying he was not aware that his firm had signed options to purchase DC-10 airlines from Douglas Aircraft when he assumed the All Nippon presidency in 1970. All Nippon later dropped the options and bought 21 Lockheed Tristars.

Ex-Premier Tanaka indicted in case— Former Premier Kakuei Tanaka was indicted by the Tokyo District Court Aug. 16 on charges of having accepted $1.6 million in bribes to arrange the purchase of Lockheed aircraft by All Nippon Airlines. Tanaka was the first Japanese to be indicted for bribery occurring while he held the position of premier.

Tanaka, in prison since his arrest July 27, was released on $690,000 bail Aug. 17 pending trial. Also freed on bail were Tanaka's secretary, Toshio Enomoto, who had been indicted Aug. 9; Hisayori Aoki, accounting chief for All Nippon, and Hiroshi Hiyama and Toshiharu Okubo, two former executives of Marubeni Trading Corp. who were accused of having paid the bribe to Tanaka.

Hiyama and Okubo had been indicted along with Tanaka, as was Hiroshi Itoh, another Marubeni executive.

The indictment charged that on Aug. 23, 1972, one month after Tanaka had become premier, Hiyama, Okubo and Itoh asked Tanaka to use his office to assure the purchase of Lockheed L-1011 Tristar passenger planes by All Nippon in exchange for a $1.6-million payment. On Oct. 10, 1972, All Nippon canceled an option to purchase McDonnell Douglas DC-10 jets and decided to buy the Lockheed plane instead. Enomoto accepted the payments on Tanaka's behalf in four installments starting Aug. 10, 1973 and ending March 1, 1974, according to the formal charge. Tanaka reportedly had admitted, under questioning in the previous three weeks, that he had received the payments but insisted that they had been legal political donations.

In previous developments, Tokuji Wakasa, president of All Nippon, and Koichi Fujiwara, the airline's managing director, were indicted July 28 on charges of having violated foreign-exchange laws by receiving Lockheed bribes. The indictment said that Wakasa had received $180,000 from a Lockheed representative in Tokyo in June and July 1974 and that both men had received another $400,000 from the firm in August of that year.

Naoje Watanabe, vice president of All Nippon, was indicted on charges of committing perjury in testimony June 16 and 24 before a parliamentary committee investigating the bribe scandal, the Wall Street Journal reported July 28. Watanabe was accused of having lied when he said he had not received reports from All Nippon that the firm had received $70,000 and $103,300 in bribe money from Lockheed in July 1974.

The Tokyo district prosecutor's office Sept. 10 indicted Tomisaburo Hashimoto, former Japanese transport minister, and Takayuki Sato, a member of the House of Representatives, on charges of having accepted payments in the Lockheed bribe scandal.

Interim report on Lockheed probe—The Japanese government Oct. 15, 1975 submitted to the Diet (parliament) an interim report on its eight-month investigation of the Lockheed payoff scandal in which it said that 14 Diet members were involved in the case but could not be prosecuted for lack of evidence or because the statute of limitations had expired. Opposition party members criticized the report on the ground that it did not go far enough and

they demanded release of the names of the officials implicated.

In making the disclosures to two House of Representatives committees, Justice Minister Osamu Inaba acknowledged that the 14 deputies had accepted $268,000 from Lockheed in payments ranging from $3,300 to $50,000 each. But he said that in some of the cases the money could be classified as political contributions or legal gifts. Three members of a parliamentary committee on air transportation who had received secret Lockheed funds could not be tried because the statute of limitations had expired, Inaba said. Two other members of the same committee, according to Inaba, also took Lockheed money, but were in no position to help the American aircraft firm. The committee had made decisions favoring Lockheed's efforts to sell its Tristar airbuses to Japan.

Inaba said the probe thus far had focused on 17 Parliament members and 460 other government officials and businessmen. The government investigators had raided 160 locations and seized 66,000 documents, he said.

Latin Americans implicated. Military and civilian officials in several Latin American countries were implicated in February 1976 in the growing scandal over the bribery of foreign officials by U.S. corporations.

The Colombian government began an investigation Feb. 8 into reports that two air force generals had received illegal payments from Lockheed Aircraft Corp. Venezuela's air force Feb. 10 began investigating reports that Lockheed had bribed some of its officers.

In addition, Lockheed was said to have paid a $75,000 bribe to a Mexican air force colonel—Mexico's defense ministry denied it—and Northrop Corp. admitted making illegal payments in Brazil, according to the Feb. 23 issue of Newsweek magazine of the U.S.

The Colombian scandal broke Feb. 8 when newspapers in Bogota printed three letters released by the U.S. Senate's Subcommittee on Multinational Corporations, which was investigating illegal payments abroad by U.S. firms. The letters, addressed to Lockheed offices in Marietta, Ga. by two Lockheed officials in Colombia, Edwin Schwartz and Jose

Gutierrez, discussed "sugar" (bribe payments) demanded by two Colombian air force generals and other officials in exchange for inducing the government to purchase Lockheed Hercules aircraft in 1968–69.

The generals—Jose Ramon Calderon and Armando Urrego, both former air force commanders in chief—allegedly exaggerated Colombia's defense needs to secure the purchases, for which they allegedly received some $200,000 from Lockheed. Both Calderon and Urrego denied the bribery charge and cooperated fully with the government investigation which began Feb. 8, according to press reports.

(Two other scandals involving Colombian officials and European companies were reported in the press. The Feb. 23 issue of Time magazine, reported that in the 1960s the West German firm Heckler and Koch had paid $200,000 to a committee of Colombian military officers to secure Colombia's purchase of army rifles which were later discovered to be inefficient and difficult to maintain. The Bogota newspaper El Bogotano reported Feb. 16 that the French firm Dassault had given its Colombian representative $200,000 to pay commissions related to Colombia's purchase of 18 Mirage jet fighters in 1972.)

The Venezuelan air force began its investigation of alleged Lockheed bribes Feb. 10, after the Mexican newspaper Excelsior Feb. 7 printed an internal Lockheed letter noting that the company had paid for a visit to Disney World, Florida in 1974 by a Venezuelan lieutenant colonel, J. M. Laurentin, and his family.

Colombia's Supreme Court Sept. 1 took over the government's lagging investigation into bribes allegedly paid to Colombian military officers by Lockheed Aircraft Corp.

The court criticized the armed forces' prosecutor, who had been in charge of the case, for not making any progress in the seven-month probe. The prosecutor, Francisco de Paula Chavez, had said Aug. 23 that the investigation was stalled because of delays in translating Lockheed documents handed over to Colombia by the U.S. government June 22. There was only one translator working on the papers, and she worked only in the afternoons, de Paula said.

The documents indicated that Lockheed had bribed three Colombian air force generals to help secure Colombian purchase of Lockheed planes in 1968–69, the Mexican newspaper Excelsior reported Aug. 24. The generals were Jose Ramon Calderon and Armando Urrego, former air force commanders, and Federico Rincon Puentes, the current commander, Excelsior said.

Dutch involvement. The Dutch cabinet confirmed Feb. 8, 1976 that Prince Bernhard was the person suspected of being the "high government official" named in U.S. Senate subcommittee testimony as the recipient of a $1.1 million gift to aid aircraft sales in the Netherlands.

Bernhard, in a statement made public Feb. 8 by the government information office, denied the allegations and asked for an investigation to clear himself of the charges. Premier Joop den Uyl, in a televised appearance shortly after the government notice was released, said that despite Bernhard's assertions to the contrary, he had concluded from private talks that the prince was implicated in the scandal. Den Uyl added that the cabinet announcement should not be taken as establishing guilt. He announced that the cabinet Feb. 9 would set up an independent commission to explore the accusations.

A three-man commission, created Feb. 9, representing each of the main Christian, liberal and socialist political currents in the country, began its investigation Feb. 11 of Prince Bernhard. In parliamentary debate the previous day all major political forces had supported the coalition government decision to conduct the probe. Only the Communists had urged Bernhard's prior resignation of his post as inspector general of the armed forces, the New York Times said Feb. 12.

In a related development, Hubert Weisbrod, a prominent Swiss lawyer, Feb. 10 denied charges that he had acted as an intermediary for Lockheed payments to Prince Bernhard.

According to Feb. 27 reports, documents had been uncovered in Washington confirming that Lockheed paid Prince Bernhard $100,000 in 1972 through a Paris connection. The money reportedly was paid into the private account of a French woman referred to only as "Poupette" and allegedly Prince Bernhard's mistress at the time.

Unconfirmed Dutch press reports April 21 alleged that Fred C. Meuser, Lockheed's former European sales manager, had given $867,327 to a former press chief of the Dutch Fokker aircraft company. The reports said that the money had been intended for Prince Bernhard.

The U.S. Department of Justice said April 14 that it had released to the Dutch government documents relating to alleged Lockheed payoffs to Dutch officials.

*Prince quits posts under fire—*Prince Bernhard was forced to resign nearly all of his military and business posts Aug. 26 after a government investigatory commission strongly criticized his relationship with officials of the Lockheed Aircraft Corp. His top military post was inspector general of the armed forces. His business positions included membership on the board of KLM Royal Dutch Airlines. He headed the World Wildlife Fund, and lent his name as an official or patron to more than 300 organizations.

The three-member government commission had spent six months investigating allegations that Bernhard had accepted $1.1 million in bribes from Lockheed for promoting a Dutch government purchase of 138 Lockheed Starfighter jets. The investigation found no evidence that the prince had accepted the money, but concluded that Bernhard had "allowed himself to be tempted to take initiatives which were completely unacceptable and which were bound to place himself and the Netherlands procurement policy in the eyes of Lockheed—and, it must now be added, also in the eyes of others—in a dubious light."

The report, saying that "[Bernhard] showed himself open to dishonorable requests and offers," cited a personal relationship with Fred C. Meuser, a Lockheed official in Switzerland, as the reason for a series of discussions that might or might not have resulted in Bernhard's acceptance of a bribe.

The report detailed Meuser's offer of a Jetstar to Bernhard "to create a favorable atmosphere for the sale of Lockheed products in the Netherlands." Bernhard refused, the report said, and Meuser then recommended that Bernhard be given the money. Payment was to be made into the Swiss bank account of a member of Bernhard's household staff.

Inexplicably, the report added, the money went astray between 1960 and 1962, when it was to have been paid. The sum was not found in Bernhard's financial records, the panel said, adding: "The possibility that Lockheed moneys could have reached the prince or persons appointed by him without going through his books can never be completely excluded."

Among other findings in the report:
■ A sum of $62,000 was disbursed to Bernhard in 1965, without any explanation of origin or reason. "The fact that the prince had not been able to explain the origin of the $62,000 impairs his credibility," the report said.
■ Lockheed officials offered Bernhard $500,000 in July 1968 in an effort to reverse the decision to buy the French Breguet Atlantique planes rather than Lockheed's P-3 Orions. Bernhard declined the offer, but Lockheed tried to offer him $100,000 anyway at a golf course near Utrecht in Sept., 1968. "The prince is said to have made no clear response to this," the report said. "He was not certain whether he could accept the offer." A check for $100,000 was drawn later in the name of Victor Baarn and placed in a Swiss bank. The report assumed the name was fictitious.

Premier Joop den Uyl detailed the report to a silent parliament Aug. 26 and announced the prince's resignation from most of his posts. "Although no evidence has been found of any influence by the prince on the procurement policy examined, the Prince's actions have damaged the national interest," den Uyl said.

In an apparent concession to Queen Juliana, Den Uyl said that Bernhard would retain his title—His Royal Highness Bernhard Leopold Frederik Everhard Julius Coert Karel Godfried Pieter, Prince of the Netherlands. Juliana had been reported Aug. 23 to be considering abdication if the report had strongly criticized Bernhard. The royal couple Aug. 23 had cut short a vacation in Italy to see the report. Queen Juliana and Bernhard flew to The Hague and met Aug. 23 with den Uyl. The queen reportedly objected both to the report's strong language and to the idea of Bernhard resigning his military and business posts. However, she did not threaten to abdicate and resumed her vacation Aug. 24.

Den Uyl read Bernhard's resignation letter to the parliament.

In the letter, Bernhard confessed that his relations with Lockheed officials had become too personal. "My friendship with several highly placed officials of that company developed along wrong lines," he said.

In addition, the prince noted that his personal relationships with Lockheed officials had failed to take into account his position as a statesman and official representative of the Netherlands. He also acknowledged that he had sent letters to Lockheed officials which he admitted he "should not have sent," and that he had not been critical enough of Lockheed's proposals.

The Dutch parliament voted by 148 to 2 Aug. 30 to reject a left-wing motion calling for criminal prosecution of Prince Bernhard for his involvement in the Lockheed bribery scandal. The only votes in favor of the motion were cast by the members of the Pacifist Socialist Party.

Leaders of all five major parties condemned Bernhard's relationship with officials of the Lockheed Aircraft Corp. and agreed that the prince's activities had harmed the interests of the Netherlands. They also agreed with Premier Joop den Uyl that prosecution could lead to Queen Juliana's abdication and a resulting constitutional crisis.

Three Dutch legislators approached—Lockheed Aircraft Corp. officials had approached three Dutch parliament members in 1974 to gain support for the sale of the company's Orion antisubmarine aircraft to the Dutch navy, according to a report submitted by Premier Joop den Uyl to the parliament Sept. 1. The parliament members named in the report were Joop van Elsen, chairman of the Second House's permanent defense committee, and Klaas De Vries and Adrianus Ploeg, members of the committee.

The report came in response to parliament's demand that a passage in the Aug. 26 report concerning Prince Bernhard's Lockheed ties be clarified. The passage had alluded to two Lockheed documents showing that the company had entertained the committee members, who were not named in the report.

A spokesman for van Elsen, who was abroad on a North Atlantic Treaty Organization tour, said Sept. 1 that the chairman had visited all aircraft companies considered by parliament. He rejected speculation about undue Lockheed pressure on van Elsen, saying the chairman had stated publicly that he was in favor of the Orion because it was the best plane.

De Vries was mentioned in the report because he had accompanied van Elsen on a September, 1974 visit to a Lockheed plant in Farnborough, England. Van Elsen also had visited Lockheed headquarters in Burbank, Calif. in May, 1974, the Financial Times (London) reported Sept. 2.

Ploeg, who also had gone on the Burbank trip, said through a spokesman Sept. 1 that he had reserved his judgment on the Orion during his visit. He also denied any undue pressure on the part of Lockheed officials.

Bernhard asked German to purchase Northrop planes—Prince Bernhard had asked West German Chancellor Helmut Schmidt in 1971 to purchase planes produced by the Northrop Corp., according to letters published Sept. 2.

One letter from Schmidt, then West German minister of defense, to Dutch Defense Minister Willem den Toon, dated Jan. 12, 1971, said that Bernhard had tried to persuade Schmidt to cancel West Germany's planned purchase of the Lockheed Starfighter and buy the Northrop Cobra. "As you know," the letter, dated Jan. 12, 1971, said, "it is difficult for us to change our choice of planes because of our interest in the M.R.C.A. [multi-role combat aircraft] plan. But on the other hand I don't reject immediately the proposal of Northrop for smaller NATO nations."

Schmidt denied Sept. 3 that Bernhard had put pressure on him. Nor, he said, did Bernhard's approach seem inappropriate.

Italian developments. Italian Interior Minister Luigi Gui Feb. 11, 1976 requested an inquiry into charges that he received more than $50,000 from the Lockheed Aircraft Corp. in connection with Italy's 1970-1971 purchase of 14 Hercules C-130 transport planes. It had been charged that Lockheed paid out $2 million to various public figures to promote the sale of the aircraft in Italy.

The 61-year-old Gui, a Christian Democrat, also resigned his ministerial post and said he would not accept a position in the newly-formed minority Christian Democratic government to avoid jeopardizing its chances of success by any political embarrassment.

Gui, who was defense minister in 1970 when the deal was concluded, was widely attacked in the Italian press as the unnamed recipient of the $50,000 bribe disclosed in the Senate subcommittee's documents.

In conjunction with Gui, Mario Tanassi, the leader of the Social Democratic Party, had also been named as a recipient of Lockheed payoffs, it was reported Feb. 12. He also denied the charges.

The New York Times Feb. 18 reported that Italian prosecutors and a parliamentary commission were investigating the charges of Lockheed bribes. Arrest warrants were issued Feb. 17 for Ovidio Lefebvre, a prominent lawyer, and Maria Fava, a business executive, in connection with the inquiry. Lefebvre had been identified in a 1970 Lockheed memo as the individual who paid $50,000 to an unnamed Italian defense minister, alleged to be Gui. Fava was mentioned as an intermediary in the payoffs.

Former premier linked to bribes—An unnamed Italian premier during the 1960s had accepted payments from Lockheed, Italian newspapers reported April 22. The accounts named as principal suspects Giovanni Leone, Aldo Moro and Mariano Rumor, all of whom served as premiers between 1968 and 1970 when the alleged payoffs were made. The three currently held top-ranking positions in the ruling Christian Democratic government: Leone as president, Moro as premier and Rumor as foreign minister. Each, in separate statements April 22, denied involvement in the Lockheed affair.

The Italian reports were apparently derived from U.S. Senate documents that had been "leaked" from a parliamentary commission investigating the Lockheed scandal. According to the documents, a former premier, code-named "Antelope Cobbler," had helped negotiate the sale of 14 C-130 cargo planes to the Italian air force in exchange for secret payments.

The disclosure was the second in weeks to touch former Christian Democratic

Party premiers. Rumor and Giulio Andreotti previously had been mentioned as alleged recipients of oil company payoffs between 1969 and 1973.

A Rome prosecutor revealed that a total of eight Italians had been charged with extortion in connection with the Lockheed scandal, it was reported March 24. Those indicted included Gen. Duilio Fanali, a former air force chief of staff; Camillo Crociani, head of a state industrial concern; Antonio and Ovidio Lefebvre, brothers who were attorneys in Rome; Maria Fava, a businesswoman, and Vittorio Antonelli, a lawyer.

Fanali and Antonio Fefebvre were arrested March 22 and taken to Rome's Regina Coeli prison. The two were released March 27 on their own recognizance, along with Antonelli who had been detained since Feb. 20.

In a related development, Mario Tanassi, a former defense minister, was reported March 26 as being under investigation by the public prosecutor's office. A parliamentary commission had voted April 2 to undertake a probe of Tanassi and Luigi Gui, another former defense minister.

In a June 11 statement, the Communist Party demanded the immediate resignation of Foreign Minister Mariano Rumor, one of three former prime ministers and members of the Christian Democratic Party who were suspected of having received bribes from the Lockheed Aircraft Corp. in the 1960s. Rumor denied involvement in the scheme June 13. He called such reports "ignoble electoral speculation" and announced plans to "stay in my office." The U.S. Senate Foreign Relations subcommittee on multinational corporations, headed by Sen. Frank Church (D, Idaho), revealed June 15 that one of the two other persons being investigated, President Giovanni Leone, had never accepted bribes from Lockheed.

Premier Andreotti linked to bribes—The Italian leftist weekly L'Espresso published letters Sept. 1 apparently showing that Premier Giulio Andreotti was the intended recipient of $43,000 in bribes from Lockheed Aircraft Corp.

The letters included one purportedly from A. Carl Kotchian, former Lockheed vice-president, to the company's Italian lawyer on Sept. 8, 1968, and an internal memorandum dated March 5, 1975. The letter purporting to have come from Kotchian authorized the payment of $28,-000 to Andreotti "to assure his and his party's valuable assistance" in the sale of 18 Orion P-3B patrol planes to the Italian navy. The memorandum referred to negotiations for the sale to Turkey of 36 Lockheed F-104 Starfighter planes made under Italian license. The memorandum authorized payment of $15,000 to Andreotti.

Andreotti, who had known in advance of the Sept. 1 date that letters would be published, denied the charges Aug. 31. He noted that at the time of the first letter he had been minister of commerce and industry and therefore had nothing to do with the Lockheed sale negotiations. "I have never been at the head of a large power group," he said." If I hadn't been unassailable from a moral point of view, I wouldn't be, after so many year, at this post."

Lockheed headquarters at Burbank, Calif., Sept. 1 released a statement that cast doubt on the documents' authenticity. "Based on discussions with knowledgeable Lockheed personnel, the company is of the opinion the documents appear to be forgeries," the statement said. "For example the handwritten memo attributed to Dale H. Daniels in April of 1970 indicating he was to set up an appointment for . . . Kotchian with . . . Andreotti, is indeed strange, since Daniels left Europe in 1964 and was employed in the United States on non-sales-related assignments through 1972.

"Furthermore, in response to inquiries on the subject, Kotchian has stated that to his knowledge he has never met . . . Andreotti nor corresponded with anyone relative to these matters."

L'Espresso said it had voiced doubts about the source of the material, but added that it had subjected the documents to handwriting and age tests and had concluded that the documents were genuine.

A parliamentary commission named to probe Andreotti's alleged involvement in the Lockheed payoff scandal voted 19-1, Oct. 13 to drop the investigation. The commission, representing all Italian political parties, based its decision on testimony by Ernest F. Hauser, a former Lockheed official. Hauser said Sept. 30 that the docu-

ments linking Andreotti to Lockheed payoffs were "not authentic."

West German developments. Former Defense Minister Franz Josef Straus, leader of the opposition Christian Social Union, Feb. 13, 1976 denied reports that he or his party had received Lockheed funds to promote the sale of its aircraft.

Strauss was reacting to allegations arising from press accounts of a diary kept by ex-Lockheed agent Ernest F. Hauser in the early 1960s, currently in the possession of the Senate subcommittee. The Washington Post Feb. 8 and Feb. 11 reported that the information in the diaries was damaging to Strauss and would soon be made public. Entries revealed that Strauss had allegedly pushed for Lockheed payments over the resistance of one of the company's officials in Germany, the Post said.

The Post's Feb. 11 account also said that Fritz-Josef Rath, a West German defense ministry official, attended the Senate subcommittee's hearings and had reported to Bonn that the subcommittee had no evidence that ex-Gen. Gunter Rall had accepted illegal Lockheed payments.

Sen. Frank Church (D, Ida.), chairman of the U.S. Senate Subcommittee on Multinational Corporations, said March 10 the panel had been unable to prove whether Lockheed had tried to bribe West German officials in the early 1960s and was ending its inquiry on the alleged payoffs.

Lockheed officials had testified that such payments were not made in West Germany.

Church said that "since there is a clear conflict, we are unable to determine who is telling the truth."

The U.S. embassy in Bonn said Sept. 22 that it considered "to be a forgery" a letter allegedly written by ex-Central Intelligence Agency (CIA) chief Allen Dulles to Strauss in November 1958. The letter alluded to "subsidies" apparently meant for Strauss in connection with West Germany's purchase of 900 Lockheed F-104 Starfighter jets in 1958.

The letter, produced by Hauser, had alleged that Strauss' opposition party, the Christian Social Union, had been the recipient of $12 million in payoffs for supporting the Lockheed purchase. Strauss had denied the charge.

The embassy statement said that it appeared "highly unlikely that [Dulles] would have acted in such a capacity. On the basis of the available evidence, therefore, the U.S. government considers the letter to be a forgery."

The West German Defense Ministry had said earlier that handwriting experts had established some other incriminating letters produced by Hauser as forgeries, the Washington Post reported Sept. 22.

Turkish involvement. A military tribunal in Ankara April 30, 1976 cleared Gen. Emin Alpkaya, the former commander of the air force, of accepting a $30,000 bribe from an Italian affiliate of Lockheed Aircraft Corp. His co-defendants—Gen. Ihsan Goksaran, Gen. Abdullah Tenekeci and Col. Sinan Bilge—were also acquitted of the formal charge of mishandling air force funds.

The three-judge tribunal also declared illegal a special investigation of alleged kickbacks. The commission had been set up by Defense Minister Ferit Melen to probe disclosures that Lockheed had paid its Ankara agent $876,000 for "gifts" to third parties.

Rejecting unofficial press allegations that the $30,000 received from Aeritalia, Lockheed's Italian affiiliate, had constituted a bribe, the ruling concluded: "The defendants acted in no way that could defame the honorable Turkish armed forces."

Alpkaya had received the check some months after Turkey purchased two squadrons of Lockheed F-104 Starfighters, for a total of 40 planes, which were built by Aeritalia under license by Lockheed. The money was said to be for Turkish earthquake victims.

Payoff to Australian official alleged. Gough Whitlam, leader of Australia's opposition Labor Party, charged April 29 that between 1958 and 1960 a former civil aviation minister in the Liberal-Country Party coalition government of Robert Menzies, who was then prime minister, received large sums of money from the U.S. Lockheed Aircraft Corp. The minister, whom Whitlam did not name, assertedly was paid a commission on one of the 13 Lockheed Electra aircraft sold to Australian airlines in that period. The civil aviation minister at that time was the late Sen. Shane Paltridge.

Whitlam did not offer any substantiation for his charges, but said that further information could be obtained from the U.S. Senate subcommittee on multinational corporations.

In response to Whitlam, Australian Foreign Minister Andrew Peacock April 29 said that contacts with the U.S. Justice Department had "revealed no evidence of payments."

Former British minister reported bribed. A former British Cabinet minister received a $1-million bribe to promote Lockheed sales in Britain, the London Daily Mail and Daily Express reported Aug. 30.

The two front-page stories, which did not name the former minister, quoted Ernest Hauser, a Lockheed customer-relations manager for Europe in 1961–64, as having said that the deal took place in 1973 or 1974, when the Conservatives were in office.

The Gulf Oil Case

SEC finds $4.2 million in Gulf bribes. Gulf Oil Corp. officials testified before the Securities and Exchange Commission (SEC) that the firm had been compelled to pay $4.2 million to foreign politicians in order to protect Gulf's oil assets, the Wall Street Journal reported May 2, 1975. Gulf officials refused to comment on the story, but SEC documents confirmed the Journal's report that Gulf had made payoffs to foreign politicians.

According to the Journal, Gulf Chairman Bob R. Dorsey told the SEC of three "specific and absolute demands made for contributions to a political party." Because "that political party still exists and the leader of that political party is still in office," Dorsey refused to reveal the identities of recipients of the payoffs, saying disclosure could jeopardize the multinational oil firm's holdings.

"In almost all other countries," Dorsey testified, "we [Gulf] are there by sufferance of governments. I think that we place a $700 million investment in severe jeopardy if I reveal the . . . ." (Dorsey's testimony was cut off at this point, according to the Journal.)

In describing the extortion demands, Dorsey said that politicians in one country demanded two cash "contributions" totaling $4 million. He "acceded" to the first request in 1966 for $1 million, Dorsey said, because he was "under a great deal of pressure." Four years later, he said, before the next election, "the demands were rather greater . . . and I think the contributions then was $3 million."

Implying that the same country was involved in extorting money on another occasion, Dorsey said that the company also had been compelled to pay $200,000 to begin operating a foreign oil "installation" in which Gulf had invested $150,000. Dorsey said that the payoff was "the only way" to obtain those operating rights, the Journal reported.

The SEC had begun an investigation of Gulf's books after disclosure of a secret, illegal $100,000 contribution made to the Nixon re-election campaign had revealed the existence of Gulf's $10.3 million slush fund. In answering an SEC complaint, Gulf admitted that $5.4 million had been distributed in cash donations to U.S. politicians and that another $4.9 million had been "distributed overseas in cash."

Venezuela, Ecuador got no bribes Dorsey says—In a message to the presidents of Venezuela and Ecuador, Dorsey said May 7 that "neither country is involved in receiving any of the political contributions reported in an American newspaper's speculative story." (The Journal stated that Gulf officials had not identified the payoff recipients but said there were hints in their testimony indicating Latin American officials may have received some Gulf cash. Dorsey's denial was limited only to this portion of the Journal report.)

"Gulf never suggested [in its] SEC testimony or at any other time that Venezuela or Ecuador were involved" in the extortion demands, Dorsey said in a statement to reporters. The text of the messages to the Venezuelan and Ecuadorean presidents was not released but a Gulf spokesman said they "included apologies."

Ecuador and Venezuela had demanded "clarification" of the allegations made in the Journal story. Venezuela had threatened to suspend's Gulf's activities there by 6 p.m. May 8 unless Gulf stated whether its politicians were involved in the payoff.

According to the New York Times May 8, disclosure of Dorsey's testimony before the SEC had caused anti-American, and anti-oil-company sentiment to emerge in Venezuela, where the government was preparing to nationalize its large oil industry with the acquiescence of multinational oil companies.

All of Venezuela's political parties signed a Congressional resolution saying that, due to the "ambiguous" nature of Dorsey's testimony before the SEC, "this could very well be a maneuver against Venezuela's decision to nationalize oil," the Times reported.

Senate probe. The Senate Subcommittee on Multinational Corporations opened hearings May 16 to investigate the reports of bribery and extortion.

The hearing's first witness was Gulf Chairman Bob R. Dorsey, who said Gulf had paid nearly $5 million abroad for political purposes. He urged Congress to pass legislation making such payments illegal so that U.S. companies would be able to resist "the very intense pressures that are placed upon us . . . and refuse the requests" for money.

Dorsey said a total of $4 million was paid to the ruling party of South Korean President Park Chung Hee after Gulf was subjected to "severe pressure for campaign contributions." "The demand was made by high party officials, and was accompanied by pressure which left little to the imagination as to what would occur if the company chose to turn its back on the request," Dorsey said. He noted that Gulf had about $300 million invested there in an oil refinery, fertilizer plant and petrochemical and shipbuilding interests.

Dorsey said a $1 million donation was made in 1966. Another $3 million payment was made in 1970 prior to the national elections after the party's original demand for $10 million was reduced during "heated discussions" in Seoul.

Park won re-election in 1971 by a narrow margin. Dorsey admitted under questioning that Gulf's contributions constituted an "unwarranted interference in the election" and made "the difference" in the outcome. Park banned all internal dissent May 13, allowing no South Korean newspapers to print an account of the Gulf payoff. Diplomatic sources speculated that the edict may have been issued in anticipation of Gulf's disclosure.

(Secretary of State Henry Kissinger said May 17 that the disclosure would have no impact on the U.S. security commitment to South Korea.)

Dorsey testified that at the time the South Korean contributions were made, he had believed they were legal, but was later advised the payments violated South Korean law.

Dorsey also told the subcommittee that $460,000 was paid to Bolivia's late President Rene Barrientos and his political party: a $110,000 helicopter had been leased for Barrientos' use during the 1966 presidential election and subsequently was purchased for him; two other payments of $240,000 and $110,000 were made to his party.

Dorsey also testified that unspecified political payments had been made in Italy and that $50,000 was contributed in 1970 through a Beirut bank for a "public education program" to promote the Arab cause in the U.S.

All of Gulf's overseas payments, Dorsey said, were charged as expenses to its now-defunct subsidiary, Bahamas Exploration Co., so that Gulf could avoid deducting the payments from U.S. tax returns.

In accepting responsibility for the payoffs, Dorsey said, "I was basically ashamed of what was going on. This is a sorrowful chapter in Gulf's long and otherwise productive and constructive history of achievement."

Dorsey's testimony before the Senate subcommittee corresponded to his earlier secret testimony given to the SEC, which was continuing to investigate Gulf's slush fund payments. Dorsey's secret SEC testimony had been reported May 2 in the Wall Street Journal, which had hinted strongly that $4.2 million in bribes had been paid to Latin American officials.

Dorsey condemned the Journal story, telling the subcommittee that as a result of its publication, Gulf was placed "in an untenable situation in almost 70 countries around the world" because governments suspected their officials might have been the recipients of the payoff money.

Ecuador had demanded clarification of Dorsey's remarks, as did Venezuela. Peru, which had not figured in the speculation, May 13 expropriated Gulf's few remaining assets there—several service stations valued at $2 million.

Bolivia seizes Gulf aide. The Bolivian government arrested the Gulf Oil Corp's local representative May 20, 1975 and said the U.S. firm would be "criminally prosecuted" for making illegal political contributions to Bolivian officials in the 1960s. Gulf's chairman was summoned to appear in Bolivian court and testify on the payments.

The Gulf representative, Carlos Dorado Chopitea, was placed under house arrest and held despite subsequent company assurances that he had "no involvement whatever" in the contributions. Gulf's chairman, Bob R. Dorsey, was offered "all necessary guarantees" to testify in Bolivia but he faced a jail term if found guilty by the court, according to La Paz District Attorney Rolando Simbron.

The government May 16 asserted it would prosecute any officials who took illegal payments from Gulf. It sent a note to Dorsey May 17 demanding that his firm, "immediately and without major delays," disclose which officials received the payments. Gulf said it would comply as soon as it completed a full investigation of the matter.

Gulf no longer operated in Bolivia, having been nationalized in 1969 by the government of Gen. Alfredo Ovando Candia, who took power after Barrientos died in a helicopter crash that year. Ovando's regime had agreed in 1970, after extended negotiations, to pay Gulf $78.6 million for its expropriated assets. Bolivia still owed Gulf $57.2 million, according to official sources.

The government had threatened May 7 to default on the remaining payments unless Gulf cleared up confusion over whether Bolivians had been among unnamed foreign politicians who had received $4.2 million worth of Gulf bribes.

Complying with the government's demand, Dorado Chopitea submitted a note May 10 denying that Bolivians had received any of the $4.2 million but adding that Gulf could not "assure that Bolivia did not receive political contributions from our company."

Gulf was criticized May 17 by a number of prominent Bolivians, including members of parties that had supported Barrientos. The archbishop of La Paz, Msgr. Jorge Manrique, said he was "offended by these attacks on dead men," and Edwin Tapia, head of a pro-Barrientos party, called Gulf's allegations "infamous and cowardly actions which reveal the spirit with which transnational corporations exploit developing nations."

Ex-President Ovando criticized Gulf from his exile home in Madrid, asserting the company had helped bring down his government in 1970 with a campaign to "paralyze foreign investment in the country, creating a climate of insecurity and a lack of confidence within the country and abroad."

Marcelo Quiroga Santa Cruz, who had been Ovando's mines minister in 1970 and now lived in Mexico, attacked not only Gulf but the current Bolivian government. He said the Gulf payments "morally invalidate" the current government officials who had also served under Barrientos, including President Banzer, who had been Barrientos' education minister, and Defense Minister Rene Bernal, who had been peasant affairs minister. Quiroga did not mention Ovando, who had been Barrientos' army commander.

Bolivia releases Gulf agent, Dorsey bars trip. The Bolivian judge who had ordered Gulf Oil Corp.'s representative there jailed after the company admitted making contributions to Bolivian politicians later ordered his release, the Wall Street Journal reported May 29. Carlos Dorado Chopitea was freed after his lawyers argued he had no legal responsibility for Gulf's actions.

Gulf Chairman Bob R. Dorsey said May 22 that he would not go to Bolivia to answer a summons for his appearance and testify about Gulf's contributions.

3 in Holland admit Gulf link. Three Dutch citizens, including one parliamentarian, admitted Jan. 11, 1976 that they had acted as paid consultants for the U.S.

Gulf Oil Co. in the Netherlands between 1972 and mid-1975 to counteract what the company reportedly felt was bad publicity it was receiving over environmental issues. The disclosures were made following the release of a U.S. report which discussed political payments of the oil company. The three people named were Bauke Roolvink, a senior member of the Anti-Revolutionary Party; Norbert Schmelzer, the former foreign minister; and Ferry Hoogendijk, the editor of Elseviers, the nation's largest weekly news magazine.

The United Brands Case

United Brands admits Honduran bribe. United Brands Co., a multinational food concern and leading banana exporter, admitted that a $1.25 million bribe was paid in 1974 to an unnamed Honduran official to win a reduction in that country's export tax on bananas. United Brands, a successor firm to United Fruit Co., marketed Chiquita brand bananas. Honduras, which supplied 25% of United Brands' banana production, was the world's third largest banana-producing country.

United Brands disclosed payment of the bribe April 8, 1975 to the Wall Street Journal, which had learned that the Securities and Exchange Commission (SEC) was investigating bribery allegations against the company. The Journal account was published April 9.

Formal charges were filed by the SEC April 9. The company was accused of issuing false reports to conceal $2 million in foreign payoffs. In addition to the Honduran bribe, the SEC also cited "cash payments approximating $750,000 to officials of a foreign government in Europe in connection with securing favorable business opportunities" since 1970. Sources described as close to the SEC investigation identified Honduran President Oswaldo Lopez Arellano and Italian officials as recipients of the United Brands bribes.

Through a spokesman, Lopez Arellano April 9 denied involvement. An Italian embassy official in Washington said the charges "must be wrong," but added that if the "very serious allegation" proved true, "it would be a matter of state prosecution."

According to the Journal, the SEC began a routine investigation of the company after United Brands' chairman and chief executive officer, Eli M. Black, jumped to his death from the company's Manhattan headquarters Feb. 3. An SEC investigation was opened customarily after the unusual death of any company's chief executive, an SEC spokesman said.

The agency's probe intensified, the Journal reported April 10, when United Brands' lawyers notified the SEC and the State Department in February of payment of the Honduran bribe. However, company officials feared that disclosure of the payoff would jeopardize its dealings in Honduras and asked the SEC not to reveal details of the payment.

According to the Journal, United Brands feared that Honduras would expropriate the firm's 28,000 acres in banana production there if word of the payoff were revealed. These fears were alluded to in United Brands' April 8 statement to the Journal. Disclosure of the $1.25 million bribe could result in "a material reduction in future earnings and a loss of substantial corporate assets, which, in turn, could affect the continuity of operations of the company," the statement said.

In its statement, United Brands also admitted that Black had authorized the Honduran payment, which the company said was made through the company's foreign subsidiaries and was not accurately identified on its books and records. According to the SEC, the money was deposited in the Swiss bank accounts of "designated [Honduran] government officials."

Under the initial understanding with the unnamed Honduran official, the company stated, an additional $1.25 million bribe was to have been paid in the spring of 1975, but United Brands' board of directors decided not to make the second payment.

United Brands also announced that a special committee would be appointed to investigate and report the circumstances of the Honduran payment, as well as "certain other payments" estimated at $750,000 "in countries outside the Western Hemisphere."

United Brands' Honduran bribe was directed at securing a reduction in that country's export tax of 50¢ a 40-pound box on bananas. Honduras had imposed the export levy in April 1974 after several Central and South American countries joined in an effort to win higher fruit prices early in 1974 when prices were severely depressed because of an oversupply of the fruit.

In an action marking the beginning of a "banana war," the producers decided to impose a $1-a-box export tax to offset their soaring fuel costs. (However, Ecuador, the world's largest banana producer, refused to enact the levy and other countries subsequently reduced their tax ceilings.)

Banana-exporting firms quickly protested the new tax and retaliated against the producing countries. United Brands undertook negotiations with Honduras, Panama and Costa Rica to win a reduction in the levy. In August, 1974, it was announced that the Honduran tax would be lowered to 25¢ a box with yearly increases beginning in 1974 depending in part on the banana market at the time. The reduction represented a savings of $7.5 million to United Brands during 1974, when the company exported an estimated 30 million boxes of bananas from Honduras.

United Brands filed a report with the SEC in September 1974 on its successful attempts to win a reduction in the Honduran tax. United Brands' failure to mention the bribe in the report was the basis of the SEC complaint that the company had filed false and misleading statements on the tax issue with the agency.

Auditor failed to disclose bribe—Price Waterhouse & Co., United Brands' outside auditor, admitted that it had known of the $1.25 million Honduran bribe, but had not required disclosure of the payoff for fear of jeopardizing the firm's Honduran operations, the Journal reported April 11. It was feared that disclosure of the payment would embarrass the government there and perhaps result in United Brands' loss of its Honduran properties, a spokesman for Price Waterhouse said.

In its audit letter, dated March 31, filed with the SEC as part of United Brands' annual report, Price Waterhouse noted that "certain information has been omitted from this annual report and is being filed separately with the SEC together with an application to the commission for a determination that such information be kept confidential."

Several stockowners' suits were filed against United Brands as a result of the SEC complaint and United Brands' admissions regarding the bribe.

Harry Neugarten, a United Brands shareholder, brought suit April 10 seeking damages payable to the company for the wrongful conversion and "spoilation" of company assets in payment of the Honduran bribe. Neugarten also sought payment of damages to himself and other shareholders who bought United Brands common stock from April 1974 to April 8, 1975.

Neugarten contended that the defendants, who included United Brands, 12 of the company's 14 current directors, two company officers and the estate of Eli Black, knew or should have known that false and misleading financial statements were issued regarding the bribe.

Lopez loses defense post. President Oswaldo Lopez Arellano's control of Honduras was threatened by his removal as armed forces commander March 31, 1975 and the report that he had taken the United Brands bribe.

The banana bribe scandal surfaced at a time of great economic difficulties in Honduras. Following the devastation by Hurricane Fifi in September 1974, which caused $450 million–$600 million in damage and destroyed 70% of United Brands' banana plantations, the government had undertaken a massive reconstruction effort based almost entirely on foreign subsidies and loans. Some observers felt the bribe scandal would discourage foreign lending agencies from contributing further to the reconstruction program, the Wall Street Journal reported April 14.

(Most high officials in the government believed the bribe charge was another move by United Brands in its "banana war" against Honduras and other countries which imposed a tax on banana exports, the Spanish news agency EFE reported April 11. One official said: "It's conceivable that, facing imminent bankruptcy, United Brands—which has a debt higher than $400 million—would make a

final move to justify its failure before a possible nationalist measure by the Honduran government." The official referred to possible expropriation of the U.S. company's banana properties, which Honduras had always denied planning.)

Lopez ousted as president. The Armed Forces Superior Council dismissed Lopez Arellano as president of Honduras April 22, after Lopez refused to cooperate fully with a government panel investigating reports that he accepted a $1.25 million bribe from United Brands.

The day before the coup, the committee investigating the bribe reports had announced publicly that Lopez had refused it permission to examine his foreign bank accounts, creating "an obstacle to the committee's work." The U.S. Securities and Exchange Commission (SEC) had reported that the United Brands bribe money was deposited in the Swiss bank accounts of unnamed Honduran officials.

Economy Minister Abraham Bennaton asserted April 12 that the bribe allegation was unjust and proved that officials who acted in defense of national interests were exposed to "slander and reprisals." He warned that if the allegation were not contested, "no one in the future will dare struggle against the transnational companies whose power extends to the information media, thus making them capable of distorting facts and events." Bennaton resigned when Lopez Arellano was replaced April 22.

The banana bribe allegation had shaken Honduras since it was first reported April 9, according to press accounts. Labor unions in the northern banana producing area called April 10 for the nationalization of the local subsidiaries of United Brands and the other U.S. banana firm, Standard Fruit.

Lopez & Bennaton named in bribe. The Honduran newspaper La Prensa reported April 29 that a government commission had received direct evidence in the U.S. that United Brands Co. had bribed ex-President Lopez Arellano in 1974 to obtain a reduction of Honduras' banana export tax.

La Prensa said the commission had received the number of a bank account belonging to Lopez where United Brands had deposited the $1.25 million bribe payment. The commission left the U.S. April 29 for Switzerland, where the bank account presumably was located.

The Wall Street Journal reported May 7 that the bribe had been extorted from United Brands by Abraham Bennaton, who served as economy minister under Lopez. Bennaton reportedly suggested to Harvey Johnson, United Brands' vice president in charge of banana operations, that Honduras would 'reduce its banana export tax in exchange for a $5 million payment from the company. Johnson reportedly turned the matter over to John Taylor, a United Brands senior vice president, who succeeded in reducing the bribe to $2.5 million and arranged to have a first payment of $1.25 million taken from the company's European operations and deposited in the Swiss bank accounts of unnamed Honduran officials.

Bennaton indicted. The Honduran investigative panel charged May 15, 1975 that Bennaton had received the $1.25 million United Brands bribe.

Bennaton was immediately indicted for tax fraud, accepting a bribe and offending the nation's dignity. He was imprisoned May 27 and released on $825 bail June 4. A court acquitted him of the tax fraud charge June 26.

Preliminary criminal charges were also filed against United Brands' Honduran subsidiary, Tela Railroad Co., and Tela's general manager, Houston Lacombe, was forbidden to leave the country, it was reported May 19.

The government panel's report on the bribe, read in a nationwide broadcast by Jorge Arturo Reina, rector of the National University, charged Bennaton had received the payment in September 1974 at a meeting in Zurich, Switzerland with John Taylor, a United Brands senior vice president.

The panel was unable to determine whether ex-President Oswaldo Lopez Arellano was involved in the bribe because Lopez refused the panel permission to examine his Swiss bank account. However, Reina said Lopez had refused a bribe of "several hundred thousand" dollars offered him in July 1974 by Taylor and Eli Black, United Brands' late chairman.

Both Bennaton and Lopez continued to deny any role in the bribe payment. Bennaton said May 15 that the money could have been transferred to his bank account without his permission. Lopez told newsmen May 20 that he considered himself "clean," and that "Bennaton is also not implicated because he had no power over the banana export tax."

Honduras cancels U.S. concessions. Honduras Aug. 15, 1975 canceled the concessions of two U.S. banana firms, United Brands and Standard Fruit, accusing the companies of committing "immoral actions detrimental to the national interests."

President Juan Alberto Melgar Castro cited as "immoral actions" the admitted bribery of a top Honduran official by United Brands, and a "boycott of national production" by Standard Fruit.

Melgar said the government's action was not a "nationalization or expropriation," but a removal of the "unjustified" privileges heretofore enjoyed by the companies, including tax breaks.

Cancellation of the concessions conformed with recommendations issued July 9 by a government commission established 45 days before in the wake of the United Brands bribe scandal. In addition to the cancellation, the commission recommended that the government nationalize United Brands and Standard Fruit and that it seek monetary compensation for the "enormous damage" done to Honduras by the bribe scandal.

Italian bribe charged. A chief state prosecutor in Rome had opened a judiciary investigation into allegations that the United Brands Co. had paid $750,000 in bribes to Italian government officials in 1970–74 to secure favored treatment for its banana exports to Italy, it was reported May 23, 1975.

EEC fines United Brands. The European Economic Community said Dec. 18, 1975 it had fined United Brands Co. the equivalent of $1.2 million for antitrust violations in the European banana market. The U.S.-based food producer also was ordered to reduce its wholesale banana price 15% in West Germany and 30% in Belgium, the Netherlands and Luxembourg.

The price cutting order marked the first time the Common Market had tried to force a price reduction. It was taken under article 86 of the Treaty of Rome, which forbade abuse of a dominant market position.

According to the EEC, United Brands' policy forbidding its wholesalers to resell bananas to other wholesalers "effectively compartmentalized the market," and constituted restraint of trade. The Common Market's antitrust investigation was based on complaints from banana wholesalers in Denmark and Ireland who claimed that United Brands restricted them from selling the company's Chiquita-brand bananas to other wholesalers who were not customers of United Brands.

Gulf Oil Action

Gulf board ousts four top officials. Gulf Oil Corp.'s board of directors, embarrassed by revelations of illegal payments, dismissed board chairman Bob R. Dorsey and three other top officials Jan. 15, 1976.

Jerry McAfee, president of Gulf Oil Canada Ltd., which was two-thirds owned by the U.S. company, was named to replace Dorsey.

The board's action followed nearly 24 hours of intense debate over a two-day period at the oil company's Pittsburgh headquarters. At the final board meeting, which ended shortly after 1 a.m. Jan. 15, the board "accepted" Dorsey's resignation and those of William L. Henry, head of Gulf's real-estate subsidiary, Fred Deering, senior vice president for finance, and Herbert C. Manning, vice president and corporate secretary, for their roles in the slush fund operation that an internal fact-finding commission had declared was "shot through with illegality."

John J. McCloy, a prominent New York lawyer who headed the three-man investigation panel, said the directors "faced up to their responsibility quite well." Their action "set a high level of corporate responsibility," he added.

It was widely reported that the five outside directors representing the Mellon family on the 14-member board engineered the high-level shake-up that resulted in Dorsey's ouster.

The Wall Street Journal Jan. 15 quoted a Mellon "ally" who said Dorsey's "firing" was "an expression of community conscience," particularly the business community, in Pittsburgh, where the Mellon family's financial, industrial and philanthropic activities were centered.

Gulf's directors issued a statement Jan. 16 denying the board had been divided over a course of action and refuting the Journal's report that Dorsey's supporters on the board had "fought to the last minute" to prevent his dismissal.

The Journal also reported that Dorsey's lawyers sought a "bargain" from the Mellon family interests that would allow him to remain as honorary chairman or part of a three-member operating team. According to the Journal, the board's Mellon representatives refused to bargain and ruled out any "Ford-type pardon" that would release Dorsey from future liability in any lawsuits arising out of the slush-fund scandal.

In its statement Jan. 16, the board stated "unequivocally that all action taken was unanimous." There was "no dissension among any of the directors" on the "basic point" that the illegal contributions cited in the McCloy report "were and are condemned in every respect," the report said.

Dorsey and director E. D. Brockett, Dorsey's predecessor as chairman, were excluded from the board's deliberations because the McCloy report declared both men were "involved" in the illegal political contributions scheme. The report also linked Henry and Deering, former Gulf comptrollers, to the slush-fund operations, and identified Henry and Manning as having received "laundered" cash used in the secret fund.

Gulf, the nation's seventh largest industrial corporation, with estimated 1975 sales of $16 billion and 50,000 employes around the world, was the largest company to become enmeshed in the widening scandal of illegal domestic political payments and business payoffs made abroad by U.S. companies.

McCloy report details political payments
—Gulf Oil Corp. made political contributions in the U.S. and abroad totaling $12.3 million, most of it donated illegally and funneled through a slush fund maintained at Gulf's Bahamian subsidiary, from the early 1960s to the early 1970s, according to a special review panel authorized by Gulf's directors to determine the extent of the company's illegal political activities.

The fact-finding commission had been established in March 1975 at the behest of the Securities and Exchange Commission, which charged Gulf with concealing the payment of at least $10.3 million to U.S. and foreign politicians, in violation of federal securities laws.

Gulf quickly accepted a consent order settling the complaint and agreed not to violate securities laws in the future. Gulf also accepted the SEC's chief condition for the settlement and agreed to an independent examination of Gulf's books and management to reveal the full extent of the company's unlawful contributions. The special review panel's report was filed with the SEC and with U.S. District Court in Washington Dec. 30, 1975 in compliance with the terms of settlement.

The report also was submitted to Gulf's board of directors and provided the basis for the board's subsequent ouster of Gulf chairman Bob R. Dorsey and three other top officials of the company.

Noting that 11 company executives admitted having some knowledge of the covert transfer of Gulf funds through the Bahamian slush fund, the McCloy report said, "The pattern and nature of this use of corporate funds, in large part not recorded on the books of the company, has raised serious questions as to the policy and management of the company in regard to this matter."

The panel was unable to prove that Dorsey was aware that Gulf's former vice president in Washington, Claude C. Wild Jr., was illegally distributing more than $5 million in laundered corporate cash to politicians; however, the report "concluded that Dorsey was not sufficiently alert and should have known Wild was involved in making political contributions from an unknown source."

The panel also blamed E. D. Brockett, who had preceded Dorsey as Gulf chairman, for failing to question Wild's "extra-curricular" activities.

Of the 11 executives with direct knowledge of the slush fund, only two remained with the company, the report stated, three having died and six retired.

The two men, William L. Henry and Fred Deering, both vice presidents of Gulf and former comptrollers with the company, denied "knowledge that company funds were being used for domestic political contributions," according to the report.

However, the commission concluded that Henry "had an obligation" as comptroller to question the covert transactions, and that Deering, also while comptroller, "did not act in a manner consistent with the responsibilities of his office in connection with the transfer of funds to the Bahamas."

Herbert C. Manning, a lawyer and secretary of the company, also was blamed for failing to make inquiries about the source of funds used to make donations. Henry, Deering and Manning were dismissed by Gulf's board in the shakeup resulting from Dorsey's ouster.

The commission was unable to pinpoint when the Bahamian slush fund was created, but believed it occurred around 1960. One of the former company officials said to have knowledge of the fund told the commission that the late William K. Whiteford, then chairman of Gulf, established the fund in 1960 "to help maintain a political atmosphere conducive to [Gulf's] foreign expansion plans" and "to give the company some 'muscle' in [domestic] politics."

The commission offered several recommendations to prevent a recurrence of the political payments scandal. These included prohibiting the use of "off-the-book [unrecorded] funds, whether legal or not"; strengthening the company's internal audit department; and giving the company's chief legal officer direct access to the chief executive and charging the lawyer with the "responsibility of calling to the attention of management any operations of the company which ... constitute illegal political activities."

The commission acknowledged, however, that these safeguards would not necessarily prevent future abuses. "The illegal use of corporate funds for political purposes was originally instituted by the top management of Gulf and in the last analysis it will be in the tone and attitude of top management that the eradication of the practice will be insured in the future," the report stated.

The commission said it was unable to trace most of the $5.4 million that the SEC said was donated illegally to U.S. politicians. However, the panel concluded that the domestic contributions made by Gulf were "shot through with illegalities."

Although the commission was unable to prove that politicians knowingly accepted corporate cash in violation of federal laws, the report said, "It is hard to escape the conclusion that a sort of 'shut-eyed sentry' attitude prevailed upon the part of both the corporate officials and the recipients as well as on the part of those charged with enforcement responsibility."

Senate Minority Leader Hugh Scott (R, Pa.) was among those whom company officials said had received laundered cash from the slush fund—$5,000 in the spring and $5,000 in the fall of each year for several years. The report noted that Scott had filed a written statement with the commission denying he "knowingly" received illegal contributions.

The commission's estimate of Gulf's total political payments differed from the SEC's figure because the report disclosed payments made in Sweden, Canada and Italy that were termed legal.

Gulf's Swedish subsidiary donated $6,000 to political parties there, and Gulf's Canada subsidiary made political contributions at the national and provincial level totaling more than $1.35 million, the report stated.

The commission classified two payments made in Italy as ordinary business expenses. However, the report also disclosed the existence of a "fondo nero," or black fund, out of which more than $10,000 was paid to newspapers, editors and journalists associated with the Christian Democratic and Socialist parties.

A "gray fund" existed in South Korea, the report stated. The fund was used to pay $33,000 from 1972-1975 to members of the South Korean president's staff, the prime minister's staff, the ministry of commerce and industry, and the South Korean central intelligence agency.

The report also revealed that a Korean oil company in which Gulf had an interest had paid kickbacks since 1971 to the South Korean ministry of national defense. Another $200,000 was paid to President Chung Hee Park "to defray" his expenses for a trip to California to meet then President Nixon.

The report also revealed that Gulf intended to pay $1.8 million to the late President Rene Barrientos of Bolivia and two other Bolivians in connection with the construction of a pipeline, but said that only $250,000 actually was paid in 1969 and 1970.

Other Oil Companies

Political payments in Italy & Canada. Exxon Corp. Chairman James J. Jamieson admitted publicly May 15, 1975 that the company had made political contributions in Italy and Canada. Exxon's disclosure was made during its annual stockholder's meeting.

Jamieson claimed that the contributions were made "openly" by Exxon affiliates through "legal" and "direct" donations to political parties. "In those areas where it is legal, we have made political contributions," Jamieson declared. "Canada is one. Italy is another," he said, but added that contributions made to these countries were the only ones he "was aware of."

Contributions were made to "two or three" political parties in Canada, Jamieson said. He was unsure when the money was donated. The Italian contributions were made several years ago, he said. "We haven't given any contributions in Italy since late 1971 or early 1972." Jamieson declined to tell stockholders how much the Canadian and Italian contributions totaled.

A proposed stockholder's resolution that would have required Exxon to make public its 1974 political contributions was defeated.

Three other U.S. oil giants, Mobil Oil Corp., Standard Oil Co. (Indiana), and Standard Oil Co. (California), told the Wall Street Journal May 19 that they also had made political contributions outside the U.S.

Mobile and Indiana Standard said their donations were made in Italy and Canada, and like Exxon, contended that the gifts represented a legal and accepted practice in those countries. Both oil companies refused to name the parties which had received the payments or say how much money was disbursed.

A spokesman for California Standard said the firm had "occasionally" made contributions "in a few countries," but declined to name them or say how much was donated.

The company denied that payments had been made in South Korea, where California Standard participated in a refinery operation with another oil firm, saying that "the company has a long-standing policy against so-called 'under the table' contributions to government officials anywhere in the world."

Other major oil firms queried by the Journal denied making foreign political contributions.

In Italy, Communist member of Parliament Ugo Spagnoli charged in a discussion televised May 30 that the oil industry had paid $32 million to parties in the government coalition to obtain favorable legislation. Spagnoli, vice chairman of a parliamentary commission investigating corruption in oil and public works, said the $32 million had bought "at least one law, six decrees and eight ministerial directives."

However, the Christian Democratic chairman of the parliamentary commission, Angelo Castelli, said May 31 that Spagnoli's charges were based only on newspaper reports, not on the commission's findings. The parliamentary probe was being conducted under the secrecy rules of pretrial procedures.

Exxon paid $46–$49 million in Italy. Exxon Corp. admitted July 12, 1975 that its political payments in Italy from 1963–1972 totaled $46–$49 million. Authorized payments made by Exxon's Italian subsidiary, Esso Italiana S.p.A., totaled $27 million. Another $19–$22 million in unauthorized payments, including $86,000 intended for the Italian Communist party, also were made through the Italian subsidiary, a company spokesman said.

Although all payments were ordered stopped in late 1971, the spokesman said, unauthorized donations continued to be made in 1972 and a company investigation of these contributions resulted in the resignation of Vincenzo Cazzaniga, then managing director of Esso Italiana.

Exxon's comptroller, Archie L. Monroe, testified on the Italian payments July 10 in a closed hearing of the Senate Subcommittee on Multinational Corporations.

In issuing the statement, a company spokesman conceded that Exxon had sought to keep Monroe's subcommittee testimony secret. "We asked for the confidentiality out of concern for the Italian political parties and citizens under investigation in Italy," the spokesman said. (A parliamentary commission was investigating charges that oil companies had bribed politicians to win government favors.)

In 1971, Exxon authorized the payment of $3 million in political contributions. Late that year, the spokesman said, "We discovered that the managing director [Cazzaniga] had made substantial unauthorized commercial arrangements, payments, and commitments over a period of years. Some of those, he indicated to us, were political contributions." The spokesman added, however, that Exxon still did not know "definitively" who received the $19-$22 million.

Exxon's spokesman said the authorized payments were made in checks and cash. Esso Italiana had indicated cash contributions were customary, he said, and added, "Some of the parties wanted it that way." "Most of the authorized contributions were entered on the books as payments to newspapers, publicity agencies, and the like," with the balance "entered under the broad category of administrative expenses. The unauthorized payments were concealed in various ways," he said.

When asked the purpose of Exxon's authorized payments, the spokesman quoted Monroe's response before the Senate subcommittee. The money was donated to "further the democratic process," he said.

Monroe amended that statement in subcommittee testimony July 16, conceding that the money was authorized to promote Exxon's "business objectives" in Italy, and that the money was earmarked on records toward efforts to reduce or defer taxes, obtain refinery licenses, win permission to import natural gas, and secure favorable locations for service stations. Monroe refused, however, to characterize the payments as bribes.

Questions at the subcommittee hearing July 16 centered on two internal Exxon audits that indicated the payments were intentionally camouflaged by Exxon officials. According to the first audit, dated August 1972, the authorized Italian payments were made out of a "special budget" Exxon "created to control payments, which by their very nature, couldn't be accurately recorded on the books of the Italian company" because Esso Italiana did not want them disclosed. "In addition to the $29 million disbursed through the special budget," the audit stated, "at least $30 million was expended in a similar manner over the last 10 years." Monroe stated that Cazzaniga, beside making unauthorized political contributions, also used the money to make "secret purchases of real estate" and "secret guarantees to banks in favor of other companies." (Discrepancies between these figures and payments Exxon admitted making were not resolved in Senate testimony.)

"These irregularities" occurring at Esso Italiana went undetected, Monroe said, "because of a failure of management and financial controls."

According to another report in October 1972 to the audit committee of Exxon's board, "the principal factor which permitted the irregularities to occur and remain undiscovered for such a long period of time was the fact that higher levels of management [regional headquarters in London and corporate headquarters in New York] condoned the falsification of records to obtain funds for confidential special payments. Bogus documentation and false accounting were accepted by many levels of management," the report stated. "Thus, the entire control system was rendered ineffective as it was virtually impossible under the circumstances to verify the validity of specific transactions."

(In a statement issued July 15, Exxon Chairman J. K. Jamieson admitted the firm had covered up political payments by its Italian subsidiary and conceded "this was a mistake." Management was "persuaded that it was necessary to make [political] contributions without disclosing the recipients, as it appears was the custom," Jamieson said. "This meant handling the payments so that they couldn't be identified as political contributions on the books of Esso Italiana.")

Although Monroe claimed Exxon had moved quickly to end the abuses in 1972, the August 1972 audit indicated that Exxon had continued to use phony accounting methods, including "dummy invoices," long after the problem had been identified several years earlier.

Monroe said Cazzaniga had assured him all the payments were legal. According to the Washington Post July 12, corporate contributions were legal in Italy. A 1974 disclosure law required the consent of the company's shareholders and the entry of payments on the company's books. Subcommittee Chairman Frank Church (D, Ida.) charged July 16 that Exxon was practicing corruption on a massive scale.

According to Exxon documents, the Christian Democratic party, which had dominated Italy's coalition governments in the post-war period, was allocated $11,948,046 from 1963–1972; the Social Democrats $5,160,952; the Socialists $1,245,028; the Liberals $591,531; the Republicans $267,521; the Italian Socialist Movement $236,106; and the Socialist Party of Proletarian Unity $71,111. Another $1,096,344 was disbursed to "others unkno vn."

The August 1972 audit identified the money earmarked in the special budget for obtaining favors from the government, including $2,350,000 for the "deferred payment" of taxes from 1969–1971; $500,000 for "tax legislation" in 1971; and $1,150,000 to secure refinery licenses from 1969–1971.

The Italian Communist Party July 16 denied having received $86,000 earmarked for it by Exxon's Italian subsidiary, but a pro-Communist newspaper in Rome admitted July 18 that its publishing house, Editrice Rinnovamento, had received money from Esso Italiana. The newspaper, Paesa Sera, said the money was paid for advertising. The publishing house also owned a pro-Communist newspaper in Sicily.

The party's denial appeared July 14 in its official newspaper, L'Unita, which was housed in the same building as Paesa Sera. The statement said, "Not only the hands but also the coffers of the Italian Communist Party are clean."

Mobil's Italian payments totaled $2.1 million. A Mobil Oil Corp. official told the Senate Subcommittee on Multinational Corporations July 17 that $2.1 million was donated to Italy's three major center-left political parties from 1970–1973 by the oil company's affiliate, Mobil Oil Italiana.

Everett S. Checket, executive vice president of Mobil's international division, conceded the disbursements were disguised on company books, but insisted the payments were made to "support the democratic process."

"All such contributions were made from Mobil's normal business accounts, by company check or bank remittance," Checket said. "These contributions were not paid from any secret fund and did not involve out-of-country financial transactions [laundering of funds]," he said. However, under questioning, Checket admitted that the payments were recorded as advertising, research or other expenses on Mobil Oil Italiana's books, at the request of the parties.

Subcommittee Chairman Frank Church (D, Ida.) charged that Mobil had "falsified" its accounts to conceal the payments, but another Mobil official objected to use of the term, contending that nobody was "defrauded or deceived" by the accounting procedure. "That's an argument only a lawyer would make," Church replied.

Checket acknowledged that the contributions were actually assessments made by Unione Petrolifera, Italy's trade association of petroleum companies. The association took a bank loan to make contributions and then set assessments on various oil companies to repay the loan based on the amount of oil each had sold Italy's state-owned electricity company, according to the testimony.

Payments to Canadian parties. Imperial Oil Ltd. of Canada, which was 70%-owned by Exxon Corp., disclosed July 15 that its political contributions to Canadian parties at the provincial and federal level had totaled $234,000 annually over the past five years.

The money was limited to three parties: the Progressive Conservative, Liberal and Social Credit parties. No individuals received contributions from Imperial, a spokesman said. The company refused to say how much money was received by each party.

Additional Exxon payments. Exxon Corp. admitted Sept. 25, 1975 that another $860,000 had been paid to government officials and others elsewhere during 1963–75.

The disclosure was contained in a preliminary prospectus, filed with the Securities and Exchange Commission, describing $400 million of securities being offered for sale by an Exxon subsidiary. The financing would be used to meet Exxon's share of building a pipeline to transport oil from Alaska's North Slope.

The company statement did not reveal where the political donations had been made, to whom, or for what purpose.

However, Exxon's chairman, Clifton Garvin Jr., said Nov. 16 that corporate funds were contributed to political parties in Australia and Japan. Garvin said all such foreign payments had ceased.

In a further statement Nov. 19, Exxon disclosed that its Japanese subsidiary had contributed $19,000 to two political parties in Okinawa in 1972, shortly after Japan assumed control of the island from the U.S. The contributions were made "to encourage healthy political activities" in Okinawa, a spokesman for the Japanese subsidiary said.

According to Exxon's prospectus, "various payments totaling about $740,000" were made from 1963–1975 "in three countries to government officials, officials of government-owned companies, or others, in connection with action by such governments or companies."

Another $13,000 was paid to "a government legislator serving in a consulting capacity." The money, which was paid from 1969 through 1975 when payments ceased, was covered up in Exxon's books "prior to 1973."

Also "improperly booked" were "political contributions [made] in 1972 in two countries totaling $31,000."

The prospectus also provided details about the previously disclosed Italian payments. Exxon said that Esso Italiana made authorized political contributions totaling $27 million. Political contributions from corporations were legal in

Italy, but a government investigation was underway there to determine if bribes were paid.

The oil company also claimed that Vincenzo Cazzaniga, former managing director of the subsidiary, made unauthorized political contributions totaling $19 million. Another $10 million of unauthorized commercial payments were made by Cazzaniga to a unit of the Italian government-controlled oil company, Ente Nazionale Idrocarburi, "under secret side agreements" related to a liquified natural gas transaction, according to Exxon.

The prospectus also revealed that Esso Italiana had instituted arbitration proceedings to invalidate the secret agreements, which could cost the subsidiary $40 million over the life of the contract, which ran till 1991. Exxon said it was trying to recover the $10 million, but had not yet decided whether to sue Cazzaniga.

The $27 million in authorized political contributions was generated through sham bookkeeping procedures, Exxon said, including the use of bogus invoices and secret bank accounts. Cazzaniga also used secret bank accounts, according to the prospectus.

Ashland Oil accused. Another major oil company was accused during 1975 of improper overseas payments.

In a civil suit filed May 16 in U.S. District Court in Washington, the SEC accused Ashland Oil Inc. and three of its top officers of failing to disclose that more than $4 million in cash had been transferred or disbursed overseas since 1967 "ostensibly for business purposes."

Ashland and the other defendants, Orin E. Atkins, chairman, William R. Seaton, a vice president, and Clyde M. Webb, a vice president, consented to a permanent injunction against filing false reports with the agency, but did not admit or deny the charges.

According to the SEC complaint, some of the foreign payments were made to "consultants, legal representatives, and others," but "inadequate records" were maintained for other payments, making it difficult to determine the funds' true use abroad. Ashland contended that the money was used in more than 35 foreign

transactions over a number of years for "a wide variety of subjects."

The SEC suit also charged that the defendants failed to disclose that they had "systematically diverted" about $780,000 "to a secret cash fund maintained by them for unlawful political contributions and other purposes."

The agency also charged that $90,000 of the secret fund "remains totally unaccounted for." Another $70,000 "in cash payments to officers and employes of Ashland," money that was unrelated to the slush fund, also "cannot be accounted for," the complaint stated.

A special panel investigating possible illegal payments made by Ashland said June 29 that $801,165 might have been used for such payments in the U.S. and abroad in 1967–74. Questionable payments included funds that went to consultants and officials in Libya, Gabon, the Dominican Republic and Nigeria.

In earlier disclosures at the firm's annual meeting, Ashland had told stockholders that $533,000, excluding an illegal $100,000 donation to the Nixon re-election campaign, had been contributed to politicians.

The investigation, by a committee of Ashland's board of directors, was initiated under court order as part of a settlement with the SEC.

In determining the extent of possible political payments, the panel said all monies that could not "be substantially accounted for" were regarded "as having been available for political contributions."

The report's findings:

Libyan payments—$100,000 was paid in 1971 to a consultant in Libya, "who may have paid that money to two Libyan nationals" employed by the Libyan National Petroleum Corp. prior to Col. Muammar el-Qadaffi's seizure of power in 1969. Another $5,000 was paid to a "minor Libyan official" in 1970.

Gabon payments—Payments of $150,-000 and $40,000 were made in 1971 to "two government officials of Gabon," where Ashland had oil-drilling rights. The company said it had been advised by an official of the African nation "that the money would be used by both recipients for social welfare and public purposes."

According to the Washington Post July 10, Gabon President Omar Bongo was the recipient of the $150,000 payment. Names of the recipients of Ashland's payments had been submitted to the board, but were not filed with the report submitted to the court and to the SEC.

Dominican Republic payment—$50,000 was paid in 1967 and 1968 to several persons in the Dominican Republic, where Ashland was considering developing a petrochemical and refinery project. The money was funneled through a consultant to a lawyer, an engineer, an "unidentified government official" and a "person identified by the consultant as an ambassador-at-large for the Dominican Republic in Europe."

Nigerian payment—$30,000 was paid in 1968 to a Nigerian consultant "in connection with general business opportunities in that country," where Ashland had struck oil and was searching for more.

(Columnist Jack Anderson July 9 published a confidential Ashland letter revealing that the firm had paid $240,000 to Saudi Arabian Prince Mishal Abdul-Aziz, a half-brother of King Khalid. The prince was retained in May 1974 to "provide aid in representations" with the government so that Ashland could obtain crude oil for its U.S. refineries, according to the company letter.)

The special panel recommended no changes be made in Ashland's management as a result of the investigation, but one of its proposals was adopted by the full board requiring that officers directly responsible for making the contributions reimburse the firm for funds disbursed.

The panel said Chairman Orin E. Atkins, who had pleaded no contest to authorizing the Nixon donation, agreed to repay Ashland $175,000 over five years. In other five-year installments, Vice Chairman William R. Seaton agreed to repay $105,000 and President Clyde M. Webb agreed to reimburse $45,000. Ashland already had been reimbursed $135,310 by some recipients and two officers, the report stated.

Report details domestic donations—Ashland made a total of $780,465 available for domestic political contributions, the special panel's report stated in disclosures published July 8. From 1967 through 1972, actual contributions made directly by the oil company totaled $612,-000 and another $105,000 was funneled through an intermediary to "selected candidates for Congress."

Among the recipients of Ashland's contributions was Gov. Hugh Carey (D, N.Y.), whose 1974 gubernatorial campaign was given $5,000. Donations made by Ashland's Canadian subsidiary to political parties there totaled $125,000 from 1970 through 1974. (Corporate contributions were legal in Canada.)

The report was ambiguous on whether Ashland's regular accountants, Ernst & Ernst, were aware of the political payments. "There is conflicting evidence which suggests, but does not establish, that Ernst & Ernst obtained knowledge during the course of its 1969 audit engagement that the corporation was making political contributions," the report stated.

Ashland took CIA money, acted as cover for spy—Ashland Oil Inc. secretly accepted nearly $100,000 from the Central Intelligence Agency and acted as a cover for covert CIA activities for five years, the Wall Street Journal reported July 9. The disclosure was made in the report filed with the SEC and federal court by the special committee of Ashland's board charged with investigating illegal corporate payments to politicians.

The CIA confirmed Ashland's admission and said other U.S. firms had been used as secret conduits for the funding of intelligence operations abroad. The Ashland case was "not an isolated practice," a CIA spokesman said, refusing to elaborate.

According to the Journal, Ashland's independent auditors, Coopers and Lybrand, informed the board on June 18 that the CIA had paid the firm $50,468 in cash from 1958 through 1971 and $48,500 in two checks, the last in March 1973. Ashland officials placed the money in an office safe and did not record it on corporate books until October 1973 when $58,-600 was deposited in a corporate bank account.

The accountants did not specify why the CIA money was paid or how it was spent, but officials of Ashland and the CIA claimed that the money was not used for illegal political payments made in the U.S. or abroad. (Other sources, however, said the CIA cash was mingled with Ashland's secret political fund and disbursed as illegal corporate contributions.) An anonymous government official told the Journal that the money probably was used to reimburse Ashland for salaries of CIA agents whose initial payments had come from the oil firm.

The official said Ashland, probably unwittingly, had purchased an unidentified small firm around 1968 that was a front for the CIA. When Ashland discovered that the firm was a cover for the agency, the oil firm agreed to pay the salaries of secret CIA employes and accept secret reimbursement from the agency.

An authoritative source told the New York Times July 9 that Ashland was paid by the CIA for allowing a secret agent to operate in Western Europe for five years, posing as one of its officials. The agent was not infiltrated into the oil company, but employed by the small firm acquired by Ashland, according to the source.

After Ashland bought the firm (in 1967), the CIA informed officials of the oil company that one of the executives in the newly-purchased firm was a secret operative and asked Ashland to continue the relationship.

After five years, the agent decided to leave the CIA, but remained in Ashland's employ. A spokesman for the oil company said no "arrangement" with the CIA currently existed.

Cash recipients listed—Bowing to SEC pressure, Ashland Oil Aug. 9 disclosed the names of the recipients of more than $1.1 million of its foreign and domestic political payments, many of them illegal, from September 1967 to January 1973.

Among those who accepted money from Ashland were President Omar Bongo of Gabon, former President Richard Nixon, the Democratic National Committee, and numerous candidates for federal, state, and local elections.

Ashland had refused to make the list public, saying Aug. 7 "no useful purpose would be served by public disclosures of the names." The SEC responded by threatening legal action against the firm.

As part of a consent judgment, Ashland had agreed to reveal the recipients of its cash payments "to the full satisfaction of the commission."

Ashland listed more than $342,000 paid in corporate cash to government officials abroad. In addition to Bongo, who received $150,000 in 1972, Francois

Nguema Ndong, Gabon's minister of state and minister of agriculture in 1972, was paid $40,000 and Paulin Ampanba Goueranque, minister of mines in 1972, received $12,000.

Prior to release of the Ashland list, the Gabon government had responded to unofficial reports of the payments by "officially and categorically" denying charges that Ashland had bribed Bongo and the two ministers in its effort to win exploration rights in Gabon.

The government statement, issued July 17, labeled the charges "ridiculous," saying they were "part of a campaign to strike at the leaders of oil-producing nations, especially those of black Africa." "Rich countries seek by all possible means to undermine the initiatives taken by third world countries to create a new international economic order . . . [and] now strive to tarnish the image of leaders of OPEC member countries," the statement said.

According to the Ashland list, other foreign government officials who accepted money from the oil company included Kaliffa Musa, Libya's former petroleum minister, who was paid $7,500; Miguel R. Garrido Alvarez, the Dominican Republic's ambassador-at-large for Europe, who was paid $800 a month for several months in 1968 in connection with Ashland's efforts to build a refinery in the Dominican Republic; Yehia Omar, a consultant in Libya, who was paid $100,-000 in 1970; and Omar Shali, informal adviser to Libya's former King Idris, who was given a $2,500 wedding gift.

Cities Service Co. admission. The Cities Service Co., Oklahoma-based oil and chemical firm, became the first major U.S. corporation to admit voluntarily to the SEC that it had made improper corporate payments abroad, the Wall Street Journal reported Sept. 24, 1975.

In July, the SEC had urged companies to come forward and reveal any questionable payments made abroad, or face possible enforcement action. Until Cities Service's announcement, no firms had accepted the SEC offer because of fear of embarrassment, business reprisals, or the nationalization of foreign holdings.

In its statement to the SEC, Cities Service said a "limited inquiry" begun in

May had uncovered that unnamed foreign subsidiaries had secretly funneled $30,000 through a Swiss bank for "political purposes." The money, authorized by high corporate officials, had been "disguised" on the subsidiary's books and improperly deducted from U.S. tax returns as a legitimate business expense.

Cities Service told the SEC that an amended tax return had been filed, that such payments would be prohibited in the future and that subsidiaries would not be allowed to make unrecorded cash transactions.

Cities Service also revealed that another $15,000 was paid against a phony invoice to a foreign lobbyist, and that "for a number of years," the company had maintained a $600,000 slush fund for overseas "business purposes," funded in part by kickbacks from brokers and suppliers.

BP, Shell Italy bribes admitted. The Royal Dutch/Shell Group and the British Petroleum Co., Ltd. (BP) April 13, 1976 confirmed reports that they had made secret payments totaling about $6.6 million to Italian political parties between 1969 and 1973. The payments were allegedly made to promote legislation maintaining the prevailing oil price structure and favoring revisions in the oil excise tax.

A statement by BP said that about $1.6 million was paid to parties of the Italian coalition governmnet over the five-year period. The payments were halted in 1973 when the company withdrew from the Italian market after sustaining $34 million in losses, BP asserted. The British government currently owned 70% of the stock in BP.

Shell, which was a private British-Dutch company, admitted in a similar statement that its Italian payoffs totaled $5 million in 1969–1973. Shell also liquidated its Italian operations in 1973.

The Shell and BP admissions followed the publication April 11 of an account in the London Times asserting that the two companies were under official investigation in Italy. A two-year-old probe by a parliamentary committee had uncovered evidence of collusion among major oil companies operating in Italy, the report said. The firms included Shell, BP, and the U.S. Exxon Corp.

According to the accounts, the companies amassed a payments fund of $8.4 million between March 1971 and February 1972 alone to be channeled to three Italian political parties. Two Christian Democrats, Giulio Andreotti and Mariano Rumor, both former premiers, were named in the articles as recipients of secret payments. Andreotti denied the charges, the Times said.

Venezuelan arrests in Occidental case. A Caracas judge July 14, 1976 ordered the arrest of seven persons on charges of "conspiring together" to use illegal means to win contracts in Venezuela for Occidental Petroleum Corp. of the U.S.

Judge Noel Pantoja said the seven were not being charged with bribery because Venezuelan officials had refused to take money from them. The case involved the award to Occidental of three 123,500-acre oil concessions in southern Lake Maracaibo in 1970.

The defendants included Alberto Flores Ortega, former Venezuelan minister to the Organization of Petroleum Exporting Countries; his father, Alberto Flores Troconis; Jose Toro Hardy, a Venezuelan oil businessman, and two U.S. citizens, Charles Hatfield and John Askew.

A Venezuelan congressional panel had issued a report June 8 saying that Askew, a former consultant to Occidental who lived in Venezuela, had made payments to the other defendants from $3 million in fees he received from the U.S. company. The money was to have been used to win favors for Occidental, but the defendants had not been in a position to influence government decisions on oil-service contracts, the report concluded.

The congressional panel said that because of Occidental's "irregular" activities, the company should not be compensated by the government for its Venezuelan assets which were nationalized Jan. 1.

Armand Hammer, Occidental's chairman, denounced the panel's report June 10. He said that its charges had no "supportive evidence," and that its recommendation against compensation for Occidental was "contrary to the constitution of Venezuela."

Hammer acknowledged that Occidental had paid Askew $3 million, but he said the money had been paid for "valuable services" rendered by Askew and not for "an irregular purpose."

Occidental again July 14, after the seven arrest warrants were issued, denied any wrongdoing. The company said it "didn't direct, authorize or have any knowledge of alleged attempts to bribe Venezuelan officials."

Venezuelan President Carlos Andres Perez Feb. 14 gave his attorney general an official report on alleged bribes by Occidental Petroleum Corp., whose assets were nationalized by the Venezuelan government Jan. 1 along with those of all other foreign oil companies. The report said that in order to secure oil exploration contracts from the previous Venezuelan government, Occidental had paid $1.6 million in bribes to seven persons including Alberto Flores.

(Venezuelan newspapers reported Feb. 17 that to secure oil contracts in 1971, Occidental had made payments to relatives of a number of officials, including $106,400 to Alberto Flores' father.)

The Northrop Case

Northrop admits bribes. The executive committee of the board of Northrop Corp., an exporter of fighter planes, admitted June 5, 1975 that the firm had paid nearly $470,000 in bribes, including $450,000 in payments to two Saudi Arabian generals, but denied allegations of widespread wrong-doing related to Northrop's earlier admission that $30 million was paid in agents' fees and commissions in connection with overseas sales.

The statement was issued, the executive committee said, to quell "speculation and often erroneous characterizations" about the confidential section of an auditor's report on the $30 million fund due to be released June 6 by the Senate Foreign Relations Committee's subcommittee on multinational corporations in preparation for hearings on the subject.

The auditor's report on the overseas payments was prepared by Northrop's outside auditor, Ernst & Ernst, after the Securities and Exchange Commission accused Northrop of maintaining a slush fund for "unlawful political contributions and other unlawful purposes." Northrop, which had earlier pleaded guilty to making an illegal $150,000 donation to the Nixon re-election campaign, settled the SEC complaint without admitting or denying the charges.

In its statement June 5, the executive committee said the company "possesses no legal right to control the ultimate disposition of funds disbursed" abroad through its sales network of agents. "Thus, contrary to certain press reports, there was no $30 million slush fund," the group contended.

The executive committee defended the role of its consultants and foreign agents, saying they "have on the whole performed valuable and legitimate services, similar in general to those provided by technical, legal, financial, and marketing consultant services and representatives in the U.S."

In addition to the Saudi Arabia payments, the executive committee said it could identify only one or two other instances of possible graft: a $15,000 gift to an unidentified politician by Northrop's Indonesian agent in 1972, and $4,400 paid to an Iranian tax assessor who demanded the payment for settling a tax liability.

Northrop's statement June 5 reflected the preliminary conclusions of the executive committee based on the auditor's investigation. The confidential section of the auditor's report was not released with the company statement.

The Senate subcommittee did release the confidential section, however. It revealed that Northrop secretly employed politicians, generals and other high-level government contacts, including some whose identities were unknown even to top Northrop officials, to penetrate foreign markets and win lucrative defense contracts.

Highlights of the report:

Khashoggi and the Saudi Arabian bribes—According to Northrop officials, money intended for two Saudi Arabian generals was solicited by Adnan Khashoggi, a Saudi Arabian businessman with close ties to the royal family.

As the chairman of the Triad Financial Establishment Co., a unit of his Luxembourg-incorporated, Beirut-based Triad Holding Corp., Khashoggi also served as consultant in the Middle East for Lockheed Aircraft Corp.,

Chrysler Corp., and Raytheon Corp., according to the Wall Street Journal June 6.

Through a Washington spokesman, Khashoggi denied that he had acted as an intermediary for the Northrop bribes. Northrop officials told the auditors they could not be certain the bribery money given to Khashoggi was ever paid to the generals.

According to the auditor's report, Khashoggi asked for $250,000 in 1971, in addition to his usual fee, to pay off a Saudi minister who could make "difficulties" for the firm. Northrop's sales there totaled $200 million at the time. Khashoggi later told Northrop officials the money was "passed along to the general."

In 1972, Khashoggi asked for another $150,000 to pay off a second general. When Northrop officials resisted, the general reacted to company personnel "in a hostile fashion," the report stated, and increased his demand to $200,000. That sum was paid in August 1973 through Triad after the consulting firm agreed that both payments would be applied against possible commissions earned on future arms sales.

In testimony before the Senate subcommittee June 9, Richard W. Millar, chairman of Northrop's executive committee, apologized to the Saudi Arabian government "for an embarrassment caused by the bribery payments."

The auditor's report stated that Khashoggi also paid a portion of his agent's fee to an unidentified Saudi Arabian prince, a registered commercial agent, who "approached" Northrop for a commission. Representatives of the Saudi Arabian government also interceded with Northrop officials there on the prince's behalf, according to the report. More than $500,000 was paid to the prince's firm in 1971 and 1973 for "unspecified services." The Journal June 6 identified the prince as Khalid bin Abdullah.

The Senate subcommittee also was studying a $45 million commission paid to Khashoggi by Northrop after Saudi Arabia purchased 60 F-5E fighter planes valued at $750 million.

Gen. Stehlin a secret consultant—Gen. Paul Stehlin, former chief of staff of the French air force and until 1974, a vice president of the French National Assembly, was secretly on the Northrop payroll from 1964–1974, reporting to Northrop

chairman and president Thomas V. Jones, the report asserted. Stehlin received up to $7,500 a year in consulting fees.

"He has usually been able to spot and identify changes in national policy as they affect defense months and even years ahead of others," Jones said of Stehlin when questioned by auditors.

In a letter to Jones in January 1973, Stehlin claimed he had provided Northrop with "exploitable elements of a good strategy," and said that during parliamentary debates, he had "made good use of the information you [Jones] have been providing me."

According to Jones, Stehlin's "primary responsibility" as a Northrop consultant was in preparing an "analysis of all political, economic and military situations in Europe, with changing relationships between principal countries and emphasis on defense-related programs." Stehlin's "secondary responsibility," Jones added, "is the alerting of Northrop to business opportunities in the defense-related areas as they arise."

Stehlin died June 22 after being hit by a bus June 7 in Paris.

Other highly-placed contacts—The report also revealed that Kermit Roosevelt, grandson of President Theodore Roosevelt, worked on Northrop's behalf in the Middle East, where he had formerly served with the Central Intelligence Agency and allegedly arranged a coup in 1953 that reinstalled Shah Riza Pahlevi in Iran.

The auditors stated that Roosevelt was "perhaps the key figure in establishing the very high-level of activity Northrop now has in the Middle East, with contract values in this area in the past seven to eight years running close to a billion dollars." Roosevelt, who had quit the CIA before 1959, currently was paid $75,000 annually by Northrop. (He also served as a consultant to Raytheon.)

Letters from Roosevelt to high Northrop officials were submitted with the report, showing that in 1965 Roosevelt claimed he had foiled Lockheed Aircraft's attempts to sell its F-104 fighter plane to Saudi Arabia when he told the late King Faisal that Lockheed had bribed certain Saudi Arabian officials in an effort to win the government contract. Saudi Arabia subsequently purchased Northrop's F-5 fighter plane.

In his letters, Roosevelt also claimed he had used his CIA contacts in Saudi Arabia and Iran on Northrop's behalf.

The report also identified other Northrop consultants:

Hubert Weisbrod was a Swiss consultant who, Jones said, gave Northrop "an unusual visibility into the highest councils of NATO, the Common Market and the many official and unofficial discussions between the highest officials in Europe." Weisbrod was paid $125,000 annually, the report stated.

A Dutch consultant, Johannes Gerritsen, acted "as a trusted communications channel between the highest levels in the Dutch government and the president of Northrop," Jones said. According to the auditor's report, senior members of the Dutch government invited Northrop to appoint a special company "ambassador" who could act as a liaison in arms deals between the aerospace firm and the Netherlands. Gerritsen's name was suggested "by several of the highest levels in the Dutch government," Jones said. Secrecy was maintained in Gerritsen's high-level contacts, he said.

Wilhelm Franz-Josef Bach, a former member of the lower house of the West German parliament, was paid for his services to Northrop through a Swiss consulting firm secretly set up by another Northrop advisor.

Gen. Adolf Galland, a former Luftwaffe combat ace in World War Two, relayed political information to Jones in code, the report stated.

U.S. military held susceptible to bribes—Frank J. DeFrancis, a lawyer and Northrop's chief Washington consultant, told the auditors that the U.S. military also was susceptible to bribery and graft. The report did not cite examples of bribes accepted by military personnel, but noted that DeFrancis claimed he had hired a former two-star general for Northrop's "protection" at $1,000-a-month.

Another consultant whom DeFrancis said he had hired for "Northrop's protection" was John R. Blandford, chief counsel for the House Armed Services Committee until 1972.

In response to auditors' questions, Jones said DeFrancis "advises and counsels the Northrop Corp. in its international dealings around the world,

but most specifically with the relationship with West Germany." According to the report, DeFrancis also was the legal advisor to the West German government through its embassy in Washington.

DeFrancis told the auditors he did not "know a damn thing about an airplane except the nose and tail," but said he "had from time to time employed people to do certain things [for Northrop] for which he made cash payments for their services." According to the report, DeFrancis "said that these people were of the type who would not want their names associated with Northrop and that this [procedure] utilized their services."

Swiss corporation promoted sales—DeFrancis told the auditors that he had been instrumental in secretly setting up the Economic and Development Corp. (EDC), a Swiss-based organization that sought to reward foreign nationals for their help in promoting Northrop sales abroad. Since the early 1970s, the report stated, Northrop had paid or committed $1.8 million to the EDC, which was originally established to promote sales in Iran.

DeFrancis said Northrop "is not interested in knowing how EDC operates and who they are in touch with, but can only measure the benefit of EDC by sales which occur." EDC worked "behind the scenes through the use of the right people at the right time," DeFrancis said.

According to the report, EDC received commissions for sales made in Brazil, Taiwan, Saudi Arabia, Malaysia, and Iran. These contracts were won, Jones said, because EDC provided "broad and high-level support at political, industrial, and economic decision-making levels that are important to selection of any major governmental procurement."

Page Communications payments in Iran—Page Communications Engineers Inc., a Washington-based subsidiary of Northrop, paid $5.9 million in "fees" to Iranian officials and others, including Prince Charam Pahlevi, a member of the Iranian royal family, to facilitate the construction of a $200 million telecommunications system being built for the Iranian government.

Northrop officials told the auditor that Pahlevi, who held no government post, was paid $705,000 for recommending architects and engineers and providing "general practical information" toward resolving a negotiating problem with the Iranian government.

Total fees paid by Page and the three other companies that were jointly building the communications project came to $10 million, according to the report. Included in that figure was a $1.1 million payment made by Page to a bank account for unknown individuals because another member of the consortium, Siemans AG, a West Germany firm, claimed that "these payments were necessary in order to obtain information and advice necessary to implement the contract and obtain approval of completed tasks thereunder."

Page officials also said that their representatives in Iran maintained a $30,-000 cash fund so that bureaucrats could be rewarded for cutting red tape.

Senate subcommittee hearings. During hearings June 9 on the Northrop disclosures, Senate subcommittee chairman Frank Church (D, Ida.) called for a "fundamental reform of Western military arms sales practices." "The competition is out of control," Church said. "We and the Europeans are in an unprincipled race to arm to the teeth the newly rich nations of the Persian Gulf."

If reforms were not instituted, Church warned, NATO "could be ruptured by greed run amuck" and "we will end up corrupting ourselves and those who deal with us."

"Symptomatic of the sickness that must be exorcised," Church said, was Northrop's secret arrangement with the Economic and Development Corp. for information-gathering and sales promotion. Northrop operated an "intelligence network" that a "government would employ to get inside information and pull strings," Church declared. [See above]

(Northrop's lawyer told the subcommittee that EDC's operations were so secret that Northrop officials had been unable to learn who the firm's chief stockholders were.)

Read into the record at the hearings were an auditor's notes of a conversation that took place with John R. Hunt, an official of a Northrop subsidiary. Hunt "and his people don't know and don't want to know where the money paid to

agents goes," the notes said. "Agents are an expensive and necessary evil of doing business in a foreign country; the agents make the necessary payments."

The basic tasks of Northrop's foreign agents, the notes said, were to peddle influence and "know whose pockets to line." Hunt said his firm paid sales commissions of 10%, but added that payments could increase if competition dictated or "if the magnitude of graft in the country was higher than usual."

Two Northrop officers testified before the Senate subcommittee. Richard Millar, chairman of the executive committee of the board, said, "An American corporation doesn't have the ability to monitor all the actions of the agent with whom it must deal and cannot be held responsible for activities or practices which the corporation doesn't know about and doesn't tacitly or explicitly approve."

In testimony June 10, Northrop president Thomas Jones said he accepted "full responsibility for all the actions of the Northrop Corp." and admitted he had "made a mistake" in not refusing to pay the Saudi Arabian generals.

The Defense Department June 21 gave some indication of the scope of commissions won by agents of U.S. aerospace firms on foreign dealings. Since 1973, agents' fees totaled more than $200 million, according to preliminary estimates submitted to the Senate subcommittee in a classified Pentagon document.

Iran, Saudi Arabia act on Northrop disclosures. Following disclosures that Northrop Corp. had paid bribes and commissions to foreign government officials in an effort to win lucrative arms contracts, Iran, one of Northrop's major client states, June 9 announced that foreign companies would be required to give written oaths that no commissions or other payoffs had been made to officials to secure government contracts.

Saudi Arabia intended to investigate Northrop's admission that bribes were paid to two Saudi generals whose approval was needed for an arms contract, United Press International reported June 9.

According to the official government statement, anyone involved in accepting the bribes would be punished. The Saudi defense ministry said it had no prior knowledge of the payments and had "never approved them." Northrop and the U.S. government were asked to supply documents on the issue.

Jones resigns Northrop post. Thomas V. Jones resigned July 16, 1975 as chairman of Northrop Corp., after the aerospace company's executive committee accused him of bearing "a heavy share of the responsibility for the irregularities and improprieties" involving bribes and other payments made by Northrop to consultants and foreign officials in connection with winning government arms contracts.

Jones also was responsible "for the atmosphere within Northrop which contributed to these shortcomings and for the failure to concern himself with the functional weaknesses and pressures within management which had brought the company to its present circumstances," the report stated.

Under a previous agreement, Jones would remain as president of Northrop. The board permitted him to stay on as chief executive and director during what the committee called "this difficult transitional period."

In its final report, Northrup's special panel confirmed only two instances of improper payments made abroad—$450,000 in bribes paid to two Saudi Arabian generals—but said Jones "either actively fostered marketing strategies without recognizing the potential for raising questions of impropriety, or he refrained from taking the initiative to supervise effectively the activities of other company personnel."

Jones' role in the Saudi Arabian bribery remained "ambiguous" despite six months of investigation, the report stated. The committee said it "isn't convinced" that Jones "recognized the seriousness of his involvement in the matter."

Jones also was criticized for failing to cooperate fully with the company's directors, auditors and the committee in efforts to uncover the extent of Northrop's improper foreign payments.

The committee again denied press reports that Northrop maintained a $30 million slush fund from which improper or illegal political payoffs in the U.S. and abroad were made. "Nearly all" of that money was paid to Northrop consultants and commission agents, the report stated.

Other issues raised in the panel's interim report about agents and their fees were not specifically resolved in the final study. The report said only that the investigation "did disclose other shortcomings in the company's relationship with certain consultants and agents and in connection with certain other matters examined. These included instances of violations of applicable law, improprieties, irregular or inadequate corporate procedures, and questionable business judgments."

The full board approved recommendations in the report for selecting and controlling consultants and sales agents, new procedures to assure that laws were not broken in maintaining corporate-client relationships, and improved communications and control throughout the company.

The investigation and report was mandated in the settlement of a class-action suit brought by stockholders following disclosure that Jones and another Northrop official had made an illegal $150,000 corporate contribution to the Nixon re-election campaign. The settlement also required that Jones quit as president within 18 months and provided for the selection of four outside directors.

Khashoggi kept bribe. Adnan M. Kashoggi admitted Sept. 1, 1975 that he had pocketed a $250,000 bribe offered in 1971 by Northrop Corp. to Gen. Hashim M. Hashim, a former commanding general of the Saudi Arabian air force who was now retired.

"I stopped a bribe. I put it in my pocket," Khashoggi told the Washington Post. He also claimed that Northrop, not he, had "cooked up" the idea of buying the general's cooperation in approving an arms deal. The bribe was offered, Khashoggi said, because Northrop was "afraid maybe Lockheed had reached" Hashim.

Khashoggi said he took the bribe himself to keep Northrop officials from "putting themselves in a bad position" by doing something "stupid." Khashoggi also claimed he deserved the bribe more than the general. "I didn't think the general had earned it," Khashoggi said. "I worked harder than he did on this."

Khashoggi denied another Northrop charge that he had also demanded a $200,000 bribe for Hashim's successor, Gen. Asad-Zuhair. Khashoggi said no payoff had been sought and none was paid, but contended that the $450,000 in corporate funds were treated by Northrop as non-interest-bearing advances on commissions due him.

Khashoggi said that shortly after Northrop issued a statement and audit on its business practices abroad, he flew to Saudi Arabia to meet with Prince Sultan, minister of defense. After the meeting, Sultan and Crown Prince Fahd issued statements condemning press reports of Northrop's allegations as politically damaging to Saudi Arabia. They also supported the right of Arab businessmen to expect reasonable compensation for their work, according to the Post.

However, the Pentagon received other messages from Sultan, indicating the government was tightening its policy on arms commissions, the Post reported. Saudi contracts now could be terminated automatically if the company involved were caught trying to bribe government officials.

Based on its reading of Sultan's new policy, the Pentagon July 9 ordered Northrop not to pay $55 million owed Khashoggi as commissions on his services in securing three contracts for the F-5E fighter plane and ground support, the Post reported.

Khashoggi said that if the dispute were not resolved within six months, Northrop would be forced to withdraw from Saudi Arabia and abandon its $1.6 billion in contracts already awarded there.

The Post reported Oct. 16 that the Federal Bureau of Investigation and the Justice Department were investigating Northrop's alleged overbilling of $6.1 billion on its defense contracts with the Pentagon.

Italian payments admitted. The Northrop Corp. disclosed Feb. 20, 1976 that its Italian subsidiary had made $861,000 in improper commission payments in five countries from 1969-75. The payments were made without the knowledge of Northrop's management, the company

said in papers filed with the SEC.

About $129,000 was paid after Northrop signed a consent decree in April 1975 settling an SEC complaint about the foreign payments.

The payments were made by Page-Europa S.p.A. of Rome, a subsidiary of the Northrop-owned Page Communications Engineers Inc. The money, paid to obtain sales in Italy, went to unidentified individuals in Italy, Greece, Somalia, Portugal and Turkey, Northrop said.

Arms & Aerospace Cases

Arms agents paid $18.7 million. Previously secret Pentagon reports showed that since 1973, six U.S. firms had paid at least $18.7 million to five agents to win weapon contracts in the Middle East valued at about $500 million.

The report was released Sept. 29, 1975 by Rep. Les Aspin (D, Wis.), who cited the Freedom of Information Act in demanding that the material be made public.

The documents, which purportedly detailed agents' fees on all military sales worth at least $25 million, did not indicate whether the money was used to bribe military or political figures in any of the countries named—Saudi Arabia, Kuwait, Jordan, Israel, Greece, Turkey and Spain.

Northrop Corp. made the largest single payment listed in the report—$8.9 million which went to Triad Financial Establishment Co., part of Saudi Arabian businessman Adnan M. Khashoggi's worldwide network of companies. Khashoggi's efforts to sell Northrop aircraft in the Middle East had been disclosed earlier in testimony before the Senate Subcommittee on Multinational Corporations.

Other payments cited in the Pentagon report, including supplemental information provided by Aspin:

■ $4.8 million paid by Raytheon Corp. to two agent firms in connection with a missile system sale to Kuwait.

■ $300,000 by Raytheon to its wholly-owned subsidiary, Middlesex International, for the sale of missiles to Israel. (This was the first known agent's fee paid for an Israeli weapons contract.)

■ $4.5 million paid by Vinnell Corp. to Ghassan Shaker, a Middle East banker, for work in winning a $100 million contract to train Saudi Arabian military forces.

■ $200,000 paid by FMC Corp. to Shahdeh S. Twal in connection with the sale of vehicles, possibly tanks, to Jordan.

■ $226,000 paid by Lockheed Aircraft Corp. to Constantine Exharhacos, a former Greek air force officer, for the sale to Greece of eight transport planes valued at $53.1 million.

■ $166,000 paid by McDonnell-Douglas Corp. to a Turkish firm in connection with a $134.8 million sale of multiple sensors on F-4 aircraft.

McDonnell-Douglas also paid an undisclosed amount to an unidentified agent for the sale of $50.6 million worth of aircraft to Spain. It was also reported that a McDonnell-Douglas employe arranged large aircraft sales to Iran and another contract with Israel. The company claimed the employe was not paid a special fee; Aspin said the man was listed with the Pentagon as an agent.

Aerospace payments. Several questionable payments overseas were reported by U.S. aerospace companies during 1976. Among the disclosures:

Boeing Co. paid $70 million in commissions to foreign representatives between 1970 and 1975 in connection with overseas sales, T. A. Wilson, Boeing chairman, told the Wall Street Journal March 5.

Wilson denied any wrongdoing. He said that the money was paid to the middlemen as "independent contractors" for their aid in negotiating sales abroad. In "four or five instances," Wilson said, commissions on aircraft sales were paid to employes of foreign governments. He declined to characterize the payments as bribes because, he said, the officials were not in a position to influence the sales.

Wilson also disclosed that Boeing had made "some foreign political contributions that we know are legal."

The SEC, which was investigating Boeing's foreign payments, filed suit Feb. 12 to compel the company to produce documents related to its overseas transactions. Boeing denied making illegal political contributions abroad, but refused to comply with the SEC request unless the court gave it protection against public disclosures and leaks. The court ruled in Boeing's favor Feb. 22, ordering the SEC to keep Boeing's documents confidential.

Lockheed Aircraft Corp. and Occidental Petroleum Co. had received similar court-ordered protection in December 1975 in connection with the SEC investigation.

Rockwell International Corp. of Pittsburgh told the SEC April 9 that a foreign subsidiary had made a questionable cash payment of $96,000 in December 1975, despite efforts by Rockwell's management to halt such payments. The money was paid for "assistance in obtaining expedited treatment" from a foreign government and was not "properly receipted," the company said.

The foreign payment was discovered during an internal investigation by Rockwell after the company had informed the SEC in December 1975 that improper payments totaling $570,000 were made from 1971–75 to foreign government officials or employes in four countries in connection with sales. At that time, Rockwell also said it was trying to block payment of another $98,000 in commission that "is or might be payable" to third parties "who are foreign government officials or employes."

Approximately $10 million in sales were connected with the improper payments, Rockwell said. Its foreign sales for the 1971–75 period were $2.2 billion.

Rockwell said its internal investigation uncovered only one instance of foreign political contributions—$8,300 donated in Canada, where such payments were legal, according to the company.

United Technologies Corp. of East Hartford, Conn. disclosed April 9 that it made nearly $2 million in improper foreign payments in 1974 and 1975.

The company said that $1.8 million of the total was paid to "independent foreign representatives," who "might, in turn" have paid "foreign government employes."

United Technologies, formerly known as United Aircraft Corp., said that another $150,000 was paid to an "independent marketing consultant" who worked for Boeing's customer, a "foreign government instrumentality."

The company said it would not claim

the payments on its 1974 and 1975 tax returns. "All foreign payments have been properly recorded on the books of the corporation," United Technologies said.

Pharmaceutical Companies

Payments admitted. Many of the U.S.' pharmaceutical companies admitted during 1976 that they had made questionable payments overseas. Among companies involved:

A. H. Robbins of Richmond, Va., a pharmaceutical manufacturer. Overseas payments totaling $130,000 were made to facilitate the processing and distributing of foreign orders, officials said April 27.

Allergan Pharmaceuticals of Irvine, Calif. Between 1972 and 1975, the company said March 19, foreign government officials in five countries had been paid a total of $17,000. The payments were made to obtain foreign sales or win government approval of Allergan's products or prices, the company said.

Baxter Laboratories Inc., an Illinois-based manufacturer of hospital supplies, disclosed Feb. 23 that it had made $2.1 million in "questionable payments" abroad since 1971. The transactions were uncovered during an internal investigation and were reported voluntarily to the SEC.

Most of the $2.1 million was paid in one unidentified country to relatives of government employes to promote Baxter's sales. The company claimed that the payments did not violate that country's laws.

Similar payments totaling $28,000 were made in five other countries. In three other nations, Baxter paid a total of $136,-800 to facilitate the payment of past due receivables.

Baxter said that its senior management had had no knowledge of the foreign payments and that no political contributions were made in the U.S.

G.D. Searle & Co. of Skokie, Ill. admitted Jan. 9 that it had paid $1.3 million to officials of foreign governments or their agents from 1973–75 to promote overseas sales. The payments, which were entered on company books as commissions, generated $11.5 million in foreign sales during the three-year period, the company said.

The payments were "unintentionally deducted" on the company's U.S. income tax returns for 1973 and 1974, Searle said, but added that amended returns were being filed. Its tax liability was estimated at $84,000, Searle said.

In a subsequent report to the SEC Feb. 20, Searle admitted that "certain members of corporate management" had authorized the overseas payments.

Johnson & Johnson, whose overseas sales and earnings were the largest of any U.S. health-care products company, disclosed March 9 that from 1971–75 it had made "improper payments" abroad totaling $990,000.

The payments were made by seven foreign subsidiaries, the New Brunswick, N.J.-based company said in a report to the SEC. Most of the money was paid as commissions on government sales. Johnson & Johnson operated in 45 foreign countries. Its overseas sales for 1975 totaled $956.7 million.

No illegal contributions in the U.S. or abroad were uncovered as a result of an internal investigation, the company said.

Merck & Co. "mistakenly deducted" from its U.S. income taxes portions of the $3.6 million that was paid to foreign governments and agencies from 1968–75, according to Merck's review committee charged with investigating the transactions.

The panel was created in 1975 after the foreign payments had been disclosed. Its report was filed with the SEC and made public March 9, 1976. (In the report the amount of foreign payments by Merck, a Rahway, N.J.-based drug and chemical firm, was revised downward from the $3.9 million reported initially.)

The committee charged in its report that Merck's outside auditor, Arthur Andersen & Co., had failed to follow up information it was given about questionable foreign payments despite knowledge that in at least one case the payments were illegal. The company, nevertheless, allowed the Andersen firm to continue as auditor.

In two other instances, the panel said, Henry W. Gadsden, Merck's chairman and chief executive officer, ignored "possible warning signals" of improprieties.

The committee said that Merck had paid an additional $264,000 in U.S. taxes as a result of the payments inquiry, but also added that the Internal Revenue Service was conducting an investigation for possible tax fraud.

Pfizer Inc. of New York City, a drug and chemicals manufacturer. In papers filed with the SEC March 19, Pfizer said that $300,000 was paid as bribes and political contributions by its foreign subsidiaries operating in three countries.

Richardson-Merrell Inc. of Wilton, Conn., which marketed its drugs in more than 160 foreign countries. An internal investigation had uncovered "a number of payments of questionable legality or propriety overseas," the company said in a Feb. 23 announcement. The information also was filed with the SEC. No dollar figure was given. The company said the amount was not "material."

Schering-Plough Corp. of Kenilworth, N.J., a drug, toiletries and cosmetics maker. Subsidiaries made improper payments in "recent years" in three foreign countries to obtain government sales, according to papers filed with the SEC Feb. 17. Schering-Plough said the total payments did not exceed $207,000 in any one year, and that sales associated with the payments were $2.3 million annually. The company reported worldwide sales of $795.3 million in 1975.

Sterling Drug Inc., whose headquarters were in New York City, told the SEC March 9 that an internal investigation of the 1970–75 period had uncovered "illegal or improper" payments in 19 of the 125 foreign countries in which it had operations. Some corporate officials "may have approved" the payments, Sterling said.

Sterling did not give the total foreign payments made during the six years but said annual payments, which were listed as commissions, ranged from $103,000 to $180,000. Additional payments, ranging from $33,000 to $252,000 in any one of the six years, were made in connection with "a variety of other government actions." The company said that these actions were "related to increasing profitability of foreign business of the company's subsidiaries." It said payments were made "to obtain governmental authorizations for price increases, product registrations, work or construction permits, or import permits." Sterling said that the disbursements

were made from two slush funds not recorded on the company's books. Amended U.S. tax returns were being filed to correct the deception, Sterling said.

Other companies in the health-care products field that reported smaller foreign payments were:

Upjohn Co. of Kalamazoo, Mich. told the SEC March 26 that $2.71 million had been paid to foreign government employes or their "intermediaries" since 1971 to promote the company's extensive drug sales abroad.

Recipients of the money were not identified. Upjohn said the transactions involved 22 countries. "No corporate political contributions of any kind in the U.S. or any foreign countries have been discovered" during the company's internal investigation, Upjohn said.

The practice was stopped in January, company officials said. R. T. Parfet Jr., Upjohn chairman, termed the payments "a demeaning cost of business."

The payments represented about 10% of total sales to the 22 countries from 1971–75, but less than 1% of the company's worldwide sales of $3.28 billion over the five-year period, Upjohn said.

Warner-Lambert Co., a Morris Plains, N.J.-based drug firm, said March 18 that an internal investigation had uncovered $2.2 million in "questionable payments" made abroad from 1971–75 by some of its subsidiaries.

"Certain of the company's foreign subsidiaries" had made payments in 14 countries, Warner-Lambert said. The payments represented less than .2% of its worldwide sales in 140 countries during the five-year period, officials said.

Most of the payments were "in the nature of commissions on sales of pharmaceutical products to foreign government agencies," the company said. It added, however, that payments also were made to expedite government action on prices, product registration, dividends, taxes and other matters.

Warner-Lambert said it would pay an additional $325,390 in U.S. income taxes and interest because some of the foreign payments were made through the U.S. but were not recorded on the firm's books. The company said that no illegal political payments had been made in the U.S. and that the practice of making foreign payments had been terminated.

Other Companies

U.S. auto makers disclose Canadian gifts. Officials of General Motors Corp. told shareholders at the firm's annual meeting that GM had made "modest" contributions to Canada's two major parties, the Wall Street Journal reported May 27, 1975. GM Chairman Thomas A. Murphy defended the gifts, made by GM's Canadian subsidiary, but refused to state how much was donated, saying only the contributions were in the "five figure" range.

"In Canada," Murphy said, corporate donations "are part of the political process just as individual contributions are here. The practice has been that the political process in Canada is supported by companies, and in Canada we conduct ourselves as a Canadian company."

Murphy said the contributions made in Canada were the company's only political payments. A company spokesman had told the Journal May 19 that GM also had given $125,000 to the South Korean National Defense Fund, but Murphy said that gift was nonpolitical. The award was toward "the movement to develop understanding of free enterprise and combat Communism," Murphy said, rather than toward the aims of a specific political party.

In response to questions May 27 from the Journal, Chrysler Corp. and Ford Motor Co. also admitted they had made contributions to Canada's political parties. Chrysler said its Canadian subsidiary gave about $5,000 to each of the two major parties for use in the 1974 national election.

About $60,000 was donated by Ford's Canadian subsidiary to that country's federal and provincial political parties. The bulk of the gifts—$20,000 each—went to the two major federal parties. Chrysler and Ford both termed their Canadian contributions "legal and customary."

Ford also detailed its donations to Australian political parties: $11,150 was given in late 1969 to four parties for an "information campaign for the electorate" and $13,380 was donated to the same parties in 1972. Ford also disclosed that contributions totaling $7,200 were made in 1972 to three "study institutes" sponsored by West German political parties. A Ford spokesman said all of the foreign contributions were legal.

Later, GM disclosed Aug. 4 that the Shinjun Group of Companies, which held joint ownership with the U.S. auto manufacturer in General Motors Korea, claimed to have made a $250,000 political contribution in South Korea "on behalf of General Motors Korea."

GM denied authorizing the donation, made in 1972, and said it had resisted repeated demands by its partner in the joint venture for partial reimbursement from GM or GM Korea funds.

GM's disclosure was made to the Senate Subcommittee on Multinational Corporations, which was investigating overseas payments made by U.S. businesses.

ITT disclosures. The International Telephone & Telegraph Corp. disclosed March 12, 1976 that it found it had "reason to believe" that its employes had made $3.8 million in unauthorized foreign payments from 1971 through 1975. The money was paid to "employes or persons closely related to foreign customers," the company said. The ITT announcement was made in a press release that gave no further details of the foreign payments. ITT did disclose that the SEC was investigating the case.

The ITT statement also cited $4,300 in domestic political payments "that could be considered to be direct or indirect contributions to federal election campaigns."

The voluntary disclosures were made under terms of the SEC's amnesty program, announced in July 1975. Companies making the voluntary disclosures generally were not ordered to reveal the names of those who received the payments. The companies also were promised they would not be prosecuted.

Federal law prohibited corporate donations to political campaigns for national office. Contributions to state and local election races were not necessarily illegal. ITT said its legal contributions since 1971 had totaled $60,000.

ITT declined to characterize its foreign payments as illegal or questionable. "In many areas of the world it isn't unusual, and [is] often accepted as normal practice, to give presents or make payments of modest value to government functionaries in order to expedite administrative action or secure procedural assistance," the company said.

"About half of ITT's total annual business is accounted for by foreign-based ·manufacturing companies whose national governments are vitally interested in export sales."

A federal judge in U.S. District Court in Washington May 5 ordered ITT to comply with an SEC subpoena for documents relating to the domestic and overseas payments; however, the judge restricted the scope of the subpoena to payments of $5,000 or more that were made since 1970. The SEC had sought material dating to 1968.

The court also granted an ITT request that its documents be kept confidential. ITT's lawyer contended that the "physical safety" of an Italian auditor had been endangered by an SEC disclosure April 16 regarding payments in Italy. The disclosure came in documents filed with the court in connection with SEC efforts to compel ITT to cooperate with the government investigation.

According to the documents, ITT subsidiaries paid about $270,000 to Italian tax agents between 1969 and 1972 to "facilitate" negotiations over the amount of corporate tax owed there.

In a subsequent development May 12, Harold S. Geneen, ITT chairman, said the company in 1970 "may have" paid $350,-000 for political purposes in Chile.

The Senate Select Committee on Intelligence had charged in 1975 that ITT contributed $350,000 to election opponents of Salvador Allende, Chile's late president. (Allende was elected in 1970.)

Geneen told stockholders at ITT's annual meeting that he had "recent information tending to show that some $350,000 of ITT funds may have been sent to Chile in the year 1970 for the purpose of supporting the democratic anti-Communist cause there, within the framework of their normal democratic process, but there is no information that even suggests any sup-

port of any irregular or violent action."

The Senate committee also had charged that ITT helped foment the 1973 coup that led to Allende's overthrow and death.

Germain Baudrin, former head of the Belgian telephone and telegraph administration, had been sentenced Feb. 23 to nine months' imprisonment for accepting bribes in 1973 from the president of Bell Telephone Co. of Belgium, a unit of International Telephone and Telegraph Corp. (ITT), to win a $60 million equipment contract for the firm.

General Tire accused. In a suit filed May 10, 1976, the SEC accused the General Tire & Rubber Co. of numerous foreign and domestic payoffs. The charges were the broadest yet in the SEC's post-Watergate investigation of management fraud.

The SEC's wide-ranging probe centered on the payment of illegal corporate contributions to U.S. politicians and on bribes paid to officials of foreign governments.

The suit was settled when consent agreements and the SEC complaints were filed simultaneously in U.S. District Court in Washington, D.C. General Tire neither admitted nor denied the charges but accepted a court injunction barring further violations of federal securities laws.

General Tire also agreed to appoint a special review committee to investigate and make a public report of any improper activities by the company or its employes.

Charges against the company involved contributions to U.S. politicians, payments of "gratuities" to military and civilian employes of U.S. agencies with which the firm did business, overseas bribes, a hidden slush fund, violations of foreign-currency laws, participation in the Arab League's boycott of Israel and the filing of false and misleading financial reports.

The company and its president, Michael G. O'Neil, also were accused of devising and directing various schemes to circumvent U.S. and foreign laws against corporate payoffs. (O'Neil also signed a consent agreement settling the SEC's charges against him.)

According to the SEC, political payments totaling at least $65,000 were made between 1968 and 1972 to candidates for federal and state office. A "substantial portion" of that sum was donated illegally, the SEC said. Recipients of the contributions were not identified.

According to the SEC, General Tire's foreign payments involved "several million dollars." The recipients included an Arab financier, a Chilean leftist, a consultant in Rumania, and officials of the Mexican and Moroccan governments.

General Tire's domestic and foreign payoffs were made from an elaborately maintained slush fund, the SEC charged. The money used for domestic purposes was called the General Tire Good Citizenship Fund. It was kept in a wall safe in O'Neil's office at the firm's Akron, Ohio headquarters.

At O'Neil's direction, the SEC charged, a percentage of executive bonuses and salaries, beginning in 1968, were paid into the domestic slush fund.

Money used for "various improper purposes in Chile, Morocco and other countries" was maintained in General Tire's other slush funds, called "611 accounts," the SEC said. The accounts, which were established in the late 1950s, and maintained at least through 1975, were kept in Akron until 1964 when General Tire acquired a Liechtenstein company. That firm then served as the conduit for the secret funds. According to the SEC, the Liechtenstein company had assets of $3.9 million which were never recorded on General Tire's books.

The money used for foreign payoffs was generated in a variety of ways, such as the overbilling of General Tire's foreign affiliates on supply contracts, the SEC said. Proceeds from the overbilling of affiliates in Morocco, Chile and elsewhere totaled at least $3 million between 1960 and 1970, the SEC charged.

Most of the foreign payoffs, the SEC said, were made to prevent competitors from obtaining operating licenses abroad, or to win government approval for price increases or plant expansion.

One of General Tire's overseas transactions involved the Arab League boycott of firms doing business with Israel or Israeli companies. The SEC charged that General Tire paid $150,000 in two installments in 1971 and 1973 to an affiliate of a company headed by Adnan Khashoggi, a Saudi Arabian businessman and Middle East arms broker for several U.S. aerospace companies. The money was paid to have General Tire's name stricken from the boycott list.

The SEC also revealed that General Tire had filed a certificate with the Arab League in 1971 pledging participation in the boycott of Israel.

Allegations that General Tire engaged in improper activities abroad first disclosed in December 1975 by a Boston group challenging a license renewal application of RKO General Inc., a Boston broadcasting firm that was wholly owned by General Tire. RKO General, which held 17 radio or television licenses, was one of the nation's largest owners of broadcast stations.

In a petition filed that month with the Federal Communications Commission, Community Broadcasting of Boston Inc. charged that General Tire had made payoffs to political parties or government officials in Chile, Morocco and Rumania. The money was funneled through slush funds maintained by General Tire's Liechtenstein subsidary, the group charged.

Community Broadcasting also charged that General Tire's activities in Morocco violated U.S. antitrust laws. According to evidence compiled by the group, General Tire paid $40,000 in 1970 to Moroccan government officials to obtain their permission to expand General Tire's plant in Morocco and to prevent Goodyear Tire and Rubber Co. from entering the Moroccan market.

In a limited response to Community Broadcasting's December charges, General Tire admitted March 12 that it had uncovered several instances of illegal or questionable transactions by its foreign subsidiaries. Its internal investigation was continuing, the company said. The disclosure came in a preliminary report filed with the SEC in which General Tire admitted that:

■ Three of its foreign subsidiaries had maintained slush funds and had disbursed $1.2 million from the secret accounts.

■ "Improper or illegal payments were made to foreign government employes" by a foreign subsidiary.

■ Another foreign subsidiary maintained hidden accounts that "appear to have violated . . . foreign-currency exchange controls."

Alcoa discloses foreign payments. Aluminum Company of America (Alcoa) said July 9, 1976 that during 1970–72 it had made $80,000 in "unlawful" payments abroad and that its foreign subsidiaries or affiliates had made nearly $270,000 in questionable payments.

Alcoa said it had detailed the payoffs in a report to the SEC. Between 1972 and 1974, the firm said, a foreign affiliate had received "excess" interest and "refund payments" totaling $400,000 from financial institutions in that country. Alcoa, said the practice was "prevalent" in the unidentified country. Nearly all of the money was used for corporate purposes, but was placed in an "off-book fund," Alcoa said.

Claims U.S. ambassador solicited funds—In its report filed with the SEC, Alcoa claimed that a U.S. ambassador solicited the payment of corporate funds to officials and political parties of a foreign country. Although Alcoa and the SEC refused to furnish further details, newspaper reports published July 16 identified the envoy as Vincent W. de Roulet, ambassador to Jamaica from 1969 to 1973. De Roulet died in August 1975 of a heart ailment.

According to the Wall Street Journal, which printed excerpts from Alcoa's 1971 report to the SEC, de Roulet asked the company to make a contribution to an "education program" in Jamaica to explain to the citizenry the advantages of U.S. investments there.

Alcoa gave de Roulet a cashier's check for $25,000, made out to Jamaica's ruling party, the Journal reported. In 1971, the Labor Party governed Jamaica. It was defeated in elections in 1972.

Quoting from Alcoa's report, the Journal said, "Subsequently, four payments, aggregating an additional $25,000, were paid by cashier's check to the order of officials or political parties in that country." Alcoa later made another $5,000 political payment, the Journal said.

Jamaica's ruling People's National Party, headed by Prime Minister Michael Manley, acknowledged July 19 that it had received $20,000 from Alcoa for its 1972 campaign. Spokesmen denied that the payment was linked to the U.S. ambassador.

Alcoa had substantial bauxite mining and processing operations in Jamaica. (Bauxite was the raw material that yielded alumina, which was processed into aluminum.) According to the Journal, Alcoa obtained 10% of its alumina requirements from Jamaica. Through a subsidiary, the company operated a 550,000-ton-a-year alumina refinery, completed in 1972.

De Roulet, a major contributor to the Nixon presidential campaigns, had been a controversial figure in Jamaica because of his lavish life style and political statements. In 1973 Manley's government declared de Roulet persona non grata after he told a congressional committee that he had made a "deal" with Manley before the 1972 election.

De Roulet said he had promised Manley that the U.S. would not intervene in the 1972 elections if Manley promised not to nationalize Jamaica's bauxite industry. Manley denied the report and De Roulet later resigned as ambassador.

Kaiser, Reynolds Metals admit payments. Two other U.S. companies with bauxite investments in Jamaica, Kaiser Aluminum & Chemical Corp. and Reynolds Metals Co., also admitted making political contributions in Jamaica.

Kaiser told the SEC June 10 that the firm had donated a total of $90,000 to Jamaica's two political parties between 1970 and 1972. A spokesman termed the contributions "legal, ethical and proper" and said the payments were "properly authorized and accounted for in the company's books."

In a report filed June 2 with the SEC, Reynolds disclosed that it had made political contributions and "other expenditures' in Jamaica, Canada, Guyana and Surinam since 1970. Reynolds said the donations were properly recorded and "permissible under applicable law."

R. J. Reynolds admits $25 million. R. J. Reynolds Industries, Inc. of Winston-Salem, N.C. admitted Sept. 10, 1976 that it had made more than $25 million in questionable corporate payments in the U.S. and abroad since 1968 to promote its business and political interests.

The voluntary disclosure was made in a report filed with the Securities and Exchange Commission. The amount made

Reynolds' payment total one of the largest disclosed by the more than 200 companies that had filed such reports with the SEC.

Reynolds said that between 1971 and 1975 its wholly-owned shipping subsidiary, Sea-Land Services Inc., had paid $19 million in "possibly illegal rebates" to "shippers, consignees and forwarding agents."

Reynolds' tobacco subsidiaries made $5.4 million in questionable payments to officials of foreign governments or to employes of companies owned or controlled by foreign governments, the report stated. Most of the overseas payments from the tobacco operations were recorded on company books as commissions, Reynolds said, adding that 75% of the questionable commissions already had been stopped. The remaining payments would be ended shortly, Reynolds said.

Reynolds also admitted paying $190,000 in corporate funds to presidential and congressional candidates between 1968 and 1973. The cash was generated "by diverting a royalty payment due from a foreign license and paying inaccurate invoices, purportedly from other foreign countries," the report said. The money was disbursed through Reynold's Washington office.

In a preliminary report filed with the SEC May 28, Reynolds had said its political contributions totaled $65,000 to $90,000. Three directors responsible for making the contributions on Reynolds' behalf had resigned and agreed to reimburse the company for the illegally disbursed funds, Reynolds said.

At the same time, Reynolds said its preliminary investigation had uncovered "questionable payments" made by Sea-Land. Reynolds also admitted making other payments, totaling $100,000, to foreign officials.

Of the $19 million paid by Sea-Land, Reynolds said, $11.5 million involved the Atlantic market, $7 million went to Pacific businesses and $500,000 was paid in the Caribbean. Reynolds said that rebates were "traditional and pervasive in the international ocean-shipping industry." Sea-Land "reluctantly joined in the practice after trying to compete without doing so," Reynolds said.

(According to the Sept. 13 Wall Street Journal, rebates paid by returning part of the posted tariff to the shipper or consignee were legal and customary in most foreign countries.)

Sea-Land unilaterally stopped paying rebates in the Pacific in 1973 and in the Atlantic in 1975, but "believes that it has lost business as a result," Reynolds said.

Although the payment of rebates had halted, Reynolds said, Sea-Land continued to pay small bribes, known as "tea money," to shipping clerks in the Pacific until 1976. In one year, the small payments totaled $730,000 according to the report. Reynolds, which had acquired Sea-Land in 1969, said it had first learned of the rebating practices in early 1975.

"Mislabeling of accounts" was involved in paying the rebates, made in part from "off-book funds," Reynolds said.

In a report filed with the SEC Aug. 23, Gamble-Skogmo Inc., a Minneapolis-based merchandiser, admitted that one or more ocean carriers had paid $130,000 in rebates to employes of its importing subsidiary. Sea-Land reportedly had made some of the payments.

Warnaco Inc., an apparel company with headquarters in Bridgeport, Conn., told the SEC Sept. 13 that one of its subsidiaries had been paid $400,000 in rebates between 1970 and 1974 by an ocean carrier. According to government sources, Sea-Land had paid the rebates. The payments were being investigated by the maritime commission, Warnaco said.

A commission official said that Reynolds' disclosure was the commission's "first big break" in its rebate investigation that began in the spring.

Admissions from many firms. Many American companies during 1975–76 admitted questionable payments. Among them:

American Home Products—American Home Products Corp., a diversified manufacturer of drugs, food and other items, announced Oct. 17, 1975 that it had voluntarily informed the Securities and Exchange Commission that "questionable payments" had been made abroad. Most of the overseas payoffs, the company said, were "commission-type payments to foreign government employes to facilitate sales to foreign government entities."

Officials said the payoffs "wouldn't have exceeded $750,000 in any one year," according to an "initial inquiry" of records for 1973, 1974 and the first three quarters of 1975. The company's worldwide sales in the U.S. and more than 35 other countries totaled $2.18 billion in 1974.

The company said an investigation was continuing into certain other payments made abroad, including those made to "foreign political campaigns."

The company filed an updated report with the SEC March 9, 1976.

After an internal inquiry, the company said, it determined that payments totaling $3.4 million had been made in 41 countries from 1971–75. Most of the payments were made as commissions. An additional $204,000 in U.S. income tax was paid to correct 1972 and 1974 tax returns, the company said.

Del Monte—Del Monte Corp., the world's largest producer of canned fruits and vegetables, paid nearly $500,000 in 1972 to a Guatemalan "consultant" to overcome the Guatemalan government's opposition to Del Monte's purchase of a banana plantation, the Wall Street Journal reported July 14, 1975. Soon after the consultant was hired, the government reversed its position and allowed Del Monte to buy the 55,000-acre plantation from United Brands Co. for $20.5 million.

Del Monte confirmed the Journal's story but gave few other details. According to the Journal, the consultant's fee was "entirely contingent on his ability to influence the balky Guatemalan government," which had delayed the sale of the plantation for 18 months.

Del Monte charged the consultant's fee to "general and administrative expenses on the books of several Panamanian shipping subsidiaries," the Journal reported.

Corporate officials believed the payment was "entirely proper," according to the Journal, and denied that bribery or illegal political contributions were involved. The consultant had assured them, the Journal reported, that no Del Monte cash went to government officials.

Guatemalan President Kjell Eugenio Laugerud ordered an immediate investigation of the consultant's fee, the Associated Press reported July 16.

Domingo Moreira, a naturalized Guatemalan from Cuba, identified himself as the Del Monte consultant, AP reported July 23. Moreiro made a written statement to the Guatemalan commission investigating the case.

General Refractories—The SEC filed a suit May 21, 1976 against the General Refractories Co., charging that it had made "payments to officials of certain foreign governments" in 1972 and 1974 without giving proper account of the payments or disclosing them to shareholders.

Fraud charges also were leveled against General Refractories, a Philadelphia-based firm that made firebrick for the steel industry, and its chairman, Joseph G. Solari. They were accused of scheming for 10 years to conceal an Austrian businessman's investment in General Refractories stock. According to the SEC, Hermann Mayer, currently a Swiss resident, directly or indirectly held about 17% of the total common stock outstanding in the firm—enough, the SEC said, to give him controlling interest. Mayer also was accused of fraud by the SEC.

The commission's complaint charged that Mayer's companies in Europe engaged in certain transactions with General Refractories that caused the U.S. firm "to incur unnecessary costs to the benefit of the Mayer concerns." "Millions of dollars" in revenues were generated from these deals, the SEC claimed.

According to SEC officials, the General Refractories case represented the first instance in which the agency had accused a foreign citizen of exerting secret influence over the operations of a U.S. company.

Among the defendants named in the SEC suit, in addition to Mayer, Solari and the firm, were Mayer's son who served as his representative on General Refractories' board, a vice president of the firm, and a Swiss lawyer for one of Mayer's companies abroad. Six of those firms also were named in the SEC suit.

General Refractories May 22 denied the SEC allegations.

International Business Machines—International Business Machines Corp. said Aug. 1, 1975 that its Canadian subsidiary had halted "its customary and legal practice" of making contributions to Canadian political parties in order to conform to a "single world-wide IBM policy" against political donations.

IBM said its Canadian subsidiary's contributions to federal and provincial campaigns had averaged $36,000 a year in the past five years. The largest amount, $67,500, was given in 1974. Names of the parties and candidates receiving the corporate contributions were not revealed.

3M—One of Minnesota Mining & Manufacturing Co.'s foreign subsidiaries paid a $52,000 bribe in June to a foreign customs agent to avoid penalties for evading customs payments, the Wall Street Journal reported Nov. 18, 1975.

Payment of the bribe was revealed by William P. Murphy, a retired Minnesota supreme court justice. Murphy was investigating whether 3M had made any other illegal political payments in the U.S. or overseas in addition to illegal political contributions made from a $634,000 slush fund uncovered in 1974.

The investigation was ordered in a consent decree, settling a Securities and Exchange Commission charge, that enjoined 3M from violating U.S. securities laws in connection with the illegal political contributions.

Justice Murphy gave no other details about the bribe because, he said, officials feared disclosure would lead to expropriation of 3M properties or other "costly harassment." He added, however, that the subsidiary's managing director, who had paid the bribe, would reimburse 3M. Murphy also said that the company would pay the foreign country any amount that an audit determined was owed.

Most of Murphy's report dealt with the methods used by 3M officials to accumulate and disburse their secret political fund. From the early 1950s to 1963, 3M's president solicited money for political contributions "from a number of well-to-do persons connected with 3M." After 1963, money was deposited in a Swiss bank, purportedly to pay foreign insurance premiums, and was withdrawn by three top officials of the company.

Murphy determined that from 1963 through 1973, illegal corporate donations totaling $197,975 went to various national Republican Party committees, and $22,650 went to national Democratic Party committees. (No records existed prior to

1963, Murphy said.)

Individual candidates received a total of $64,460 from the slush fund, Murphy said. The largest contributions went to three Republicans—former California Sen. George Murphy, the late Illinois Sen. Everett Dirksen, and former Minnesota Rep. Clark MacGregor.

Rollins—The U.S.-based advertising agency Rollins, Inc. admitted March 3, 1976 that it had paid more than $100,000 in bribes to municipal authorities in Mexico City and that it "expected" to continue making payments "because it is a custom" there.

List of Companies Mounts

SEC lists paying firms. In a report filed May 12, 1976 with the Senate Banking Committee, the Securities and Exchange Commission identified 79 companies that had admitted making, or had been formally charged with making, foreign payments of questionable legality.

The SEC named another 24 companies that had admitted making domestic political contributions.

The first part of the three-part SEC report was a list of 89 companies that had filed with the agency public documents relating to foreign and domestic payments. The SEC emphasized that the disclosures were not based on its independent investigations. When no statement on a particular issue was made, the chart simply showed "not indicated."

The second part summarized reports prepared by six special-review commissions that had been established under court order by American Ship Building Co., Ashland Oil Inc., Gulf Oil Corp., 3M Co., Phillips Petroleum Co. and Northrop Corp. The SEC had filed charges against the six companies, charging that they had violated federal securities laws by concealing their domestic and/or foreign payments. All six consented to court injunctions barring future violations of securities laws, but the firms neither admitted nor denied the SEC charges.

In the third part of the report, the SEC summarized allegations made in enforcement actions against eight other companies whose special review panels had not yet completed their reports. The eight firms were Braniff International Corp., General Tire and Rubber Corp., Kalvex Inc., Lockheed Aircraft Corp., Missouri Public Service Co., Sanitas Service Corp., United Brands Co. and Waste Management Inc.

According to the SEC's tabulations of the 95 companies that had made disclosures of questionable or illegal corporate payments, 66 were manufacturing companies. The two largest groups were drug manufacturers and oil companies, each represented by 12 firms.

The most common transactions reported, the SEC said, were payments, disclosed by 54 companies, to foreign officials. In two other categories of questionable foreign payments, 17 companies reported making political payments and 29 said they had paid sales-type commissions.

Twenty-six companies reported making domestic political contributions, many of which were identified as illegal. Fifteen companies reported "other domestic matters" of a questionable or illegal nature.

The SEC said that 42 companies indicated that the disclosure of their corporate payments had led to adjustments in their federal tax liability or discussion of the issue with the Internal Revenue Service.

A "particularly disturbing fact" revealed in the report, the SEC said, was the disclosure that in 46 companies "at least some member or members of corporate management had knowledge of, approved of or participated in the questionable and illegal activities reported."

The SEC also noted that "most of the instances of reported abuse also involved some falsification of corporate records or the maintenance of records that appear to be inadequate."

According to the SEC, 19 of the 95 companies specifically said that the cessation of their payment practices "would have no material effect on their total revenues or overall business." For this reason, the SEC said, an end to the practice of making foreign payments "will not seriously affect the ability of American business to compete in world markets."

Domestic and Foreign Corporate Payments

(From reports filed with the SEC by April 21, 1976)

Corporation	Domestic Political Contributions or Other Domestic Payments	Questionable Foreign Payments
Abbott Laboratories	None	$680,000 (1973–75)
Allergan Pharmaceuticals	None	51,899 (1970–75)
American Airlines Inc.	Guilty plea to Watergate special prosecutor for illegal contributions of $55,000. Other payments of $50,975 from 1971–73 believed legal. Another $117,474 believed contributed during period beginning as early as 1964.	Not indicated
American Cyanamid Co.	None	More than 1,200,000 (1971–75)
American Home Products Corp.		6,462,000 (1971–75)
American Ship Building Co.[1]	Selected employes were paid bonuses of $30,000 in 1970, $25,000 in 1971 and $42,325.17 in 1972. After paying taxes on the bonuses, the employes were directed to contribute the remainder to various political figures.	Not indicated
American Standards Inc.	None	More than 266,500 (1973–75)
AMF Inc.	Not indicated	1,500,000 (1971–75)
American Telephone & Telegraph Co.	Pending investigation concerning political contributions to obtain favorable treatment from state commissioners.	Not indicated
Ashland Oil Inc.[1]	Political contributions totaled $850,000 from 1967–72. A total of $25,700 expended from 1972–74 constituted legal contributions. The following sums were reported but not identified as legal:	679,500 (1967–74)

Corporation	Domestic Political Contributions or Other Domestic Payments	Questionable Foreign Payments
	1967—$66,500, 1968—$239,600, 1969—$46,300, 1970—$71,700, 1971—$54,500, 1972—$256,815. A subsidiary paid $15,000 in 1970 in response to an extortionate demand by a local government. Between 1967–72, another $71,700 was "presumed to have been used" for political contributions.	
Baxter Laboratories Inc.	None	2,160,220 (1970–75)
The Boeing Co.	None	*
Braniff International Inc.[2]	Guilty plea to the Watergate special prosecutor for illegal political contributions of $40,000.	More than 900,000
Bristol-Myers Co.	Not indicated	"Some payments"
Browning-Ferris Industries Inc.	Apparent $10,000 contribution in a "jurisdiction in which corporate political contributions are not unlawful." Contribution was made against management orders.	Not indicated
Burroughs Corp.	Not indicated	1,500,000 (1973–75)
Butler National Corp.	$302,000†	
Carnation Co.	Not indicated	1,261,000 (1968–76)
Carrier Corp.	None	2,614,000 (1972–75)
Castle & Cooke Inc.	Money was passed through special checking account in connection with anticipated port strike. Some $140,000 paid to contractor to arrange for unloading vessels. Payment believed legal.	110,000
Celanese Corp.	Not indicated	Not indicated
Cerro Corp.	Not indicated	*
Cities Service Co.	Not indicated	645,000 (1973–75)
Coastal States Gas Corp.	None yet discovered	8,000,000
Coherent Radiation	Not indicated	20,388
Colgate-Palmolive Co.	None	865,000 (1971–75)
ComBanks Corp.	President made contributions of some $100,000 from 1967–73 to federal, state and local officials from account maintained by officer of affiliated bank.	Not indicated
Cook Industries Inc.	Investigation not complete but company believes that certain of its employes may have been involved in violations relating to grain transactions and other such matters as bribery and intimidation of federally licensed grain officials.	Not indicated
Cook United Inc.	6,163†	
Core Laboratories Inc.	None	184,485
Del Monte Corp.	Not indicated	*
Diamond International Corp.	Revealed voluntary disclosure to federal authorities of illegal political contributions and guilty plea of company and a vice president to contributions of $6,000.	Not indicated
Diversified Industries Inc.	Allegation in civil suit that cash fund of some $270,000 was maintained from 1972–75, and that payments of $200,000 made to company employes. A $5,000 payment alleged in another company division for unknown purposes. Remainder not verified but $35,000 returned to general funds.	Not indicated
Dresser Industries Inc.	Not indicated	24,000
Electronic Associates Inc.	Possibly some $1,150 paid to domestic political parties by	83,000 (1971–75)

Corporation	Domestic Political Contributions or Other Domestic Payments	Questionable Foreign Payments
	former officer who was reimbursed by firm.	
Exxon Corp.	Not indicated	56,771,000 (1963-75)
Fairchild Industries Inc.	Not indicated	*
Gardner-Denver Co.	None	96,200 (1971-76)
General Telephone & Electronics Corp.	None	13,257,483 (1971-75)
General Tire & Rubber Co.[2]	Investigation under way	1,349,000
The B. F. Goodrich Co.	None	124,000 (1971-1975)
The Goodyear Tire & Rubber Co.	A foreign bank account, funded from volume discounts in foreign sales, was used as the source of domestic contributions. The account was started in 1964. Over six years, some $260,000 was transferred to the U.S. and used as political contributions. Chairman and company pleaded guilty to making an illegal $40,000 contribution in 1972.	846,000 (1970-75)
Gulf Oil Corp.[1]	Political contributions totaled $1.4 million from 1960-72. Another $5.4 million returned to U.S. from foreign countries in off-book transactions to be used for political contributions. Disposition of $4 million of this total not determined.	6,900,000 (1960-73)
Harrah's	Contributions of $17,500 in possible violation of federal law. Company reimbursed by chairman.	Not indicated
Honeywell Inc.	Nominal state and local contributions that were legal were made and discontinued in 1974.	1,840,000 (1971-75)
Hospital Corp. of America	Not indicated	"Some payments"
Ingersoll-Rand Co.	Not indicated	Not indicated
Intercontinental Diversified Corp.	Not indicated	329,320 (1970-72)
International Telephone & Telegraph Corp.	From 1971-75 various subsidiaries expended some $4,300 in purchasing tickets in fund-raising events, incurring other minor expenses and making minor contributions that could be considered directly or indirectly to be contributions to federal election campaigns. ITT's foreign and domestic contributions totaled $64,300 from 1971-75, of which $60,000 was made in jurisdictions where legal.	3,864,300 (1971-75)
Johnson & Johnson	None	1,002,300 (1971-75)
Kalvex Inc.[2]	Kickbacks to senior officers†	Not indicated
Koppers Co. Inc.	None	1,500,000
Kraftco Corp.	Contributions totaling $550 from 1972-76 that may have been illegal.	699,500 (1969-75)
Levi Strauss & Co.	Not indicated	75,000 (1974-75)
Lockheed Aircraft Co.[2]	Not indicated	25,000,000 (1967-75)
McDonnell Douglas Corp.	None	2,500,000 (1971-76)
Mercantile Bankcorp. Inc.	Officers established fund, existing from 1968-75, for political contributions. Bank did not participate and did not reimburse officers. Contributions averaged $10,000 a year and were not coerced.	Not indicated
Merck & Co. Inc.	None	3,761,319 (1968-75)
Missouri Public Service Co.[2]	Contributions of $51,865 from 1968-76 made by club formed by senior employes.	Not indicated

Corporation	Domestic Political Contributions or Other Domestic Payments	Questionable Foreign Payments
NCR Corp.	Not indicated	300,000 (1967–75)
Northrop Corp.[1]	Contributions totaled at least $501,928 from 1962–73. Another $119,000 was disbursed from Northrop's eastern office from a "hidden fund of cash" from 1971–73. A $40,000 consulting fee was paid to a congressional staff member.	30,704,400 (1969–75)
Northwest Industries Inc.	Not indicated	582,000 (1973–75)
The Offshore Co. (A subsidiary of Southern Natural Resources Inc.)	None	169,000
Ogden Corp.	Unannounced candidates provided services of company plane until 1974 at cost of $40,000. Former subsidiaries made illegal contributions of $16,200.	2,415,000 (1970–75)
Otis Elevator Co.	Not indicated	*
Pacific Vegetable Oil	Not indicated	1,170,000 (1974–75)
Pfizer Inc.	Not indicated	262,000 (1972–75)
Phillips Petroleum Co.[1]	Contributions totaled $585,000 from 1964–72.	1,258,000
Public Service of New Mexico	Grand jury investigation regarding possible violation of federal law in connection with $9,656 paid to private company that may have been passed on to candidate.	Not indicated
Pullman Inc.	None	2,275,665 (1973–75)
Republic Corp.	Not indicated	*
Richardson-Merrell Inc.	None	"Some payments"
Rockwell International	Not indicated	676,300 (1971–75)
Rohm & Haas Co.	None	749,400 (1971–75)
Rollins Inc.	Not indicated	127,000 (1971–75)
Sanders Associates Inc.	Not indicated	"Some commissions"
Sanitas Service Corp.[2]	$1.2 million†	Not indicated
Santa Fe International Corp.	Investigation under way	66,140 (1972–75)
Schering-Plough Corp.	No illegal contributions	207,000 (annually)
G.D. Searle & Co.	No illegal contributions	1,303,000 (1973–75)
Security New York State Corp.	Officers received fees which were later allegedly contributed to political campaigns. Investigation of possible violations of New York election laws.	Not indicated
The Singer Co.	Grand jury indictment involving $15,000 contribution charging company and lower-level employes.	Not indicated
Smith International Inc.	Not indicated	13,349
Southern Bell Telephone & Telegraph Co. (A subsidiary of American Telephone & Telegraph Co.)	Former employes made allegations of illegal contributions. North Carolina commission found $142,000 was improperly accounted for. Purpose of money not disclosed.	Not indicated
Standard Oil Co. (Indiana)	Probably illegal state contribution of $10,000 in 1970; $10,000 payment in 1970 to trade association for political contribution. Aggregate of $289,000 in promotional allowances from supplies not recorded as assets.	1,359,400 (1970–75)
Stanley Home Products Inc.	None	50,000
Sterling Drug Inc.	None	136,000 (1970–75)
Sybron Corp.	Not indicated	76,500 (1974–75)
Tenneco Inc.	Subsidiaries made lawful contributions of $180,000 in California. Some $3,000 contributed illegally by subsidiary in Louisiana. Payments of $2,000 a month to	865,480

	Louisiana sheriff presently under investigation. Contribution to U.S. Senator may have been paid to obtain influence in General Service Administration decision.	
3M Co.[1]	Between 1963 and 1969, $633,997 was misappropriated and placed in a secret fund, of which $545,799 was disbursed for political contributions from 1963–72. Vast majority was contributed illegally.	52,000 (1975)
UOP Inc. (A subsidiary of Occidental Petroleum Corp.)	None	290,000 (1971–75)
United Brands Co.[2]	Not indicated	2,000,000
United Technologies Corp.	None	2,040,000 (1973–75)
Upjohn Co.	None	2,736,000
Warner-Lambert Co.	None	2,273,000 (1971–75)
Waste Management Inc.[2]	$36,000†	Not indicated
Westinghouse Electric Corp.	Not indicated	223,000
White Consolidated Industries Inc.	None	1,190,000 (1974–75)
Whittaker Corp.	Contributions totaling $585 to congressional candidates by middle level employes from 1970–75. A total of $47,328 paid from 1970–75 paid to a customer in connection with sales, possibly illegal.	133,425 (1970–71)

Source: Securities and Exchange Commission and Congressional Quarterly, Aug. 28, 1976.

[1]Information based on court-ordered report prepared by special review commission.
[2]Information is a description of SEC allegations because the court-ordered report had not been completed.
*Company reported that alleged improper payments were under investigation by a government agency or by the company.
†Report did not identify payments as either domestic or foreign.
Quotes indicate excerpt from company report.

Legislative Action

Ford submits payments disclosure bill. President Ford submitted to Congress Aug. 3, 1976 legislation to require companies to disclose payments, whether "proper or improper," that they had made to officials of foreign governments to foster sales abroad.

The proposal was the Administration's latest response to the widening foreign-payments scandal.

Under the Administration bill, reports of all foreign payments would be made to the secretary of commerce. The reports would be kept confidential for one year and then made public unless the secretary of state or attorney general issued a written declaration that "considerations of foreign policy or judicial process dictate against disclosure."

The commerce secretary could make the payments reports available at an earlier time to the State Department, the Justice Department, the Securities and

Exchange Commission, the Internal Revenue Service and "appropriate Congressional committees." Information in the reports also could be released to foreign governments.

Proposed penalties for violations were a $100,000 civil fine for failing to disclose payments and a $500,000 criminal penalty for deliberately failing to make the required disclosures.

In a message to Congress that accompanied the bill, Ford said the legislation "will help deter would-be foreign extorters from seeking improper payments from American businessmen" and "will help reverse the trend toward allegations or assumptions of guilt-by-association impugning the integrity of American business generally."

The SEC, which had been the source of nearly all the disclosures of foreign bribes and payments made by U.S. companies, would continue to require the filing of financial reports on information it deemed necessary for investors.

In citing the need for federal legislation

dealing with foreign payments, the Administration noted that only 9,000 of the 30,000 companies doing international business were under SEC jurisdiction and that the SEC did not necessarily require the naming of recipients of foreign payments.

The Administration bill was the product of more than four months of work by the White House Task Force on Questionable Corporate Payments Abroad, a Cabinet-level group appointed March 31 by Ford. Commerce Secretary Elliot L. Richardson headed the task force.

At an Aug. 3 press conference on the bill, Richardson said that a basic solution to the payments problem would require a new international treaty, which the U.S. was promoting within the framework of the United Nations.

(As a preliminary step, the Organization for Economic Cooperation and Development had adopted a voluntary code of conduct for multinational corporations. The code barred the offering and soliciting of bribes.)

Richardson said that the Administration had rejected as unenforceable efforts to legislate an outright ban on foreign payments. The Administration position was severely criticized by Jimmy Carter. It conflicted with the views of Sen. William Proxmire (D, Wis.), chairman of the Senate Banking Committee and sponsor of an anti-bribery bill before the Senate.

The fiscal 1976–77 foreign-aid bill, passed June 25 and signed by Ford June 30, required the disclosure to the secretary of state, and through him to Congress, of "political contributions, gifts, commissions and fees paid, offered or agreed to be paid" in connection with foreign arms sales.

ITT & Chile

The International Telephone & Telegraph Corp. was accused of having misused its money and power in Chile. Initially, it was charged, ITT tried to prevent the election of Marxist leader Salvador Allende as the country's president. After Allende had become president, it was reported, ITT sought to build up his opposition and have him deposed.

Senate committee's probe. The Special Senate Subcommittee on Multinational Corporations in March 1973 began hearings on ITT's activities in Chile.

John A. McCone, former director of the Central Intelligency Agency (CIA) and a consultant to the agency since his retirement in 1965, told the subcommittee March 21 that he had met with Henry A. Kissinger, President Nixon's national security adviser, and Richard Helms, then director of the CIA and a "close friend," in mid-1970 to offer the U.S. government $1 million in financial aid from ITT. The money would be used to block the runoff election of Salvador Allende Gossens as president of Chile.

Allende, a Socialist, was elected Sept. 4, 1970 by a small plurality. He headed a left-wing coalition dominated by the Chilean Communist party. Allende took office in October 1970 after a joint session of Congress elected him president.

A year after his election, Allende expropriated the ITT-controlled telephone company in Chile.

ITT had filed a claim for $92 million with the U.S. government's Overseas Private Investment Corp., which insured U.S. firms against foreign takeovers; however, any "provocation or instigation" by a client company, unless requested by the U.S. government, could invalidate the insurance claim.

McCone made the $1 million offer in his capacity as a director of ITT. The money had been authorized by ITT President and Chairman Harold S. Geneen. McCone denied that the money was intended for "surreptitious" purposes or would be used to create "economic chaos."

"What he [Geneen] had in mind was not chaos but what could be done constructively. The money was to be channeled to people who support the principles and programs the U.S. stands for against the programs of the Allende-Marxists," McCone testified.

The money would be used in Chile, McCone said, for programs such as housing projects and technical agricultural assistance.

"International communism has said time and again that its objective is the destruction of the free world, economically, politically, militarily. . . . That was what Mr. Geneen was thinking of," according to McCone.

Members of the subcommittee expressed incredulity at McCone's testimony. Sen. Clifford P. Case (R, N.J.) noted that the U.S. had already given Chile more than $1 billion in economic aid over the past 10 years and that Allende had been elected anyway.

"How can a man of Mr. Geneen's intelligence possibly think that $1 million for these kinds of purposes in six weeks could make any difference?" Case asked.

The ITT plan proposed to Kissinger and Helms was termed the "Alessandri Formula." It called for financial support to be given to a coalition of the conservative National party, headed by Jorge Alessandri Rodriguez, and the Christian Democratic party, led by Radomiro Tomic. It was planned that they would oppose Allende in the expected runoff election and that Allesandri would be elected. He would then resign and call for new elections, permitting former President Eduardo Frei Montalva to challenge Allende in the subsequent two-man race.

"A number of people were trying to explore alternatives about what might be done. The Chilean military was discussing the Alessandri Plan. Mr. [William V.] Broe [director of clandestine operations in Latin America for the CIA] had a shopping list and the staff of the CIA had a shopping list," McCone told the subcommittee.

The plan was abandoned when Alessandri withdrew from the runoff race because of his lack of support in the Chilean Congress where the final decision would be made.

McCone testified that Helms had told him "the matter was considered by an interdepartmental committee of senior representatives of the Defense and State Departments as well as the CIA, and the decision was reached that nothing should be done."

Although the ITT plan was rejected, McCone said that at his request, Helms put Geneen in contact with Broe. This corresponded with testimony given the previous day.

William R. Merriam, vice president of ITT and former director of its Washington office, had testified March 20

that ITT President Geneen had arranged to establish a working relationship between the corporation and the CIA in order to prevent the election of Allende as president of Chile, and, failing that, to bring about the "economic collapse" of Chile.

Merriam said his association with the CIA's Broe began at a Washington meeting held July 16, 1970 which was arranged and attended by Geneen. Geneen instructed him to "stay in touch" with Broe, Merriam testified, and subsequent phone conversations and meetings with the CIA agent occurred "many times."

Merriam told the subcommittee that Broe was impressed with the quality of information gathered by ITT operatives in Latin America. When shown a Sept. 17, 1970 cable from ITT officials Bob Berrellez and Hal Hendrix, Broe "approved" the recommendation, Merriam declared.

The cable urged ITT "and other U.S. firms in Chile" to head off Allende's election by contributing advertising funds to a conservative Chilean newspaper in financial difficulties. The report also recommended that ITT "bring what pressure we can" on the U.S. Information Agency to circulate the Chilean newspaper's editorial in Latin America and Europe. (In testimony given March 21, Hendrix claimed the plan was never carried out because its intent was too obvious.)

According to an ITT memo dated late September 1970 when the Chilean election results were still in doubt, ITT Senior Vice President Edward Gerrity told Geneen that Broe had suggested the company "apply economic pressures" to influence the voting.

Broe "indicated that certain steps were being taken, but that he was looking for additional help aimed at inducing economic collapse," Gerrity told Geneen, "Realistically I don't see how we can induce others involved to follow the plan suggested," Gerrity concluded.

As part of this plan, Merriam said the CIA made "repeated calls to firms such as General Motors, Ford Motor Co. and banks in California and New York." All refused to cease or reduce operations in Chile, according to ITT documents submitted to the subcommittee.

Merriam testified that ITT, at the instigation of the Anaconda Copper Co., organized an "Ad Hoc Committee on Chile" which met in his office in February 1971. "The thrust of the meeting was toward the application of pressure on the [U.S.] government wherever possible to make it clear that a Chilean takeover wouldn't be tolerated without serious repercussions following," according to Ronald Raddatz, a representative of the BankAmerica Corp., who was present. Others represented were Anaconda, Kennecott Copper Corp., W. R. Grace & Co., Pfizer Inc., and Ralston Purina Co.

No conclusions were reached, according to Merriam and he discounted the significance of the meeting itself. "We were just kicking around some ideas. We have these ad hoc committees all the time in Washington."

After the expropriation of the ITT company in September 1971, Merriam wrote White House assistant Peter Peterson that there were "numerous justifiable leverages" the government could exert to protect American property in Chile.

The 18 suggestions included fostering "discontent" in the Chilean military, cutting off bank loans, restricting Chilean travel and slowing trade between the U.S. and Chile. "Everything should be done quietly but effectively to see that Allende doesn't get through the crucial next six months," the memo concluded.

Merriam justified the corporation's actions saying, "If Allende was faced with economic collapse, he might be more congenial toward paying us off."

In other testimony and documents submitted to the subcommittee, Merriam indicated that he made at least 25 visits to the State Department and had conferred for a "year" with officials in Kissinger's office.

According to another ITT memorandum submitted to the committee March 21, President Nixon had given the U.S. ambassador to Chile, Edward M. Korry, a "green light" in September 1970 to do everything possible short of military intervention to prevent the victory of Allende.

Geneen admits ITT offers—ITT chairman Geneen admitted to the Senate sub-

committee April 2 that he had twice offered money to the U.S. government to prevent Allende's election.

Geneen's admission regarding the first offer of funds was cautious. Having "no recollection to the contrary," Geneen told the subcommittee he would accept the testimony of William V. Broe, director of covert operations in Latin America for the Central Intelligence Agency (CIA), that the money was offered at a July 1970 meeting and was intended to finance a CIA effort to stop Allende.

Geneen justified the gesture as an "emotional reaction" resulting from his conversations with Broe in which the CIA representative said the U.S. planned no efforts to circumvent the Chilean election of Allende, who was running on a Socialist-Communist platform.

According to Geneen, this policy of nonintervention represented the reversal of a 14-year U.S. "policy to maintain a democratic government in Chile." Geneen said he had been particularly disturbed by the talks with Broe because ITT had invested in Chile as part of the U.S. government's economic assistance policy to develop the country. In contrast to its past encouragement, the Nixon Administration appeared unwilling to aid ITT when the company anticipated the expropriation of its Chilean properties.

The matter "died right there," Geneen claimed, although he admitted making a second offer to the government in September 1970 when Allende had won his first election test and required ratification by the Chilean Congress in an October vote.

Geneen was unable to clarify contradictory testimony given earlier regarding the use of the slush fund. He claimed that the "amount mentioned of up to seven figures was intended to show a serious intent and to gain serious attention from the government" to finance "some socially constructive joint private industry and government projects" to induce Allende to make adequate compensation for ITT properties in Chile.

John A. McCone, former director of the CIA and currently an ITT director, had testified March 21 that the $1 million offer by ITT was earmarked for support of an anti-Allende coalition in the runoff period before the October 1970 vote.

This offer was never clearly explained to the Administration, Geneen explained, because ITT officials at the firm's Washington office did not receive explicit instructions from him detailing the proposal.

The hearings recessed following Geneen's appearance but earlier testimony elicited further information regarding the extent of ITT's involvement in Chile's internal affairs.

ITT memo cites efforts—An ITT memorandum submitted to the subcommittee March 22 revealed that ITT had attempted to obtain compensation for the firm's telephone company in Chile, expropriated in September 1971 by President Allende, at the expense of other U.S.-owned companies also slated for nationalization.

The memo detailed a mutual assistance pact in which ITT would be compensated for loss of property and Allende would benefit politically by demonstrating his willingness to conclude a "fair deal" with the U.S. firm.

According to the memo, ITT hoped to persuade Allende that favorable world opinion would then allow him to confiscate the copper companies owned by Kennecott Corp. and Anaconda Copper Co. under the pretext that the seizures involved crucial natural resources and were distinct from the deal concluded with ITT.

The Chile plan failed when the Allende government broke off negotiations after columnist Jack Anderson made public ITT documents revealing ITT's intervention in the 1970 presidential elections in Chile aimed at the defeat of Allende.

According to the ITT memo, the company claimed success for its arrangement in 1968 when it had "handled the situation in Peru" on the "same basis." A petroleum subsidiary of the Exxon Corp. had been confiscated without compensation while ITT had received payment for the takeover of its telephone company.

ITT Senior Vice President Edward J. Gerrity gave testimony March 22 which contradicted the public statements of ITT director McCone that he had offered $1 million to U.S. officials to finance an anti-Allende coalition.

Gerrity said he was "baffled" by McCone's disclosures. "The first I heard about it [the covert purpose of the fund] was here yesterday." Gerrity said ITT had intended that the money be used to finance "constructive" humanitarian programs in Chile.

Gerrity claimed that Jack D. Neal, ITT's director of international relations, had conveyed the offer of social assistance to the National Security Council and the State Department during September 1970.

In testimony March 20, Neal had said he "didn't elaborate" on the purpose of the money in his talks with government officials.

Arturo Matte Larrain, a prominent conservative Chilean politician, corroborated McCone's testimony March 23. Matte said he had rejected an offer by Robert Berrellez, an ITT official, to help anti-Allende forces block the final presidential vote in October 1970.

Matte, campaign manager for Jorge Alessandri who was opposing Allende in the runoff race, said Berrellez "offered assistance but money was not mentioned. We turned him down."

Broe testified before a closed session of the subcommittee March 27. Portions of the proceedings were made public March 28 after review by the CIA.

Broe described Geneen's offer made at a July 16, 1970 meeting in Washington to provide a "substantial fund" for the support of Alessandri's candidacy. The money was rejected, Broe testified, because the CIA refused to "serve as a funding channel."

"I also told him that the United States government was not supporting any candidate in the Chilean election," Broe said. He added that Geneen never suggested at that time that the money be used for social assistance programs.

According to Broe, Geneen told him that ITT and other American companies had raised money to influence the 1964 Chilean election of Eduardo Frei but that CIA Director John A. McCone had refused the offer.

After the Sept. 4, 1970 election in Chile when Allende won a small plurality of the vote, the CIA altered its policy of neutrality and met with ITT officials to devise anti-Allende plans, Broe testified.

During the same period in 1970, ITT held a board of directors meeting Sept. 8–

9 when Geneen asked McCone to repeat the offer of financial assistance to the government with the new aim of funding an anti-Allende coalition before the second presidential vote.

Broe admitted devising a series of secondary proposals in September 1970 for Gerrity which would create economic chaos in Chile, also with the aim of preventing Allende's presidential victory.

Broe claimed he had acted with the full knowledge of CIA Director Richard Helms and that Geneen had initiated the company's first contact with the CIA in 1970.

Broe met with Geneen Sept. 29, 1970 to discuss plans for accelerating Chile's economic deterioration in order to "influence a number of Christian Democratic [party] congressmen who were planning to vote for Allende." Among the proposals Broe presented were delays in bank credits and delivery of spare part shipments, and withdrawal of technical assistance.

Broe also confirmed the testimony of another top ITT official, William M. Merriam, who had said Broe gave his approval Sept. 29, 1970 to a plan supporting an anti-Allende newspaper and "propagandists."

Other portions of the Broe testimony were released March 29 relating to the September 1970 conversations with Gerrity. Broe insisted that the CIA plan for the disruption of the Chilean economy had been approved by superiors in the intelligence gathering agency.

Former Commerce Secretary Peter Peterson, then presidential adviser on international economic affairs, confirmed March 29 that he had met with Geneen Dec. 14, 1971 to discuss ITT's plan to cripple the Chilean economy. Gen. Alexander Haig, presidential security adviser Henry Kissinger's principal adviser, was also present at the meeting. Peterson said the ITT proposal was never seriously considered by the Administration.

Edward Korry, U.S. ambassador to Chile from 1967 to 1971, testified March 27. He revealed that the CIA had commissioned polls to determine the outcome of the 1970 election and voiced his disagreement with the survey results.

Korry declined to answer other questions related to intervention in Chilean politics by the U.S. government or U.S.

businesses. However, he did state that an ITT document claiming that President Nixon had given him a "green light" to oppose Allende was "erroneous."

OPIC rejects ITT claim. The Overseas Private Investment Corp. (OPIC) April 9 denied International Telephone & Telegraph Corp.'s (ITT) insurance claim for $92.5 million sought as indemnity for its Chilean subsidiary seized in 1971 by the government of President Salvador Allende.

OPIC, a quasi-governmental agency which insured investments of U.S. companies from political risks abroad, based its rejection on ITT's "noncompliance with contractual obligations." It charged the firm with failing to "disclose material information to OPIC. In addition, ITT increased OPIC's risk of loss by failing to preserve administrative remedies as required by the contracts, and by failing to protect OPIC's interests as a potential successor to ITT's rights."

Allende: no compensation—Chilean President Allende asserted April 10 that Chile would pay no compensation to ITT because of the revelations which emerged from the Senate subcommittee hearings.

"No one can dream that we are going to pay even half a cent to this multinational company which was on the verge of plunging Chile into civil war," Allende declared. He added that he "now could say North American officials and agencies of the U.S. tried to thwart the will of the Chilean people."

In making his address before a meeting of the World Labor Union Assembly, attended by 1,500 representatives from 70 countries, Allende extended his remarks on "imperialist" corporations to include Anaconda, Kennecott Copper Corp. and Cerro Corp., whose properties also had been seized.

Senators score ITT. The Senate Subcommittee on Multinational Corporations issued a final report June 21, 1973 following its hearings on ITT actions in Chile.

The subcommittee concluded that ITT had "overstepped the lines of acceptable corporate behavior" in seeking covert CIA aid to prevent Allende's election.

ITT's offer of $1 million to the CIA "to manipulate the outcome" of the 1970 Chilean election was not illegal, according to the subcommittee; however, proposed legislation included in the report would make any recurrence of the offer a criminal offense. The bill would prevent a U.S. citizen or resident from offering money to any U.S. agency in order to influence the outcome of any foreign election. Government solicitation of any money was also barred.

The subcommittee proposed that clandestine operations of the CIA be subject to review by the executive branch and by "the appropriate Congressional committees."

Securities Frauds & Abuses

Vesco & IOS

SEC charges Vesco stock fraud. A two-year investigation by the Securities and Exchange Commission (SEC) culminated Nov. 27, 1972 in charges that Robert L. Vesco, ex-chairman of the International Controls Corp. (ICC), and 20 individuals and 21 firms associated with him diverted more than $224 million in assets from four mutual funds holding American companies' securities. It was also alleged that the defendants filed false and incomplete reports with the SEC and failed to make full disclosures of their actions to their stockholders.

The case, which the SEC termed "rife with self-dealing," grew out of the 1971 sale of the Swiss-based, mutual funds complex, Investors Overseas Services Ltd. (IOS), by its founder, Bernard Cornfeld, to Vesco after Vesco had rescued the failing corporation with a loan of $5.5 million in 1970. Also named in the suit was James Roosevelt, the eldest son of the late President and a former IOS director.

According to the civil suit filed in New York, after ICC took control of IOS in October 1971, IOS was broken down into component mutual funds and real estate, banking and natural resources companies, some of which were later sold.

However, it was alleged that the "sales" were "a device to conceal their intended misappropriation of the assets of the [funds] managed by IOS subsidiaries and of the assets of two closed end real estate funds."

It was also charged that while appearing to have resigned all IOS offices, Vesco actually retained control, creating a "shell" corporation to obtain 6.6 million shares of IOS stock sold in January 1971 by Cornfeld.

The SEC claimed that the $224 million in cash and securities siphoned from the Fund of Funds, the Venture Fund (International), the Transglobal Growth Fund and the International Investment Trust (IIT) had been "spirited" away to two banks in the Bahamas and Luxembourg which allegedly were controlled by Vesco.

The SEC won a temporary restraining order Nov. 30 against any further drain on the assets of the four mutual funds.

Vesco and IOS' president, Milton F. Meissner, had been arrested in Geneva Nov. 30, 1971 on charges of influencing a misappropriation of shares when they were directors of a former IOS bank subsidiary. The complaint was filed by David Tucker, a former IOS senior sales executive.

Tucker's complaint alleged that Vesco and Meissner had arranged to remove IOS preferred shares, deposited by Tucker with Overseas Development Bank in Geneva as loan collateral, so they could be used by Vesco in a proxy fight to retain control at the IOS annual

163

meeting. The shares were apparently among IOS preferred stock sold to Hemispheres Financial Services Ltd. and then voted to defeat Tucker's dissident management slate at the annual IOS meeting June 30. Three Swiss directors of the bank had testified before a Swiss court in July, when the complaint was first filed, that the shares had been transferred during their absence. Another Swiss director, Ulrich Strickler, was jailed Nov. 30 along with Vesco and Meissner on the same charges. The three men were freed on bail Dec. 1 after pleading innocent.

Swiss Federal Banking Commissioner Emile Duperrex confirmed Dec. 3, 1971 that the bank commission had requested the resignations of Vesco and Meissner from the Geneva bank's board of directors in October. He said the two had agreed to make their resignations effective at the end of the year. On Oct. 25, IOS announced the sale of Overseas Development Bank and other IOS banking subsidiaries to International Bancorp Ltd., a holding company in the Bahamas. However, Vesco and Meissner apparently remained on the newly "reconstituted" board of Overseas Development.

A Vesco codefendant in the SEC suit, James Roosevelt, Feb. 9, 1973 signed a consent agreement that severed him from the trial on condition that he resign from the boards of three mutual funds managed by Investors Overseas Services, Ltd. and that he cooperate with the SEC's investigation.

Vesco, who had gone to Costa Rica following a New York grand jury investigation of criminal fraud charges, appeared March 6 on a television program in San Jose to charge that the SEC had "unleashed the most cruel of persecutions" against him and his associates.

"They pretend that I have misused funds administered by the mutual funds, because I have tried, instead of continuing to finance large North American companies with money collected in underdeveloped countries, to invest those funds in property, companies and healthy securities in poor countries that need help so much," Vesco declared.

The Washington Post reported March 19 that Vesco and a group of associates, led by the Bahamas Commonwealth

Bank, had obtained majority control in many diverse companies, such as automobile dealerships, liquor stores, pharmacies and travel agencies, located in the Bahamas.

Costa Rican president & Vesco. President Jose Figueres of Costa Rica told a radio and TV audience May 23, 1973 about his financial dealings with Vesco.

Domestic political considerations in Costa Rica forced Figueres to make the disclosures. His opponents had charged that Vesco-owned companies had placed $300,000 in Figueres' personal bank account in the National Bank of North America in New York. The charges were based on a report in the Wall Street Journal May 16. According to the newspaper, SEC documents showed that Figueres' account had increased by $325,000 between August 1972, when Vesco increased his operations in Costa Rica, and early 1973. The information indicated that Figueres had acted as a conduit, transferring $255,000 from companies in Costa Rica and the Bahamas which were linked to Vesco, to a Vesco-controlled bank, Bahamas Commonwealth Bank. The bank previously had been identified by the SEC as a transfer point for $224 million diverted from four mutual funds controlled by Vesco.

The Journal also reported that SEC documents showed that $70,000 in Figueres' New York bank had been released to the account of a Costa Rican company in which Vesco held 30% ownership and the Figueres family 10% ownership.

In his televised address, Figueres accounted for funds totaling $436,000 in the New York account. "Some of this money" originated with the Bahamas Commonwealth Bank, Figueres admitted.

Figueres said other funds in the personal account were intended for endowment of a national symphony for Costa Rica, "interesting scientific experiments" in Phoenix, Ariz., and a Costa Rican factory producing prefabricated houses.

A special committee of the Costa Rican Congress, established to investigate Vesco's investments there, cleared him of charges of wrongdoing May 16. "There was no doubt cast on the legality of Mr. Vesco's operations," the report declared.

The study showed that Vesco had invested $5.25 million in Costa Rican nationalized banks; $1.5 million in a government housing institute; $1 million in a government waterworks institute; and an undisclosed amount in private homes, a coffee plantation, timber works and low-income housing construction. Vesco claimed his Costa Rican investments totaled $25 million since 1969.

Figueres admitted July 9 that he had helped draft a speech Vesco had delivered over national television defending his presence in Costa Rica.

Figueres was responding to charges by a prominent San Jose lawyer, Fernandez Duran, that he had served as Vesco's "adviser and intellectual collaborator" in writing "substantial parts" of speech. Figueres congratulated Duran for "discovering that I am helping investors transfer their capital to Costa Rica."

Extradition denied—The Costa Rican Supreme Court July 24 upheld a lower court's refusal to turn Vesco over to U.S. authorities. The lower court had ruled June 22 that a 1922 extradition treaty did not cover attempted fraud. The treaty also did not cite obstruction of justice charges as a basis for extradition.

Vesco's Bahamas activities—Vesco's investments in the Bahamas reportedly were extensive.

The New York Times reported June 2 that Vesco had made major cash contributions and loans to politicians in the Bahamas. Prime Minister Lynden O. Pindling July 8 confirmed reports that Vesco had contributed a "good sum" to his 1972 campaign, but he declined to reveal the amounts.

Vesco's banking interests in the Bahamas were closely linked to the U.S. charges of criminal and civil wrongdoing. In a secret indictment, the government charged that Vesco had arranged the transfer of $250,000 in cash from the Bahamas Commonwealth Bank, which he controlled, to Barclays Bank in New York April 6, 1972. Vesco intended to repay the Bahamas bank with money fraudulently obtained from International Controls Corp., it was alleged.

According to the Times, Bahamas Commonwealth Bank acquired another Nassau bank, Butler's Bank, which held

a $500,000 note on a building owned by Prime Minister Pindling. (Pindling claimed to have sold the property.) Other Butler interests absorbed into Vesco's investment network included pharmacies, car dealerships, liquor stores, a hotel and a daily newspaper.

Butler also played a major role in Vesco's takeover of Investors Overseas Services Ltd., which the SEC charged had been defrauded of $224 million. According to the SEC, Bahamas Commonwealth Bank also had served as a transfer point for the money Vesco had diverted to shell companies and dummy corporations.

Secret indictments. Vesco was secretly indicted by a federal grand jury in New York (announced June 13, 1973) on charges of wire fraud and of trying to defraud the International Controls Corp. (ICC) and its stockholders of $250,000.

The money had been donated to President Nixon's re-election campaign in 1972 while Vesco was under investigation by the Securities and Exchange Commission (SEC).

There were further repercussions when Vesco was indicted May 10 by a federal grand jury on criminal charges of obstructing justice. The allegations stemmed from his 1972 political contribution, of which $200,000 was a secret cash donation. Participants in that transaction, former Attorney General John N. Mitchell, Nixon finance committee chairman Maurice Stans and New Jersey politician Harry L. Sears, also were accused of attempting to block the SEC investigation as part of a quid pro quo settlement.

The secret indictment against Vesco, accusing him of illegal use of the telegraph, was the basis of U.S. ambassador Viron P. Vaky's request that Costa Rica order Vesco's extradition. He had fled to Costa Rica to avoid prosecution in the SEC suit and had evaded three bench warrants ordering his arrest.

Later in 1973, Vesco was again secretly indicted by a federal grand jury in New York (reported Oct. 16). The charge was using $50,000 in ICC funds as part payment for Investors Overseas Services (IOS) stock in January 1972.

Bahamas denies extradition. A Bahamian magistrate refused Dec. 7, 1973 to order Vesco's extradition.

Emmanuel Osadebay granted a defense motion to dismiss the case without hearing evidence presented on Vesco's behalf. U.S. Attorney Paul J. Curran, whose office had won three indictments against Vesco from a federal grand jury in New York, said Dec. 11 that no appeal would be made.

The U.S. had based its case against Vesco on affidavits from Laurence Richardson, a former ICC president, Robert Ost, a former ICC accountant, and C. Henry Buhl 3rd, a former director of Investors Overseas Services Ltd., an ICC unit. According to Buhl's testimony, he agreed in December 1971 to sell Vesco 375,000 IOS shares for $140,000. Buhl claimed that he had received a $50,000 deposit by wire for the sale Jan. 4, 1972. (The balance was paid in the form of a loan from the Bahamas Commonwealth Bank, another firm controlled by Vesco.)

Osadebay ruled that the U.S. had not proven that Vesco had ordered $50,000 in ICC funds transferred from a U.S. bank to Buhl's account in Switzerland for the private stock sale.

Vesco, who had been free on $75,000 bail since his arrest Nov. 6 in Nassau, had attended every session of the month-long hearing, but he was not present for the reading of the final decision.

His Costa Rican passport, obtained when he established legal residence there in 1972, was returned to him after the hearing. His U.S. passport had been canceled when he fled the U.S. in early 1973 to take up residence in Nassau and Costa Rica.

Mitchell, Stans acquitted. John N. Mitchell and Maurice H. Stans, former Cabinet officials in the Nixon Administration and directors of President Nixon's 1972 re-election campaign, were acquitted by a federal district court jury in New York City April 23, 1974 of all charges stemming from a secret Vesco cash campaign contribution.

The government had accused Mitchell and Stans of conspiracy, obstruction of justice and perjury for attempting to block the SEC investigation of Vesco and

of lying to a grand jury about it.

The Finance Committee to Re-elect the President had been found guilty June 20, 1973 of three misdemeanor counts for concealing a $200,000 cash contribution from Vesco.

Casey denies wrongdoing—In a development related to the Vesco case, Undersecretary of State William J. Casey said May 17, 1973 that while he was SEC chairman, he had been unaware of Vesco's political contribution to the Nixon re-election committee and had taken no part in deleting a reference to the campaign gift from the SEC's complaint against Vesco's financial activities, filed in November 1972.

Casey's sucessor at the SEC, G. Bradford Cook, had resigned May 16 because the federal grand jury indictment against Stans had implicated Cook in an Administration attempt to suppress the SEC fraud case against Vesco. The indictment also charged that Mitchell had "attempted" to induce Casey to bring influence on the prosecution of the SEC suit on Vesco's behalf.

Casey claimed he had given final approval to filing of the commission's suit against Vesco in early November 1972 before the SEC had learned of the secret political gift.

Casey added May 18 that he had turned down a request by then White House counsel John W. Dean 3d in November 1972 to seek a postponement in subpoenas relating to the SEC's case.

Other Cases

Ex-Westec Officers Sentenced. A U.S. District Court in Houston sentenced James W. Williams, ex-chairman of the Westec Corp., to 15 years imprisonment (reported Oct. 3, 1968). Ex-President Ernest M. Hall Jr. got eight years, Malcolm G. Baker Jr. 18 months, and Lester L. Lilley, Hall's brother-in-law, a one-year jail term. All 4 had been convicted July 11 of manipulating and falsifying the company's financial reports and stocks.

Westec, a geophysical instrument manufacturer and natural resources company, was suspended from trading Aug. 25, 1966, when an $8 million order to buy shares through the American Stock Exchange could not be met. A court-appointed trustee had been charged with reorganizing the company, but trading on the exchange had not been resumed.

Wolfson guilty. A federal jury in New York Aug. 8, 1968 found Florida financier Louis B. Wolfson, 55, and 3 of his associates guilty of violating the Securities & Exchange Act in connection with sales and purchases of stock of the Merritt-Chapman & Scott Corp., a ship-building, construction, chemicals and money-lending concern currently in the process of liquidation.

In the trial, which began June 16, Wolfson, chairman and chief executive officer of Merritt-Chapman (he owned more than 800,000 shares of Merritt-Chapman stock), and Elkin B. Gerbert, 49, a director of the corporation, were convicted of conspiracy, perjury and 2 counts of issuing false and misleading annual reports to the SEC. The other 2 convicted were Marshall G. Staub, 45, Merritt-Chapman president, who was found guilty of conspiracy and issuing false reports, and Joseph Kosow, 51, a Boston financier whose business operations had been bought by Merritt-Chapman in 1962. A 5th defendant, Alexander Rittmaster, 51, former consultant to Merritt-Chapman, had pleaded guilty to the conspiracy charges June 19. Rittmaster, Wolfson and the 3 others had pleaded not guilty to the conspiracy charge at the time of their indictment in 1966. The indictment had accused all the defendants of involvement in agreements that Kosow buy Merritt-Chapman stock at fixed prices and that Merritt-Chapman repurchase the stock at guaranteed profits to the defendants. Kosow had realized a profit of more than $3 million from Merritt-Chapman stock purchased by him on the open market in 1961–3, the indictment said. An additional charge against all the defendants, involving their alleged defrauding of the company's stockholders, had been dismissed by Judge Edmund L. Palmieri July 24.

Wolfson and Gerbert had been convicted Sept. 29, 1967 of stock conspiracy in connection with shares of Continental Enterprises, Inc.

Wolfson was sentenced Dec. 6, 1968 to 18 months in prison and was fined $32,000 in the Merritt-Chapman case. Staub received a one-year suspended sentence, one-year probation and $30,000 fine, and Kosow, received a one-year in jail term and $10,000 fine. Gerbert received an 18-month term and $32,000 fine Jan. 21, 1969, and Rittmaster a four-month sentence and $5,000 fine.

Texas Gulf loses plea. A U.S. Court of Appeals in New York Aug. 13, 1968 reversed a lower court decision and upheld the Securities and Exchange Commission's contention that the Texas Gulf Sulphur Co. had violated disclosure rules by buying stock in a mineral concern before informing the public. The court ruled that officials of Texas Gulf, after the discovery of an ore mine in Canada in November 1963, had not publicly announced the find until after the company had bought shares or received stock options that were substantially affected by the find. The company allegedly also had played down stock market rumors of the discovery Apr. 12, 1964, when it announced that the reports were "premature and possibly misleading." 4 days later, the company said it had made "a major discovery."

The decision was regarded as a landmark in the area of "inside" trading. The ruling reportedly indicated that officials must disclose all pertinent information about their company before they can accept stock options or trade its shares.

The SEC's suit was a civil action, and no punitive measures were taken against the Texas Gulf officials.

Hutton Liable for Hopkins Loss. A federal court in Baltimore ruled that the brokerage firm of W. E. Hutton & Co. had been guilty of "material misrepresentation" in its $1.3 million sale of oil investments to Johns Hopkins University in 1961 (reported Aug. 16, 1968). Hutton was ordered to repay the university for the amount, in addtion to 6% interest accrued from 1961. In return, Hutton was to receive any income that the university had acquired from the investment.

SEC Penalizes Merrill Lynch. Merrill Lynch, Pierce, Fenner & Smith, Inc., the largest U.S. brokerage house, was penalized by the Securities and Exchange Commission Nov. 26, 1968 for giving "inside" data to 14 investments firms that were said to have used it to make profits or avoid losses totaling $4.5 million.

The case stemmed from Merrill Lynch's role as managing underwriter for the Douglas Aircraft Co. in June 1966. At that time, Douglas was planning to offer a $75 million debenture. Merrill Lynch learned that Douglas' earnings for fiscal 1966 were down sharply, and the brokerage house informed the investment companies of this fact on June 20, 1966. The investment concerns then sold short or sold outright more than 190,000 shares of Douglas. The price of Douglas shares, which had sold for about $90 June 20, dropped to $78 within 2 days. After Douglas publicly announced its earnings report June 24, the stock continued to fall and reached $69 June 27. Those who sold short reaped substantial earnings.

The SEC's penalties included the suspension of the firm's New York sales office for 21 days, and its West Coast underwriting office for 15 days. (SEC sources indicated that the suspension might cost Merrill Lynch as much as $1 million.) Archangelo Catapano, a vice-president and specialist on aerospace companies, was censured (the lighest sanction the SEC could apply) and ordered suspended for 60 days without pay. Phillip F. Bilbao, another vice-president, was censured and suspended without pay for 21 days. Similar action was taken against 5 salesmen. Other Merrill Lynch officials were also censured.

At SEC hearings involving the investment companies Dec. 16, Donald W. Douglas Jr., ex-president of Douglas and presently vice-president in charge of administration for the McDonell Douglas Corp. (Douglas had merged with McDonell in 1967) confirmed that he had telephoned Merrill Lynch June 20, 1966 to inform the brokerage house of Douglas' lowered earnings for fiscal 1966.

SEC Penalizes Hubshman. The Hubshman Management Corp. and its president were penalized by the Securities & Exchange Commission March 21, 1969 for alleged violations of the antifraud provisions of federal security laws. The firm's broker-dealer registration was revoked for 30 days, and Louis Hubshman Jr. was suspended from trading for the same period.

The SEC charged that the firm, improperly using its status as investment adviser and principal underwriter of the Hubshman Fund, Inc., a mutual fund, had received kickbacks from a portion of the fund's brokerage transactions and that certain Hubshman Management expenses had been paid by the fund. Hubshman Management consented to the findings and penalties but neither admitted nor denied the charges.

The SEC ordered Hubshman Management to pay the fund $63,351 and to relinquish $36,000 of investment advisory fees received in 1969.

Supreme Court rulings. The Supreme Court May 19, 1969 upheld a decision that corporation officers were liable for damages for misleading corporate financial statements even if the officers had not engaged in stock transactions. The suit under review had been filed in 1965 after officers of Applied Devices Corp., then known as Belock Instrument Corp., had been indicted on federal charges of making false statements in connection with defense contracts. Two of the officers were convicted and one was acquitted.

Three stockholders had filed the suit against Belock and its directors, accountant and investment bankers. A circuit court ruled that Belock had violated securities and exchange laws and was liable to stockholders for damages. The circuit court based its decision on its Aug. 13, 1968 ruling in a case involving Texas Gulf Sulphur Corp. The circuit court had said then that a company was liable when it made false or misleading statements "in a manner calculated to influence the investing public."

The Supreme Court May 19 let stand a lower court ruling that foreign companies were subject to U.S. laws against stock fraud if they were listed on American exchanges. A suit had been brought against Aquitaine Co. of Canada, Ltd.

and certain officers of Banff Oil, Ltd., a Canadian company, charging that Aquitaine had used inside knowledge of a 1965 oil discovery to profit from purchase of Banff stock. The suit had been brought by a Banff minority stockholder for Banff's benefit.

The justices in effect ruled that U.S. securities laws applied to Banff even though the company did no business in the U.S. Banff was listed on the American Stock Exchange.

Cohn, 2 Associates Acquitted. Roy M. Cohn, a former aide to the late Sen. Joseph R. McCarthy, and two associates were acquitted by a federal jury in New York Dec. 12, 1969 on charges of conspiracy, bribery and extortion. Cohn, John A. Kiser and John F. Curtin had been indicted by a federal grand jury Jan. 17 on charges of extorting stock to gain control of the city's Fifth Avenue Coach Lines.

The charges against Cohn, his former law partner Kiser, and Curtin, a transportation engineer, involved New York City's takeover of the Fifth Avenue Coach Lines to end a strike in 1962. The prosecution argued that the three defendants had conspired to bribe city-appointed appraiser Bernard Reicher, who had been assigned to determine how much the city should pay for the bus routes. (Reicher was indicted with the three but was to be tried separately.)

Most of the testimony presented during the 11-week trial centered on the charge that Cohn had bribed the appraiser to obtain confidential information for the Coach Lines. The case had come under federal jurisdiction because the charges against Cohn and his two associates allegedly involved the use of interstate transportation and the U.S. mails.

Cohn was again acquitted by a federal jury in New York Oct. 15, 1971 on a charge of violating federal securities law. In the 1971 trial, Cohn was cleared of charges of making false statements to the SEC to conceal information about $350,000 his law firm had obtained from Fifth Avenue Coach Lines.

The charges were based on federal security laws which required formal disclosure of any material interest that a company's official had in money distributed by the company.

Specifically, Cohn had been accused of concealing the required information in two proxy statements and a report to the SEC and the bus line's stockholders when he was the line's general counsel.

Wilson quits Justice Department over Texas bank fraud. Will R. Wilson, chief of the Justice Department's Criminal Division, resigned Oct. 15, 1971 because of his association with a Texas banker involved in a stock scandal.

Wilson, 60, said he was quitting to spare embarrassment to the Nixon Administration.

Wilson had acknowledged Aug. 25 that he had received a $30,000 interest-free loan in 1970 from a bank owned by Frank W. Sharp, a Houston financier who was being investigated by federal authorities on suspicion of stock fraud.

Wilson had asserted that his association with Sharp was proper and entirely innocent.

The criticism of Wilson all related to Sharp, who had pleaded guilty to selling unregistered securities and making false entries in a bank ledger. In addition, the Securities and Exchange Commission had accused Sharp of "systematically looting" banks and insurance firms by manipulating stock in the National Bankers Life Insurance Company.

In pleading guilty to two charges, Sharp drew a suspended sentence and was placed on probation. He was granted immunity by the Justice Department as it sought to unravel a major stock swindle.

Fourteen persons, among them Speaker of the Texas House of Representatives Gus F. Mutscher Jr., had been indicted by Texas grand juries for their alleged role in the stock fraud. Mutscher was indicted Sept. 23 with three other persons, including a state representative and a Mutscher aide.

3 acquitted in Four Seasons case. A U.S. district court jury in Oklahoma City acquitted three of four defendants Feb. 8, 1974 of securities- and mail-fraud charges involving the Four Seasons Nursing Centers of America Inc. The jury was unable to reach a decision on charges involving accountant Kenneth J. Wahrman, who, along with two of the other defendants, also accountants, was accused of certifying audits of Four Seasons that he knew to be false. The accountants acquitted were Edward J. Bolka and Jimmie E. Madole.

The fourth defendant, James P. Linn, former president of the Four Seasons subsidiary, Four Seasons Franchise Corp., was also acquitted.

The nine-count indictment had essentially charged that the men had participated in a conspiracy to inflate the price of Four Seasons' stock through false financial reports and profit projections based on fictitious earnings from building nursing homes and contrived sales of nursing homes and franchises.

Thomas J. Gray, a co-founder of Four Seasons, had pleaded no contest in 1973 to one count of mailfraud and had agreed to cooperate with the prosecution in exchange for a suspended sentence. He was sentenced March 21, 1974 to one year in prison and was fined $10,000.

Glenn R. Miller and Gordon H. McCollum, former officials of Walston & Co., investment banker for Four Seasons, were fined $40,000 each by U.S. District Court Judge Thomas P. Griesa Feb. 27 for stock fraud and conspiracy. They had pleaded guilty to the charges in 1973.

Jack L. Clark, former president of Four Seasons, had been sentenced Sept. 19, 1973 to a year in prison.

Clark had pleaded guilty in June to the main count of a 65-count indictment alleging he and seven other corporate officers conspired to inflate the price of Four Seasons' stock by falsifying earnings reports.

The sentence imposed by U.S. District Court Judge Thomas P. Griesa drew criticism from Gary P. Naftalis, the U.S. assistant attorney heading the case. Naftalis asserted that Clark had profited by $10 million and had "stashed" $4 million in a secret trust account.

National Student figures sentenced. Cortes W. Randell, founder of the National Student Marketing Corp. who pleaded guilty to stock fraud charges Aug. 20, 1974, was sentenced to 18 months in prison and fined $40,000 in New York federal court Dec. 27.

In addition, a partner and a former employee of Peat, Marwick, Mitchell & Co., the nation's largest accounting firm, were sentenced for making false and misleading statements involving National Student Marketing in a proxy statement filed with the Securities and Exchange Commission (SEC) in 1969. The accounting firm's partner, Anthony M. Natelli, was sentenced to 60 days in jail and fined $10,000; Joseph A. Scansaroli, who worked for Peat Marwick in 1968 and 1969, was sentenced to 10 days in jail and fined $2,500. Both men were found guilty in a November trial on charges they had falsely portrayed National Student Marketing as a company with extremely large sales and earnings.

Two former sales executives of National Student Marketing, Dennis M. Kelly and Robert C. Bushnell, who had also pleaded guilty to stock fraud charges, were sentenced. Kelly was given a 10-month prison term and a fine of $10,000, Bushnell was fined $4,000 with a suspended six-month prison sentence.

(NSM's collapse as a glamor stock in 1970 was believed to have cost Peat, Marwick investors more than $100 million, according to the Wall Street Journal Jan. 18.)

The SEC, in a suit filed in Washington Feb. 3, 1972, had charged that the following firms defrauded shareholders in a "fraudulent scheme" involving National Student Marketing's acquisition of Interstate National Corp. and 24 other companies during 1969–1970: National Student Marketing's law firm, White & Case of New York; Interstate National's law firm, Lord, Bissell & Brook of Chicago; and Peat, Marwick, Mitchell & Co., auditors for National Student Marketing. The 15 individuals involved in the suit were members of the firms cited in the complaint.

The two law firms were accused of misleading shareholders with false information in order to consummate the merger of National Student Marketing and Interstate National Oct. 31, 1969. The SEC charged that the firms had failed to inform shareholders that Peat-Marwick had recommended "significant" adjustments in National Student Marketing's financial reports prior to the merger, and had issued opinions that legal requirements of the merger had been fulfilled.

The SEC argued that the law firms and Peat-Marwick should have insisted that their client amend its financial report, should have withdrawn from the case if the client did not comply and should have advised the SEC of the impropriety.

GeoTek figure pleads guilty. Jack P. Burke, former president of GeoTek Resources Fund Inc., pleaded guilty Nov. 13, 1974 to one criminal violation of federal securities laws. A 17-count indictment had been filed June 17, accusing him of conspiring to defraud more than 2,000 investors of $30 million in an oil drilling tax shelter venture set up through GeoTek. Burke pleaded guilty to filing a false affadavit with the Securities and Exchange Commission (SEC). Conspiracy and fraud charges were dropped. Jacqueline Aldrich, the firm's former chief accountant who had pleaded guilty to one count of perjury, cooperated with the prosecution. She was fined $750.

Burke was sentenced Jan. 20, 1975 to 30 months in jail and was fined $5,000.

Otis Chandler, publisher of the Los Angeles Times, won dismissal March 17 as a defendant in the SEC's continuing civil fraud case against others linked to the GeoTek swindle. Neither the SEC nor Chandler admitted nor denied the charges in accepting the dismissal arrangement.

Chandler agreed to comply in the future with securities laws and promised he would not "receive fees or commissions from any issuer, underwriter or dealer in connection with the purchase or sale of securities without fully describing such fees or commissions." Chandler had been accused of secretly accepting stock and $109,000 in cash finder's fees from GeoTek in return for introducing wealthy friends and prospective investors to Burke.

Westinghouse accused. The SEC filed fraud charges Aug. 12, 1975 against Westinghouse Electric Corp., alleging that the company had made false public statements about the 1974 sale of its major ap-

pliance division and that an official of the firm had bought Westinghouse stock on the basis of inside information.

Filed in federal district court in New York, the suit charged that in August 1974 when Westinghouse was "seriously negotiating" the sale of its major appliance division to White Consolidated Industries a Westinghouse executive was telling company employes that the firm was "in the major appliance business to stay." An unidentified Westinghouse official was alleged to have used his knowledge of the impending sale of the major appliances division to buy company stock for an employe stock-purchasing program. The agency also charged Westinghouse with having issued inaccurate news releases and of failing to correct releases made inaccurate by subsequent events.

Westinghouse settled the case by signing a consent decree Dec. 23.

The decree, which required Westinghouse neither to admit nor deny the government allegations of stock fraud, enjoined the company from further alleged violations of the fraud provisions of federal securities law and obliged it to employ an independent trustee to handle purchases for all its employe stock plans.

U.S. Financial, Inc. case. Four officials of the bankrupt U.S. Financial, Inc. real estate conglomerate pleaded no contest during 1975 to an indictment handed down in San Diego Dec. 30, 1974. They were accused in an alleged $100 million scheme to defraud investors in U.S. Financial Inc., a real estate, land development and housing firm now in bankruptcy.

The defendants were accused of conspiring to inflate U.S. Financial's earnings in 1970–73 through sham land sales, "shell corporations and straw men" in an effort to attract investors, cause stock prices to rise and conclude advantageous business transactions.

Richard W. Arneson, a company official, pleaded no contest to felony charges involving the sale of land through what the government called a "shell" corporation. At the same time Dennis P. Hill, another U.S. Financial official, pleaded to aiding and abetting fraud in the sale of securities, it was reported Feb. 19, 1975. Arneson, who pleaded to charges of conspiracy to inflate the earnings of U.S. Financial, was sentenced Nov. 3 to two years in prison with all but six months suspended. Arneson's company, the Coastal Land Corp., which pleaded no contest to a conspiracy charge, was fined $10,000. Robert H. Walter, former chairman of U.S. Financial, pleaded no contest to conspiracy and filing a false report with the SEC, it was reported Sept. 5. The company's president, John B. Halverson, was sentenced to seven years in prison on his no contest plea to fraud charges Sept. 9. Walter was sentenced Feb. 3, 1976 to three years in prison.

Equity Funding fraud. Stanley Goldblum, co-founder and former chairman and president of the Equity Funding Corp. of America, was sentenced March 18, 1975 to serve eight years in prison and pay $20,000 in fines for his part in the multimillion dollar Equity insurance and securities fraud uncovered in 1973. Goldblum had pleaded guilty in October 1974 to five violations of federal law.

Five other defendants, all former top Equity executives, also were ordered to serve jail sentences. Judge Jesse Curtis of U.S. District Court in Los Angeles sentenced Fred Levin, former executive vice president of the parent company and president of the insurance subsidiary, to a five-year prison term. He had pleaded guilty to conspiracy, wiretapping and two counts of mail fraud. Arthur S. Lewis, Lloyd D. Edens and James H. Banks, each were ordered to serve three years in jail after pleading guilty to conspiracy, mail fraud and telegraph fraud charges. James C. Smith Jr. was sentenced to a two-year term for three counts of conspiracy and mail fraud.

Twelve other former Equity officials and employes were sentenced March 25. Their sentences and charges to which they pleaded guilty: Samuel B. Lowell, five years in jail for one count of conspiracy and four counts of mail fraud; Michael E. Sultan, two years in jail for conspiracy, filing false bank statements and mail fraud; David J. Capo, two years in jail for conspiracy and mail fraud; Lawrence G. Collins, two years in jail for conspiracy, securities fraud and illegal electronic surveillance; William Mercado, six months in jail, 1½ years' probation for conspiracy;

Donald McClellan, six months in jail and three years' probation for conspiracy and stock fraud; Lester M. Keller, three months in jail and one year and nine months' probation for conspiracy and mail fraud; Alan L. Green, three months in jail and three years' probation for conspiracy and mail fraud; Jerome H. Evans, $5,000 fine and two years' probation for conspiracy; William E. Symonds, $1,000 fine and three years' probation for conspiracy; Mark C. Lewis, three years' probation for conspiracy; and Gary S. Beckerman, $1,000 fine and three years' probation for conspiracy.

Three accountants, the last remaining defendants in the Equity Funding fraud, were each sentenced to three months in prison in U.S. District Court in Los Angeles July 17. They were Julian S. H. Weiner, Marvin A. Lichtig and Solomon Block. They were the only defendants to stand trial in the case that saw 19 others plead guilty and 11 imprisoned.

Frederick Levin, a former Equity officer, pleaded guilty to state charges in Lake County Circuit Court in Illinois and was given a two-to-eight-year prison term, the Wall Street Journal reported April 14. Goldblum pleaded guilty to charges of forgery in the Illinois court and was sentenced Sept. 9 to imprisonment of three to 10 years. The indictment arose from the forgery of a letter by Goldblum and other Equity officials giving the impression the firm had $24 million of corporate bonds in Illinois.

Background—The story of the Equity Funding frauds had first been disclosed publicly in the Wall Street Journal April 2, 1973. Equity Funding, a leader in the insurance and mutual funds industry, handling $6.5 billion in life insurance at the end of 1972, was accused of engaging in a fraud involving at least 56,000 bogus insurance policies, forged bonds and death certificates and $120 million in nonexistent assets.

The scandal threatened to involve other insurance firms which had bought Equity's fraudulent policies, paying Equity commissions of 180%–200% on the value of the policies' first year premiums. The plan's intent, according to the Journal, was to create the appearance of an enormously profitable operation, thereby inflating the price of Equity stock and eventually allowing the company to buy a reputable insurance company.

Equity shares (8,000,000 outstanding), once traded at prices up to $80, were held in large blocks by banks, pension funds and other institutional investors. As rumors of an impending scandal began to circulate, large amounts were unloaded, forcing the price down from $25 to $14.

Equity, considered an outstanding investment in 1972 because of the company's record of rapid and aggressive expansion, filed a petition for bankruptcy April 5, 1973.

The firm had been ordered to file for bankruptcy April 4 by the U.S. district court in Los Angeles. The court issued its order after holding hearings at which Securities and Exchange Commission (SEC) officials, state insurance regulators and representatives of the nation's largest banks gave testimony on recent investigations into the firm's operations.

The information leading to disclosure of the apparent swindle was gathered by Raymond L. Dirks, a securities analyst and officer with the Wall Street research firm of Delafield Childs, Inc. Dirks' information prompted the SEC to begin its probe of Equity.

The alleged deception was participated in by many Equity employes at all levels of the company and the effects extended throughout the securities and insurance industries. Involved were several prestigious auditing firms which reportedly had been deceived by the use of elaborate false computer codes; state insurance regulatory agencies charged with watchdog responsibilities over Equity's various affiliates; stock market analysts who had refused to accept or corroborate the evidence uncovered by Dirks despite mounting rumors of fraud; insiders, who, it was charged, had dumped millions worth of Equity stock after obtaining confidential information on the impending scandal; and the public and institutional stockholders, who had invested heavily in the former glamour stock.

According to Dirks, his inquiry into Equity was precipitated by a phone call March 6 from Ronald H. Secrist, a former officer of the conglomerate's key subsidiary, Equity Funding Life Insurance Co. and another affiliate, Bankers Na-

tional Life Insurance Co. Secrist provided Dirks with an outline of the plot, which Secrist said had been known to him "for a couple of years."

After investigating the charges, Dirks confronted Equity's President, Stanley Goldblum, March 21. Goldblum contended that Dirks' allegations were "preposterous," and cited recent auditing reports which indicated no financial irregularities in the company. Dirks held a followup meeting with Equity's current and former auditors, who also rejected the charges.

Goldblum sought a second meeting with him March 26, Dirks said, but no action was taken because SEC had begun its independent investigation.

In an agreement concluded with unusual speed, Equity signed a consent judgment (involving no admission of wrongdoing) with the SEC April 3. That same day, the federal agency filed charges of major securities violations by Equity in the federal district court in Los Angeles.

A court-approved "special investigator" was named in the consent decree to recover "diverted or misappropriated assets" (estimated at $120 million) resulting from the alleged swindle. Further securities violations were also barred in a permanent injunction obtained by the SEC.

During late March, the Illinois Insurance Department conducted a surprise audit of Equity's life insurance affiliate. The move triggered similar investigations by state agencies in California, Massachusetts, Ohio, Pennsylvania, Washington, New York and elsewhere. Illinois insurance officials discovered April 4 that $25 million in bonds, reportedly on deposit at the American National Bank and Trust Co. in Chicago, were "nonexistent." California regulators uncovered 56,000 fake policies and 35,000 genuine ones April 6.

The New York Stock Exchange (NYSE) suspended trading in Equity stock March 27 as a result of a probe begun March 19 into illegal inside dealing in the shares. The inside traders allegedly had benefitted from knowledge of the company's financial difficulties in exchange transactions.

The exchange heard testimony from Dirks April 9 and filed disciplinary action against him April 12 on the grounds he had violated rules designed to prevent the spread of rumors in stock trading. Dirks was also accused of giving clients advance warning of his discoveries before the information became available to the public and with failing to notify the NYSE of his investigations.

By April 17, it had been revealed that at least four Equity officers had sold large holdings of stock in the company just prior to the suspension of trading by the NYSE.

Indictment—A federal grand jury in Los Angeles handed up a 105-count indictment Nov. 1, 1973 against 22 persons involved in the Equity Funding scandal.

According to the Justice Department, Equity officials conspired to create nonexistent life insurance policies to "fraudulently increase the market price of [Equity] stock and support investor confidence in [Equity], thereby enabling [Equity] to borrow money from banks, make successful debenture offerings and conclude mergers. . . . The scheme enabled various defendants to sell their [Equity] stock at artificially inflated levels."

Goldblum was charged with periodically setting earnings and sales goals for Equity that he knew could not be met by lawful means. To bring about the fraud, the indictment alleged, Goldblum and others fabricated bogus insurance policies and sold them to reinsurers, rigged computor printouts and records, forged death claims and policy files, counterfeited bank documents, bank stationery, securities purchase confirmations and bonds, and prepared false financial data.

The auditors were charged with intentionally conducting incomplete and insufficient audits at Equity.

The conspiracy occurred between January 1965 and April 1973, the Justice Department said. Electronic eavesdropping took place in March 1973 when state insurance examiners began to investigate Equity's books. Some of the defendants were charged with attempting to learn the scope of the investigation by illegally intercepting the examiners' conversations.

The indictment capped a 7-month investigation by the SEC, the Federal Bureau of Investigation, the Postal Inspection Service, the Illinois and California Departments of Insurance, the U.S. attorney's office in Los Angeles and the Illinois attorney general's office.

SEC charges Hughes with fraud. The Securities and Exchange Commission (SEC) filed a civil suit in U.S. District Court in San Francisco March 27, 1975 charging Howard R. Hughes, the billionaire recluse, and several of his associates with fraud and manipulation in connection with his acquisition of Air West in 1968. (Criminal indictments stemming from the Air West take-over were twice dismissed in 1974.)

The complaint sought to enjoin Hughes and the other defendants from further violations of federal securities law and "disgorgement of all monetary benefits" from the acquisitions, which the SEC estimated might total $48 million.

Essentially, the complaint charged that Hughes obtained controlling interest in Air West by mounting a publicity campaign to induce the directors and shareholders of Air West to approve a cash-purchase agreement, under which Hughes would buy their holdings at $22 a share. The campaign was misleading, the complaint said, as it failed to disclose that the offer was contingent on Air West's net worth rising to $21 million. Hughes, who eventually paid $8.75 a share, knew or should have known of Air West's inability to comply with the condition, the complaint alleged.

The suit also alleged that the defendants and their agents gave contributions to certain politicians—not identified by the SEC—who made statements in favor of the take-over. Throughout the publicity campaign, the suit said, it was made to appear that persons advocating the acquisition were acting without any connection to the defendants.

Other tactics cited in the complaint were lawsuits ostensibly filed by independent shareholders but actually brought by the defendants to pressure recalicitrant directors of Air West to endorse the Hughes purchase offer before it expired.

Those named in the suit were Hughes; Summa Corp., Hughes' personal holding company; Hughes Airwest; Herman Greenspun, owner and publisher of the Las Vegas Sun; David Charnay, president of a Los Angeles-based television and movie company; George Crockett, a long-time friend of Hughes; Robert A. Maheu, one-time head of Hughes interests in Nevada, but later the winner of a multimillion-dollar slander suit against Hughes; Chester C. Davis, chief counsel to Summa Corp.; Jimmy "the Greek" Snyder, the Las Vegas oddsmaker, whose publicity firm had assisted Hughes in the take-over; and Patrick J. Hillings, a former Republican congressman from California, who was an Air West director during 1968–70 and who, the suit alleged, did not disclose that he had been paid by Hughes and Summa more than $50,000 during that time.

Antitrust Enforcement

Conglomerates, Mergers
& Big Business Under Fire

Federal agencies in the late 1960s and the 1970s continued their long-standing but sporadic programs of investigations to see whether mergers, the creation of conglomerates and the behavior of big business in general violated antitrust or other laws designed to protect consumers and the entire business community.

FTC studies conglomerates. The Federal Trade Commission (FTC) announced July 8, 1968 that it was beginning a major investigation "of the causes, effects and implications" of conglomerate corporate consolidations. It said that it was undertaking the study at a time when "the merger movement appears to have reached the highest levels in American industrial history."

Three types of such mergers were identified by the FTC: market-extension mergers, which combined companies that were in the same business but were located in different geographical areas; product-extension mergers, involving acquisitions of concerns in related businesses; all other mergers, including those between companies in unrelated lines of business.

The FTC said that the inquiry had as its major aim the prevention of acquisi-

tions or mergers "that may substantially lessen competition or tend to create a monopoly in any line of commerce in any section of the country," and would determine the need for new legislation "to bring the conglomerate merger movement under control." The new study was an expansion of a previous investigation of "horizontal" mergers (those involving direct competitors) and "vertical" mergers (involving suppliers and their customers). The new study was to cover the "relationship between conglomerate mergers and technical or business efficiencies, [the] economic performance of conglomerate firms in the same market place [and] effect of conglomerate mergers on the competitive vigor of enterprises by their change in status from independent firms to subsidiaries or divisions of conglomerates." The agency planned to review recent merger developments to seek ways "to prevent increases in the concentration of economic power, to encourage internal growth as a competition-promotion process, to preserve the competitive opportunities of medium-sized and small businesses, and to eliminate monopolistic tendencies in their incipient stages."

The first indication that the FTC was planning the study had come in March, when the agency, in its annual report on corporate mergers, said it intended to "focus special attention" on conglomerates. According to the report the number of corporate acquisitions had increased from 1,746 in 1966 to 2,384 in 1967, "the sharpest increase in merger activity in modern industrial history." The report, which showed that mergers of manufacturing and mining companies had risen from 995 in 1966 to 1,496 in 1967, noted that conglomerate-type mergers comprised about 83% of all "large" mergers in 1967.

Merger guidelines. The Justice Department May 30, 1968 issued guidelines that set standards under which corporate acquisitions or mergers become subject to prosecution under Section 7 of the Clayton Antitrust Act. According to Atty. Gen. Ramsey Clark, the purposes of the guidelines were to inform the public on the department's current antitrust policies and to promote a continuing dialogue between government and business on the role of antimerger enforcement in the maintenance of a competitive economy.

Conglomerates Under Attack. Government antitrust officials sought to curb the spread of conglomerate corporate mergers in 1969 by bringing suit under existing legislation.

Richard W. McLaren, newly-appointed chief of the Justice Department's Antitrust Division, announced March 6 that the government would "go after big-company mergers" under provisions of the Clayton Act. McLaren told the annual antitrust conference of the National Industrial Conference Board, held in New York, that the department intended to investigate both conglomerates and corporate reciprocal buying practices. In testimony March 12 before the House Ways and Means Committee, McLaren asserted that he expected to probe and possibly bring suit against some conglomerate mergers already in effect.

McLaren further clarified the government's stand when he repeated in a New York Times interview March 18 that the antitrust division would mount a campaign against reciprocal corporate dealings which tended to "freeze out the little guy." The antitrust chief asserted that he intended to go after conglomer-

ates on every level, not limiting his actions only to antitrust issues. But he told the antitrust section of the American Bar Association March 28 that while more antitrust suits would be filed to prevent "very large" corporations from buying leading companies in other industries, the government would not challenge big companies that acquire "smaller" concerns in other industries.

In a speech before the Town Hall of California in Los Angeles May 28, McLaren charged that some types of joint business ventures posed "serious threats to competition" and would be subject to the conglomerate investigation.

In the wake of McLaren's statements, the Nixon Administration appeared to give tacit endorsement to a task force report ordered by Pres. Lyndon B. Johnson in December 1967 and delivered to him in July 1968. (Johnson had refused to let the report be made public.) The Justice Department released the report May 21. The report's recommendations, which would require divestitures by General Motors, Ford Motor Co., Chrysler Corp. and firms in the steel and computer and other industries, called for prohibition on acquisition of one company dominant in an industry by a company dominant in another industry. If concentration should be found to exist, the companies would be given one year to take voluntary steps to reduce their dominance. Failing this, the government could then order steps to reduce to a 12% maximum the market share held by each of the companies.

In a major policy address June 6 to a Georgia Bar Association meeting in Savannah, Attorney General John N. Mitchell attacked the "danger that this super-concentration [giant mergers] poses to our economic, political and social structure." Mitchell asserted that the government probably would oppose any and all voluntary mergers or involuntary takeovers among the nation's biggest business giants. The attorney general listed as specific government targets: corporate reciprocity; anti-competitive effects of big firms' "nationwide marketing structure, capital resources and advertising budgets"; and the trend toward a "community of interest" among giant companies.

Jailing urged for price-fixing. Assistant Attorney General Donald I. Baker said Nov. 20, 1976 that the Justice Department's antitrust division would ask federal judges to impose 18-month prison sentences on most corporate officials convicted of price-fixing under a 1974 law.

In passing the 1974 law, Congress had made price fixing a felony offense and had tightened penalties so that an individual violator faced a maximum three-year prison sentence and a $100,000 fine. Corporations found guilty of price-fixing under the 1974 law could be fined up to $1 million. Under previous laws that made price-fixing a misdemeanor violation, corporations could have been fined a maximum $50,000 and individuals faced a maximum one-year jail term and a $50,000 fine.

Speaking at an antitrust conference in Boston, Baker said imposition of stiff prison sentences was necessary "to put hard-core price-fixing on a par with embezzlement and stock fraud." Currently, he said, there wasn't "any sufficient deterrent for such conduct."

In 1975, Baker said, persons convicted of stock fraud received an average sentence of 45.7 months, bank embezzlers got an average 22.6 months and income-tax evaders an average 15.4 months. The 75 defendants convicted in 1975 of antitrust misdemeanors received a total of 75 days in jail, Baker said.

"A higher percentage of persons convicted of violating [federal] migratory bird laws were sentenced to prison, for longer terms, than those who violated the antitrust laws," Baker said.

A person convicted of price-fixing and sentenced to 18 months in jail would be eligible for parole after six months. Baker said that the government would recommend imposition of a high fine, often the maximum $1 million, for a convicted corporation that had a prior record.

Food Industry

Greyhound-Armour upheld. The Supreme Court June 1, 1971 upheld Greyhound Corp.'s takeover of Armour & Co. The court ruled 4 to 3 that the action did not violate a 1920 consent decree against Armour and other meatpackers prohibiting them from "dealing in" or acquiring any company that dealt in a lengthy list of non-meat food products.

The decision ended a two-year legal battle over whether companies dealing in the other food products could acquire Armour. (Greyhound, which operated restaurants and catering services was deemed to be in the food business.) In 1970, the Justice Department had asked the Supreme Court to rule on the take-over of Armour by General Host, which was also dealing in other food products, but by the time the case reached the court,

General Host had sold its Armour stock to Greyhound.

In the majority opinion, Justice Thurgood Marshall interpreted the 1920 decree as barring Armour's acquisition of other food lines, not Armour's acquisition by another company in the food business.

Cereal companies accused. The Federal Trade Commission (FTC) voted, 3–2, Jan. 2, 1972 to file a proposed complaint against the nation's four largest breakfast cereal companies for illegally monopolizing the market, preventing "meaningful price competition" and forcing consumers to pay "artificially inflated" prices. The FTC attached a proposed consent order that would require divestiture of some or all of the firms' manufacturing assets to permit new competitors to enter the industry.

The FTC said the four companies— Kellogg Co., General Mills Inc., General Foods Corp. and the Quaker Oats Co.— comprised 91% of the ready-to-eat cereals market.

The proposed complaint did not charge the firms with conspiracy, but accused them of individually violating Section 5 of the Federal Trade Commission Act which prohibited restraint of competition. They were charged with "proliferation of brands and trademark promotion; artificial differentiation of products; unfair methods of competition in advertising and product promotion; restrictive retail shelf space control programs and acquisitions of competitors."

The complaint was signed by Chairman Miles W. Kirkpatrick and Commissioners Paul R. Dixon and Mary Gardiner Jones. Commissioners Everette MacIntyre and David S. Dennison Jr. dissented.

A commission staff study estimated that cereal prices would be 20%–25% lower in a competitive market.

A&P guilty on meat prices. A federal jury in San Francisco July 25, 1974 found the Great Atlantic & Pacific Tea Co. (the A&P supermarket chain) guilty of conspiring to fix wholesale and retail beef prices. The jury awarded actual damages of $10.9 million to six livestock producers, and the damages were automatically trebled under antitrust law.

The verdict came in a suit filed in 1968, in which the plaintiffs accused A&P of conspiring with other major food chains to set high, noncompetitive retail prices and low wholesale prices paid to packers. The suit had also charged that A&P conspired to restrain trade by allocating geographical territories to preclude competition.

Two other defendants, Safeway Stores Inc. and Kroger Co., had settled out of court in 1973, agreeing to pay only plaintiffs' attorneys fees.

The damages covered the 1964-68 period, although the plaintiffs had contended that the practices continued through early 1973.

Dairy companies indicted. Four major dairy-product companies and six current or former company officials were indicted by a federal grand jury Aug. 16, 1974 on charges of conspiring to fix prices, rig bids and allocate customers in Arizona. The Justice Department filed a companion civil suit with the indictment.

The violations, which the department said had occurred since "before 1966," included submission of rigged bids to schools, hospitals, military installations and other government agencies. The department said the companies had sales of $80 million in Arizona in 1973, or about 90% of the state's wholesale dairy business.

The companies were: Borden Inc., Carnation Co., Foremost-McKesson Inc. and Shamrock Foods Co.

ITT baking unit accused of monopoly bid. The Federal Trade Commission filed a complaint Dec. 10, 1974 against ITT Continental Baking Co., the maker of Wonder Bread and a subsidiary of International Telephone & Telegraph Corp. The baking unit was accused of trying to monopolize the wholesale bread baking industry. ITT was also charged with joining in "most or all" of the anticompetitive practices alleged against ITT Continental.

According to the FTC, ITT Continental and its predecessor, Continental Baking Co., had tried since 1952 to monopolize regional and local bread markets by selling bread below cost in areas where there was serious competition, while subsidizing the losses incurred by marking up bread prices in areas where there was little competition. Most of these predatory pricing practices were still in use, the FTC charged.

The FTC contended that ITT Continental's alleged anticompetitive practices had driven 43 wholesale baking concerns out of business since January 1972 and caused closure of 80 wholesale bakery plants.

ITT Continental, which had been acquired by ITT in 1968, was the "world's largest bread baker," according to the FTC. The firm had operations in 30 states. In 1973, its net sales of bread totaled about $475 million, up 47% from 1968 and 50% greater than its nearest competitor.

The Supreme Court Feb. 19, 1975, reversing two lower court decisions, ruled, 5-4, that ITT Continental Banking must pay daily civil penalties for acquiring three other bakeries in violation of an FTC consent order.

In 1962, Continental Baking Co. had settled an FTC antitrust complaint by signing a consent order that prohibited it for 10 years from acquiring other bakeries without FTC permission. In 1968 the government sued ITT Continental Baking—Continental had merged with International Telephone & Telegraph Corp. (ITT) earlier in the year—charging that Continental's acquisition of assets in three companies had violated the 1962 order. The government sought, among other things, civil penalties of $1,000-a-day for each acquisition, as well as divestiture of the three companies.

Subsequently, the U.S. 10th Circuit Court of Appeals ruled that the consent order had barred only the acquisition. Consequently, the appellate court said, ITT Continental was liable for a single penalty of $5,000 for each violation and did not have to divest itself of the three companies.

In reversing the appellate court, the Supreme Court concerned itself only with the matter of penalties. The appeals court decision would undermine the deterrent effect of the penalty, the court said, and convert it "into a minor tax upon a violation which could reap large financial benefits to the perpetrator." The court also decided that the 1962 consent order had included both purchase and retention of the assets.

A federal grand jury in San Diego June 24 returned price-fixing indictments against ITT Continental, five other wholesale bakery companies and five executives.

The indictment charged conspiracy to fix the price of bread in the San Diego area, running from 1966 to 1974. Conspiracy to reduce or eliminate discounts to retail customers also was charged, as well as lack of competitive activity for orders to large customers, including the federal government. A companion civil suit filed by the Justice Department sought damages for violation of federal law against rigged bidding on federal contracts.

The companies and individuals named in the indictment, in addition to ITT Continental: Richard L. Walker, San Diego plant manager for ITT Continental (a unit of International Telephone & Telegraph Co.); Interstate Brands Co. and Samuel Tatum, its regional plant manager; American Bakeries Co. and John E. McCarthy, regional vice president; Towntalk Baking Co. and William J. Thompson, sales manager; Snowflake Baking Inc. and Louis Kahn, president; Akervik & Salmon (which ceased operations in 1973).

6 sugar firms indicted. Six U.S. sugar firms were indicted Dec. 19, 1974 by a federal grand jury in San Francisco on charges of fixing prices in 23 Western and Midwestern states.

Two criminal indictments and two companion civil suits, filed by the Justice Department, accused the defendants of engaging in separate price fixing conspiracies in two regional markets on the West Coast and in the Midwest. Named as defendants were Great Western Sugar Co.; American Crystal Sugar Co.; Holly Sugar Corp.; California and Hawaiian Sugar Co.; Amalgamated Sugar Co.; and Consolidated Foods Corp.

A third civil suit, filed against Utah-Idaho Sugar Co. and the National Sugar Beet Growers Federation, alleged a similar conspiracy in Western and Mountain states.

Justice Department spokesmen said the charges grew out of an 18-month investigation into pre-1973 pricing practices of the $2.5 billion U.S. sugar market, and were not related to the current high price of sugar.

According to the government, sales of refined sugar in the California-Arizona market totaled $268 million in 1972. The defendants accounted for 69% of this market.

In the Chicago-West regional market, the Justice Department said, sales totaled $770 million in 1972, with the defendants accounting for more than half of that figure. In the mountain state area, the defendants shared 86% of the market, in which sales totaled about $50 million, according to the government.

The two indictments alleged that "purchasers of refined sugar have been deprived of free and open competition in the sale of refined sugar" and that competition for sugar sales "has been restricted, suppressed and restrained."

Nestle violations alleged. The Federal Trade Commission filed a complaint Jan. 21, 1975 against Nestle Alimentana S.A., charging the world's second largest food processor with violating U.S. antitrust laws through its acquisition of Stouffer Corp., the leading U.S. maker of frozen foods. According to the FTC, Nestle's purchase of the firm from Litton Industries Inc. for $105 million in 1973 reduced competition in the frozen food market. The agency sought Nestle's divestiture of Stouffer.

The FTC also announced that it had closed its investigation into Nestle's earlier acquisition of Libby, McNeil & Libby, a U.S. producer of canned foods, deciding that the purchase was not anticompetitive. Nestle, a Swiss-based firm with food plants in 70 countries and nearly 90,000 employes, had sales equal to $5.5 billion a year.

IBM Under Attack

Divestiture sought. The Justice Department said Oct. 16, 1972 that it would ask the federal court in New York to order the breakup of the International Business Machines Corp. (IBM) into "several discrete, separate, independent and competitively balanced entities" if government charges of monopoly were sustained by the court in a forthcoming trial.

The government's intention, which was revealed in a court-ordered memorandum at a pretrial hearing, indicated the scope of the antitrust suit which was originally filed Jan. 17, 1969, the last working day of the Johnson Administration.

The Justice Department memorandum based its complaint on several new charges which had not formed part of the original suit. The new charges of monopolizing the computer business related to IBM's foreign market operations, computer leasing and peripheral equipment.

The Justice Department filed its pretrial brief Nov. 6, 1974.

According to the government, IBM sold 73% of the computers used in the U.S. and had established such dominance in the field that other computer makers, even large firms such as General Electric and RCA Corp., either operated at a loss and quit the field or were forced to provide more services and equipment than a new entrant in the computer business could afford.

The brief cited a 1970 General Electric document which said, "In the absence of now unanticipated severe constraints on IBM, any competitor over time will exist at the tolerance of this dominant company." An RCA document cited in the government's brief charged that "to attack IBM head-on amounts to attacking a well-led army with a commando company in an open field."

The IBM case had been scheduled to go to trial Oct. 7, but was delayed at the request of the government. In its brief, the Justice Department warned that the trial "can be expected to be a long one . . . in part because IBM's power base in the relevant markets is very broad, touching a very large percentage of the commercial establishments that are the heart of U.S. commerce and industry."

Judge David N. Edelstein, who had been presiding over the case, said Oct. 4 that it could take up to one year to try the case and another year for him to reach a decision. (The case would be tried without a jury.) Both parties to the suit had said they intended to call a total of about 600 witnesses.

Control Data suit settled. Control Data Corp. Jan. 16, 1973 announced the settlement of a four-year-old antitrust suit it had filed against IBM.

Under the agreement, IBM would sell its subsidiary, Service Bureau Corp., to the rival computer company for $16 million in cash as well as make payments totaling $96 million over the next 10 years to Control Data for expenses, services and contracts.

Control Data, the fifth largest computer manufacturer in the U.S. and responsible for 4.5% of the nation's installed value of data processing equipment, also won a pledge from IBM not to re-enter the data service business in the U.S. for six years.

The settlement, which provided for destruction of Control Data's legal "work product," was a setback to the antitrust suits against IBM still pending, according to the Washington Post Jan. 20.

The Justice Department had been using a computerized index of 27 million IBM documents compiled over three years by Control Data, which was destroyed with lawyers' research. Preparation of another index could delay the trial another two—three years, the Post reported.

The government charged in the 2nd Court of Appeals Jan. 24 that the two companies made a secret agreement to destroy the index and claimed that if a Justice Department lawyer had been present at the St. Paul court, IBM would not have been able to insist upon destroying the file.

Telex decision reversed. The 10th Circuit Court of Appeals Jan. 24, 1975 reversed a lower court ruling that IBM had engaged in predatory pricing practices and other anticompetitive actions against the Telex Corp. In overturning the antitrust conviction against IBM, the court also set aside a $259.9 million civil damages award that IBM had been ordered to pay Telex, plaintiff in the original suit against IBM.

The appeals court in Denver also affirmed the lower court's separate ruling against Telex in a countersuit that had been brought by IBM. Telex, which had been convicted of misappropriating and pirating IBM's computer trade secrets, had been ordered to pay IBM $20.9 million in compensatory damages. The appeals court reduced the penalty to $17.5 million, but upheld a $1 million punitive damage award that Telex also had been ordered to pay IBM.

In a brief summary of its findings, the appeals court said that its decision to reverse the charges and damages levied against IBM was based on "this court's determination that the trial court [the U.S. District Court in Tulsa] erred in defining relevant markets or market as the term is used in the antitrust laws. . . . This fundamental misconception affected the remainder of the court's decision."

The appeals court also concluded that "IBM's actions constituted valid competitive practices and were neither predatory . . . nor otherwise violative of the antitrust acts."

The court released its 94 page ruling Jan. 29. In explaining its decision, the court stated that the "record shows that the acts of IBM were part of the competitive scene in this volatile business inhabited by aggressive, skillful businessmen seeking to market a product cheaper and better than that of their competitors."

U.S. District Court Judge A. Sherman Christensen in Tulsa, Okla. Sept. 17, 1973 had originally ordered IBM to pay treble damages of $352.5 million to Telex for alleged antitrust violations harmful to the latter company. He also ordered Telex to pay IBM $21.9 million in damages for copyright violations. But Christensen admitted Oct. 9 that he had made a "substantial error" in calculating the damages, and he cut the sum to $259.5 million.

Christensen had found IBM guilty of "possessing and exercising monopoly power," by utilizing a "strategy" that was "sophisticated, refined, highly organized and methodically processed and considered. In this day and age, such conduct is hardly less acceptable than the naked aggressions of yesterday's industrial powers if unlawfully directed against competition." Christensen added: It may "pose more danger under modern conditions than instantly more obvious strategies."

Telex had charged that IBM maintained a monopoly on attachments that plugged into or could be used with IBM central data processing equipment. IBM had countered, claiming that the peripheral devices did not constitute a separate market within the industry, but were part of the larger electronic data processing market, in which IBM held a lesser overall share.

Telex, a Tulsa-based firm, had entered the booming computer field in the late 1960s, offering price cuts for customers leasing IBM units under 30-day cancellable leases. IBM responded by packaging lower prices with long-term leases and stiff penalties for customers breaking the leases.

Telex, which had suffered a net fiscal loss in 1973, had sought an estimated $1.1 billion in damages.

In a 222-page decision, Christensen ruled that IBM had tried to "substantially constrain or destroy its plug peripheral competition by predatory pricing actions and by market strategies bearing no relationship to technological skill, industry, appropriate foresight or customer benefit."

Telex was found guilty of undertaking a "programmed and massive invasion" of IBM's trade secrets. The company was ordered to return all IBM documents and confidential IBM information in its possession and to destroy Telex manuals infringing on IBM copyrights; to refrain from hiring or soliciting any IBM employes for two years without court approval; and to refrain from assigning any former IBM employe "to the development or the manufacture of products functionally equivalent or similar to those on which such employe worked at IBM."

Ampex suit settled. IBM announced July 28, 1974 that it had agreed to pay $13 million to the Ampex Corp. to settle a dispute involving allegations against IBM of patent infringement and antitrust violations.

Under the agreement, Ampex was to drop charges that IBM had infringed on tape and disc patents and violated antitrust laws in marketing peripheral and memory equipment used in computers. The companies also agreed to an exchange of existing and future patent licenses covering their data-processing interests.

The settlement avoided another suit against IBM based on principles set down in a 1973 judgment in favor of Telex Corp.

Broadcasting & the Press

Networks win suit dismissal. Judge Robert J. Kelleher of U.S. District Court in Los Angeles dismissed an antitrust suit brought against the three major television networks by former Attorney General John Mitchell in 1972, it was disclosed Nov. 15, 1974.

The suit charged that the networks had monopolized prime time programming by broadcasting only those shows which they produced or in which they had substantial interests. The government had asked that the networks be prohibited from obtaining financial interests in programs from independent producers.

Lawyers for CBS Inc., American Broadcasting Cos. and National Broadcasting Co., a unit of RCA Corp., argued that the suit had been filed by the Nixon Administration to harass the networks because they had broadcast news that the Administration did not like.

(The Watergate special prosecutor's office had informed that court Nov. 8 that its investigation had uncovered no evidence that the antitrust suit was politically motivated.)

The judge granted the defense motion for dismissal. The networks had sought the dismissal after they were unable to obtain access to President Nixon's papers, which the defense contended would prove that the suit was "improperly motivated."

The suit was dismissed "without prejudice," leaving the government free to refile the charges.

The suit had been filed April 14, 1972 against all three of the major commercial television networks and against a television program distributor formerly owned by one of the networks. The suits sought to prevent the networks "from carrying network-produced entertainment programs, including feature films,

and from obtaining financial interests in independently produced entertainment programs," with the exception of first-run exhibition rights. The defendants claimed that the suit was superfluous in light of recent Federal Communications Commission (FCC) rulings that already, they claimed, had sharply reduced their control of entertainment programming.

CBS, NBC and ABC were charged with violating Sections 1 and 2 of the Sherman Antitrust Act. Viacom International, Inc., a former CBS subsidiary that controlled some CBS program syndication rights, was also named as a defendant.

According to the Justice Department, the networks "have used their control of access to air time to monopolize prime time television entertainment programming and to obtain valuable interests in such programming," depriving "the viewing public, independent program suppliers, and advertisers" of "the benefits of free competition."

In particular, the suit alleged that the networks' entry into motion picture production threatened free competition in that industry as well.

The Department said the networks had spent $840 million for programs in 1969 and received $1.5 billion in revenues. In 1967, the suit charged, ABC had ownership interest in 86% of the entertainment programs it broadcast during prime time (which the suit defined as 6–11 p.m., and the networks considered 7–11 p.m.), NBC had interests in 68% and CBS in 73%.

Network officials, reacting to reports of the suits published the day before they were filed, claimed that the situation had changed drastically since 1967. In the last quarter of 1971, a CBS spokesman said April 13, the network had financial interests in only two of its prime time entertainment programs, and its own production accounted for only 8.2% of its prime time schedule. NBC and ABC spokesmen said over 90% of their prime time programs in the last quarter of 1971 were bought from outsiders.

An April 13 ABC statement cited a 1970 ruling by the FCC requiring every station to buy at least one hour of prime time entertainment from non-network sources. Other rulings issued by the

FCC had barred the networks from equity ownership in all shows produced or televised in 1971 or thereafter, and curbed network control over syndication, the sale of programs to individual stations. The latter decision had caused the separation of Viacom from CBS.

ABC vice president Eugene S. Cowen disputed the Justice Department's income figures April 13. He said about $500 million of total network revenues were distributed to affiliates as station compensation, and about $60 million more was paid to the American Telephone & Telegraph Co. for line charges.

The Justice Department, in a statement April 14, said its suits had resulted from an investigation dating back to the 1950's, but suspended during an 11-year FCC inquiry. The New York Times said April 15 that the suits had been approved by former Assistant Attorney General Richard W. McLaren more than a year and a half before they were filed. They were said to have been revived after repeated complaints by Antitrust Division staff lawyers about delays in antitrust enforcement, and after the controversy surrounding the out-of-court settlement of antitrust suits against the International Telephone & Telegraph Corp.

TV networks sued again—The Justice Department Dec. 10, 1974 filed separate civil antitrust suits against the three major television networks, accusing them of using their control over access to network air time to restrain and monopolize prime time television entertainment programming.

FCC announces media merger curbs. The Federal Communications Commission, after a two-year study, announced March 26, 1976 that it would prohibit any new combinations of radio and television ownership in the same city. The commission said that in granting future broadcast licenses, it would follow a "single market" rule, "designed to prevent undue influence on local public opinion by relatively few persons or groups."

The commission also proposed new regulations that would give media combinations five years to divest themselves of ownership of more than one mass medium in a single community—an AM-FM radio combination, a television station or a daily newspaper. These proposed curbs would be applied only to media concentration on a local level, not on a state or national level.

According to an FCC report released the week of March 22, 256 daily newspapers in the U.S. were owned jointly by broadcast license holders in the same city; in 68 relatively small communities the only commercial radio station and the only daily paper were jointly owned; and in 11 cities the only TV station and the only newspaper were jointly held.

Merger barred. The Supreme Court ruled March 10, 1969 that the joint commercial operation of two competing newspapers in Tucson, Ariz. was in violation of antitrust laws.

Under an agreement formed in 1940, the Arizona Daily Star, a morning paper, and the Tucson Daily Citizen, an evening paper, shared facilities for production and distribution of the papers and set common circulation and advertising rates. The court upheld the ruling of Federal District Judge James A. Walsh that the papers would have to abandon joint advertising and circulation operations. The order would allow the two dailies to continue to print and distribute the papers jointly.

Justice William O. Douglas declared in his majority opinion that the anticompetitive practices of the two papers could be justified only under the "failing company" doctrine, an antitrust exception permitted by the Supreme Court in 1930 during the Depression, and that the papers did not meet the requirements of the doctrine. Some newspaper interests had urged Congress to pass a "failing newspaper" bill that would permit joint ventures if one newspaper would otherwise be in serious financial trouble. The American Newspaper Publishers Association had submitted a friend-of-court brief listing 44 newspapers operating under similar arrangements that might be affected by the court's decision.

Boston Globe to share material. The Boston Globe agreed March 5, 1975 to share feature material distributed by news syndicates with other papers in the New

England area. Under a proposed consent decree worked out with the Justice Department in connection with a civil antitrust suit filed in 1973, the paper agreed to reduce the geographic region over which it claimed exclusive rights over rival papers to the syndicated material.

Globe Newspapers Co., publisher of the Boston paper, had been accused of violating federal antitrust laws by signing agreements with news syndicates that prevented them from selling their features to papers in eastern Massachusetts and surrounding states.

Under the consent decree, the Globe agreed to limit its claim to features exclusivity to five counties in the Boston area, enabling about 50 other papers in the region to buy features currently monopolized by the Globe from the syndicates.

In order to keep its exclusive contracts, the consent decree would require that the Globe maintain daily circulation of at least 5,000 copies in a county and 20% of the households in that area. Papers with circulation of less than 11,750 would be able to share the Globe's syndicated features.

S.F. papers settle suits. Five antitrust suits brought against San Francisco's two daily newspapers and their commonly owned printing company by a total of 17 local plaintiffs were settled out of court for about $1.4 million, the Wall Street Journal reported May 27, 1975.

The suits had questioned the legality of a 1965 agreement by which the San Francisco Chronicle and the San Francisco Examiner, both owned by Hearst Corp., had formed the San Francisco Newspaper Printing Co. According to the Wall Street Journal, the suits had challenged the constitutionality of the federal 1970 Newspaper Preservation Act, allowing joint printing companies, which was upheld by a federal judge in 1972.

Automobile Industry

Nader charges GM trust suit withheld. In letters to the chairmen of the House and Senate antitrust subcommittees Dec. 23, 1970, consumer advocate Ralph Nader charged that the Justice Department's antitrust unit suppressed recommendations on file for antitrust suits against General Motors Corp. and Ford Motor Co. The letters to Rep. Emanuel Celler (D, N.Y.) and Sen. Philip A. Hart (D, Mich.) urged that Congress begin a "full-fledged inquiry" of the antitrust division, which Nader accused of "bureaucratic cowardice and anticipatory politics" because of its inaction in regard to the two auto giants.

Most notable among the recommendations was a memorandum submitted by Donald F. Turner, the department's antitrust chief 1965–68, while he was serving as a Justice Department consultant after resigning. Turner, according to Nader, had recommended that a suit be brought under the Sherman Antitrust Act to dissolve GM into three separate companies and divide Ford into two new companies. Turner, a professor at Harvard Law School, confirmed that he had written a "highly confidential memo" about a possible suit against the auto industry. Edwin M. Zimmerman, Turner's successor, said the memo had been turned over to the unit's staff for further evaluation.

Ford spark plug case. The Supreme Court March 29, 1972 upheld, by 5–2, a lower court ruling forbidding the Ford Motor Co. from manufacturing its own spark plugs for 10 years as a penalty for illegally acquiring the Electric Autolite Co. in 1961.

Upon its acquisition by Ford, Electric Autolite became known as the Autolite Spark Plug Division of Ford.

Pollution control charges dismissed. In a decision made public Nov. 26, 1973, Judge Manuel L. Real in U.S. District Court in Los Angeles dismissed 34 consolidated antitrust suits that had accused the nation's automobile manufacturers of conspiring to delay development of pollution control devices. The suits had been filed by a number of states and localities.

Real said there was a "temptation" to depart from traditional application of antitrust law because of the seriousness of auto pollution. He decided, however, that antitrust laws were meant to preserve "free and unfettered competition" and were not intended as a "panacea" for all social damage caused by industry.

However, Real criticized the auto makers, charging them with conduct "that occasionally bordered on the legerdemain" in their response to public pressure to reduce air pollution. He said the industry's "cross-licensing agreement" on control technology might have hampered development. The result, Real said, was a "less than spectacular" cooperative effort among the manufacturers.

Acquittal on fleet sale charge. General Motors Corp. and the Ford Motor Co. were acquitted by a federal jury in Detroit Dec. 19, 1973 of criminal charges of conspiracy to fix prices in the automobile fleet sales market. U.S. District Court Judge John Feikens Dec. 13 had found the automakers not guilty of charges they had plotted to monopolize the fleet sales market.

In his instructions to the jury Dec. 19, Feikens said no one had testified that Ford and GM had conspired to eliminate price competition. He pointed out that the firms had been within their rights to watch each other's pricing activities as well as change prices so long as there was no express agreement between them. Similarly, Feikens had ruled the automakers were not guilty of the monopoly charges because the government had failed to produce sufficient evidence.

Feikens Sept. 26, 1974 dismissed a companion civil complaint filed by the Justice Department against the two auto manufacturers.

The indictment alleged that in 1969 and 1970 the companies, supported by two co-conspirators, the National Automobile Dealers Association and Peterson, Howell & Heather, Inc., the nation's largest automobile leasing company, conspired through public statements and talks to third parties in the industry to end the practice of discount pricing on fleet cars. The Chrysler Corp. originated the discount policy in 1962, and only partially curtailed it when GM and Ford moved out of the discount market.

Summit meetings charged. The Justice Department Jan. 17, 1973 accused 97 officials of the three major car makers, including the company chairmen, of holding secret meetings in 1969 and 1970 to exchange confidential cost information.

The government, which revealed the charges at the Detroit price-fixing trial against General Motors Corp. and Ford Motor Co., declared that some of the "foothill" and "summit" meetings held also with Chrysler Corp. executives dealt with mutual assistance pacts in the event of strikes during 1970 auto negotiations.

The auto makers lost a plea to keep the government's bill of particulars secret in order to avoid embarrassment and pretrial publicity.

EC fines GM. The European Commission Dec. 20, 1974 fined the Belgian branch of General Motors 100,000 units of account ($120,000) for violating EEC fair competition rules, a Commission official disclosed Dec. 21. The Commission ruled that General Motors Continental of Antwerp had charged excessive prices for certificates of conformity for GM cars, mostly Opels, brought into Belgium by independent importers. The certificates were required for use of the cars in Belgium, and GM Continental had sole rights to issue them for GM cars.

AT&T Breakup Sought

Trust suit filed. The Justice Department filed a civil antitrust suit Nov. 20, 1974 against American Telephone & Telegraph Corp. (AT&T), the world's largest privately owned corporation.

AT&T and two other defendants—Western Electric Co. Inc., AT&T's wholly owned subsidiary which manufactured telecommunications equipment for the Bell System, and Bell Telephone Laboratories Inc., the nation's largest industrial laboratory and owned equally by AT&T and Western Electric—were accused of combining and conspiring to monopolize telecommunications service and equipment in the U.S., in violation of the Sherman Act.

The suit, which was filed with U.S. District Court in Washington, asked the divestiture of Western Electric by AT&T and the division of Western Electric into two or more competing firms, if necessary, to assure competition in the manufacturing and sale of telecommunications equipment.

The government also sought to promote competition with its request that "some or all" of AT&T's Long Lines Department, which handled long distance calls, be separated from "some or all" of the 23 local Bell Telephone Operating Cos., which together with the three defendant firms made up the Bell System. The local Bell companies were named co-conspirators in the antitrust suit.

Under the divestiture plan submitted by the government, the Long Lines Department could be divested from the Bell System, or some or all of the Bell Operating Companies could be divested by AT&T as separate and independent firms.

According to a government spokesmen, the suit did not challenge the concept of exclusive franchises for the provision of local exchange telephone service.

The Justice Department said that "in terms of assets," the antitrust suit was the largest ever filed by the government, surpassing the 1911 suit that led to the breakup of Standard Oil Co., and the 1969 suit against International Business Machines Corp.

The Bell network and its dominance of the telecommunications field were without parallel. AT&T, with assets of $67 billion, had annual revenues of $23.53 billion in 1973; Western Electric's sales in 1973 totaled more than $7 billion. With earnings of $315 million, Western Electric was one of the 12 largest manufacturing firms in the nation. The 23 Bell operating subsidiaries served 112.3 million telephones, about 80% of the nation's total. (There were 1,705 independent phone companies, but none of them competed directly with AT&T for phone customers, because like the AT&T subsidiaries, they operated within specific geographic areas under a monopoly franchise.)

AT&T's Long Lines Department transmitted more than 90% of the nation's long distance telephone calls, and the Bell System transmitted most of the nation's data, television shows and other com-munications. Western Electric manufactured most of the nation's telecommunications equipment and was the largest maker of telephone equipment in the world, producing about 11 million units in 1973.

The government had filed another antitrust suit against AT&T in 1949, also seeking the divestiture of Western Electric. A consent judgment was finally accepted in 1956, but the Bell System was left intact.

Critics of the government's 1956 settlement charged that the consent decree was a mere "slap on the wrist" for the giant company. AT&T settled the suit with an agreement that Western Electric would be restricted to the manufacture of telephone equipment, and would relinquish units that produced nontelephone equipment, such as railroad dispatch machinery and movie gear. AT&T also agreed to license all of its existing patents.

It was later revealed during 1958 House subcommittee hearings that Herbert Brownell, attorney general in the Eisenhower Administration, had given AT&T's vice president and general counsel, T. Brooke Price, a "little friendly tip" on how to settle the case. The "tip" was that AT&T should examine its operations and tell the Justice Department about "practices that we might agree to have enjoined with no real injury to our business."

AT&T officials had testified at the Congressional hearings that the patent licensing requirement would greatly reduce its dominance in the telephone business.

AT&T's competitors won a landmark victory with the "Carterfone" decision in 1968 when a small company won the right to sell a device, a cradle-like apparatus called the "carterfone," that connected a mobile radio into the phone network. The ruling allowed makers of non-Bell equipment to hook into the Bell system. In a 1971 ruling, the Federal Communications Commission created a new classification of specialized common carriers licensed to provide interstate communications facilities on a private line basis, thereby allowing customers to bypass the Bell dial network.

Competing firms which attempted to take advantage of these rulings later charged that AT&T impeded their efforts. Antitrust suits were pending to decide whether AT&T could require non-Bell equipment makers to use a Bell-produced, installed and leased interface to hook into the Bell network. In regard to the 1971 FCC ruling, a court had recently ordered that Bell provide its private line rivals with linkage service necessary to connect non-Bell interstate customers to the non-Bell interstate system.

Other Cases

USM suit settled. Under a consent decree agreed to in January 1969, the Justice Department's antitrust suit against USM Corp., formerly the United Shoe Machinery Corp., ended Feb. 20 after more than 20 years of court litigations. The decree required USM to divest itself of shoe machinery business accounting for $8½ million in revenues.

In compliance with the decree, USM established two new shoe machinery subsidiaries. One of the new companies, the Transamerican Shoe Machinery Corp., would sell and lease shoe machines in 22 model categories mainly using the welt process. The other new company, Inter-Coastal Shoe Machinery Corp., would sell and lease 15 model categories chiefly using sole and lasting attaching operations. Ultimately, USM would be required to dispose of the two companies.

Hazeltine-Zenith suit. The Hazeltine Corp. and its subsidiary, Hazeltine Research, Inc., agreed April 30, 1971 to pay Zenith Radio Co. $22.5 million in cash and credits to settle a 13-year-old antitrust suit. In addition, Zenith would receive licenses for all Hazeltine inventions being used for consumers home entertainment electronic products with royalty obligations chargeable against a $6 million credit set forth by the settlement.

Zenith had charged that Hazeltine Research had entered foreign patent pools to exclude Zenith products from Canadian, English and Australian markets.

Tire firms' break-up sought. The Justice Department filed antitrust charges Aug. 9, 1973 against the U.S.' largest tire manufacturers, Goodyear Tire & Rubber Co. and Firestone Tire & Rubber Co., charging that the firms had made independent attempts to monopolize the $2 billion market in replacement tires bought directly by consumers.

In a rare request, the government asked federal district court in Cleveland to order the breakup of Goodyear and Firestone in an effort to restore competition to the tire industry.

The companies were accused of making substantial price reductions, beginning in 1959 and continuing until 1966. During that period, they allegedly engaged in reciprocal trade agreements to restrict the market of its smaller competitors, which also were unable to match the lower tire prices. Subsequently, the weakened firms were acquired by Goodyear and Firestone during the 1959–1966 period, according to the government. It was alleged that the two large manufacturers maintained the artificially low prices until 1966, when it had eliminated its competitors.

The Justice Department claimed that as a result of monopolistic practices, Goodyear increased its share of the consumer tire market from 23% in 1959 to 28% in 1973; Firestone's share was reported to have increased from 15% to 25% during the same period.

Drug makers acquitted. U.S. District Court Judge John M. Cannella acquitted three drug firms Nov. 30, 1973 of all charges they had conspired to fix prices and monopolize the market for the broad spectrum drug Tetracycline in violation of the Sherman Antitrust Act.

The pharmaceutical firms were Chas. Pfizer & Co., American Cyanamid Co. and Bristol-Meyers Co.

Cannella's decision ending 12 years of antitrust prosecution came after the three firms and two others—Upjohn Co. and Squibb Corp., both unindicted coconspirators—had paid or had agreed to pay $196 million to settle 150 lawsuits prompted by the federal action. A number of lawsuits, including ones by North Carolina and the federal government, remained in litigation.

A New York federal jury in 1967 had

found the three major drug companies guilty of conspiring to fix prices and monopolize production and distribution of broad-spectrum antibiotics, principally Tetracycline. Later, however, the Second U.S. Circuit Court of Appeals had thrown out the conviction on grounds that U.S. District Court Judge Marvin E. Frankel had misinformed the jury on the law applicable to the case. The court also held, in effect, that the companies could not be convicted solely on the circumstantial evidence which was the basis of the Justice Department's case.

In arguments before the Supreme Court, the department contended that Frankel's jury instructions had been "exemplary" and asked the court to reinstate the convictions with an accompanying declaration that reviewing courts should treat trial judges in complex cases more generously. It also said the appeals court decision had placed a "serious burden" on the government's prosecution of antitrust cases because there was rarely "direct proof of the conspiracy and the government almost invariably has to rely upon circumstantial evidence."

A 3-3 tie vote of the Supreme Court Jan. 24, 1972 had automatically affirmed the appellate court's ruling.

Interlocking directorships. The FTC Nov. 24, 1972 charged the Aluminum Co. of America (Alcoa), Kennecott Copper Corp. and Armco Steel Corp. with violating the law that bars interlocking directorships.

The agency charged that Russell De-Young, chairman of the Goodyear Tire and Rubber Co., was a board member of both Alcoa and Kennecott and that John A. Mayer, chairman of the Mellon National Bank & Trust Co., was a board member of both Alcoa and Armco.

The Clayton Antitrust Act forbade individuals from serving as directors of competing companies with revenues in excess of $1 billion. The FTC, which admitted that the charges constituted a "new wrinkle" in antitrust litigation, alleged that copper and steel and aluminum and steel were interchangeable industrial metals and that those companies were, therefore, competitors.

The FTC announced April 22, 1975 that 12 corporations in the petroleum and gas business had agreed to the resignation of seven men charged with serving at the same time on the boards of directors of two competing firms. The order also instructed the companies to obtain from current and prospective directors, for a period of five years, the names of other corporations on whose boards they were also serving.

The companies and individuals involved were: Standard Oil Co. (Ohio) and the Diamond Shamrock Corp. (Horace A. Shepard), Amerada Hess Corp. and the Newmont Mining Corp. (William B. Moses Jr.), El Paso Natural Gas Co. and Transcontinental Gas Pipeline Corp. (Alfred C. Gassell Jr. and Franz Schneider), Dixilyn Corp. and the Austral Oil Co. Inc. (William H. Johnson), the General American Oil Co. of Texas and Pauley Petroleum Inc. (Paul A. Conley), Kerr-McGee and the Oklahoma Natural Gas Co. (Dean A. McGee).

The FTC July 21 charged two pairs of companies with operations in the food industry for having interlocking directorates. The firms and individuals named in the complaint were: Kraftco Inc. and SCM Corp. (Richard C. Bond) and United Brands Co. and Kane-Miller Corp. (Joseph M. McDaniel Jr.)

GE guilty on prices. A federal district court in New York ruled May 9, 1973 that the General Electric Co.'s (GE) consignment agency system for marketing household light bulbs violated Sherman antitrust provisions against price fixing. GE sold $150 million worth of bulbs annually, according to the court. The antitrust case brought by the Justice Department had been in litigation since 1966.

Continental Can in consent accord. The Justice Department and Continental Can Co. filed a consent agreement June 27, 1974 under which the firm, without admitting past wrongdoing, agreed not to engage in future reciprocal purchasing agreements with some of its suppliers.

The consent judgment settled a suit, filed the same day, in which the Justice Department accused the company of violating antitrust law by entering into agreements to buy products and services from suppliers on condition that the suppliers purchase containers from Continental. The suit charged that Continental had engaged in such practices since 1949.

Kodak, Bell & Howell settle. The federal court in Chicago July 8, 1974 approved an agreement settling Bell & Howell Co.'s antitrust suit against Eastman Kodak Co.

Under the agreement, Kodak would provide competitors with notice of new film or cartridge product developments at least 18 months before such products were to be marketed. Bell & Howell had charged that many of its camera products had been rendered instantly obsolete when Kodak secretly developed new film products which did not fit existing cameras or projectors marketed by Kodak's competitors.

The agreement provided that Bell & Howell and other companies wishing to participate would pay a $10,000 fee for each advance disclosure. The company receiving the information would be required to keep it confidential. The accord did not apply to Kodak innovations in cameras, projectors or self-developing photography. The agreement was limited to six years.

8 chemical firms plead no contest. Eight major chemical firms pleaded no contest Oct. 18, 1974 to charges that they had conspired since 1970 to fix dye prices in the U.S. The criminal indictment and a related civil complaint had been filed July 18 in U.S. District Court in Newark, N.J.

Named in the indictment and pleading no contest were the E.I. du Pont de Nemours & Co.; Verona Corp.; Allied Chemical Corp.; American Cyanamid Co.; BASF Wyandotte Corp.; CIBA-GEIGY Corp.; Crompton & Knowles Corp.; and GAF Corp. A ninth defendant, American Color & Chemical Corp., pleaded not guilty Oct. 18.

According to the one-count indictment, du Pont officials discussed a "proposed across-the-board increase in the price of dyes with each of the other defendants." By the end of 1970, all had agreed to a price increase. Du Pont initiated the action in January 1971, announcing a 10% across-the-board price rise, which was quickly followed by similar announcements from each of the other defendants.

The eight companies were fined a total of $360,500 Dec. 15.

Two of the defendants, E. I. du Pont de Nemours & Co. and Verona Corp., were fined $50,000 each. Fines imposed on the other six defendants ranged from $40,000 to $45,000 each.

Major book publishers charged. The Justice Department accused 21 of the nation's largest book publishers of conspiring with a British publishing association to divide the English-speaking world into exclusive territories for book sales.

The trust suit was filed Nov. 25, 1974 in U.S. district Court in New York. Publishers Association, which, according to the Justice Department included "virtually all" of the publishing firms in Great Britain, was named an unindicted co-conspirator in the case.

According to the government, the defendants had maintained an illegal market allocation agreement with the British organization since 1947, in violation of the Sherman Act. The court was asked to issue an injunction against the practice because it suppressed competition between U.S. and British publishers, deprived book buyers of open competition and restrained international trade in English language books.

In its suit, the government described the operation of the market allocation agreement, which insured that U.S. copyrighted books were sold in Britain only by British publishers and that British copyrighted books were sold in the U.S. only by U.S. publishers.

The division of territories applied to approximately 70 countries, all present or former Commonwealth nations. If a U.S. publisher wished to market a book in Britain or in any of those countries, rights to produce, distribute and sell the book would be sold to a British firm. Conversely, British publishers agreed not to directly enter the U.S. market.

Named as defendants:
Simon & Schuster Inc., Random House Inc., Prentice-Hall Inc., McGraw-Hill Inc., Macmillan Inc.,

Houghton Mifflin Co., Harper & Row Publishers Inc., Bantam Books Inc., CBS Inc., Dell Publishing Co., Grosset & Dunlap Inc., Harcourt Brace Jovanovich Inc., Litton Educational Publishing Inc., Oxford University Press Inc., Viking Press Inc., John J. Wiley & Sons Inc., Addison-Wesley Publishing Co., Doubleday & Co , Intext Inc., Penguin Books Inc. and Times Mirror Co.

Engineers guilty of price fixing. The National Society of Professional Engineers was convicted Dec. 19, 1974 of violating federal antitrust laws by prohibiting its 69,000 members from bidding competitively for contracts.

Judge John L. Smith Jr. of U.S. District Court in Washington ruled that a provision in the group's code of ethics banning competitive bidding was "in every respect a classic example of price fixing in violation of the Sherman Act."

The ban had been enforced by the society since 1964. In defending the practice, the engineers had contended that they were not engaged in trade or commerce, but in a "learned profession," which was exempt from antitrust action because it was state regulated.

Judge Smith rejected the argument, saying, "It would be a dangerous form of elitism, indeed, to dole out exemptions to our antitrust laws merely on the basis of the education level needed to practice a given profession, or for that matter, the impact which the profession has on society's health and welfare."

Airlines indicted. Braniff Airways and Texas International Airlines were indicted Feb. 14, 1975 by a federal grand jury on charges they conspired to monopolize airline business in the Dallas-Fort Worth, Houston and San Antonio areas by attempting to exclude Southwest Airlines from operating at those airports.

The criminal indictment was returned in U.S. District Court in San Antonio. Braniff and Texas International denied the charges. The alleged conspiracy against Southwest began before May 1971 and continued until "at least 1973," the indictment stated.

Braniff and Texas International were accused of trying to prevent Southwest from obtaining the three Texas routes and attempting to increase the cost of Southwest's entry into the three regional markets as a competitor. The indictment also charged that the defendants exchanged information on schedules and fares "to disadvantage and injure Southwest" and undertook a boycott against Southwest by preventing passengers from cancelled flights from switching to Southwest flights.

Clothiers fined after pleading no contest. A U.S. District Court judge in New York Feb. 27, 1975 imposed the maximum antitrust fine on three New York City clothing stores accused of fixing the prices of women's clothing.

The stores, Saks Fifth Avenue, Bergdorf Goodman and Genesco Inc., which operated Bonwit Teller, had entered not guilty pleas before the court in November 1974, but filed a motion to change the pleas to no contest the following month. (Increases in maximum antitrust penalties took effect during December 1974. Alleged price-fixing conspiracies carried on before that period faced the previous maximum.) The Justice Department opposed the change in plea, but Judge Harry F. Worker rejected the government's motion.

Barrie Somerfield, Saks Fifth Avenue vice president, changed his plea from not guilty to no contest March 26; he was fined $15,000 April 30 and sentenced to one day of unsupervised probation. Leonard Hankin, executive vice president of Bergdorf Goodman, changed his plea from not guilty to no contest June 25; he was fined $25,000 and sentenced to one day of unsupervised probation.

The five defendants had been charged with conspiring since the late 1960s to fix retail prices for women's ready to wear clothing by adopting uniform mark up lists. They were also accused of compelling clothing manufacturers to use the same mark up lists in devising their "suggested retail prices," thereby forcing other retailers to maintain the same high prices.

In imposing the $50,000 fine on each defendant, Judge Werker said the stores' management had "bilked" the public, adding that "it seems to me that [the public's] patronage may have been misplaced." (Seven class-action suits had been filed against the stores by consumers seeking treble damages for alleged price fixing violations.)

Revlon cleared of price fixing charges. U.S. District Court Judge Inzer B. Wyatt March 7, 1975 ruled Revlon, Inc. not guilty of federal antitrust charges filed in 1962. Revlon had been accused of conspiring to fix prices in restraint of trade.

However, Wyatt granted the government's request for an injunction barring the cosmetic maker from restricting the rights of beauty products jobbers and retailers in reselling its products. Until 1963, Revlon had limited the jobbers' sales territory and set conditions on resale.

The case had been tried without a jury in 1967.

Car renters accused. The Federal Trade Commission June 12, 1975 accused the nation's three largest car rental firms of having conspired to monopolize automobile rentals and keep prices artificially high at airports throughout the U.S.

The companies specified in the FTC complaint were Hertz Corp., a subsidiary of RCA Corp.; Avis Rent-A-Car System Inc., a unit of Avis Inc.; and National Car Rental System Inc., subsidiary of Household Finance Corp.

According to James T. Halverson, an official of the FTC, the three companies named had developed since 1968 a "highly concentrated, non-competitive market structure" which forced U.S. consumers "to pay substantially higher prices for the rental of passenger automobiles." The arrangement allowed the firms to obtain "profits and returns on investment substantially in excess of those they would have obtained in competitively structured" markets. Halverson said the three firms, which in 1968 controlled 99% and in 1973 96% of a market now believed to exceed $500 million a year, had submitted to airports common bid specifications and contractual provisions designed to exclude their smaller competitors. They were able, for example, he said, to get airports to require that car rental concessionaires have a national reservation network and credit card arrangements. In addition, each company was charged with having entered into an "exclusive arrangement" for advertising subsidies with the three major automobile manufacturers—Hertz with the Ford Motor Corp., Avis with Chrysler Corp.,

and National with General Motors Corp. —although the auto makers were not named as respondents in the complaint. Halverson said one of the rental firms had received subsidies from Detroit of up to $5 million a year.

Three states query fertilizer prices. The attorneys general of Washington, Idaho and Montana filed civil suits against eight multinational corporations, charging them with fixing fertilizer prices over the past ten years, it was reported June 12, 1975.

The states alleged that price-fixing and anti-competitive activities by the eight firms, among them the creation of an artificial fertilizer shortage during the energy crisis, had placed farmers in the Pacific Northwest at a disadvantage because prices in that area were higher than elsewhere.

Those named as defendants were Chevron Chemical Co., a subsidiary of Standard Oil Co., of California; Phillips Pacific Chemical Co., subsidiary of Phillips Petroleum; Western Farm Service, subsidiary of the Shell Oil Co.; Union Oil Co., of California, and a subsidiary, Collier Carbon & Chemical Co.; J.R. Simplot Co. and Simplot Industries Inc., both of Boise, Idaho; and Cominco American Inc., subsidiary of Consolidated Mining & Smelting Ltd., Vancouver, Canada.

Xerox consent order. The Federal Trade Commission July 30, 1975 settled an antitrust complaint against the Xerox Corp. by adopting a consent order it had announced on a trial basis in April. The settlement was described as a stronger version of the one the FTC had rejected in February after accepting it in November 1974.

Although the FTC did not require Xerox to divest itself of its foreign holdings, as the commission's original complaint had specified, the order directed the firm to license to others in the office copier field its 1,700 patents and to share its manufacturing and technological expertise. Xerox's right to obtain patents from its competitors was limited, and it was instructed to forgive all past liability for patent infringement by any company taking a license under the FTC order.

Xerox was required to give up its policy of offering group prices to volume customers that rented both its more popular copiers and those less in demand.

In its final order, the FTC said that although Xerox had admitted no wrongdoing and there had been "no formal adjudication of ultimate or subsidiary legal or factual questions," the settlement would "eliminate the principal sources of Xerox's dominance of the office copier industry." Firms wishing to compete with Xerox "will have a more meaningful chance to do so." It expressed the view that "implementation now of the provisions of the negotiated order is a better approach to bringing significant relief to the industry than protracted litigation would be."

Richard Sexton, vice president and general counsel for the SCM Corp., which had a private antitrust suit pending against Xerox in federal district court in Connecticut, criticized the FTC order July 30, calling it "a failure of federal antitrust enforcement and a knuckling under to Xerox." (Xerox and Litton Industries Inc. were reported by the Wall Street Journal April 4 to have settled their private litigation out of court with the exchange of patent licenses and a net payment to Litton of $11.6 million. Litton had opposed the earlier FTC consent order.)

Gypsum firms guilty. A federal court jury in Pittsburgh, Pa. July 15, 1975 found four gypsum manufacturers and three officers guilty of conspiring to fix prices on $4.8 billion of products over a 14-year period. The maximum $50,000 fine was assessed against the firms by Judge Hubert I. Teitelbaum. The individuals were given fines, ranging from $1,000 to $50,000, and suspended prison terms.

The convicted companies: U.S. Gypsum Co., National Gypsum Co., Georgia-Pacific Corp., and Celotex Corp. The individuals convicted were Colon Brown, chairman of National Gypsum; J. P. Nicely, vice president of National Gypsum; Andrew J. Watt, executive vice president of U.S. Gypsum.

Flintkote Co. and Kaiser Gypsum Co., Inc. had pleaded no contest Jan. 16 and were fined $50,000 each. Seven individual

defendants also pleaded no contest: three were fined $40,000, given a six-month suspended jail sentences and placed on probation; four others were fined $20,000, given 30-day suspended sentences and also placed on probation.

Bag makers charged. A federal grand jury Oct. 29, 1976 charged five companies that manufactured paper-bag products and seven of their officials with conspiring since 1950 to fix the prices of certain of their products. The criminal indictment, which was filed in U.S. District Court, Philadelphia, was the government's first major case brought under the 1974 law that made price-fixing a felony.

Named as defendants were Continental Group Inc. of New York City (formerly Continental Can Co. Inc.), and three of its executives, James K. Cooper, Peter J. Weggeman and David Mawicke; American Bag & Paper Corp. of Philadelphia and its president, Stanley A. Schottland; Chase Bag Co. of Greenwich, Conn. and its vice president, Harrison B. Rue; Harley Corp. of Spartanburg, S.C., and St. Regis Paper Co. of New York City, and two officials, William H. Versfelt and Edward W. Weikum.

The indictment charged that the defendants had engaged in "continuing combination and conspiracy in unreasonable restraint of trade ... [to] raise, fix, maintain and stabilize the prices, terms and conditions of sale" of their products. (The bags were used chiefly to package such consumer items as coffee, cookies and pet food.) The government estimated the corporations' combined sales in 1974 at about $42 million.

In a companion civil suit, the government asked the court to issue a permanent injunction barring continuation of the alleged price-fixing scheme.

The grand jury returned a second indictment in the case Nov. 4 when three individuals were charged with conspiring to fix prices. The defendants were George K. Landon Jr., a Continental vice president; Eugene P. Alexander of Chase, and Frederick W. Kiendl, a former Chase official.

Because the grand jury found "insufficient evidence" of their participation in the alleged conspiracy after Dec. 21, 1974, when the tougher new law made price-fixing a felony, the defendants were charged with misdemeanor violations of the antitrust law. The five companies were named as unindicted co-conspirators in the case against Landon, Alexander and Kiendl.

Judge James B. Persons Nov. 30, 1976 imposed prison terms, probation and fines on 47 paperboard-company officials who had pleaded no contest to price-fixing charges filed by the Justice Department.

R. Harper Brown, president of Container Corp. of America, a unit of Mobil Oil Corp., received the harshest sentence—60 days in jail and a $35,000 fine. The maximum penalty for a person convicted of the misdemeanor antitrust violation was a $50,000 fine and one year in jail.

Fourteen other executives also were ordered to serve jail sentences and fined. The officials and their sentences were: John F. Allen, retired chairman and chief executive officer of Hoerner Waldorf Corp., indicted for his actions as executive vice president, 45 days in jail and a $35,-000 fine; William E. Mastbaum, senior vice president, Container Corp., 30 days and $20,000; George V. Bayly Sr., senior vice president, Tenneco Inc.'s Packaging Corp. of America, 30 days and $20,000; Paul Wilch Jr., division vice president, Diamond International Corp., 15 days and $20,000; William J. Koslo, executive vice president, Diamond International, 10 days and $20,000, and Paul H. Wolff, vice president and general manager, Alton Box Board Co., 10 days and $20,000.

Also, Frank D. Bergstein, president, Interstate Folding Box Co., 10 days in jail and a $10,000 fine; Charles L. Hamilton, vice president, Packaging Corp., seven days and $10,000; R. F. Krause, vice president, Packaging Corp., seven days and $10,000; J. Donald Scott, vice president, Container Corp., five days and $10,000; Carl M. De Faria, vice president and regional general manager, Federal Paper Board Co., five days and $10,000; Donald H. Wedin, sales and marketing director, American Can Co., five days and $5,000; Gordon Dilno, sales vice president, Brown Co., five days and $5,000, and Jack D. Tovin, vice president, Container Corp., five days and $5,000.

Because of age, one official was given a 90-day suspended sentence, fined $30,000 and placed on three months' probation. Another 16 executives were fined and placed on probation for up to six months. Fifteen executives received only fines. Sentencing was deferred until December for William S. Hart, national sales director for Fibreboard Corp.

Before handing down the sentences, Parsons noted that paperboard boxes were used to package products ranging from frozen food to camera film. "Because of this kind of price accommodation, the manufacturer of each pays more for cartons than he would if there were clean competition between the producers," Parsons said. "Presumably, this additional cost is passed along to the ultimate consumer."

Of the 23 companies and 50 executives indicted on the antitrust charges, only one corporation, Consolidated Packaging Corp. of Chicago, and two executives, Vern A. Kepford of Potlach Corp. and Paul J. Van Keuren of St. Regis Paper Co., had pleaded not guilty.

.

Other Business Corruption Developments

Grain Export Scandal

Large companies probed. A year-long investigation by the Justice Department that had yielded 20 federal grand jury indictments of individuals and corporations in the New Orleans and Houston areas was reported June 24, 1975 to have begun probing the affairs of two of the world's largest grain exporting firms. News sources said high-level federal agricultural officials had attempted to ignore earlier charges that U.S. grain was being shipped abroad with grades and weights misrepresented and that a variety of other corrupt practices had become entrenched. Widespread cancellation of orders by foreign companies was threatened.

The background to the grain export investigation was presented in June 19 testimony before the Senate Agriculture Committee's subcommittee on foreign agricultural policy by Carl W. Belcher of the Justice Department's criminal division. Belcher said the investigation was begun in the spring of 1974 after the U.S. attorney for the eastern district of Louisiana, which included New Orleans, was informed that "inspectors licensed by the U.S. Department of Agriculture [USDA] may have been receiving bribes from certain companies involved in the grain shipping business." The matter was placed under the supervision of U.S. At-

torney Gerald J. Gallinghouse, who used the resources of the Federal Bureau of Investigation, the USDA's Office of Investigation, the Internal Revenue Service and a federal grand jury. The grand jury indicted 10 persons in August 1974. These included seven USDA-licensed inspectors, a marine surveyor, the president of a ship-cleaning company, Dean Leslie Peterson, and his company, Peterson Maritime Services, Inc. Belcher told the subcommittee that five more persons were indicted in New Orleans May 29. He said that in the first of two separate indictments a USDA-licensed inspector, his brother, a corporation and a resident of New Orleans were charged with "conspiring together to violate federal wire-fraud and transportation-of-stolen-and-fraudulently-obtained-property statutes." A second indictment that day charged a grain elevator employe with "improperly influencing" the inspector.

(The New York Times May 30 identified the inspector as Richard M. Blades of Metairie, La., employed by the New Orleans Board of Trade, and his brother as Dewey F. Blades Jr. of Picayune, Miss. The Times said the corporation was Le Trac Land, Inc., of La Place, La.; the New Orleans resident was Carey T. Lindsay and the grain elevator employe was Rufus J. Hebert of Port Barre, La. The paper reported that the defendants were charged with having concocted fraudulent accounts and false inspection certificates in order to sell non-existent soybeans to the Peavey Company of Alton, Ill.)

Belcher revealed that five USDA-licensed inspectors in Houston had been indicted March 24 on charges of "accepting gratuities."

Senate told of bribes—Sen. Richard Clark (D, Iowa), a member of the subcommittee, said June 9 in the text of a speech scheduled for delivery in the Senate the following day that he had been told of a "pervasive system of bonus payments" by grain elevator owners to operators who accumulated grain by inflating shipment reports and holding back the excess. Clark declared: "As I understand the practice, a company owning the elevator will pay its operators an annual bonus for grain that they have been able to save by shaving on reported shipments."

Times articles—William Robbins, continuing in the New York Times a series of articles on the grain export investigation he had begun in that newspaper in May, said June 14 that an official of the USDA's internal investigative agency had been discouraged in 1972 from going ahead with a probe of department practices similar to the current inquiry. Robbins said Willard W. Griffin, now retired and then employed by the Office of the Inspector General—since divided into the Office of Investigation and the Office of Audits—had been called a scandal monger by the department when he tried to take evidence of alleged wrongdoing to the office of the U.S. attorney in New Orleans. According to Robbins, when he noted in an interview with Ervin L. Peterson, administrator of the Agricultural Marketing Service (whose jurisdiction included the grain division) that the department's internal agents had conducted over 100 official investigations since 1964, he was told by Peterson, "That record is an indictment of the grain division—an indictment of management. But we're positioned now to begin to move."

Robbins reported June 16 that a 1973 probe by the Office of the Inspector General had concluded that the grain division, responsible for the safety and quality of U.S. grain shipments, was not fulfilling some of its primary duties. The 1973 inquiry report said it "has not been

the practice of the grain division to inform the Food and Drug Administration of grain found to contain deleterious substances such as mercury-treated kernels, crotalaria seeds, aflatoxin or adulterants such as rodent excreta and insect-damaged kernels." The division was further criticized for "unapproved shortcuts" taken by some of its inspectors, for failure to develop a safety code that would protect employes against health hazards in the fumigated holds of ships and for an inspection rule allowing 10% of a cargo to be made up of off-grade grain. Robbins said that when asked about the 1973 findings Peterson declared: "I think you could say that what we haven't corrected, we're well on the way to correcting." Peterson said the 1973 report "was the genesis of my close and continuing surveillance of the grain division," which led among other results to the recent replacement of Howard H. Woodworth, its chief executive, by David R. Galliart, his deputy. (The Washington Post June 15 said a February 1969 report submitted to Woodworth on complaints by European grain dealers had described the division's inspection system as "subject to bribery or fraudulent issuance of certificates.")

Weight rigging described—In a July 6 report in the New York Times on testimony given to federal investigators in New Orleans, Robbins described a number of illegal practices current in grain elevators.

After the grain was dried, cleaned and blended in the elevators it was moved by conveyor belts to ships and weighed. Robbins quoted one witness, who declared: "They tell you it's a fool-proof system, huh? Look, all you have to do is put these scales on hold, see. Then you reach under the keyboard and trip a lever, and you can punch any weight you want to on the tape." The testimony reportedly indicated that much of the grain accumulated through weight rigging was stolen, in many cases by grain elevator employes. Another witness was quoted as saying: "From the day you go to work as an inspector, it's bred into you that your job is to help the elevator. They say you've got to bend with the wind. You only draw the line when it gets too bad."

Another former inspector reportedly told investigators of being asked by the managers of a grain elevator to allow the blending of 20,000 bushels of ruined soybeans with higher quality beans. He asked them not to "overdo it," but soon"they were running that bad stuff 50–50 with the good." Sometimes, according to one witness, "whatever we had in the house went on the ships, no matter what the contract called for." In one case of a ship certified as loaded with No. 2 grade wheat, elevator managers had to go outside to purchase a small amount of wheat that might serve as an example of the shipload.

Robbins said July 9 that David R. Galliart of the Agriculture Department's grain division had written the office of the department's general counsel to ask about procedures for withdrawing the authority of a private grain inspection agency. Three inspectors from Delta Weighing and Inspection Bureau, Inc., the agency, had been indicted on charges of accepting bribes.

Louisiana aides on grain payroll—Louisiana Gov. Edwin W. Edwards confirmed June 27 that between the time of his election and inauguration in 1972 two members of his staff had been paid by the Lake Grain Co., now being investigated by the Internal Revenue Service.

In a related development, Sen. Richard Clark (D, Iowa) said July 3 that the Bunge Corp. had loaned at least $10,000 to Bryan J. Lehmann Jr., a former state representative, when he founded the Destrehan Board of Trade, now being investigated by the Justice Department.

Clark, in New Orleans interviewing witnesses in the probe, commented on the "sweetheart relations" between grain companies and private inspection agencies, like Destrehan, and said he was "surprised by the pervasiveness of corruption" in the grain trade.

Cook official suspended. The suspension "pending investigation" of Melvin L. Hibbets, vice president for operations of Cook Industries, Inc., was confirmed July 6, 1975 by the firm. Cook Industries was reported in June to have become, along with another major grain exporting company, the subject of a growing Justice Department probe into allegations of corruption in the industry.

Continuing a series of articles in the New York Times on the burgeoning grain scandal, reporter William Robbins said June 28 that Hibbets had been named in a 1972 report by an Agriculture Department official as someone with "a long history of being involved in apparent irregularities." The report, written by J. L. O'Brate, then acting chief of the grain division's inspection branch, cited 26 complaints from foreign customers "resulting from grain shipped" from the St. Charles Grain Elevator Co. during the period when Hibbets was manager there. At one point the division had recommended prosecution of the company for "layering grain sorghum and off-grade grain on export loading belts in such a manner that samplers could not obtain representative samples."

In 1969 Hibbets went to work for the Bayside Warehouse Co., a wholly owned Cook subsidiary. The Times reported July 2 that in 1970 he wrote a letter to the captain of the freighter Sincerity, which was returning to the Bayside elevator corn rejected by Mexican buyers, asking him to insure "complete secrecy" when the ship docked and "to prohibit sampling of the cargo and the taking of photographs." Hibbets claimed "these precautions are essential to our future relations with the Mexican government," which had rejected the corn because it contained a large quantity of broken kernels.

(Robbins reported July 4 that in 1964 Louis LaCour, then the U.S. attorney for the area, had been presented with evidence of grain thefts that included photographs, reports from spotter planes, identification of trucks and personal testimony but that his office and the Federal Bureau of Investigation had not followed up on the information because the barges from which the grain was said to have been stolen were "at rest," which meant the grain was neither interstate nor foreign commerce and therefore not subject to federal jurisdiction.)

The New York Times reported July 16 that accounts kept by the Destrehan Board of Trade appeared to indicate that Cook Industries, Inc. sold over a period of years more grain than it had bought. The Times also said Cook had purchased monthly from Degelos & Associates as many as 40 boxcars of rice hulls, an adulterant often mixed with grain shipments.

Dozens indicted. The Bunge Corp., one of the world's largest grain exporting firms, was indicted by a federal grand jury in New Orleans July 21, 1976 on charges of theft. Also indicted were 13 persons described as former or current employes of the company.

Adnac, Inc., a corporate affiliate of two major grain concerns, was indicted in August together with 33 persons, including another group of defendants from Bunge and officials of a loading elevator operated by Adnac. The charges, many of them falling concurrently on the same individuals, described a variety of fraudulent practices.

The July 21 allegations against Bunge were that the company had conspired between 1961 and 1973 to steal grain by short-weighting exports and had then disguised the thefts by a system of falsified interoffice accounts. Walton F. Mulloy, vice president of Bunge for its Kansas City regional headquarters, and Clayton E. Wilcox, a former vice president for the St. Louis region, were among those indicted.

Multiple charges were handed up August 7 against Adnac, the manager of its New Orleans area grain elevator, Robert W. Edgeworth, and other local employes. Adnac, a joint venture of the Archer Daniels Midland Co. of Decatur, Ill. and the Garnac Grain Co., was a Swiss-owned U.S. company. The manager of the St. Charles Elevator, operated by Adnac, and five other employes were charged with conspiracy to commit theft from 1971 to 1975 and with using an electronic device to circumvent inspection. At the same elevator, two employes and an official of a grain inspection agency were alleged to have sold Archer Daniels Midland fictitious barge loads of grain by interstate teleprinter transmissions. Each of the three was said to have deposited about $100,000 in a bank in the Bahamas. Nine defendants at the Mississippi River Grain Elevator were charged with carrying out similar fraud against the Pillsbury Co. of St. Louis and Tabor & Co. of Decatur, Ill. Four employes of the Bunge Corp. were said to have conspired to make profit by selling to a local company a higher-quality grain than it had agreed to buy. In each of the alleged schemes, except the one involving Edgeworth and his co-defendant, the ac-

cused were reported to have had dealings with Degelos & Associates and two other local firms with the same address and telephone numbers.

Charges involving the St. Charles Elevator were first brought Aug. 5 when two former employes, an assistant superintendent and a barge foreman, were accused of fraudulent sales and of evading taxes on income earned from the sale of stolen grain. Two former officials of the Bunge Corp. who had been indicted in July were indicted again Aug. 5. Also charged that day were present and former officials of the Mississippi River Grain Elevator and employes of two inspection companies, the Delta Weighing and Inspection Bureau, Inc. and the South Louisiana Port and Weighing Board, Inc.

Bunge license suspended, restored—The U.S. Department of Agriculture (USDA) temporarily revoked July 25 the federal warehouse licenses of Bunge Corp. grain elevators in Destrehan, La. and Galveston, Tex. The suspension was reported July 29 to have been lifted.

The announcement of USDA's action in revoking the licenses was made by James H. Lauth, a department official, who explained the move as having been a result of indictments of Bunge employes earlier in the week. Suspension of the licenses meant the warehouses were unable legally to store grain for other parties, although they could store Bunge's grain.

The Washington Post July 29 reported that the licenses had been reinstated two days earlier after it was determined that the persons named in the grand jury indictment no longer worked for Bunge.

Chief grain inspector indicted. Louis H.C. Matherne, chief grain inspector for Delta Weighing and Inspection Bureau Inc., was indicted by a New Orleans federal grand jury Aug. 15, 1975 on charges of bribery and making false statements to the grand jury. Matherne's employer was licensed by the U.S. Agriculture Department (USDA) to inspect grain at the Myrtle Grove, Louisiana export elevator owned and operated by the Mississippi River Grain Elevator Inc.

The indictment alleged that Matherne took separate payments of $1,500 and

$5,000 in 1972 and 1973 from an official of Tabor and Co., a Nevada corporation engaged in the merchandising and export of grain. The indictment also charged Matherne with distributing some of the alleged bribery money to other Delta inspectors. (Matherne pleaded guilty to the bribery charge March 5, 1976.)

In a related development, the Agriculture Department announced Aug. 26 that it had suspended the weighing and inspection licenses of Matherne. The announcement also indicated that the licenses of three other Delta inspectors charged in federal grand jury indictments Aug. 5 had been suspended or cancelled.

In a separate announcement Aug. 18, the USDA said the weighing licenses of six employes of the St. Charles elevator at Destrehan, La. had been suspended, as had the weighing license of Robert P. Nicholas, chief weigher for the South Louisiana Port Inspection and Weighing Board Inc., the private inspection agency at St. Charles. The St. Charles elevator was operated by Adnac, Inc., which had been indicted Aug. 7.

Grain trade corruption outlined. Former grain inspectors and other witnesses told the Senate Agriculture Committee Aug. 14-15 that corruption was a way of life in international grain trading. They said that grain was constantly being misgraded and misweighed to maximize the profits of grain companies and that grain containing poisonous substances was sometimes shipped overseas without so much as a cursory inspection.

The committee hearings, held in Bondurant and Walcott, Iowa, focused on the relationship between large grain companies that shipped grain overseas and privately owned concerns that weighed, inspected and graded the grain.

Among the witnesses testifying was Harlan Ryan, chief supervisory officer for the Agriculture Department's grain division in New Orleans, who said Aug. 14 that the main weakness of the private grain inspection system was the close relationship between the inspection agencies and the grain elevators. Noting that private inspectors worked under contract with the elevators, Ryan testified that the inspectors' livelihood depended on the elevators doing a good business. As a re-

sult, Ryan said, the private inspectors' loyalty lay with the elevators and not with federal standards.

Bunge pleads no contest. Bunge Corp. Oct. 8, 1975 pleaded no contest to the federal indictment charging conspiracy in the systematic theft of grain and in the cover-up of the thefts. Judge Jack M. Gordon, who accepted Bunge's plea in federal district court in New Orleans, said that a plea of no contest was equivalent to a plea of guilty for purposes of punishment.

After entering its plea, Bunge was fined a maximum of $10,000 on each of the counts by Judge Gordon. In addition, Bunge agreed to implement an affirmative action program over the next three years, under which the company would undertake a program of self-regulation to prevent recurrence of the alleged abuses in its grain handling operations.

The program, expected to cost $2 million, would entail improved external and internal accounting procedures; automation of the company's scales at its Destrehan, La. and Galveston, Tex. elevators; and increased supervision of company operations by the U.S. Agriculture Department. (Bunge's commitment was the result of plea bargaining that allowed the company to plead no contest and avoid a trial, which would have brought out details of the thefts that occurred, according to the indictment, between 1961 and 1973.)

Bunge 'abuses' described. A former Bunge employe, Drebing A. Negrotto, told a New Orleans grand jury that he had been present at a June 1969 meeting at which two top Bunge executives discussed means of covering up grain thefts. According to a Nov. 14 New York Times interview with Negrotto, the alleged meeting took place in the office of Bunge's grain-elevator manager in Destrehan, La., a suburb of New Orleans. Negrotto said he was one of four junior executives in attendance. Also present, he claimed, were Bunge's president, Walter C. Klein, and its vice president, Roger Noall. Bunge's law firm, and Noall himself, denied the charges to the Times.

Negrotto was employed at Bunge as a grain elevator manager and supervisor. He was one of 13 employes indicted on theft-conspiracy charges as the result of federal inquiries. The charges were dropped, however, when he became a government witness. He did plead guilty to a separate count of evasion of income taxes on more than $100,000 in income from grain thefts, and was given a suspended sentence.

Negrotto told the Times Nov. 21 that he had personal knowledge of extensive abuses related to the government's Food for Peace program. Food for Peace provided food-aid to needy countries.

He said that ships bound for India were systematically short-weighted, often by as much as 10,000 bushels of grain, and that he knew of one ship that had been short-weighted by 28,000 bushels. (Poor countries, the Times noted, often lacked facilities to weigh the grain properly once it arrived.)

Grain exporters also frequently misgraded food-aid shipments, according to Negrotto. He said Food for Peace cargoes often contained inferior grain, while the companies charged for high-quality grain. Negrotto related a 1968 incident in which he bribed grain inspectors with $1,000 to overlook a cargo infested with weevils. The bribe money, he said, came from a shipping agent.

Negrotto's charges were the first specific allegations to emerge publicly from the government's investigation into the Food for Peace program.

Food-aid abuse—One aspect of the U.S. Agriculture Department (USDA) probe of the Food for Peace program was the overpayment of shipping subsidies to foreign grain buyers. Parts of a USDA Office of Audit draft report on shipping subsidies were revealed by the New York Times Dec. 7. The report found that subsidies totaling millions of dollars in overpayments had been authorized routinely for years.

Food for Peace operated under the 1954 Cargo Preference Act which required that at least half of food-aid cargoes travel on American-flag vessels (ships under U.S. registry). The carrying rates of American-flag vessels had been traditionally higher than those of foreign vessels. Since foreign buyers had to pay all transportation costs, a system of government subsidies was established to make up the difference. About $1 billion in subsidies has been paid

out in the last 21 years.

The USDA Office of Investigation had been looking into reports that foreign and U.S. ship owners had been trading information and rigging bids to widen the difference between foreign and American rates, thus increasing the subsidy. Foreign embassy officials empowered to award bids for carrying food-aid cargo were suspected to be cooperating in the manipulation and receiving kickbacks.

Bunge aide pleads guilty. A former assistant vice president of the Bunge Corp., Clayton C. Wilcox, pleaded guilty Dec. 12, 1975 in New Orleans to two misdemeanor counts of conspiring to weigh grain improperly for the company. Felony charges against Wilcox were dropped in return for his cooperation in the continuing federal investigation of widespread corruption in the grain export industry.

Federal Bureau of Investigation agents testified that Wilcox knew of illegal short-weighting practices at Bunge's Destrehan, La. grain elevator and didn't act to stop the activities, although he did not receive any personal gain from it.

"Ghosting" investigated—Three stevedoring companies owned by large grain corporations came under local and federal investigation, the New York Times reported Dec. 17. The coordinated inquiry was part of a wide-scale probe into grain export corruption. Stevedore companies hired longshoremen to load and unload cargo ships. The companies under investigation, Grain Stevedores Inc., Rogers Terminal and Shipping Corp. and St. John's Shipping Co. were owned respectively by Bunge Corp., Cargill Inc., and Cook Industries Inc.

The investigation centered mainly on the practice of "ghosting." Ghosting was an activity by which a dockworker not present during a workshift was paid for work he did not do. Ghosting, the article said, required the involvement of stevedore foremen, who were in charge of the daily "shape-ups," or hirings.

Four foremen and one time-keeper were indicted for accepting kickbacks from the pay of nonworking longshoremen.

Defendants penalized. Six former Bunge Corp. employes were given probationary sentences by a federal district judge in New Orleans Feb. 4, 1976.

The six had pleaded guilty to misdemeanor charges of conspiring to misweigh grain. They were: Clayton E. Wilcox, a former vice president of Bunge, sentenced to one year's probation and a $500 fine; Harry O. Dolsen Sr., former superintendent and manager of an elevator in Destrehan, La., sentenced to three months' probation on the conspiracy charge and the same on a tax violation; Daniel G. Delaney, a former manager of a Galveston, Tex., elevator, sentenced to three years' probation; Willie E. Horn, former foreman and assistant superintendent of the Galveston elevator, sentenced to 18 months' probation; Edwin L. Wolf, former assistant superintendent of the Destrehan elevator, sentenced to 18 months' probation; and Andrew J. Voelkel, former superintendent of the Destrehan elevator, sentenced to 18 months' probation. The government attorney told the judge that the six had cooperated fully with the government's investigations into the grain trade. Other felony charges against the defendants were dismissed.

The Archer-Daniels-Midland Co., the Garnac Grain Co. and a company jointly-owned by the other two, the St. Charles Grain Elevator Co. were indicted, pleaded no contest, and fined $10,000 each by a U.S. district court judge in New Orleans March 4. The charges stemmed from alleged shortweighing and misgrading of grain at an elevator at Destrehan, La.

A government investigator told the court that the shortweighing saved the companies about $450,000 worth of grain annually and the misgrading added $1.2 million a year to grain receipts. The companies agreed to put new measures into effect to prevent a recurrence of the abuses, at an estimated cost of $2 million a year.

Advertising & Selling Deception

Ad claims found wanting. Federal Trade Commission (FTC) Chairman Miles W. Kirkpatrick told the Senate Consumer Affairs Subcommittee May 16, 1972 that 60% of data submitted by 32 companies to support 282 advertising claims was either inadequate or "so technical in nature" that neither consumers nor the FTC staff could judge its validity.

The companies, manufacturers of automobiles, television sets, air conditioners and electric shavers, had been ordered in 1971 to file reports supporting claims that the FTC considered could be factually verified. The commission planned the program to aid consumer choice, and to encourage manufacturers to contest exaggerated claims by competitors.

When the claims were analyzed by FTC staff, about 30% raised "serious questions" about adequacy of supporting material, and at least an additional 30% could not be verified. Kirkpatrick said, however, that the staff finding did not in itself constitute grounds for charges of deceptive advertising.

Car ads evaluated. Another independent evaluation of FTC advertising data, performed by the engineering firm of Bolt Beranek & Newman, Inc. and released Oct. 6, 1972 by Consumers Union, indicated that 65% of documentation submitted to the federal agency by auto makers was irrelevant and inadequate.

The FTC moved against nine car makers and advertisers and air conditioner makers Oct. 12, charging that their ads were "misleading and unfair."

Named in the action, which culminated a 15-month campaign to obtain substantiation for advertisements, were General Motors Corp., Volvo of America Corp., Fedders Corp. and Whirlpool Corp.

Ads for TV sets scored. A public interest law group at Georgetown University in Washington charged in a report Dec. 3, 1972 that television set advertisers failed to substantiate nearly 70% of their ads questioned by the FTC.

The group, using 1971 data from 10 manufacturers and two retailers supplied by the FTC under a campaign aimed at verifying the claims of advertisers, found that 41 of 59 ads could not be substantiated.

Advertising "promises, misleads and

tempts, but it does not do much in the way of informing the public," the report concluded.

Publishing companies charged. The Federal Trade Commission (FTC) and the Justice Department took separate actions against Cowles Communications Inc. for deceptive practices in the sale of magazine subscriptions. Cowles and five of its magazine sales subsidiaries were fined $10,000 each Jan. 18, 1971 after they pleaded no contest in a Des Moines, Iowa federal district court to 10 criminal and civil counts of mail fraud. The FTC said Jan. 21 it had filed formal complaints against Cowles and the Hearst Corp., also for deceptive sales practices.

Both actions charged that door-to-door salesmen and telephone callers had misrepresented to prospective customers the cost and terms of the magazine subscription contracts.

In the federal court action Jan. 18, Cowles and its five Des Moines-based subsidiaries agreed to a permanent injunction barring them from continuing the fraudulent practices cited. The five subsidiaries were Home Reference Library Inc., Home Readers Service Inc., Mutual Readers League Inc., Civil Readers Club Inc. and Educational Book Club Inc.

Chrysler accord. The FTC announced Jan. 11, 1971 agreement by the Chrysler Corp. to cease alleged truth-in-lending violations in its advertising of Simca and Sunbeam cars. The agency charged that Chrysler's advertisements cited monthly installment rates not usually used by dealers selling Simcas or Sunbeams and did not publish legally required credit information.

The agency said it provisionally accepted Chrysler's agreement to stop advertising installment payments unless commonly offered by dealers and to henceforth disclose the car's cash price, the down payment required, the number of payments and the interest rate.

Enzyme detergent accord. The FTC March 3, 1971 announced agreement by the three largest detergent manufac-turers to halt advertising that misled consumers into believing enzyme detergents removed all stains. Under terms of the agreement contained in a consent order provisionally accepted by the agency, Proctor & Gamble Co., Colgate-Palmolive Co. and Lever Brothers Co. Inc. accepted FTC proposals for advertising and packaging their enzyme products.

Without admitting guilt, the three companies agreed to implement the following requirements after nine months: (1) disclosure on the packages of the types of stains the product can and cannot remove, (2) acknowledgement in their media advertising that all types of stains will not be removed by the products and (3) elimination of claims that an additive in a product removed stains when in fact the product could have done the job alone. Products affected by the FTC action included Drive, Amaze, Punch, Axion, Ajax, Gain, Biz and Tide.

Plastics accord. The FTC announced July 29, 1974 that 25 companies and a trade association—the Society of the Plastics Industry Inc.—had agreed to stop claiming that cellular plastic products were non-burning or self-extinguishing and to inform the public of fire hazards associated with the products. The agreement was the result of a class action complaint filed in 1973.

The products, primarily foamed polyurethanes and polystyrenes, were widely used in construction, furniture and airplane interiors.

Under the agreement, the companies would: cease use of misleading terms about the products' performance under actual fire conditions; attempt to notify all purchasers since Jan. 1, 1968 of fire hazards and take advertisements in popular and trade magazines warning of dangers; and establish a $5 million program for research into improving safety of the products.

The FTC said that once ignited, the plastics often created greater fire hazards than conventional materials by producing dense smoke, faster spreading of flames, extreme heat and toxic or flammable gases. The Federal Aviation Administration had found such gases to be the possible cause of death in airplane crashes, the New York Times reported May 31, 1973.

The FTC contended that the industry had known of the hazards as early as 1967 but had continued to promote them as safe on the basis of small-scale tests by the American Society for Testing and Materials. The manufacturers and the trade group—the Society of the Plastics Industry, Inc.—had helped set the testing standards, the commission alleged.

Banking Abuses

Ex-AMA chairman admits bank fraud. Dr. John R. Kernodle, who resigned as chairman of the board of the American Medical Association in Sept. 1973, was sentenced to 18 months in a federal penitentiary Dec. 29, after he pleaded guilty to charges of misapplication of bank funds.

Kernodle, former chairman of the North State Bank of Burlington, N.C., and the bank's former president, Norman Graham Smith, who pleaded guilty to bank fraud and received two concurrent 18-month prison terms, were accused of making indirect loans for their own purposes, concealing the purposes of the loans, and misapplication of funds with the intent to defraud the bank. Three other Burlington businessmen also admitted taking part and received sentences up to one year in prison.

14 indicted in Norfolk bank collapse. Thomas J. Jones, former Virginia state banking commissioner; Boyd D. Wilkins, former senior bank examiner, and 12 others were indicted May 6, 1975 by a Circuit Court grand jury in Norfolk, Va. The indictment alleged that systematic efforts by bank officials, and the deliberate failure of state officials to halt the illegal activities, led to the loss of $12 million in bank funds and the ultimate collapse of the Norfolk Savings and Loan Corp. in January 1973.

The bank's president, Leon C. Hall; its vice president, Frank F. Warren, and 10 other former employees and business people who had dealings with the bank were charged with, among other crimes,

setting up companies without assets or purpose to siphon off millions of dollars in loans. Hall and Warren had already been convicted of similar charges in 1974. Criminal action was said to have extended back to the 1950s. According to a story in the Washington Post May 7, Wilkins and his associate, Jones, ignored several state and federal examinations of Norfolk Savings and Loan, which had determined that the bank was in poor financial condition. (Because their deposits were uninsured, 3,500 depositors received none of their money when the bank closed and were now scheduled to receive only 55 cents on the dollar, according to a court-appointed receiver.)

C. A. Smith, associate, sentenced in fraud case. C. Arnholt Smith, 76, friend of ex-President Richard Nixon, pleaded no contest June 12, 1975 to charges that he had defrauded his own bank of $27.5 million. The maximum prison term of two years was imposed but was suspended and he was placed on probation for five years. In addition, the U.S. District Court in San Diego, Calif. imposed the maximum fine of $30,000.

Philip A. Toft, former president of the Smith-controlled Westgate-California Corp., also pleaded no contest June 12 to charges of conspiring to defraud Smith's now-defunct U.S. National Bank by misapplication of bank funds and using a false statement for the sale of real estate. Toft's one-year prison sentence was also suspended and he was placed on probation for five years. His fine, also the maximum, was $25,000. The charges against both defendants had been reduced.

Smith had been indicted in 1974 on criminal conspiracy charges of misapplying $170 million in bank funds. The fraud charges stemmed from one of the largest bank failures in U.S. history—the collapse of U.S. National Bank of San Diego, owned by Smith. He was accused of fraudulently obtaining loans from the bank for use by subsidiaries in his now defunct financial empire, headed by the Westgate-California Corp. (Westgate had filed for bankruptcy in February.)

Shipowners accused. Among federal grand jury actions in New York during 1975:

Two Greek shipowners and five of their business associates were indicted in Manhattan Sept. 15 along with four former bank officials on charges of obtaining bank loans fraudulently. The shipowners were Charalambos (Harry) Amanatides, president of the defunct Tidal Marine International Corp., and Amilcas Ion Livas, its chairman. The business associates named in the suit were James D. Hanlon, an admiralty lawyer for Tidal Marine; Costas Naslas and Paul Katritsis, two employes of the firm; Michael Blonsky, who had operated a London office for the two principal defendants, and Michael A. Panayotopulos, president of International Mining and Abrasives Inc. Three of the former bank officers had worked in the ship loan department of the National Bank of North America—Gregory Spartalis, Joseph Metzger and John J. Shevlin. The other, Francis A. Marone, had been vice president of Bank of America International. As an example of the method used in the scheme, news accounts mentioned the purchase by a Livas-owned company of a Norwegian tanker called the Thorhild for $795,000. The name was changed to Aquario and the vessel "was reconveyed through companies controlled by the defendants at increasing prices and was refinanced at National Bank of North America for $1.5 million," according to Paul J. Curran, U.S. attorney for the southern district of New York. Curran added that a "fabricated 3½-year time charter with Shell of Venezuela" was pledged as collateral.

Franklin aides jailed. Six former Franklin National Bank executives were sentenced in New York March 9, 1976 on charges stemming from the bank's loss of more than $30 million in unauthorized foreign currency speculation.

In U.S. District Court, Judge Thomas P. Griesa sentenced the six men, each of whom had pleaded guilty to one count in the Franklin National case, to terms ranging from three to six months in prison.

Andrew N. Garofalo was sentenced to six months; Arthur Slutzky, Donald Emrich and Martin Keroes were sentenced to four months; Michael Romersa and Paul Sabatella were sentenced to three months.

According to the indictment, the defendants between January and May 1973 "caused the bank to sell, for future delivery, more foreign currencies than it purchased, resulting in an enormous and unauthorized short position with a dollar value exceeding $400 million."

Nixon '68 campaign aide sentenced. William M. Rentschler, manager of former President Richard M. Nixon's 1968 presidential campaign in Illinois, pleaded guilty in Chicago April 20, 1976 to a count of defrauding Citibank.

Rentschler, who admitted having submitted a false financial statement to the bank, was ordered by a U.S. district judge to begin serving a one-year sentence on May 19.

Lefferdink sentenced. Allen J. Lefferdink, a financier whose international dealings included control of the Capital National Bank of Miami, was sentenced in U.S. Court there April 26, 1976 to eight years in prison after having been found guilty in March of wire fraud, mail fraud and conspiracy. Lefferdink had illegally used at least $5 million in bank assets to back up a conglomerate of insurance companies and mutual funds that he operated.

Land-Sale Swindles

FTC files land-sale complaints. The Federal Trade Commission announced separate complaints March 19, 1975 against two major land companies charging "unfair and deceptive practices" in the sale of lots from large tracts in five states. The companies named were the Horizon Corp. of Tucson, Ariz. and AMREP Corp. of New York. The properties involved covered 900 square miles in Arizona, Florida, Missouri, New Mexico and Texas, where approximately 215,000 customers had purchased property since the 1950s at prices ranging from $2,000 to $5,000 a lot.

The complaints charged misrepresentation about the "all-inclusive" purchase price of lots and about development of sites. The FTC proposed an end to such practices, a "cooling-off" period in which purchasers could cancel contracts without penalty and a limit on a buyer's liability in event of default. It also sought contract warnings in bold-face, for example, that certain lots should not be considered as an investment since there was virtually no resale market for the land.

Both companies named defended their business practices as legal and proper.

Rio Rancho case. A large real estate group was indicted Oct. 28, 1975 on charges of one of the biggest land swindles in U.S. history. The 80-count federal indictment charged that over 45,000 people from 37 states were fraudulently sold $200 million worth of "undeveloped semi-arid desert lots" in a New Mexico land development, Rio Rancho Estates.

The indictment resulted from a 20-month investigation by the office of the U.S. Attorney into land sales practices by the AMREP Corp. and two of its subsidiaries, the ATC Realty Corp. and Rio Rancho Estates, Inc. The attorney's office said the companies bought 91,000 acres of desert land outside of Albuquerque in 1961 for about $180 an acre. The land was in turn sold to individuals for up to $11,800 an acre for a "home site" and up to $25,000 an acre for "commercial" lots.

It was charged that the realtors duped buyers into thinking the land investment would yield substantial profits when resold, whereas it was found by prosecutors to be "an exceptionally poor, risky and dangerous investment." AMREP called the charges "wholly unwarranted and legally and morally unjust."

Other Cases

Stock theft hearings. The Senate Government Operations Subcommittee on Permanent Investigations held hearings in June 1971 on organized crime's role in the theft of negotiable securities.

Attorney General John N. Mitchell and New York Police Commissioner Patrick V. Murphy were among those who testified June 8. Mitchell told the subcommittee that more than $400 million in securities had been stolen without discovery in 1969 and 1970. Mitchell

laid the chief responsibility for deterring the thefts on the industry. However, Murphy said banks and brokerage houses had shown reluctance to report the thefts.

Murray J. Gross, assistant district attorney for New York County (New York City), said June 9 that organized crime had a "virtual monopoly" on the disposition of stolen securities, often in collusion with certain New York banks. Gross, who had been in charge of investigations and prosecutions of securities thefts in New York for the past five years, charged that some banks had added stolen securities to their assets to improve their financial position, while loan officers took bribes to make loans with stolen securities as collateral. Gross later told reporters that several small brokerage houses, "generally over-the-counter houses," were suspected of being "created and controlled" as conduits for organized crime.

DuPont grip on Delaware denounced. A two-volume study, entitled "The Company State" and compiled by law students working under Ralph Nader, accused E. I. duPont de Nemours & Co. and the powerful duPont family of using their domination over "virtually every major aspect of Delaware life" for selfish interests.

Among the allegations of the study Nov. 26, 1971, the team of "Nader's Raiders" charged that the nation's 18th largest industrial corporation and members of the duPont family: did not pay their fair share of property and income taxes; used their control over community charities in Wilmington to sway decisions on projects irrespective of public sentiment; ignored problems of air and water pollution; condoned racism in Wilmington; prevented dissent by "a virtual monopoly" over the news through control of Delaware's two largest newspapers, the Morning News and the Evening Journal in Wilmington; nurtured a "business-coddling" judiciary; allowed a "disgraceful state of health and education for all but the well-to-do"; and curbed the social, political and professional freedom of action of its employees.

Charles B. McCoy, duPont's chairman and president, issued a statement

Nov. 29 in Wilmington, denouncing the results of the year-long study as "completely one-sided" so as to "twist" the company's motives "to fit the authors' preconceived notions."

Copeland case cited—As an example of undue duPont influence, the report cited a $3,718,925 loan by Wilmington Trust Co. in April 1969 to Lammot du-Pont Copeland Jr., secured by $500,-000 in collateral and a $3,350,000 guarantee from former duPont Board Chairman Lammot duPont Copeland Sr., also a board member of Wilmington Trust. Copeland Sr. had stepped down April 19 as duPont's chairman (he was succeeded by McCoy) and as a member of its finance committee because of personal interests, which included those of Copeland Jr. who in 1970 had filed one of the largest personal bankruptcy actions in history.

When the $3.7 million loan fell due in 1970 with a $3.4 million balance, Wilmington Trust acted on the advice of its lawyer William S. Potter, also Copeland Sr.'s attorney and a duPont in-law, to obtain judgment on the loan June 19, 1970—121 days before Copeland Jr. filed his bankruptcy petition. The timing of the judgment and the bankruptcy petition protected the bank and $3 million of Copeland Jr.'s assets from a federal bankruptcy law, which required creditors who obtained judgments less than 120 days prior to bankruptcy filing by the debtor to seek his settlement from a court-approved reorganization plan.

Cable firm guilty of bribery. Irving B. Kahn, former head of Teleprompter Corp., the biggest cable TV company in the U.S., was sentenced in federal court in New York Nov. 30, 1971 to five years in prison on charges that he had obtained an exclusive cable TV franchise by bribing Johnstown, Pa. officials.

A jury Oct. 20 had found Tele-prompter and Kahn guilty on chargers of paying $15,000 in bribes to three town officials, two of them had pleaded guilty.

General Dynamics acquitted re F-111s. A Fort Worth federal jury July 2, 1973 found the General Dynamics Corp. not guilty of conspiring to defraud the government of $114,000 for faulty metal plates for the F-111 fighter-bomber.

During the two-week trial, Frank Davis, a vice president of the Fort Worth-based firm, testified that conviction "could very well close the [local General Dynamics] plant and mean loss of millions of dollars to the economy as well as the loss of thousands of jobs in the Forth Worth area." General Dynamics was Fort Worth's largest employer.

U.S. District Court Judge Leo Brewster had ruled that the jury could take Davis' testimony into account.

According to testimony, the company had destroyed the plates made by Selb Manufacturing Co. of Walnut Ridge, Ark. and then filed for repayment from the Air Force. The government claimed that General Dynamics should have held Selb liable for the faulty plates.

Airline executive sentenced. Walter J. Rauscher, former executive vice president of American Airlines, who pleaded guilty to participating in a kickback scheme in 1973, was sentenced to six months in prison by U.S. District Judge Robert J. Ward March 5, 1974. According to a federal indictment charging one count of conspiracy, Rauscher aided and participated in kickbacks paid by several firms seeking contracts from American.

Juan Homs Jr., former director of sales promotion for American, remained a fugitive from a warrant for his arrest. Believed in Portugal, Homs was accused in the indictment of organizing the kickback scheme.

Penn Central ex-officials indicted. Two former officials of Penn Central Railroad and three other persons were indicted by a federal grand jury Sept. 11, 1974 on charges that they had conspired to misapply $4.2 million in funds from the bankrupt Penn Central.

The defendants were former Penn Central Chairman David C. Bevan, former Penn Central Vice President William R. Gerstnecker, Fidel Gotz, a West German financier living in Liechtenstein, and two brothers, Joseph H. Rosenbaum and Francis N. Rosenbaum, both lawyers.

According to the government, the defendants defrauded the Penn Central and a syndicate of West German banks by obtaining a $10 million loan under false pretenses and diverting $4.2 million of the loan to a dummy Liechtenstein company.

In a related Penn Central lawsuit, Goldman, Sachs & Co., a major New York investment firm, Oct. 9 was ordered to pay $3 million in damages to three firms which had contended that Goldman Sachs had fraudulently sold them a total of $3 million of Penn Central commercial paper despite being aware of the railroad's financial troubles. A fourth plaintiff in that suit, Financial Investors Inc., had settled in July when Goldman Sachs agreed to pay more than 25% of its claim.

Credit abuses. The FTC charged Sept. 11, 1974 that five major department store chains had over the past five years retained more than $2.8 million in unclaimed credit balances owed to charge account customers.

According to the FTC, customers who established credit balances would, over several months, receive statements showing the amounts in their favor. But unless the customers requested refunds or made offsetting purchases, the stores eventually cleared the accounts and kept the money. The FTC said the amounts owed individual customers were relatively small.

The five chains and amounts involved were: Gimbel Brothers Inc., $1,158,000; Genesco Inc., $740,000; Carter Hawley Hale Stores Inc., $509,740; Associated Dry Goods Corp., $405,275; and Rapid American Corp., $75,000.

Beef packer guilty in bribe scheme. Iowa Beef Processors Inc. and its co-founder and co-chairman, Currier J. Holman, were found guilty in State Supreme Court in New York Oct. 8, 1974 of conspiring to bribe butchers' union officials and supermarket chain executives to get the firm's boxed beef products into the New York market.

However, Judge Burton B. Roberts discharged Holman without sentence, reasoning that "there are very few people in American business who would have acted differently in these circumstances."

Roberts called Holman "a victim of extortionate practices" of the union officials and supermarket executives. Iowa Beef, the world's largest packer, was fined $7,000.

"Sadly, like a modern-day Dr. Faustus, Currier J. Holman sold his soul to Moe Steinman," Roberts said. Steinman, alleged kingpin of New York meat racketeering, pleaded guilty April 22 to one count of income tax evasion.

The Iowa Beef case was one of a series of federal and state prosecutions relating to alleged illicit cash payments by meat companies to supermarket executives to get them to select the companys' products and to union officials to win labor goodwill.

(Steinman was sentenced to a year in prison and fined $1,000 for being the "moving force" behind a bribery conspiracy, it was reported May 19, 1975. The penalty imposed on the former vice president of the Shopwell supermarket chain was the maximum allowed under the state misdemeanor charge. Steinman was charged with running brokerages that raised the wholesale price of meat and using the proceeds to bribe meat buyers. It was reported June 5 that he had been sentenced to an identical penalty for filing a false income tax return. The federal penalty would be served concurrently with the state sentence.)

Six found guilty in California credit scheme. A phony real estate credit agency was unmasked and six persons associated with it were convicted on federal charges, it was reported Sept. 9, 1975. Among those found guilty was former (1957–70) California Republican State Senator Richard Dolwig. A seventh defendant was acquitted.

The jury deliberated nearly 4½ days in San Francisco after hearing four weeks of testimony about the scheme. The man considered the key figure in the case, David Kaplan, 45, was found guilty on all 21 counts against him.

According to the indictment, the defendants falsely told potential credit seekers that their corporation, Eurovest Ltd., could get them letters of credit from prime U.S. banks. The defendants falsely backed up their promises by saying that Eurovest had $10 million in securities to place with banks as collateral for the issuance of credit.

It was further alleged that the defendants required their clients to pay a $25,000 advance fee for each $1 million in credit desired. This sum was supposedly insured and would be returned if credit was refused. However, when the letters of credit did not, in fact, materialize, the advance fees were not returned. The indictment cited 16 parties who fell victim to the scheme.

Airlines fined for rebates. Nineteen international air carriers pleaded no contest Sept. 29, 1975 to criminal charges of illegal fare-cutting and were fined a total of $655,000 in federal district court in Brooklyn.

The Justice Department complaint grew out of the 1974 arrest of a man at Kennedy International Airport in New York with $80,000 concealed on his person. Subsequent investigation determined that he was a travel agent who had taken part in a scheme to sell cut-rate airline tickets to persons ineligible for them and then pay the full rate to the airlines; later, he would visit airline offices to be given a cash rebate. The scheme also involved transporting charter passengers on scheduled flights at charter rates.

David Trager, U.S. attorney for the Eastern District, said he had accepted the consent decree because the relevant statute had never been enforced and because the agreement met the basic objectives of his department's investigation.

The airlines pleading no contest were Air France, Air India, Alitalia, British Airways, British Caledonian, El Al, Iberia, Icelandic, Japan, KLM Royal Dutch, Lufthansa, Olympic, Pakistan International, Pan American, Sabena, Scandinavian, Swiss Air, TAP Portuguese and Trans World Airways. Each company was fined $35,000 except for British Caledonian, which paid $25,000. Irish International, Finnair, Aeroflot and Czechoslovak Airlines did not offer pleas in the case.

L.A. title insurer indicted. The T.I. Corp. of California (Ticor), one of the nation's largest title insurance firms, was indicted Jan. 14, 1976 by a federal grand jury in Los Angeles on charges involving check-kiting of more than $100 million. (Check-kiting was described as the misuse of the check clearing process at banks.)

The fraud allegedly took place in the first three months of 1973, when Ticor was said to have used accounts at six California banks and one New York City bank to artificially inflate its balances. By passing checks drawn on insufficient funds between the banks, Ticor was able to obtain millions of dollars in bank money without the knowledge of the seven banks involved.

According to the indictment, Ticor used the money to purchase "millions of dollars in prime short-term interest-bearing money market investments."

The company was charged with eight counts of wire fraud and two counts of mail fraud.

The investigation leading to the indictment was conducted by the Federal Bureau of Investigation and the Securities and Exchange Commission.

In a related development, the California department of insurance had commenced administrative proceedings against a Ticor unit, the Title Insurance and Trust Company, charging it with intentionally overdrawing it's accounts, the Associated Press reported from Los Angeles Feb. 2. The company was also accused of violating anti-rebate provisions of California insurance laws. The U.S. attorney's office had refused to accept a no contest plea on the charges.

ABP, ex-official found guilty. A federal district court judge in Omaha, Neb. Jan. 21, 1976 found American Beef Packers, Inc. guilty of 32 counts of mail and wire fraud in connection with the company's scheme to defraud its largest creditor and principal financing source, General Electric Corp. of Stamford, Conn. ABP was fined $3,200.

Frank R. West, the former chairman and president of ABP, was also found guilty the same day of 24 counts of mail and wire fraud. He was sentenced to 24 concurrent two-year prison terms but the sentence was suspended. Instead, West was placed on two years' probation and fined $24,000.

Conviction in GM warranty-fraud case. The former manager of a General Motors Corp. auto dealership was convicted April 1, 1976 of defrauding the auto maker by submitting fake or inflated new-car-warranty claims to GM for reimbursement.

The manager, George O. Edgerly, had worked for the Gordon Butler Chevrolet Inc. dealership in Lowell, Mass. The firm, one of the largest in the Northeast, had come under investigation in 1974 following the slaying of a GM service representative who had been probing false warranty claims.

In the decision returned by a jury in Middlesex County (Mass.) Superior Court, Edgerly was convicted on a specific charge of larceny exceeding $100, but he also faced murder charges in the slaying.

Action also was pending on a number of other criminal and civil suits resulting from the warranty-fraud case. The Lowell dealership and its owner, R. Gordon Butler, and two other men faced fraud and conspiracy charges. GM also had filed a civil suit against Butler and his dealership seeking to recover the $600,000 allegedly obtained by Butler's firm in bogus claims. Butler had countersued GM.

The company also had ordered wholesale firings of GM employes in one New York City area office and dismissed other employes in New York state, Boston, and Detroit as a consequence of its own internal investigation into the warranty scandal. The scope of the fraud case prompted some observers to call it "GM's Motorgate Affair."

Nursing-home operators sentenced. New York nursing-home operator Eugene Hollander was sentenced in U.S. District Court May 4, 1976 and in state court May 18 for Medicare and Medicaid fraud.

Hollander had pleaded guilty Feb. 2 to parts of federal and state indictments alleging total fraud of $1.2 million. The largest single fraud was said to have been Medicaid reimbursement for $637,000 worth of linen that Hollander had never purchased.

U.S. District Judge Jack B. Weinstein sentenced Hollander in Brooklyn May 4 to spend five nights a week in jail for up to six months. Weinstein also ordered Hollander to sever all connections with the nursing-home industry for inflating medicare reim-

bursement claims by more than $100,000.

The judge also fined Hollander $10,000, suspended a five-year prison term and put him on probation for five years. The probation depended on Hollander's repaying all money and assets he obtained illegally and on his renouncing any occupation involving the custody or care of other people, Weinstein said.

Justice Milton Mollen, sitting in New York State Supreme Court, Brooklyn fined Hollander $250,000 and put him on probation for five years May 18 on condition that he pay the state $1 million in illegally obtained medicaid funds and that he stay outside the nursing-home industry and all related fields. Hollander was given six months to make restitution and pay the fines.

Mollen said that a prison sentence for Hollander would have been "the equivalent of a death sentence." The judge noted reports by medical experts who agreed that Hollander might commit suicide or suffer severe aggravation of a heart ailment if he were jailed.

Nursing-home operator Bernard Bergman was sentenced June 17 in U.S. District Court in Manhattan to four months in prison for tax evasion and defrauding $1.2 million in medicaid funds.

Immediately after Judge Marvin E. Frankel handed down his decision, Charles J. Hynes, special state prosecutor in the nursing-home investigation, accused Bergman of reneging on a plea bargain and threatened to reopen the case.

Calling the sentence "special justice for the privileged," Hynes said Bergman was "in significant violation" of an agreement made in March, in which he pleaded guilty to reduced charges and was promised concurrent sentences on the federal and state charges. In return, Bergman had agreed to cooperate fully with the nursing home investigations and to make full restitution of the stolen money. The 64-year-old rabbi and his family also were granted immunity from further prosecution.

Subsequently, Bergman offered to repay only $367,000 of thefts totaling $2.5 million and had failed to provide valuable testimony about political involvements in nursing-home conspiracies, Hynes said.

Bergman had faced a possible eight-year maximum prison term. Judge Frankel described the four-month sentence as "stern" in light of Bergman's age and "illustrious public life and works."

Four convicted in payola case. Four Brunswick Record Corp. executives were sentenced to jail and fined April 12, 1976 by a federal judge in Newark. Sentencing followed their conviction Feb. 29 on charges of conspiracy and fraud in connection with the payment of bribes to radio station personnel.

Nat Tarnopol, 45, president of Brunswick, was sentenced to three years in jail and fined $10,000. Peter Garris, 51, vice president, Irving Wiegan, 65, secretary, and Lee Shep, 44, a production manager, were each sentenced to two years in jail and fined $10,000.

The four men were found guilty of one count of conspiracy each, alleging that they had defrauded the Internal Revenue Service of taxes, their own creative personnel of royalties and radio stations of the proper services of the employes who were bribed. Each was also convicted on more than 20 counts of mail fraud.

The trial was the result of a two-year investigation of violations of laws against payola, the practice of giving cash to radio station personnel to promote certain records.

Fruehauf officials sentenced. William E. Grace, 68, Fruehauf Corp. board chairman, and Robert D. Rowan, 53, Fruehauf president, were sentenced in Detroit June 30, 1976 to six months in prison and fined $10,000 on charges of conspiring to evade more than $12.3 million in federal excise taxes owed by the truck-trailer manufacturer.

The two men and the company had been convicted in July, 1975, five years after a federal grand jury in Detroit charged that between 1956 and 1965 the Fruehauf officers and two unindicted co-conspirators had evaded payment of excise taxes by using deceptive invoices.

Charles J. Muller, the government's chief attorney in the case, said that the sentencing marked "the first time the government has prosecuted and obtained a criminal conviction of a major corporation and its officers in a tax case." He said

that the government had "hoped desperately" that the judge would impose a jail sentence "for its deterrent value."

SEC sues Foremost-McKesson. The Securities and Exchange Commission filed a complaint July 7, 1976 against Foremost-McKesson Inc. of San Francisco, the nation's largest distributor of wines and liquors, over alleged kickbacks paid from 1971 through 1976. The SEC accused the firm of making $6 million in illegal payments to wholesalers and retailers to induce them to carry Foremost's products.

In Washington July 7, Foremost accepted a court order enjoining the company from violating anti-fraud, reporting and proxy provisions of federal securities laws, but neither admitted nor denied the SEC charges.

Foremost had admitted July 3 that its divisions had "extended" $6,067,000 in "trade discounts and other business-related payments that appear consistent with competitive practices in the industry, but which are subject to question under certain liquor laws and regulations."

According to the SEC complaint, Foremost falsified corporate records by concealing the payments as travel expenses, advertising costs and other legitimate business items. In its complaint, the SEC also said that the Internal Revenue Service had moved to disallow $750,000 in Foremost's tax deductions that "allegedly constituted illegal rebates."

Foremost also admitted that it had paid $231,000 to undisclosed officials of foreign governments. The SEC said the cash payments were made "to affect or attempt to affect government policy with respect principally to Foremost's pharmaceutical- and chemical-product lines."

In its statements July 3, Foremost also said it had made domestic political contributions to local or state candidates totaling $137,800 from 1971–76, of which $5,000 was of questionable legality.

The SEC suit against Foremost was the agency's first alleging the payment of kickbacks by a distributor of alcoholic beverages. The SEC earlier had sued Emersons Ltd., a restaurant chain that allegedly received kickbacks from brewers and beer distributors.

Index

X

Y

Z

Facts on File Reference Books on Contemporary Issues

GOVERNMENT AND POLITICS

The CIA & the Security Debate/1971-75 (Vol. 1)

The shadowy world of the CIA and other semi-secret federal agencies. Wiretapping, personal dossiers, IRS harassment of dissenters and military domestic spying are also covered in detail. $12.50

The CIA & the Security Debate/1975-76 (Vol. 2)

The Senate Report on the CIA, the Daniel Schorr affair, Attorney General Levi's attempts to investigate the FBI, CIA covert missions in Italy and Angola, the death of CIA station head Welch in Athens, President Ford's firing of Colby and reorganization of the CIA. $12.50.

Political Profiles Series
The Kennedy Years
The Johnson Years

Unique modern reference series based wholly on the biographical approach. For the first time, the biographies of more than 2500 of the most politically influential men and women of the postwar era will be available to readers in a systematic, convenient and permanent reference work.

Each profile is a rounded and readable portrait that gives shape and meaning to the public career of its subject, set against the major themes and events of a presidential administration.

The Kennedy Years, single volume $45.
The Johnson Years, single volume $45.
Set price for both books: $79.90.

Government & the Media in Conflict/1970-74

Chapters cover the Pentagon Papers case, the Nixon Administration's attacks on the media, the equal-time and fairness doctrines, judicial challenges to confidentiality and other major issues. Clothbound $11.50/Paperbound $4.50.

Presidential Succession/Ford, Rockefeller & the 25th Amendment

Background of the 25th amendment, the events that ended in the Agnew and Nixon resignations, the appointment of Gerald Ford as Vice President, his succession to the Presidency and his appointment of Nelson Rockefeller as the second unelected Vice-President. $9.95.

Watergate & the White House

This widely-acclaimed series offers an overall perspective on the Watergate story—from the break-in through the pardon.
Volume 1: June 1972-July 1973/$13.50
Volume 2: July-December 1973/$13.50
Volume 3: January-September 1974/$17.50
3-Volume Clothbound Set: $40.00
3-Volume Paperbound Set: $14.25

SOCIAL PROBLEMS

Job Bias
Job discrimination based on race, sex, age, religion and ethnic background. Major legislation, court decisions, union behavior, government practices and enforcement, affirmative action, case studies. $9.95.

Welfare & the Poor
The situation of the poor and the nation's efforts to help them. Federal and state activities in the field of welfare, including the food-stamp program. Medicaid, legal aid, rise of welfare rights organizations, economic strains on the system. $8.95.

Corruption in Business
Dishonesty in business and instances of industrial and political business corruption. The major international bribery scandals, anti-trust law conspiracies and political contribution illegalities will be covered as well as such case studies as the events leading to the resignation of Spiro Agnew as Vice President. $8.95.

New York & the Urban Dilemma
An overview of the financial crisis and the other critical problems facing New York and other American cities: strikes, pay cuts, massive layoffs, the welfare load, shrinking tax bases, crime, "white flight." $9.95.

War on Privacy
How the CIA, FBI, and other organizations—governmental and private—have intruded into the personal lives of American citizens. $9.95.

Consumer Protection
Government protection of consumers from dishonest business practices has been a recurrent theme in American life. Consumer Protection records these efforts during the past decade, including detailed information on attempts to outlaw false advertising, dangerous products, harmful or valueless drugs, deceptive packaging and usurious loans. $8.95.

Health Care / An American Crisis
Proposals and progress made since Medicare and other government-sponsored programs were established. The soaring costs, payment scandals and many other aspects of the crisis are examined in detail. $8.95.

The School Busing Controversy / 1970-75
A detailed month-by-month record of the court decisions, local controversies and the political debate from early 1970 through mid-1975. Clothbound $12.50/ Paperbound $5.25.

All titles are clothbound unless otherwise specified. Prices subject to change without notice. Write for free catalog to:

Facts On File
119 W. 57th St.
New York, N.Y. 10019